Basic and Clinical Science Course
Section 9

Intraocular Inflammation and Uveitis

1999-2000

LEO

LIFELONG
EDUCATION FOR THE
OPHTHALMOLOGIST

American Academy of Ophthalmology

The Basic and Clinical Science Course is one component of the Lifelong Education for the Ophthalmologist (LEO) framework, which assists members in planning their continuing medical education. LEO includes an array of clinical education products that members may select to form individualized, self-directed learning plans for updating their clinical knowledge. Active members or fellows who use LEO components may accumulate sufficient CME credits to earn the LEO Award. Contact the Academy's Clinical Education Division for further information on LEO.

This CME activity was planned and produced in accordance with the ACCME Essentials.

The Academy provides this material for educational purposes only. It is not intended to represent the only or best method or procedure in every case, nor to replace a physician's own judgment or give specific advice for case management. Including all indications, contraindications, side effects, and alternative agents for each drug or treatment is beyond the scope of this material. All information and recommendations should be verified, prior to use, with current information included in the manufacturers' package inserts or other independent sources, and considered in light of the patient's condition and history. Reference to certain drugs, instruments, and other products in this publication is made for illustrative purposes only and is not intended to constitute an endorsement of such. Some material may include information on applications that are not considered community standard, that reflect indications not included in approved FDA labeling, or that are approved for use only in restricted research settings. The FDA has stated that it is the responsibility of the physician to determine the FDA status of each drug or device he or she wishes to use, and to use them with appropriate patient consent in compliance with applicable law. The Academy specifically disclaims any and all liability for injury or other damages of any kind, from negligence or otherwise, for any and all claims that may arise from the use of any recommendations or other information contained herein.

Each author states that he or she has no significant financial interest or other relationship with the manufacturer of any commercial product discussed in the chapters that he or she contributed to this publication or with the manufacturer of any competing commercial product.

Basic and Clinical Science Course

Thomas A. Weingeist, PhD, MD, Iowa City, Iowa
Senior Secretary for Clinical Education

Thomas J. Liesegang, MD, Jacksonville, Florida
Secretary for Instruction

M. Gilbert Grand, MD, St. Louis, Missouri
BCSC Course Chair

Section 9

Faculty Responsible for This Edition

Narsing A. Rao, MD, *Chair,* Los Angeles, California

Scott Cousins, MD, Miami, Florida

David Forster, MD, Falls Church, Virginia

David Meisler, MD, Cleveland, Ohio

E. Mitchel Opremcak, MD, Columbus, Ohio

Paul Turgeon, MD, Canton, Ohio
Practicing Ophthalmologists Advisory Committee for Education

Recent Past Faculty

H. Jane Blackman, MD
Brent E. Chalmers, MD
William W. Culbertson, MD
David H. Fischer, MD
Rudolph M. Franklin, MD

Alan H. Friedman, MD
Priscilla E. Perry, MD
John D. Sheppard, Jr., MD
Robert S. Weinberg, MD
Sue Ellen Young, MD

In addition, the Academy gratefully acknowledges the
contributions of numerous past faculty and advisory
committee members who have played an important role in
the development of previous editions of the Basic and
Clinical Science Course.

American Academy of Ophthalmology Staff

Kathryn A. Hecht, EdD
Vice President, Clinical Education

Hal Straus
Director, Publications Department

Margaret Denny
Managing Editor

Fran Taylor
Medical Editor

Maxine Garrett
Administrative Coordinator

American Academy of Ophthalmology
655 Beach Street
Box 7424
San Francisco, CA 94120-7424

CONTENTS

GENERAL INTRODUCTION

The Basic and Clinical Science Course (BCSC) is designed to provide residents and practitioners with a comprehensive yet concise curriculum of the field of ophthalmology. The BCSC has developed from its original brief outline format, which relied heavily on outside readings, to a more convenient and educationally useful self-contained text. The Academy regularly updates and revises the course, with the goals of integrating the basic science and clinical practice of ophthalmology and of keeping current with new developments in the various subspecialties.

The BCSC incorporates the effort and expertise of more than 70 ophthalmologists, organized into 12 section faculties, working with Academy editorial staff. In addition, the course continues to benefit from many lasting contributions made by the faculties of previous editions. Members of the Academy's Practicing Ophthalmologists Advisory Committee for Education serve on each faculty and, as a group, review every volume before and after major revisions.

Organization of the Course

The 12 sections of the Basic and Clinical Science Course are numbered as follows to reflect a logical order of study, proceeding from fundamental subjects to anatomic subdivisions:

1. Update on General Medicine
2. Fundamentals and Principles of Ophthalmology
3. Optics, Refraction, and Contact Lenses
4. Ophthalmic Pathology and Intraocular Tumors
5. Neuro-Ophthalmology
6. Pediatric Ophthalmology and Strabismus
7. Orbit, Eyelids, and Lacrimal System
8. External Disease and Cornea
9. Intraocular Inflammation and Uveitis
10. Glaucoma
11. Lens and Cataract
12. Retina and Vitreous

In addition, a comprehensive Master Index allows the reader to easily locate subjects throughout the entire series.

References

Readers who wish to explore specific topics in greater detail may consult the journal references cited within each chapter and the Basic Texts listed at the back of the book. These references are intended to be selective rather than exhaustive, chosen by the BCSC faculty as being important, current, and readily available to residents and practitioners.

Related Academy educational materials are also listed in the appropriate sections. They include books, audiovisual materials, self-assessment programs, clinical modules, and interactive programs.

Study Questions and CME Credit

Each volume includes multiple-choice study questions designed to be used as a closed-book exercise. The answers are accompanied by explanations to enhance the learning experience. Completing the study questions allows readers both to test their understanding of the material and to demonstrate section completion for the purpose of CME credit, if desired.

The Academy is accredited by the Accreditation Council for Continuing Medical Education to sponsor continuing medical education for physicians. CME credit hours in Category 1 of the Physician's Recognition Award of the AMA may be earned for completing the study of any section of the BCSC. The Academy designates the number of credit hours for each section based upon the scope and complexity of the material covered (see the Credit Reporting Form in each individual section for the maximum number of hours that may be claimed).

Based upon return of the Credit Reporting Form at the back of each book, the Academy will maintain a record, for up to 3 years, of credits earned by Academy members. Upon request, the Academy will send a transcript of credits earned.

Conclusion

The Basic and Clinical Science Course has expanded greatly over the years, with the addition of much new text and numerous illustrations. Recent editions have sought to place a greater emphasis on clinical applicability, while maintaining a solid foundation in basic science. As with any educational program, it reflects the experience of its authors. As its faculties change and as medicine progresses, new viewpoints are always emerging on controversial subjects and techniques. Not all alternate approaches can be included in this series; as with any educational endeavor, the learner should seek additional sources, including such carefully balanced opinions as the Academy's Preferred Practice Patterns.

The BCSC faculty and staff are continuously striving to improve the educational usefulness of the course; you, the reader, can contribute to this ongoing process. If you have any suggestions or questions about the series, please do not hesitate to contact the faculty or the managing editor.

The authors, editors, and reviewers hope that your study of the BCSC will be of lasting value and that each section will serve as a practical resource for quality patient care.

OBJECTIVES FOR BCSC SECTION 9

Upon completion of BCSC Section 9, *Intraocular Inflammation and Uveitis,* the reader should be able to:

- Outline the immunologic and infectious mechanisms involved in the occurrence and complications of uveitis and related inflammatory conditions, including acquired immunodeficiency syndrome

- Identify general and specific pathophysiological processes that affect the structure and function of the uvea, lens, intraocular cavities, retina, and other tissues in acute and chronic intraocular inflammation

- Choose appropriate examination techniques and relevant ancillary studies

- Develop appropriate differential diagnoses for ocular inflammatory disorders

- Describe the principles of medical and surgical management of uveitis and related intraocular inflammation, including indications for and complications of immunosuppressive agents

INTRODUCTION TO SECTION 9

This section of the BCSC is divided into two parts. Part 2, Intraocular Inflammation and Uveitis, will come as no surprise to the reader opening a volume of the same name. Part 2 introduces the clinical approach to uveitis, devotes a chapter each to the different forms of uveitis as classified anatomically and to endophthalmitis, and discusses the complications of all forms of uveitis in a separate chapter. The final chapter of Part 2 covers the ocular involvement in AIDS, offering the most complete summary of this topic in the BCSC series.

The reader may, however, not expect to find one third of the book, Part 1, Immunology, going into such great depth. Why are so many pages given to this topic; what relevance does it have to Part 2? Progress in basic immunology, as well as in the regional immunology of the eye, has translated into major advances in recent years. Our understanding of the mechanisms by which uveitis and other intraocular diseases develop has helped clinicians to identify and establish uveitis entities and to develop specific treatments directed at altered immune processes. These clinically relevant advances include the discovery of unique immune responses in the intraocular cavities and subretinal space; the delineation of the association between HLA and various uveitis entities; and the detection of infectious agents by immunologic methods such as Western blot, ELISA, and others. Lymphocytic studies for cell surface markers and in vitro studies based on antibodies have helped in clearly separating those uveitis entities that are mediated by immune mechanisms, in particular those resulting from organ-specific antibodies, from those caused by altered lymphocyte functions. The latter mechanism appears to be prevalent in posterior uveitis, and altered cell-mediated immunity can be directed to retinal proteins or other ocular antigens in these intraocular inflammations. Such findings have led to the introduction of potential therapeutic modalities such as oral tolerance, a promising though still experimental approach.

The section on immunology has been rewritten and expanded to describe basic aspects of the human immune response, including responses specific to the ocular structures; the effector mechanisms of immunity, including antibody-mediated and lymphocyte-generated mechanisms; and the various pro- and anti-inflammatory cytokines and other effector molecules, including reactive oxygen species and nitric oxide products. Clinical examples are interspersed throughout the immunology text, discussing the clinical relevance of the issues covered in diagnosis and management of uveitis. A clear understanding of the immune mechanisms will enhance an appreciation of the clinical features and principles behind the management of uveitis triggered by either an infectious agent or another insult.

PART 1

IMMUNOLOGY

Chapters I through V discuss the human immune system and its ocular effects in detail. Many specific terms are used, and some may be defined only briefly in an early chapter and then explained in depth in a later chapter. Similarly, abbreviations that may be unfamiliar to the reader often are used after the term has been spelled out at first mention. The following glossary and list of abbreviations are designed to provide the reader with a handy reference to terminology used in Part 1, especially those terms discussed in later chapters and abbreviations that appear far from their original descriptions, and not as comprehensive listings.

Glossary

Antibody   A glycoprotein that is able to bind biochemically to a specific antigenic substance.

Antigen   Foreign substance that activates an adaptive immune response.

Antigen-presenting cells   Specialized cells that carry antigen to a lymph node, process it into fragments, and present the fragments to T-cell antigen receptors.

Chemotaxis   Attraction generated in macrophages, neutrophils, eosinophils, and lymphocytes by substances released at sites of inflammatory reactions, such as lymphokines, complement, and various mediators.

Complement   Effector molecules used to amplify inflammation for both innate and adaptive immunity.

Cytokine   A generic term for any soluble polypeptide mediator synthesized and released by cells for the purposes of intercellular signaling and communication.

Epitope   Each specific portion of an antigenic molecule to which the immune system responds.

Fc receptor   The Fc domain of each immunoglobulin monomer contains the attachment site for effector cells and complement activation.

Hapten   A small molecule, not antigenic by itself, that can react with antibodies when conjugated to a larger antigenic molecule.

Isotype   Different subclasses of immunoglobulin.

Leukotriene   A compound formed from arachidonic acid that functions as a regulator of allergic and inflammatory reactions, probably contributing significantly to inflammatory infiltration.

Lymphatics   Common term for *afferent lymphatic channels,* which drain extracellular fluid to a regional lymph node, conveying immune cells and whole antigen, and *efferent lymphatic channels,* which drain to the circulatory system.

Mediator   Substance released from cells as the result of the interaction of antigen with antibody or by the action of antigen with a sensitized lymphocyte.

Abbreviations

ACAID anterior chamber–associated immune deviation
ADCC   antibody-dependent cellular cytotoxicity
ANCA   antineutrophil cytoplasmic antibody
APC   antigen-presenting cell(s)
CAM   cell-adhesion molecule(s)
CTL   cytotoxic T lymphocytes
DC   dendritic cells
DH   delayed hypersensitivity
HLA   human leukocyte antigen
IL   interleukin
INF   interferon
LC   Langerhans cells
LPS   lipopolysaccharide
MAC   membrane attack complex
MALT   mucosa-associated lymphoid tissue
MHC   major histocompatibility complex
PAF   platelet-activating factor(s)
PG   prostaglandin
PMN   polymorphonuclear leukocytes, or neutrophils
Th   T helper cell, as in *Th0, Th1,* etc.
TGF   transforming growth factor
TNF   tumor necrosis factor

CHAPTER I

Basic Concepts in Immunology

Definitions

In general, an immune response is a sequence of cellular and molecular events designed to rid the host of an offending stimulus, usually from a pathogenic organism, toxic substance, cellular debris, or neoplastic cell. Two broad categories of immune responses have been recognized: *adaptive* and *innate*. Simply put, adaptive immunity, also called *specific* or *acquired immunity,* can be conceptualized as "user programmable." Within an individual, adaptive responses react to specific environmental stimuli (i.e., unique antigens) with a stimulus-specific (i.e., antigen-specific) immunologic response. In contrast, innate immune responses, also called *natural immunity,* are "factory preprogrammed." All individuals are endowed with a genetically predetermined set of responses to a wide range of noxious environmental stimuli. Different stimuli can often trigger the same responses.

Adaptive Immune Response

Adaptive immunity is a host response set in motion by a specific stimulus, or antigen. An antigen usually represents an alien substance completely foreign to the organism, and the immune system must generate, de novo, a specific receptor against it that must, in turn, recognize a unique molecular structure in the antigen for which no specific preexisting gene was present. The organism attempts to defend itself by the following steps:

- Recognizing the unique foreign "antigenic" substance as distinguished from "self"
- Processing the unique antigen with receptors newly created by specialized tissues (the immune system)
- Generating unique antigen-specific immunologic effector cells (especially T and B lymphocytes) and unique antigen-specific soluble effector molecules (antibodies) whose function is to remove the specific stimulating antigenic substance from the organism while ignoring the presence of other irrelevant antigenic stimuli

Thus, the adaptive immune system is not genetically predetermined but evolves as an ongoing way for an individual's B and T lymphocytes to continually generate new antigen receptor genes through recombination, rearrangement, and mutation of the germline genetic structure. A "repertoire" is created of novel antigen receptor molecules that vary tremendously among individuals within a species, representing a spectrum of recognition.

The immune response to a mutated virus is the classic example of this process. Viruses such as influenza virus are continuously evolving or mutating new antigenic structures. The susceptible host could not possibly have evolved receptors for recognition to these new viral mutations. However, these new mutations do serve as antigens that stimulate a specific adaptive immune response by the host to the virus. The adaptive response recognizes the virus in question and not other organisms, such as polio virus. Following environmental exposure, the adaptive immune response has been "programmed" to adapt to the new specific antigen.

Innate Immune Response

Innate immunity is a pattern recognition response by the organism to

- Identify various offensive stimuli (especially infectious agents, toxins, or cellular debris from injury) in an antigen-independent manner
- Respond in a stereotyped, preprogrammed fashion determined by the preexistence of receptors for the stimulus
- Generate generic biochemical mediators and cytokines that recruit nonspecific effector cells, especially macrophages and neutrophils, to remove the offending stimulus in a nonspecific manner through phagocytosis or enzymatic degradation

The stimuli of innate immunity interact with receptors that have been genetically predetermined by evolution to recognize and respond to molecular "motifs" on triggering stimuli. These motifs often include a specific amino acid sequence, certain lipoproteins, certain phospholipids, or other specific molecular patterns. The receptors of innate immunity are identical among all individuals within a species. In this way the receptors on monocytes, neutrophils, and sometimes parenchymal tissues resemble the receptors for neurotransmitters or hormones.

The innate immune response to acute infection is the classic example of this process. For example, in endophthalmitis, bacteria-derived toxins or host cell debris stimulate the recruitment of neutrophils and monocytes, leading to the production of inflammatory mediators and phagocytosis of the bacteria. The triggering mechanisms and subsequent effector response to staphylococcus are nearly identical to those of other organisms. Nonspecific receptors that recognize families of related toxins or molecules in the environment determine this response.

Similarities Between Adaptive and Innate Immune Responses

Receptor activation   Both responses use receptors present on white blood cells to recognize the offending stimulus, but the recognition receptors are fundamentally different (see next page).

Inflammatory or noninflammatory responses   Both responses can trigger inflammation, but they usually operate at a subclinical level so that the individual is unaware of the response.

Nonspecific effector cells and molecules   Although only the adaptive immune response employs T and B lymphocytes as antigen-specific effector cells, both forms of immunity use neutrophils, eosinophils, and monocytes as nonspecific effector cells and the same chemical mediators as amplification systems.

Differences Between Adaptive and Innate Immune Responses

Triggering stimuli   Adaptive immunity is triggered by antigen, usually in the form of a protein, although carbohydrates or lipids can sometimes be antigenic. Innate immunity is triggered by bacterial toxins and cell debris, often in the form of carbohydrate, phospholipid, and other nonprotein molecules.

Recognition receptors   The antigen receptors of adaptive immunity, such as antibody molecules and T-cell antigen receptor molecules, are specific for each antigen, recognizing unique molecular regions of an antigen called *epitopes*. The receptors used by innate immunity, such as scavenging receptors or toxin receptors, recognize conserved molecular patterns or motifs shared among various triggering stimuli.

Time of onset after triggering   Because adaptive immune responses are acquired, they require recognition, processing, and effector phases that need several days for activation. Therefore onset is delayed. Innate immunity is preprogrammed, requiring only the direct activation of a cellular receptor to initiate an effector response, which induces release of mediators or recruitment of cells within hours.

Memory   Adaptive immune responses demonstrate memory, so that on second exposure to the same antigen the release of effectors is more vigorous and rapid than during the original response. Innate responses are genetically preprogrammed to react in a stereotyped manner to each encounter. Memory implies that the secondary, or repeat encounter, immune response is regulated by mechanisms different from the primary, or initial "virgin" encounter, immune response, specifically by memory T and B cells.

Specificity   Adaptive immune responses demonstrate specificity for each unique offending antigen. Innate responses do not. Specificity is maintained through the use of antibodies and antigen-specific B and T cells that recognize specific biochemical information, such as three-dimensional geometry for B cells and linear amino acid sequences for T cells. Subtle biochemical changes (i.e., amino acid substitutions) in the structure of the antigen remove specific recognition for memory responses but preserve overall antigenicity for a new primary response. In contrast, similar subtle changes in toxin structure or other stimuli for innate immunity do not necessarily alter the innate response if the changes do not involve the pattern recognition sites within the molecule.

Immunity Versus Inflammation

An immune response is the process for removal of an offending stimulus. When this response becomes clinically apparent within a tissue, it can be termed an *inflammatory response*. More precisely, an inflammatory response is a sequence of molecular and cellular events triggered by innate or adaptive immunity resulting in five characteristic "cardinal" clinical manifestations:

□ Pain

□ Hyperemia

□ Edema

□ Heat

□ Loss of function

These clinical signs reflect two main physiologic changes within a tissue: cellular recruitment and altered vascular permeability. Inflammatory response is associated with the following typical pathologic findings:

- Infiltration of effector cells mediated by and resulting in release of biochemical and molecular mediators/amplifiers of inflammation, such as cytokines (i.e., interleukins and chemokines) and lipid mediators (i.e., prostaglandins and platelet-activating factors)
- Presence of oxygen metabolites (i.e., superoxide and nitrogen radicals)
- Presence of granule products as well as catalytic enzymes (i.e., collagenases and elastases)
- Activation of plasma-derived enzyme systems (i.e., complement components such as anaphylatoxins)

See chapter III for a more detailed discussion.

In practice, many clinicians use the term *immune response* to mean adaptive immunity and the term *inflammation* to imply innate immunity. However, it is important to remember that both innate and adaptive immune responses usually function physiologically at a subclinical level without overt manifestations. For example, in most individuals, ocular surface allergen exposure that occurs daily in all humans or bacterial contamination during cataract surgery that occurs in most eyes is usually cleared by innate or adaptive mechanisms without overt inflammation. Similarly, both innate and adaptive immunity can trigger inflammation, and the physiological changes induced by each form of immunity may be indistinguishable. For example, the hypopyon of bacterial endophthalmitis, which results from innate immunity against bacterial toxins, and the hypopyon of lens-associated uveitis, which presumably results from an inappropriate adaptive immune response against lens antigens, cannot be clearly distinguished clinically or histologically.

Roitt IM. *Essential Immunology*. 9th ed. Malden, MA: Blackwell Science; 1997.

Components of the Immune System

Leukocytes

White blood cells, or leukocytes, are nucleated cells that can be distinguished from one another by the shape of their nuclei and the presence or absence of granules. They are further defined by their reactions to various stains.

Neutrophils Neutrophils, also called *polymorphonuclear leukocytes (PMN)*, are the most abundant granulocytes in the blood. They are efficient phagocytes that readily clear tissues and degrade ingested material. They act as important effector cells through the release of granule products and cytokines. Through specific receptors, such as complement receptors, PMN can be recruited and triggered by immune mechanisms. Nonimmune mechanisms also recruit and activate PMN at sites of injury through poorly characterized receptors and their ligands. Chapter IV discusses PMN activation and recruitment in greater detail.

PMN dominate the infiltrate in experimental models and clinical examples of active bacterial infections of the conjunctiva, sclera (scleritis), cornea (keratitis), or vitreous (endophthalmitis). PMN are also dominant in many models of active viral infections of the cornea (herpes simplex virus keratitis) and retina (HSV retinitis) and in some human viral infections. PMN also represent the principal cell type in lipopolysaccharide (LPS)–induced inflammation and after direct injection of most cytokines into various ocular tissues.

Eosinophils Eosinophils, like PMN, also contain abundant cytoplasmic granules and lysosomes. However, the biochemical nature of the granules in eosinophils consists of more basic and binding acidic dyes, and eosinophils differ from PMN in the way they respond to certain triggering stimuli. Eosinophils have receptors for and become activated by many mediators; interleukin-5 (IL-5) is especially important. Eosinophil granule products, such as major basic protein or ribonucleases, are ideal for destroying parasites, and not surprisingly, these cells accumulate at sites of parasitic infection. Eosinophils are numerous in skin infiltrates during the late-phase allergic response and atopic lesions and in lung infiltrates during asthma. T-cell production of IL-5 within the infiltrated site is probably an important regulator of eosinophil function locally, although many of the specific mechanisms for regulation of eosinophil recruitment, activation, and function remain unknown.

Eosinophils are abundant in the conjunctiva and tears in many forms of atopic conjunctivitis, especially vernal and allergic conjunctivitis. However, they are not considered major effectors for intraocular inflammation, except during helminthic infections of the eye, especially acute endophthalmitis caused by toxocariasis.

Basophils and mast cells Basophils are the bloodborne equivalent of the tissue-bound mast cell. Mast cells exist in two major subtypes, connective tissue and mucosal, both of which can release preformed granules and synthesize certain mediators de novo. Connective tissue mast cells contain abundant granules with histamine and heparin, and they synthesize the prostaglandin PGD_2 upon stimulation. In contrast, mucosal mast cells require T-cell cytokine help for granule formation, and they therefore normally contain low levels of histamine. Mucosal mast cells synthesize mostly leukotrienes after stimulation. The tissue location can alter the granule type and functional activity, but the regulation of these important differences is not well understood.

Basophils and mast cells differ from other granulocytes in several important ways. The granule contents are different from those of PMN or eosinophils, and mast cells express high-affinity Fc receptors for the immunoglobulin IgE. *Fc,* from "fragment, crystallizable," refers to the region of immunoglobulin that mediates cell-surface receptors. Mast cells act as major effector cells in IgE-mediated immune-triggered inflammatory reactions, especially allergy or immediate hypersensitivity. They may also participate in the induction of cell-mediated immunity, wound healing, and other functions not directly related to IgE-mediated degranulation (i.e., release of cell contents). Thus other stimuli, such as complement or certain cytokines, may also trigger degranulation.

The normal human conjunctiva contains significant numbers of mast cells localized in the substantia propria but not in the epithelium. In certain atopic and allergic disease states, such as vernal conjunctivitis, not only does the number of mast cells increase in the substantia propria, but the epithelium also becomes densely infiltrated. Careful anatomical studies have shown that the choroid and anterior uveal tract also contain significant densities of connective tissue–type mast cells, whereas the cornea has none.

Monocytes and macrophages Monocytes, the circulating cells, and macrophages, the tissue-infiltrating equivalents, are important effectors in all forms of immunity and inflammation. Monocytes are relatively large cells (12–20 μm in suspension but up to 40 μm in tissues) that travel through many normal sites. Most normal tissues have at least two identifiable macrophage populations: tissue-resident macrophages and blood-derived macrophages. Although many exceptions exist, in general, tissue-resident macrophages represent monocytes that migrated into a tissue during embryologic development, thereby acquiring tissue-specific properties and specific cellular markers. In many tissues, resident macrophages have been given tissue-specific names: Kupffer's cells in the liver, alveolar macrophages in the lung, or microglia in the brain and retina. Blood-derived macrophages usually represent monocytes that have recently migrated from the blood into a fully developed tissue site.

Macrophages serve the following three primary functions:

☐ Scavengers to clear cell debris and pathogens

☐ Antigen-presenting cells (APC) for T lymphocytes

☐ Inflammatory effector cells

In vitro studies seem to indicate that "resting" monocytes can be "primed" through various signals into efficient APC and, upon additional signals, "activated" into effector cells. Effective activation stimuli include exposure to various bacterial toxins such as LPS, phagocytosis of antibody-coated or complement-coated pathogens, or exposure to mediators released during inflammation such as IL-1 or interferon gamma (INF-γ).

Only on full activation do macrophages become most efficient at the synthesis and release of inflammatory mediators and the killing and degradation of phagocytosed pathogens. At some sites of inflammation macrophages undergo a morphologic change in size and histologic features into a cell called an *epithelioid cell.* Epithelioid cells can fuse into multinucleated *giant cells.* Macrophages are extremely important effector cells in both innate and adaptive immunity, with or without overt inflammation. They are often detectable in acute ocular infections, even if other cell types such as PMN are more numerous. Chapter IV discusses these issues in more detail.

Dendritic cells and Langerhans cells Dendritic cells (DC) are terminally differentiated, bone marrow–derived, circulating mononuclear cells that are distinct from the macrophage-monocyte lineage. They make up approximately 0.1%–1.0% of blood mononuclear cells. However, in tissue sites, DC become large (15–30 μm) with cytoplasmic veils that form extensions two to three times the diameter of the cell, resembling the dendritic structure of neurons. In many nonlymphoid and lymphoid organs, dendritic cells become a system of antigen-presenting cells. These sites recruit DC by defined migration pathways, and DC in each site share features of structure and function. DC function as accessory cells that play an important role in the processing and presentation of antigens to T cells; their distinctive function is to initiate responses in quiescent lymphocytes. Thus, DC may act as the most potent leukocytes for generating primary T cell–dependent immune responses.

Epidermal Langerhans cells (LC) are the best-characterized subset of DC. LC represent about 3%–8% of cells in most human epithelia including the skin, conjunctiva, nasopharyngeal mucosa, vaginal mucosa, and rectal mucosa. They are identified on the basis of their many dendrites, electron-dense cytoplasm, and Birbeck granules. LC are not active APC, although activity develops after in vitro culture with certain cytokines. As a result, LC transform and lose their granules and thus fully resemble blood and lymphoid DC. Evidence suggests that LC can leave the skin and move along the afferent lymph to draining lymphoid organs. LC are important components of the immune system and play a role in antigen presentation, control of lymphoid cell traffic, differentiation of T cells, and induction of DH. Elimination of LC from skin before antigen challenge inhibits the induction of the contact hypersensitivity response. In the conjunctiva and limbus, Langerhans cells are the only ones that constitutively express class II major histocompatibility (MHC) molecules. Many kinds of irritation to the cornea can result in central migration of the peripheral LC.

Lymphocytes   Lymphocytes are small (10–20 μm) cells with large dense nuclei also derived from stem-cell precursors within the bone marrow. However, unlike other leukocytes, lymphocytes require subsequent maturation in peripheral lymphoid organs. Originally characterized and differentiated based on a series of ingenious but esoteric laboratory tests, lymphocytes can now be subdivided based on detection of specific cell surface proteins (i.e., *surface markers*). These markers are in turn related to functional and molecular activity of individual subsets. Three broad categories of lymphocytes have been identified: B cells; T cells; and non-T, non-B lymphocytes. These subsets are discussed in greater depth below.

> Gallin JI, Snyderman R, eds. *Inflammation: Basic Principles and Clinical Correlates.* 3rd ed. Philadelphia: Lippincott; 1999.

Lymphoid Tissues

Primary lymphoid tissues   The bone marrow is the site for replenishment and maturation of all leukocyte and lymphoid precursors. Thus, pluripotential stem cells differentiate into various myeloid or lymphoid precursor cells, which then differentiate into monocyte precursors, T- and B-lymphocyte precursors, and so on. B lymphocytes mature within the bone marrow, whereas immature T lymphocytes exit the bone marrow and mature within the thymus. Mature B and T lymphocytes then exit into the blood where they enter secondary lymphoid tissues. Granulocytes and monocytes exit the bone marrow directly as functional effectors, although some monocyte subpopulations can further differentiate in peripheral tissues.

Secondary lymphoid tissues   The central lymphoid structures—lymph nodes and spleen—are very important to the adaptive immune response. Mature but naive lymphocytes, those that have not been exposed to antigens, enter lymph nodes through specialized postcapillary venules and take up residence in specialized areas (follicles for B cells and paracortical region for T cells) until antigen exposure occurs. They can recirculate and travel between different nodes. Certain sites termed *peripheral lymphoid structures,* especially mucosa and skin, are important for initial interaction with antigen because of their location as barrier to the outside world.

CHAPTER II

Immunization and Adaptive Immunity: The Immune Response Arc

To understand the clinically relevant features of the adaptive immune response, the reader can consider the sequence of events that follows immunization with antigen using the skin, which is the classic experimental method of introduction of antigen to the adaptive immune response. Several general immunologic concepts, especially the concept of the immune response arc, the primary adaptive immune response, and the secondary adaptive immune response, are involved in this process.

Overview of the Immune Response Arc

Interaction between antigen and the adaptive immune system at a peripheral site, such as the skin, can be subdivided using the concept of the immune response arc into three phases:

□ Afferent

□ Processing

□ Effector

Each is analogous to the three phases of the neural reflex arc (Fig II-1). For example, in the neural response to the patellar deep tendon reflex, the *afferent response* begins with the recognition of a stimulus (the activation of the stretch receptor by percussion of the patellar tendon), followed by transformation of the stimulus into a neural signal that is conveyed along an afferent neuron into the central nervous system. In the CNS complex neural *processing* occurs. Finally, along an efferent neuron, the neural signal is conveyed back to the site (quadriceps muscle), which is activated to contract (i.e., an *effector response*).

   Similarly, in the adaptive immune response, antigen is recognized during the *afferent* phase of the immune response, when the antigenic information is conveyed through the lymphatics and APC to the lymph node. There, *processing* of the antigenic signal occurs, resulting in release of immune messengers (antibodies, B cells, and T cells) into efferent lymphatics and venous circulation. The intent of the immune system is conveyed back to the original site where an *effector response* occurs (i.e., immune complex formation or delayed hypersensitivity reaction). In the following discussion the important aspects of each phase are covered in more detail.

NEURAL REFLEX ARC

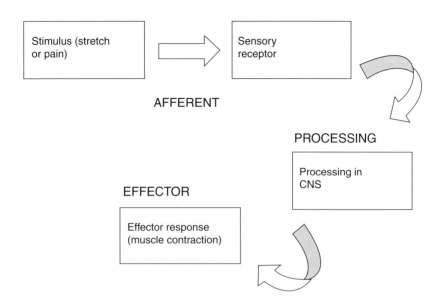

IMMUNE RESPONSE ARC

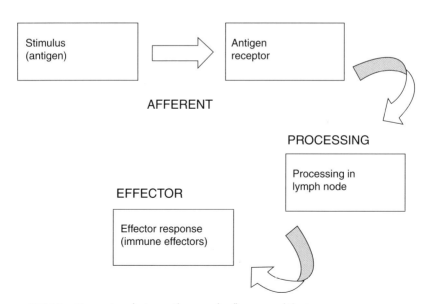

FIG II-1—Comparison between the neural reflex arc and the immune response arc.

Phases of the Immune Response Arc

Afferent Phase

The initial recognition, transport, and presentation of antigenic substances to the adaptive immune system constitutes the afferent phase of the immune response arc. Traditionally, the term *antigen* was reserved for those foreign substances that combined with antibody, and the term *immunogen* was used for those substances capable of activating an adaptive immune response. Today, most immunologists tend to use antigen to refer to both situations. The term *epitope* refers to each specific portion of an antigenic molecule to which the immune system is responding. A complex three-dimensional protein will probably have multiple antigenic epitopes against which different antibodies might bind, as well as many other sites that remain invisible to the immune system. In addition, such a protein often can be enzymatically digested into many different peptide fragments, some of which contain molecular information to serve as antigenic epitopes for T-cell recognition, and some of which are not recognized at all by the immune system.

Afferent lymphatic channels   Also referred to as simply *lymphatics,* afferent lymphatic channels are veinlike structures that drain extracellular fluid (i.e., lymph) from a site into a regional node. Lymphatics serve two major purposes: to convey immune cells and to carry whole antigen from the site to a lymph node.

Antigen-presenting cells   Specialized cells that take up antigen at a site and carry it to the lymph node, antigen-presenting cells (APC) then "process" the antigen, which is almost always in the form of a protein, into fragments (i.e., intracellular enzymatic digestion into peptides of 7–11 amino acids), place the peptide antigen fragments into a specialized antigen-binding "groove" within human leukocyte antigen (HLA) molecules, and "present" antigen peptide fragments within the pocket of the HLA molecules to T-cell antigen receptors, thereby beginning the activation process of adaptive immunity. Different HLA molecules vary in their capacity to bind various peptide fragments within the groove, and thus the HLA type determines the repertoire of peptide antigens capable of being presented to T cells. APC from one individual cannot present to T cells derived from a second individual unless the two individuals share a common HLA haplotype that can bind the antigen in question. See chapter V for discussion of HLA molecules. Table V-1 gives a short history of research on the HLA system.

Class II MHC molecules (i.e., HLA-DR, -DP, or -DQ) serve as the antigen-presenting "platform" for CD4, or helper, T cells (Fig II-2). All APC for CD4 T cells must express the class II MHC molecule, and the antigen receptor on the helper T cell can recognize peptide antigens only if they are presented with class II molecules simultaneously. However, only certain cell types express class II MHC on their plasma membrane. Macrophages and dendritic cells are the two most important class II APC. B cells can also function as class II–dependent APC, especially within a lymph node. Any cell that is induced to express MHC class II molecules also can potentially serve as an APC, although this topic is beyond the scope of this discussion. In general, class II–dependent APC are best for processing extracellular protein antigens that have been endocytosed from the external environment, such as bacterial or fungal antigens.

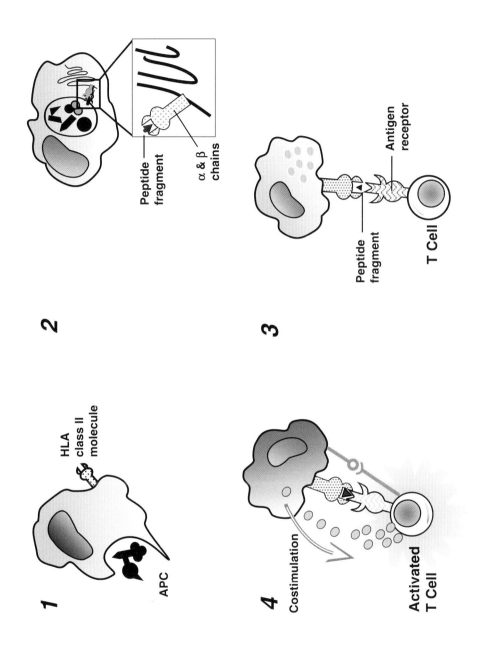

1

HLA class II molecule

APC

2

Peptide fragment

α & β chains

3

Antigen receptor

Peptide fragment

T Cell

4

Costimulation

Activated T Cell

FIG II-2—Class II–dependent APC. *1*, APC endocytose exogenous antigens into the endosomal compartment. *2*, There, the antigen is digested into peptide fragments and placed into the groove formed by the α and β chains of the class II HLA molecule. *3*, The CD4 T-cell receptor recognizes the fragment–class II complex. *4*, With the help of costimulatory molecules such as CD28/B7 interactions and cytokines, the CD4 T cell becomes "primed," or partially activated. (Illustration by Barb Cousins, modified by Joyce Zavarro.)

19

Class I MHC molecules (i.e., HLA-A, -B, or -C) serve as the antigen-presenting platform for CD8, or suppressor, T cells (Fig II-3). Class I molecules are present on almost all nucleated cells, indicating that most cells have the potential to stimulate CD8 T cells. The CD8 T-cell antigen receptor must recognize its own class I type before it can respond to tumor or viral antigens on the appropriate target cell, and therefore CD8 T cells from one individual will not respond to a target cell from another individual if the class I MHC molecules do not correspond. In general, class I APC are best for processing peptide antigens that have been synthesized by the host cell itself, including most tumor peptides or viral peptides after host cell infection.

Several other important topics that greatly influence the afferent phase are beyond the scope of this book. The immunology texts listed as references can be consulted for more detail concerning the following:

☐ The nature of antigen

☐ The immunologic microenvironment of different tissues (anatomical and functional differences among sites in APC, growth factors, immunoregulatory molecules, blood–tissue barriers, etc.

☐ Expression of HLA molecules on tissues other than leukocytes

Processing Phase

The conversion of the antigenic stimulus into an immunologic response through "priming" of "naive" B and T lymphocytes within the lymph nodes and spleen occurs during the processing phase of the immune response arc. This process is also called *activation* or *sensitization* of lymphocytes. Processing involves regulation of the interaction between antigen and naive lymphocytes, B cells or T cells that have not yet encountered their specific antigen, followed by their subsequent activation (Fig II-4). Immunologic processing has been the topic of extensive research, and the details are beyond the scope of this book. This discussion focuses on a few key concepts.

Preconditions necessary for processing   Helper T lymphocytes are the key regulatory and functional cell type for immune processing. Most helper T cells express CD4 molecule on the cell membrane. As mentioned above, T cells have an antigen receptor that detects antigen only when a trimolecular complex is formed consisting of APC-HLA molecule, processed antigen fragment, and T cell–T cell antigen receptor. The CD4 molecule serves to stabilize binding and enhance signaling between the HLA antigen complex and the T cell receptor. When helper T cells specific for an antigen become primed and partially activated, they acquire new functional properties including cell division, cytokine synthesis, and cell membrane expression of "accessory molecules" such as cell-adhesion molecules or costimulatory molecules. The synthesis and release of immune cytokines, especially IL-2, by T cells is crucial for progression of initial activation and functional differentiation of T cells. The primed T cell produces IL-2, which can then stimulate the same cell to become further activated in autocrine fashion.

Helper T-cell differentiation   At the stage of initial priming, CD4 T cells are usually classified as *T helper 0,* or *Th0,* cells. However, CD4 T cells can differentiate into functional subsets based on differences of gene activation and secretion of specific panels of cytokines. One subset called *T helper 1,* or *Th1,* becomes capable of

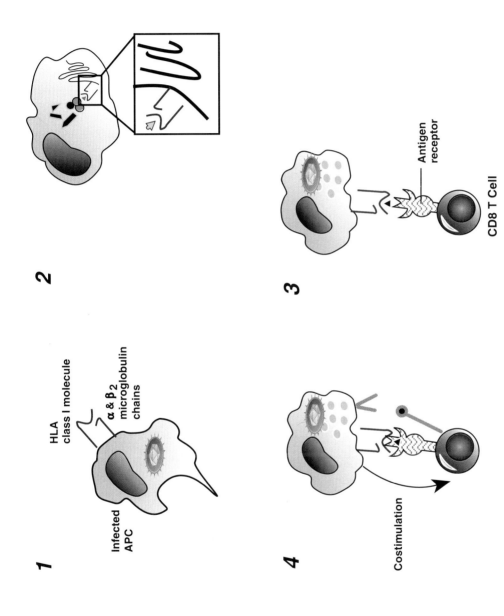

FIG II-3—Class I–dependent APC. *1*, APC is infected by a virus, which causes the cell to synthesize virus-associated peptides that are present in the cytosol. *2*, The viral antigen must be transported (through specialized transporter systems) into the endosomal compartment where it encounters class I HLA molecules. The fragment is placed into the pocket formed by the α chain of the class I HLA molecule. Unlike class II molecules, the second chain, called β2-microglobulin, is constant among all class I molecules. *3*, The CD8 T-cell receptor recognizes the fragment–class I complex. *4*, With the help of costimulatory molecules such as CD28/B7 interaction and cytokines, the CD8 T cell becomes primed, or partially activated. A similar mechanism is used to recognize tumor antigens that are produced by cells after malignant transformation. (Illlustration by Barb Cousins, modified by Joyce Zavarro.)

Immune Processing

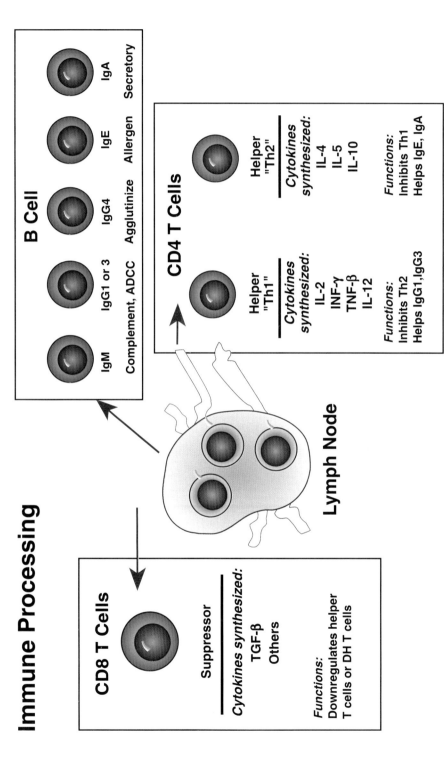

FIG II-4—Schematic illustration of immune processing of antigen within the lymph node. On exposure to antigen and APC within the lymph node, the three major lymphocyte subsets—B cells, CD4 T cells, and CD8 T cells—are activated to release specific cytokines and perform specific functional activities. B cells are stimulated to produce one of the various antibody isotypes, whose functions include complement activation, antibody-dependent cellular cytotoxicity, agglutinization, allergen recognition, or release into secretions. See chapter IV for a detailed discussion. CD4 T cells become activated into T helper 1 (Th1) or T helper 2 (Th2) subsets. Th1 cells function to help B cells to secrete IgG1 and IgG3; to inhibit Th2; and to release cytokines such as interleukin-2 (IL-2), interferon-gamma (IFN-γ), tumor necrosis factor–beta (TNF-β), and IL-12. Th2 cells function to help B cells to secrete IgE and IgA; to inhibit Th1 cells; and to synthesize cytokines such as IL-4, IL-5, and IL-10. CD8 T cells become activated into suppressor T cells that function by inhibiting other CD4 T cells, often by secreting cytokines such as TNF-β. (Illustration by Barb Cousins, modified by Joyce Zavarro.)

22

secreting interferon-gamma (INF-γ), tumor necrosis factor–beta (TNF-β), and IL-12 but *not* IL-4, IL-5, and IL-10. The other subset, *T helper 2*, or *Th2*, becomes capable of secreting IL-4, IL-5, and IL-10 but not Th1 cytokines.

These subsets are important because the different cytokines produced by Th1 or Th2 profoundly influence immune processing, B-cell antibody synthesis, and cell-mediated effector responses (see below). For example, cytokines such as INF-γ produced by Th1 cells block the differentiation and activation of Th2 cells, and vice versa. The regulation determining whether a Th1 or a Th2 response develops in response to exposure to a particular antigen is not entirely understood, but presumed variables include cytokines preexisting in the microenvironment, the nature or amount of antigen, and the type of APC. For example, IL-12 that is produced by macrophage APC might preferentially induce Th1 responses.

B-cell activation   One of the major regulatory functions for helper T cells concerns B-cell activation. B lymphocytes are responsible for producing antibodies, which are glycoproteins able to bind biochemically to a specific antigenic substance. B cells begin as naive lymphocytes bearing on the cell surface antibodies IgM and IgD, which serve as the B-cell antigen receptor. Through these surface antibodies, B cells can detect epitopes on intact antigens and thus do not require antigen processing by APC. After appropriate stimulation of the B-cell antigen receptor, helper T cell–B cell interaction occurs, leading to further B cell activation and differentiation. B cells acquire new functional properties, such as cell division, cell surface expression of accessory molecules, and the ability to synthesize and release large quantities of antibodies. Most important, activated B cells acquire the ability to change antibody class from IgM to another class (e.g., to IgG1, IgA, or another immunoglobulin). This shift requires a molecular change of the immunoglobulin heavy chain class at the genetic level, which is regulated by specific cytokines released by the helper T cell. For example, treatment of an antigen-primed B cell with the cytokine INF-γ will induce a switch from antibody IgM to IgG1. Treatment with IL-4 will induce an IgM to IgE switch. Chapter IV discusses the importance of the different antibody classes in immune reactivity.

Role of suppressor T cells   The regulation of the B-cell and helper T-cell response has recently been clarified, and the role of antigen receptors, tolerance, and immune microenvironments is discussed in chapter V. The immunoregulatory role of suppressor T cells has become partially clarified, especially through the induction of immunosuppressive cytokine synthesis by regulatory T cells. Classically, suppressor T cells were observed to express the CD8 marker and to become activated during the initial phases of processing. More recently, certain CD4 T cells have also been observed to have suppressive functions. In many cases both CD8 and CD4 suppressors appear to operate by the release of immunosuppressive cytokines such as TGF-β, which have the capacity to inhibit or alter the helper or effector function of other T cells. Other classic mechanisms of suppressor T-cell function, such as complicated antigen-specific T-cell "circuits" and release of antigen-specific suppressor molecules, have received less attention. The mechanism for activation of suppressor T cells is under investigation, but immunization of antigens orally or through an anterior chamber injection are two immune response arcs that preferentially induce suppressor T cells (see below). The relationship between CD8 suppressor T cells and CD8 cytotoxic effector cells is unclear, and probably these two represent different subpopulations of CD8 T cells.

Effector Phase

During the effector phase the adaptive immune response (e.g., get rid of offending foreign antigen) is physically carried out. Antigen-specific effectors exist in two major subsets:

□ T cells

□ B cells plus their antibodies

A third population of *non-T, non-B effector lymphocytes,* formerly called *null cells,* is sometimes also grouped with immune effectors, although these cells are not antigen specific and might be considered part of the innate immune system.

In general, effector lymphocytes require two exposures to antigen:

□ The initial exposure, often called *priming* or *activation,* occurring in the lymph node

□ A second exposure, often called *restimulation,* happening in the peripheral tissue in which the initial antigen contact occurred

This second exposure is usually necessary to fully exploit the effector mechanism within a local tissue. All of these effector mechanisms are described in much more detail in chapter IV.

Effector T lymphocyte subsets can be distinguished into two main types by functional differences in experimental assays or by differences in cell surface expression of marker molecules (Fig II-5). *Delayed hypersensitivity (DH) T cells* usually express CD4 marker and release specific cytokines such as INF-γ and TNF-β. They function by homing into a tissue, recognizing antigen and APC, becoming fully activated, and releasing cytokines and mediators that then recruit other nonspecific, antigen-independent effector cells such as neutrophils, basophils, or monocytes. As for helper T cells, Th1 and Th2 types of DH effector cells have been identified.

Cytotoxic T lymphocytes (CTL) are the other type of major effector T cell. CTL express CD8 marker and serve as effector cells for killing tumors or virally infected host cells through release of cytotoxic cytokines or specialized pore-forming molecules. The subset of effector lymphocytes formerly called null cells but now grouped as non-B, non-T lymphocytes includes natural killer cells, lymphokine-activated cells, and killer cells.

Antibodies, or *immunoglobulins,* are soluble antigen-specific effector molecules of adaptive immunity. After appropriate antigenic stimulation with T cell help, B cells secrete IgM antibodies, and later other isotypes, into the efferent lymph fluid draining into the venous circulation. Antibodies then mediate a variety of immune effector activities by combining with antigen in the blood or in tissues.

Immune Response Arc and Primary or Secondary Immune Responses

Concept of Immunologic Memory

Immunologic memory is probably the most distinctive feature of adaptive immune responses and is in many ways synonymous with the idea of protective immunization. Classically, immunologic memory was the concept used to explain why serum antibody production for a specific antigen increased markedly after reexposure to that antigen but not after exposure to a different antigen. Later it was learned that the concept of memory applied not only to antibody production by B cells but also to T lymphocytes as well.

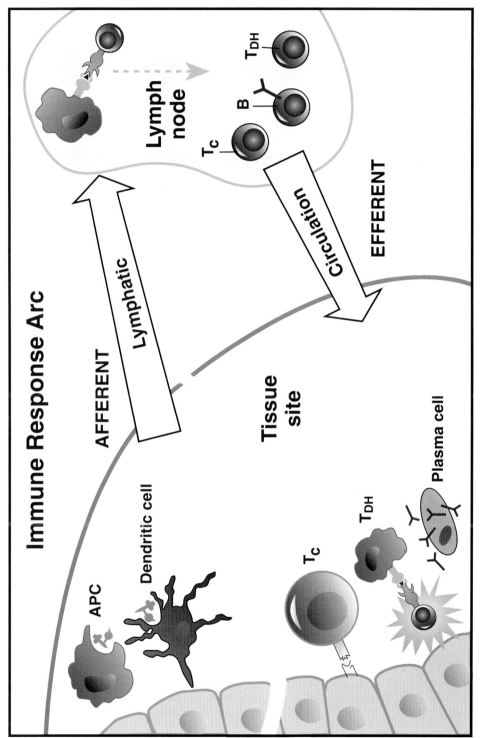

FIG II-5—Schematic representation of effector mechanisms during adaptive immunity. Not only is the immune response initiated within the tissue site, but ultimately the immune response arc is completed when effectors encounter antigen within the tissue after release into the circulation from the lymph node. The three most important effector mechanisms of adaptive immunity include cytotoxic T cells (T_C), delayed hypersensitivity T cells (T_{DH}), and antibody-producing B cells, especially plasma cells. (Illustration by Barb Cousins, modified by Joyce Zavarro.)

Differences in primary and secondary responses   Memory implies that the second encounter with an antigen is regulated differently from the first encounter. Differences in the primary and secondary immune response arc, especially in the processing and effector phases, offer partial explanation. During the processing phase of the primary response, antigen must find the relatively rare specific B cell (perhaps 1 in 100,000) and T cell (perhaps 1 in 10,000), then stimulate these cells from a completely resting and naive state, a sequence that requires days. The secondary processing response for T and B cells is shorter for at least three reasons:

- Upon removal of antigen, T and B lymphocytes activated during the primary response may gradually return to a resting state, but they retain the capacity to become reactivated within 12–24 hours of antigen exposure. That is, they are now memory cells rather than naive cells.

- Because stimulated lymphocytes divide, the population of potential antigen-responsive T or B cells will have increased manyfold, and these cells will have migrated to other sites of potential encounters with antigen.

- In some cases such as mycobacterial infection, low doses of antigen may remain in the node or site, producing a chronic, low-level, continuous antigenic stimulation of T and B cells.

For antibody responses, another memory function dependent upon antibody requires even less time and operates primarily at the level of effector phase. IgM produced during the effector phase of the primary response and released into the blood is often too large to passively leak into a peripheral site. However, during the secondary response, antibody class switching has occurred so that IgG or other isotypes that have passively leaked into a site or have been actively produced there can combine with an antigen immediately, causing the secondary response triggered by antibody to be very rapid *(immediate hypersensitivity)*.

Homing   Memory also requires that lymphocytes demonstrate a complex migratory pattern called *homing*. Thus, lymphocytes pass from the circulation into various tissues from which they subsequently depart and then pass by way of lymphatics to reenter the circulation. Homing involves the variable interaction between lymphocytes and endothelial cells using multiple *cell-adhesion molecules (CAM)*, which are discussed in chapter IV. Usually, the major types of lymphocytes that migrate into tissue sites are memory lymphocytes that express higher levels of certain CAM, such as the integrins and immunoglobulin superfamily, than do naive cells. Naive lymphocytes tend to migrate to lymphoid tissues where they have the chance of meeting their cognate antigen. Inflammation, however, changes the rules and serves to break down homing patterns. At inflammatory sites the volume of lymphocyte migration is far greater and selection much less precise, although migration of memory cells or activated lymphocytes still exceeds that of naive cells.

Regional Immunity and Immunologic Microenvironments

Regional Immunity

The idea that each organ and tissue site has its own particular immune response arc, which may vary significantly from the classic cutaneous response, is called *regional immunity*. Regional immunity of the tissue site can characterize all three phases—afferent, processing, and efferent—of the responses involved. For instance, the immune response arc for oral immunization (e.g., polio vaccine) will differ from intramuscular immunization (e.g., mumps/measles/rubella vaccine), which differs from cutaneous vaccination (e.g., bacille Calmette-Guérin vaccine). Regional immunity also affects the transplantation of donor tissue, such as a kidney or cornea. Such transplantations require the recipient to produce afferent, processing, and effector responses to the transplant, all modified by the unique location. Chapter III describes regional immune concepts relevant to the eye. See also BCSC Section 8, *External Disease and Cornea,* for discussion of the regional immunity of the cornea in Part 11, Corneal Transplantation.

Immunologic Microenvironments

Regional immunologic differences occur because different tissue sites are composed of different *immunologic microenvironments.* The concept of immunologic micro-environment incorporates a broad range of anatomical and physiologic differences among tissues or organs that regulate the immune response:

☐ The presence of well-formed lymphatics

☐ Specialized immunologic structures (Peyer's patches or conjunctival follicles)

☐ Blood–tissue barriers to macromolecules or cell migration

☐ Type of resident APC

☐ Constitutive synthesis of immunoregulatory cytokines or molecules by the parenchymal cell types

☐ Many other factors

The analysis of immunologic microenvironments has become important for understanding the immunology of transplantation, infection, or autoimmunity for gene therapy or many organ systems.

Clinical Examples of the Concept of the Immune Response Arc

The concept of the immune response arc is a powerful tool to understand clinically relevant immunologic phenomena. The two examples of cutaneous immunity on pp 28 and 29 illustrate this feature. Throughout the discussion in chapters III, IV, and V, such clinical examples will be interspersed with text to provide similar illustrations.

Male DK, Cooke A, Owen M, et al. *Advanced Immunology.* 3rd ed. St Louis: Mosby; 1996.

Roitt IM. *Essential Immunology.* 9th ed. Malden, MA: Blackwell Science; 1997.

Primary response to poison ivy toxin   The first encounter with the poison ivy resin urushiol and contact on the epidermal surface of an exposed extremity, such as the forearm, triggers the immunologic mechanisms of poison ivy dermatitis. The *afferent phase* of this primary response begins when the toxin permeates into the epidermis where much of it binds to extracellular proteins, forming a protein-toxin conjugate technically called a *hapten*. Some of the toxin is taken up by APC (especially Langerhans cells), and over the next 4–18 hours the toxin-stimulated LC leave their normal location in the basal epidermis and migrate along afferent lymphatics into the draining lymph nodes. During this time, the toxin is internalized into endocytic compartments and processed by the LC so that it can be recognized by helper T cells within the node. Some of the free toxin or hapten is also carried by lymph into the node.

In the lymph node the *processing phase* begins. The urushiol-stimulated LC interact with T cells, seeking over the next 3–5 days the rare T cell that has the correct specific antigen receptor. Once located, the naive T cell becomes primed. It is induced to undergo cell division, to acquire new functions such as cytokine secretion, and to upregulate certain surface molecules and receptors of the plasma membrane. These primed cells ultimately either function as helper cells or become effector cells that leave the node through efferent lymphatics, accumulate in the thoracic duct, and then enter venous blood where they recirculate.

Free toxin or hapten not taken up by APC experiences a different fate during the processing phase. It enters a zone of the lymph node populated by B cells. These naive B cells express membrane-bound antibody (IgM and IgD) that serves as antigen receptor. If a chance encounter occurs between the correct antibody and the toxin, the B cell becomes partially activated. However, completion of the B-cell activation requires further interaction with helper T cells, which release cytokines inducing B cells to undergo cell division and to increase production of antibodies, releasing antitoxin antibody into the lymph fluid and ultimately the venous circulation.

The *effector phase* begins when the primed T cells, primed B cells, or antibody leave the lymphatics and enter the peripheral site of the original antigen encounter. By 5–7 days after exposure, much of the urushiol toxin might have already been removed through nonspecific clearance mechanisms such as desquamation of exposed epidermis, washing of involved skin, and subclinical effects of innate immunity. When toxin-stimulated APC do remain at the site, primed T cells become further activated into effector cells, releasing inflammatory mediators to recruit other leukocyte populations. This represents the contact hypersensitivity type of delayed hypersensitivity. Rarely, if adequate free toxin is present, IgG antitoxin immune complexes can form and mediate inflammation (see below). However, if most of the antigen is already cleared, then the primed T cell may enter the skin but become inactive, retaining memory. Or the T cell may exit the skin through afferent lymphatics to reenter the lymph node. Similarly, antibody or antibody-producing B cells may remain in the skin or reach the lymph nodes.

Secondary response to poison ivy toxin   The immunologic mechanisms work much faster after the second encounter with poison ivy toxin. The *afferent phase* of this secondary response begins when the toxin permeates the epidermis. Again, some of the toxin is taken up by the LC and internalized over the next 4–18 hours into endocytic compartments and processed in a way that can be recognized by T cells. If a memory T cell is present at the cutaneous site, the *processing* and *effector phases* will occur within 24 hours at the site, as the memory T cell becomes activated upon interacting with the LC. In addition, some LC will leave the skin, enter the draining node, and encounter memory T cells there.

Processing during the secondary response is much quicker, and within 24 hours restimulated memory cells enter the circulation and migrate to the toxin-exposed cutaneous site. Since abundant toxin remains, additional T cell–LC stimulation occurs, inducing vigorous T-cell cytokine production. The inflammatory mediators, in turn, recruit neutrophils and monocytes, leading to a severe inflammatory reaction within 12–36 hours after exposure, causing the typical epidermal blisters of poison ivy. Since the response is delayed by 24 hours, it is considered delayed hypersensitivity, and in this case a specific form of DH called *contact hypersensitivity*.

Primary and secondary response to tuberculosis   The primary and secondary immune response arcs can occur at different sites, as with the immunologic mechanisms of the first and second encounter with *Mycobacterium tuberculosis* antigens. The *afferent phase* of the primary response occurs after inhalation of the live organisms, which proliferate slowly within the lung. Alveolar macrophages ingest the bacteria and transport the organisms to the hilar lymph nodes where the *processing phase* begins. Over the next few days, as T and B lymphocytes are primed, the hilar nodes become enlarged because of the increased number of dividing T and B cells as well as generalized increased trafficking of other lymphocytes through the node. The *effector phase* begins when the primed T cells recirculate and enter the infected lung. T cells interact with macrophage-ingested bacteria, and cytokines are released that activate neighboring macrophages to fuse into giant cells, forming caseating granulomas. Meanwhile, some of the effector T cells home to other lymph nodes throughout the body, where they become inactive memory T cells, trafficking and recirculating throughout the secondary lymphoid tissue.

A secondary response using the immune response arc of the skin is the basis of the tuberculin skin test to diagnose TB. The *afferent phase* of the secondary response begins when purified protein derivative (PPD) reagent, antigens purified from mycobacteria, is injected into the dermis, where the PPD is taken up by dermal macrophages. The secondary *processing phase* begins when these PPD-stimulated macrophages migrate into the draining lymph node where they encounter memory T cells from the previous lung infection, leading to memory T-cell reactivation. The secondary *effector phase* commences when these reactivated memory T cells recirculate and home back into the dermis and encounter additional antigen/macrophages at the site, causing the T cells to become fully activated and release cytokines. Within 24–72 hours these cytokines induce infiltration of additional lymphocytes, monocytes, and fibrin clotting. This process produces the typical indurated dermal lesion of the TB skin test, called the *tuberculin form* of DH.

CHAPTER III

Ocular Immune Responses

Just as regional differences in immune responses occur because of differences in the immunologic microenvironments of various tissue sites, regional differences can be identified for specific locations within and around the eye. Such areas as the conjunctiva; anterior chamber, anterior uvea (iris and ciliary body), and vitreous; cornea and sclera; and retina/RPE/choriocapillaris each seem to have differences in immunologic microenvironment that affect immune responses in health and disease (Table III-1).

Immune Responses of the Conjunctiva

Features of the Immunologic Microenvironment

The conjunctiva shares many of the features typical for mucosal sites. It is composed of two layers: an epithelial layer and a connective tissue layer called the *substantia propria*. The conjunctiva is well vascularized and has good lymphatic drainage to preauricular and submandibular nodes. The tissue is richly invested with Langerhans cells, other dendritic cells, and macrophages to serve as potential APC. Conjunctival follicles that enlarge after certain types of ocular surface infection or inflammation represent collections of T cells, B cells, and APC. Observation of the function of similar sites, such as Peyer's patches of the intestine, suggests that follicles might represent a site for localized immune processing of antigens that permeate through the thin overlying epithelium to be processed by B cells and T cells locally within the follicle.

The conjunctiva, especially the substantia propria, is richly infiltrated with potential effector cells, predominately mast cells. All antibody isotypes are represented, and presumably local production as well as passive leakage occurs. IgA is the most abundant antibody in the tear film. Soluble molecules of the innate immune system are also represented, especially complement. The conjunctiva appears to support most innate and adaptive immune effector responses, especially antibody-mediated and lymphocyte-mediated responses, although IgE-mediated mast cell degranulation is one of the most common and important. Chapter IV discusses these mechanisms in greater detail. See also Part 4 of BCSC Section 8, *External Disease and Cornea*.

Immunoregulatory Systems

The most important immunoregulatory system for the conjunctiva is called *mucosa-associated lymphoid tissue (MALT)*. The concept MALT refers to the interconnected network of mucosal sites (the epithelial lining of respiratory tract, gut, genitourinary

TABLE III-1

COMPARISON OF IMMUNE MICROENVIRONMENTS IN VARIOUS NORMAL OCULAR SITES

	CONJUNCTIVA	CORNEA/SCLERA	ANTERIOR CHAMBER, ANTERIOR UVEA, VITREOUS	SUBRETINA/RPE/CHOROID
Anatomical features	Lymphatics, follicles	Lymphatics at limbus, none centrally Macromolecules diffuse through stroma	No lymphatics, antigen clearance through trabecular meshwork Partial blood–uveal barrier	No lymphatics Blood–retinal barrier Uveal circulation permeable
Resident APC	Dendritic and Langerhans cells, macrophages	Langerhans cells at limbus No APC in central cornea No APC in sclera Epithelium/endothelium can be induced to express class II MHC	Many dendritic cells and macrophages in iris and ciliary body Hyalocytes are macrophage-derived	Microglia in the retina Dendritic cells and macrophages in choriocapillaris RPE can be induced to express class II MHC
Specialized immune compartments for localized immune processing	?? Follicles	None	None	None
Resident effector cells	Mast cells, T cells, B cells, plasma cells, rare PMN	Centrally—none Sclera—none	Rare to no T cells or B cells, rare mast cells	Retina—normally no lymphocytes Choroid—mast cells, some lymphocytes
Resident effector molecules	All antibody isotypes, especially IgE, IgG subclasses, IgA in tears Complement and kininogen precursors present	Peripherally Igs but minimal IgM Centrally minimal antibody, some complement present Sclera: low antibody concentration, minimal IgM	Kallikrein but not kininogen precursors Some complement present, but less than in blood Minimal Igs in iris, some IgG in ciliary body and aqueous humor	Retina—minimal to no Igs Choroid—IgGs and IgA
Immunoregulatory systems	Mucosa-associated lymphoid tissue	Immune privilege—Fas ligand, avascularity, lack of central APC	Immune privilege—anterior chamber–associated immune deviation, immuno-suppressive factors in aqueous, Fas ligand	Immune privilege—?? mechanisms

tract, and the ocular surface and its adnexae) that share certain specific immunologic features:

□ Rich investment of APC

□ Specialized structures for localized antigen processing (i.e., Peyer's patches or tonsils)

□ Unique effector cells (i.e., intraepithelial T cells and abundant mast cells)

However, the most distinctive aspect of MALT is the distribution and homing of effector B and T cells induced by immunization at one mucosal site to all MALT sites because of the shared expression of specific cell-adhesion molecules on postcapillary venules of the mucosal vasculature. MALT immune response arcs tend to favor Th2-dominated responses that result in production of predominantly IgA and IgE antibodies. Immunization of soluble antigens through MALT, especially in the gut sites, often produces oral tolerance, presumably by activating Th2-like regulatory T cells that suppress Th1 DH effector cells (see p 96).

Immune Responses of the Anterior Chamber, Anterior Uvea, and Vitreous

Features of the Immunologic Microenvironment

Numerous specialized anatomical features of the anterior region have an impact on ocular immune responses. The anterior chamber is a fluid-filled cavity; circulating aqueous humor provides a unique medium for intercellular communication between cytokines, or immune cells, and resident tissue cells of the iris, ciliary body, and corneal endothelium. Although aqueous humor is relatively protein depleted compared to serum (about 0.1%–1.0% of serum total protein), even normal aqueous humor contains a complex mixture of biological factors, such as immunosuppressive cytokines, neuropeptides, and complement inhibitors, that are capable of influencing immunologic events within the eye.

A partial blood–ocular barrier is present. Fenestrated capillaries in the ciliary body allow a size-dependent concentration gradient of plasma macromolecules to permeate the interstitial tissue; smaller plasma-derived molecules are present in higher concentration than are larger molecules. The tight junctions between the pigmented and the nonpigmented ciliary epithelium provide a more exclusive barrier, preventing interstitial macromolecules from permeating directly through the ciliary body into the aqueous humor. Nevertheless, low amounts of plasma macromolecules bypass the nonpigmented epithelium barrier and may permeate by diffusion anteriorly through the uvea to enter the anterior chamber through the anterior iris surface.

The inner eye does not contain well-developed lymphatics. Rather, it depends on the aqueous humor outflow channels for clearance of soluble substances and on endocytosis by trabecular meshwork endothelial cells or macrophages for clearance of particulates. Nevertheless, antigen inoculation into the anterior chamber results in efficient communication with the systemic immune response. Intact soluble antigens gain entrance to the venous circulation where they communicate with the spleen.

The iris and ciliary body contain a rich investment of macrophages and dendritic cells that serve as APC and possible effector cells. Immune processing is unlikely to occur locally, but APC leave the eye by the trabecular meshwork and

Immune response to viral conjunctivitis Conjunctivitis caused by adenovirus infection is a common ocular infection (see BCSC Section 8, *External Disease and Cornea*). Although details of the immune response after conjunctival adenovirus infection remain unknown, they can be inferred from knowledge of viral infection at other mucosal sites and from animal studies. After infection with adenovirus, the epithelial cells begin to die within 36 hours. Innate immune mechanisms that can assist in limiting infection become activated soon after infection. For example, infected cells produce cytokines such as interferons that limit spread of infectious virus and recruit nonspecific effector cells like macrophages and PMN.

However, the adaptive immune response to adenovirus infection is considered more important in viral clearance. The primary adaptive response begins when macrophages and dendritic cells presumably become infected or take up cell debris and viral antigens. Both APC and extracellular antigenic material are conveyed to the preauricular and submandibular nodes along lymphatics where both vigorous helper T-cell and antibody responses are activated, producing lymphadenopathy. Local immune processing may also occur within the follicle if virus invades the epithelial capsule. During the early effector phase of the primary B-cell response, IgM antibodies are released into the blood that will *not* be very effective in controlling surface infection, although they will prevent widespread viremia. However, IgM-bearing B cells eventually infiltrate the conjunctival stroma and may release antibody locally in the conjunctiva. Later, during the primary effector response, class switching to IgG or IgA may occur to mediate local effector responses, such as neutralization or complement-mediated lysis of infected cells.

The most active effector response later in acute viral infection comes from natural killer cells and CD8 cytotoxic T lymphocytes (CTL), which kill infected epithelium. However, adenovirus can block the expression of class I MHC on infected cells and thereby escape being killed by CTL. Adaptive immunity can also activate macrophages by antiviral DH mechanisms later during infection, and DH response to viral antigens is believed to contribute to the development of the corneal subepithelial infiltrates that occur in some patients late in adenovirus infection.

The secondary response of the conjunctiva, assuming a prior primary exposure to the same virus at some other mucosal site, differs in that antibody-mediated effector mechanisms dominate. Because of MALT, antivirus IgA will be present not only in blood but also in tears as a result of differentiated IgA-secreting B cells in the lacrimal gland, the substantia propia, and follicles. Thus, recurrent infection is often prevented by preexisting neutralizing antibodies that had disseminated into tears or follicles following the primary infection. However, if the inoculum of recurrent virus overwhelms this antibody barrier, or if the virus has mutated its surface glycoproteins recognized by antibodies, then epithelial infection does occur. Additional immune processing can occur in the follicle and draining nodes. Specific memory effector CTL are effective in clearing infection within a few days.

Nathanson N, ed. *Viral Pathogenesis.* Philadelphia: Lippincott; 1996.

Pepose JS, Holland GN, Wilhelmus KR, eds. *Ocular Infection and Immunity.* St Louis: Mosby; 1996.

home to the spleen where processing occurs that favors a Th2 response and preferential activation of CD8 suppressor T cells. Few resident T cells and some mast cells are present in the normal anterior uvea. B cells, eosinophils, and PMN appear to be absent. Very low concentrations of IgG, complement components, and kallikrein occur in normal eyes.

The vitreous has not been characterized as carefully as the anterior chamber, but it probably manifests most of the same properties with several notable exceptions. The vitreous gel can electrostatically bind charged protein substances and may thus serve as an antigen depot as well as a substrate for leukocytes' cell adhesion. Since the vitreous contains type II collagen, it may serve as a depot of potential autoantigen in some forms of uveitis related to arthritis in which type II collagen in the joint is an autoantigen. See also BCSC Section 12, *Retina and Vitreous.*

Immunoregulatory Systems

The anterior uvea has an immunoregulatory system that has been described as *immune privilege.* The modern conception of immune privilege refers to the observation that tumor implants or allografts unexpectedly survive better within an immunologically privileged region, while a similar implant or graft is rapidly rejected by immune mechanisms within the skin or other nonprivileged sites. Other immune-privileged sites are the subretinal space, the brain, and the testes. Although the nature of the antigen involved is probably important, immune privilege of the anterior uvea has been observed with a wide variety of antigens, including alloantigens (i.e., transplantation antigens), tumor antigens, haptens, soluble proteins, autoantigens, bacteria, and viruses.

Immune privilege is mediated by influences on both the afferent and the effector phases of the immune response arc. Immunization using the anterior segment as the afferent phase of a primary immune response arc results in a unique generation of immunologic effectors. Immunization as with lens protein or other autoantigens through the anterior chamber does not result in the same pattern of systemic immunity as does immunization by skin, contrary to intuitive assumptions. Immunization by an anterior chamber injection in experimental animals results in an altered form of systemic immunity to that antigen called *anterior chamber–associated immune deviation (ACAID).*

Following injection of antigen into the anterior chamber, the afferent phase begins when specialized macrophages residing in the iris recognize and take up the antigen. The APC function of these uveal macrophages has been altered by exposure to immunoregulatory cytokines normally present within aqueous humor and uveal tissue, especially TGF-β2. The process by which aqueous humor factors convert macrophages into ACAID-inducing APC is unknown. The TGF-β–exposed antigen-stimulated ocular macrophages leave by the trabecular meshwork and Schlemm's canal to enter into the venous circulation, where they preferentially migrate to the spleen. Here, processing of the antigen signal occurs, with activation of not only helper T cells and B cells but also suppressor T cells. The CD8 suppressor cells serve to alter CD4 helper T-cell responses in the spleen and to downregulate CD4 T-cell DH responses to the specific *immunizing* antigen at all body sites. Thus, the resulting effector response is characterized by a selective suppression of antigen-specific DH and a selectively diminished production of complement-fixing isotypes of antibodies. The other antibody isotypes and cytotoxic T-cell precursors are the same as those after conventional cutaneous immunization.

In addition, several other mechanisms for ACAID have been proposed. A small percentage of intact antigen can leave the eye to enter the blood, where it tends to be processed within the spleen. Low doses of intravenous antigens produce a form of immunosuppression that has been called *low-zone tolerance*. Various mechanisms for immunoregulatory T-cell activation within the eye have been suggested as well.

Especially important to the clinician is the capacity of a tissue site to sustain the secondary effector phase of the immune response arc, since the primary immune response arc in autoimmune diseases might have occurred outside of the eye. In this regard the secondary effector phase of the anterior segment is also immunosuppressive and has been termed *effector blockade*. Because various immunoregulatory systems are normally present within the eye, intact immunologic effectors that are functional elsewhere, in the skin, for example, are *partially* blocked from activation and function within the anterior segment. Thus, Th1 DH T cells, cytotoxic T cells, NK cells, and complement activation appear to function less effectively in the anterior uvea than elsewhere. For instance, the anterior uvea is *relatively* resistant to induction of a secondary PPD DH response after primary immunization with mycobacteria in the skin. Mechanisms for effector blockade are multifactorial but include production of the following:

☐ Immunosuppressive cytokines, produced by ocular tissues

☐ Immunosuppressive neuropeptides, produced by ocular nerves

☐ Functionally unique APC

☐ Complement inhibitors in aqueous humor

☐ Other factors

Recently, investigators have demonstrated the expression of a molecule called *Fas ligand* (FasL, or CD95 ligand) on iris and corneal endothelium. FasL is normally expressed in the thymus and a few other immune-privileged sites such as the testes. FasL is a potent trigger of programmed cell death, or *apoptosis,* of lymphocytes. Thus, FasL can induce apoptotic killing of infiltrating T cells, thereby preventing T-cell effector function. The loss of these protective mechanisms is presumed to occur prior to the development of uveitis.

The vitreous cavity has not been so well characterized immunologically, but preliminary experimental evidence suggests that an ACAID-like primary immune response arc probably applies to the vitreous as well, especially in a postvitrectomy eye. The existence of effector blockade in the vitreous is controversial, but this form of immunosuppression might be stimulated by vitrectomy. Other rationales for performing vitrectomy in eyes with uveitis are

☐ To remove any depot of antigen, including type II collagen, trapped in the gel

☐ To remove the gel substrate for cell-adhesion molecules to recruit and adhere leukocytes

☐ To allow circulation of immunosuppressive factors in aqueous humor

Therapeutic potential of immune privilege It is unknown whether ACAID has practical consequences for clinical diseases, although ACAID is believed to play a role in immunologic tolerance to lens crystallins after cataract surgery and in immunologic acceptance of corneal transplantation (see below). ACAID can influence the immune response to ocular autoantigens. Animals immunized through the anterior chamber with the retinal autoantigens S-antigen or interphotoreceptor retinol-binding protein develop ACAID, and they are then protected from experimental autoimmune uveitis in the contralateral eye after subsequent conventional cutaneous immunization. Recently, ACAID has been reproduced by infusion of monocytes that were first treated with TGF-β and antigen extracorporeally, suggesting a potential clinically relevant method for immunotherapy.

Ferguson TA, Griffith TS. A vision of cell death: insights into immune privilege. *Immunol Rev.* 1997;156:167–184.

Immune Responses of the Cornea

Features of the Immunologic Microenvironment

The cornea is unique in that the periphery and the central portions of the tissue represent distinctly different immunologic microenvironments (Fig III-1). Obviously, only the limbus is vascularized. Whereas the limbus is richly invested with Langerhans cells, the peripheral, paracentral, and central cornea are normally devoid of APC. However, various stimuli such as mild trauma, certain cytokines (e.g., IL-1), or infection can recruit APC to the central cornea. Plasma-derived enzymes (i.e., complement), IgM, and IgG are present in moderate concentration in the periphery, but only low levels of the IgGs are present centrally.

Corneal cells also appear to synthesize various antimicrobial and immunoregulatory proteins. Effector cells are absent or very scarce in the normal cornea, but PMN, monocytes, and lymphocytes can readily migrate through the stroma if appropriate chemotactic stimuli are activated. Lymphocytes, monocytes, and PMN can also adhere to the endothelial surface during inflammation, giving rise to keratic precipitates or the classic Khodadoust line of endothelial rejection (Fig III-2). Localized immune processing probably does not occur in the cornea. See also BCSC Section 8, *External Disease and Cornea*.

Immunoregulatory Systems

The cornea also demonstrates a form of immune privilege different from that observed in the anterior uvea. Immune privilege of the cornea is multifactorial. Normal limbal physiology is a major component, especially the maintenance of avascularity and lack of APC in the mid and central cornea. The absence of APC and lymphatics partially inhibits afferent recognition in the central cornea, and the absence of postcapillary venules centrally can limit the efficiency of effector recruitment, although both effector cells and molecules can ultimately infiltrate even avascular cornea. Another factor is the presence of intact immunoregulatory systems of the anterior chamber (i.e., ACAID), to which the corneal endothelium is exposed.

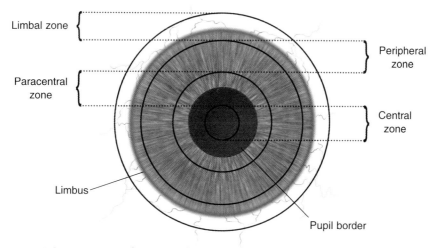

FIG III-1—Topographic zones of the cornea. (Illustration by Christine Gralapp.)

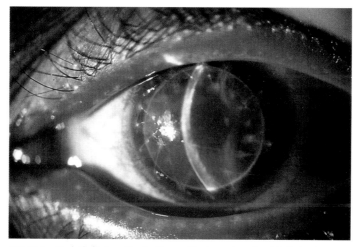

FIG III-2—Endothelial graft rejection with stromal and epithelial edema on the trailing aspect of the migrating Khodadoust line.

Corneal allograft rejection Penetrating keratoplasty, the transplantation of foreign corneal allografts, enjoys an extremely high success rate (over 90%) even in the absence of systemic immunosuppression. This rate compares favorably to the transplantation rates of other donor tissues. The mechanisms of corneal graft survival have been attributed to immune privilege. In experimental models factors contributing to rejection include the following:

- Presence of central corneal vascularization
- Induction of MHC molecule expression by the stroma, which is normally quite low
- Contamination of the donor graft with donor-derived APC prior to transplantation
- MHC disparity between the host and donor
- Preimmunization of the recipient to donor transplantation antigens

In addition, loss of immunoregulatory systems of the anterior chamber can apparently influence corneal allograft immunity, and the expression of FasL on corneal endothelium has recently been observed to greatly influence allograft protection. Rapid replacement of donor epithelium by host epithelium removes this layer as an antigenic stimulus. Once activated, however, antibody-dependent DH and CTL-related mechanisms can target transplantation antigens in all corneal layers.

Streilein JW. Regulation of ocular immune responses. *Eye.* 1997;11:171–175.

Immune Responses of the Retina, RPE, and Choroid

Features of the Immunologic Microenvironment

The immunologic microenvironments of the retina, retinal pigment epithelium (RPE), choriocapillaris, and choroid have not been well characterized. The retinal circulation demonstrates a blood–ocular barrier at the level of tight junctions between adjacent endothelial cells. The vessels of the choriocapillaris are highly permeable to macromolecules, allowing transudation of most plasma macromolecules into the extravascular spaces of the choroid and choriocapillaris. The tight junctions between the RPE cells probably provide the true physiologic barrier between the choroid and the retina. Well-developed lymphatics are absent, although both the retina and the choroid have abundant potential APC. In the retina resident microglia, bone marrow–derived cells related to monocytes, are interspersed within all layers and can undergo physical changes and migration in response to various stimuli. The choriocapillaris and choroid are richly invested with certain potential APC, especially macrophages and dendritic cells.

RPE can be induced to express class II MHC molecules, suggesting that RPE may also interact with T cells. The presence of T lymphocytes or B lymphocytes within the normal posterior segment has not been carefully addressed, but effector cells appear to be absent from the normal retina. The density of mast cells is moderate in the choroid, especially around the arterioles, but lymphocytes are present only in very low density. Eosinophils and neutrophils appear to be absent. Under various clinical or experimental conditions, however, high densities of T cells, B cells, macrophages, and PMN can infiltrate the choroid, choriocapillaris, and retina. The RPE and various cell types within the retina and the choroid (i.e., pericytes) can synthesize many different cytokines (e.g., TGF-β) that may alter the subsequent immune response. Local immune processing does not appear to occur. See also BCSC Section 12, *Retina and Vitreous.*

Immunoregulatory Systems

Recently, it has been demonstrated that a form of immune privilege is present after subretinal injection of antigen. The mechanism is unclear but is probably similar to ACAID. This observation may be important because of growing interest in retinal transplantation and gene therapy. The capacity of the choriocapillaris and choroid to function as unique environments for the afferent or effector phases has not yet been evaluated.

CLINICAL EXAMPLES

Retinal transplantation   Transplantation of retina or RPE is being investigated as a method for regeneration of retinal function in various disorders. In experimental animals subretinal transplantation of fetal retinal tissue or various kinds of RPE allografts often shows longer survival than the same grafts implanted elsewhere, even without systemic immunosuppression. The afferent phase recognition of alloantigens is likely performed by retinal microglia or recruited blood-derived macrophages from the choriocapillaris.

The subretinal cytokine environment remains unknown, since transplantation is performed in the setting of retinal diseases, such as retinitis pigmentosa or macular degeneration, in which the blood–retinal barrier is altered and retinal cell/RPE injury is present. However, injured RPE can still synthesize either immunosuppressive or inflammatory cytokines. The site of immune processing is unknown, but the spleen or some other secondary compartment outside of the eye is probably involved. When rejection does occur, the effector mechanisms are also unclear. In mice with fetal retinal grafts, immune rejection occurs by an unusual slowly progressive cytotoxic mechanism not involving typical antibody-mediated cytolysis or DH T cells. In humans and nonhuman primates, rejection of RPE allografts has been observed to occur in both subacute and chronic forms.

Retinal gene therapy   Retinal gene therapy is the therapeutic use of intentional transfection of photoreceptors or RPE with a replication-defective virus that has been genetically altered to carry a replacement gene of choice. This gene becomes expressed in any cell infected by the virus. Immune clearance of the virus has been shown to cause loss of expression of the transferred gene in other body sites. If immune privilege protects the viral vector or the protein synthesized by the transferred gene from immune clearance, then subretinal gene therapy might enjoy greater success in the eye than elsewhere. This topic is currently under intense investigation.

CHAPTER IV

Mechanisms of Immune Effector Reactivity

Immunologists have long been fascinated with all three phases of the adaptive immune response as well as related issues such as developmental biology and the ontogeny of lymphoid precursors. From the clinician's perspective, however, the effector phase is the most important aspect of both innate and adaptive immune responses, since patients who present with inflammation presumably have already experienced the afferent and processing phases of adaptive immunity, or they are in the midst of the triggering mechanisms of innate immunity. In the following discussion immune effector responses are subdivided into three categories:

☐ Innate immune effector responses: bacterial triggers, nonspecific effector molecules, neutrophil activation, macrophage activation

☐ Adaptive immune effector responses: antibody-dependent responses, lymphocyte-dependent responses, combination antibody/cellular responses

☐ Amplification mechanisms relevant to both immune responses: inflammatory mediators, cytokines, related topics

Effector Reactivities of Innate Immunity

Whereas adaptive immune responses use a complex afferent and processing system to activate effector responses, innate immune responses generally use more direct triggering mechanisms. Four of the most important triggering or response mechanisms to initate an effector response of innate immunity are reviewed here (Table IV-1).

Bacteria-Derived Molecules That Trigger Innate Immunity

Bacterial lipopolysaccharide (LPS)   Bacterial lipopolysaccharide, also known as *endotoxin,* is an intrinsic component of most gram-negative bacterial cell walls. One of the most important triggering molecules of innate immunity, LPS consists of three components:

☐ Lipid A

☐ Lipopolysaccharide

☐ A protein core

Lipid A is responsible for most of the inflammatory effects of LPS.

TABLE IV-1

EFFECTOR REACTIVITIES OF THE INNATE IMMUNE RESPONSE IN THE EYE

Bacteria-derived molecules that trigger innate immunity
    Lipopolysaccharide (LPS)
    Other cell wall components
    Exotoxins and secreted toxins

Nonspecific soluble molecules that trigger or modulate innate immunity
    Plasma-derived enzymes
    Acute phase reactants
    Local production of cytokines by parenchymal cells within a tissue site

Innate mechanisms for recruitment and activation of polymorphonuclear cells
    Cell adhesion and transmigration
    Activation mechanisms
        Phagocytosis of bacteria

Innate mechanisms for recruitment and activation of macrophages
    Cell adhesion and transmigration
    Activation mechanisms
        Scavenging
        Priming
        Activation

LPS is an important cause of morbidity and mortality during infections with gram-negative bacteria and is the major cause of shock, fever, and other pathophysiologic responses to bacterial sepsis. The pleiotropic effects of LPS include activation of monocytes and PMN, leading to upregulation of genes for various cytokines (IL-1, IL-6, TNF); degranulation; activation of complement through the alternative pathway; and direct impact on vascular endothelium. The cellular effects of LPS are the result of interactions with specific cell receptors, such as CD18/CR3, an LPS scavenger receptor on macrophages and lymphocytes. In addition, a circulating LPS-binding protein has been identified. Binding by the LPS-binding protein complex with the CD14 molecule on the macrophage surface leads to activation.

Other bacterial cell wall components   The bacterial cell wall and membrane are complex, with numerous polysaccharide, lipid, and protein structures that can initiate the innate immune response whether or not they act as antigens for adaptive immunity. Such toxins may include

- Muramyl dipeptide
- Lipoteichoic acids, in gram-positive bacteria
- Lipoarabinomannan, in mycobacteria
- Other poorly characterized soluble factors, such as heat shock proteins, common to all bacteria

Killed lysates of many types of gram-positive bacteria or mycobacteria have been demonstrated to directly activate macrophages, making them useful as adjuvants. Some of these components have been implicated in various models for arthritis and uveitis. In many cases the molecular mechanisms are probably similar to LPS.

LPS-induced uveitis Humans are intermittently exposed to low doses of LPS that are released from the gut, especially during episodes of diarrhea and dysentery, and exposure to LPS may play a role in dysentery-related uveitis, arthritis, and Reiter syndrome. Systemic adminstration of a low dose of LPS in rabbits, rats, and mice produces a mild acute uveitis; this effect occurs at doses of LPS lower than those that cause apparent systemic shock. In rabbits a breakdown of the blood–ocular barrier occurs because of leakage of plasma proteins through uveal vessels and loosening of the tight junctions between the nonpigmented ciliary epithelium. Rats and mice develop an acute PMN and monocytic infiltrate in the iris and ciliary body within 24 hours.

The precise mechanism of LPS-induced ocular effects after systemic administration is unknown. One possibility is that LPS circulates and binds to the vascular endothelium or other sites within the anterior uvea. Alternatively, LPS might cause activation of uveal macrophages or circulating leukocytes, leading them to preferentially adhere to the anterior uveal vascular endothelium. Degranulation of platelets is among the first of histologic changes in LPS uveitis, probably mediated by eicosanoids, platelet-activating factors (PAF), and vasoactive amines. The subsequent intraocular generation of several mediators, especially leukotriene B_4, thromboxane B_2, prostaglandin E_2, and IL-6, correlates with the development of the cellular infiltrate and vascular leakage.

Not surprisingly, direct injection of LPS into various ocular sites can initiate a severe localized inflammatory response. For example, intravitreal injection of LPS triggers a dose-dependent infiltration of the uveal tract, retina, and vitreous with PMN and monocytes. Injection of LPS into the central cornea results in the development of a ring infiltrate as a result of the infiltration of PMN circumferentially from the limbus.

Exotoxins and other secretory products of bacteria Various bacteria are known to secrete products such as *exotoxins* into the microenvironment in which the bacterium is growing. Many of these products are enzymes that, although not directly inflammatory, can cause tissue damage that subsequently results in inflammation. Examples include

◻ Collagenases

◻ Hemolysins such as streptolysin O, which can kill PMN by causing cytoplasmic and extracellular release of their granules

◻ Phospholipases such as the *Clostridium perfringens* alpha toxins, which kill cells and cause necrosis by disrupting cell membranes

Intravitreal injection of a cytolytic toxin derived from *Bacillus cereus* can cause direct necrosis of retinal cells. In addition, the metabolic byproducts of bacterial physiology can result in nonspecific tissue alterations that predispose to inflammation, such as altered tissue pH.

Role of bacterial toxin production and severity of endophthalmitis The effect of toxin production by various bacterial strains on the severity of endophthalmitis has recently been evaluated in experimental studies. It has been known for nearly a century that intraocular injection of LPS is highly inflammatory and accounts for much of the enhanced pathogenicity of gram-negative infections of the eye. Using clinical isolates or bacteria genetically altered to diminish production of various types of bacterial toxins, investigators have recently demonstrated that toxin elaboration by the living organism in gram-positive or -negative endophthalmitis greatly influences inflammatory cell infiltration and retinal cytotoxicity. This research suggests that sterilization with antibiotic therapy alone, in the absence of antitoxin therapy, may not prevent activation of innate immunity, ocular inflammation, and vision loss in eyes infected by toxin-producing strains.

Booth MC, Atkuri RV, Gilmore MS. Toxin production contributes to severity of *Staphylococcus aureus* endophthalmitis. In: Nussenblatt RB, Whitcup SM, Caspi RR, et al, eds. *Advances in Ocular Immunology.* New York: Elsevier; 1994:269–272.

Jett BD, Parke DW 2nd, Booth MC, et al. Host/parasite interactions in bacterial endophthalmitis. *Zentralb Bakteriol.* 1997;285:341–367.

Some bacteria secrete small formyl peptide molecules related to the tripeptide N-formylmethionylleucylphenylalanine (FMLP). These formyl peptides are potent triggering stimuli for innate immunity. FMLP interacts with specific receptors on leukocytes, resulting in their recruitment into the site. In vitro FMLP activates PMN, causes degranulation, and stimulates chemotaxis. Injection of FMLP into the cornea, conjunctiva, or vitreous produces infiltration with PMN and monocytes, which can be prevented by pretreatment with corticosteroids, cyclo-oxygenase inhibitors, and competitive inhibitors of FMLP.

Gallin JI, Goldstein M, Snyderman R, eds. *Inflammation: Basic Principles and Clinical Correlates.* 2nd ed. Philadelphia: Raven; 1992.

Other Triggers or Modulators of Innate Immunity

As discussed in earlier chapters, the adaptive immune response employs one main family of soluble effector molecules: antibodies specific for antigen. Although no similar mechanism exists for innate immunity, various *nonspecific* soluble protein molecules are used by the innate immune response.

Plasma-derived enzyme systems, especially *complement,* are discussed below under amplification systems since they are effector molecules used to amplify inflammation for both innate and adaptive immunity. However, it is important to emphasize that complement, especially when activated through the alternative pathway, is a major effector molecule for innate immunity. Thus, stimuli that activate the alternative pathway, such as microbial cell walls, plastic surfaces of IOLs, or traumatized tissues, are potential triggering mechanisms of innate immunity.

Another important family of molecules for innate immunity is the group of *acute phase reactants,* such as C-reactive protein and α_2-macroglobulin. Although generally synthesized by the liver and released into blood, many of these molecules are also made by macrophages or produced locally in tissues. α_2-macroglobulin is especially interesting: it is a natural scavenging molecule, capable of binding various types of proteins and substances presumably for clearance from the host. α_2-macroglobulin is present in aqueous humor during uveitis and is synthesized by various ocular parenchymal cells of the eye as well. Enzyme systems in tears, such as lysozyme and lactoferrin, also play a role in ocular surface defenses.

Finally, various traumatic or toxic stimuli within ocular sites can trigger innate immunity. For example, trauma or toxins interacting directly with nonimmune ocular parenchymal cells, especially iris or ciliary body epithelium, RPE, retinal Müller cells, or corneal or conjunctival epithelium, can result in a wide range of mediator, cytokine, and eicosanoid synthesis (see Table IV-7 on pp 80–81), and this mechanism probably should be considered a form of innate immunity. Thus, phagocytosis of staphylococcus by corneal epithelium, microtrauma to ocular surface epithelium by contact lenses, chafing of iris or ciliary epithelium by an IOL, or laser treatment of the retina can each stimulate ocular cells to produce mediators that assist in the recruitment of innate effector cells such as PMN or macrophages.

CLINICAL EXAMPLE

Uveitis-glaucoma-hyphema (UGH) syndrome One cause of postoperative inflammation following cataract surgery, UGH syndrome is related to the physical presence of certain IOL styles. Although UGH syndrome was more common when rigid anterior chamber lenses were used during the early 1980s, it has also been reported with posterior chamber lenses. The pathogenesis of UGH syndrome appears to be related to various mechanisms for activation of innate immunity. One of the most likely mechanisms is cytokine and eicosanoid synthesis triggered by mechanical chafing or trauma to the iris or ciliary body. Plasma-derived enzymes, especially complement or fibrin, can enter the eye through vascular permeability altered by surgery or trauma and can then be activated by the surface of IOLs, especially those composed of polymethylmethacrylate (PMMA). Adherence of bacteria and leukocytes to the surface has also been implicated. Toxicity caused by contaminants on the lens surface during manufacturing has become rare. Recent research suggests that surface modification of IOLs, such as coating with heparin, might diminish the capacity of IOL materials to activate innate immune effector mechanisms. Nevertheless, even many noninflamed eyes with IOLs can demonstrate histologic evidence of low-grade foreign body reactions around the haptics.

Pepose JS, Holland GN, Wilhelmus KR, eds. *Ocular Infection and Immunity.* St Louis: Mosby; 1996.

Innate Mechanisms for the Recruitment and Activation of Neutrophils

Neutrophils, referred to here as *polymorphonuclear leukocytes,* or *PMN,* are among the most efficient effectors of innate immunity following trauma or acute infection. PMN are categorized as either *resting* or *activated,* based on secretory and cell membrane activity. Cellular recruitment of resting circulating PMN by the innate immune response occurs rapidly in a tightly controlled process requiring two main mechanisms:

□ PMN adhesion to the vascular endothelium through cell-adhesion molecules (CAM) on leukocytes as well as on endothelial cells in postcapillary venules

□ Transmigration of the PMN through the endothelium and its extracellular matrix mediated by various chemotactic factors

For resting PMN to escape from blood vessels, an essential adhesion with activated vascular endothelial cells must occur, which is triggered by various innate stimuli such as LPS, physical injury, thrombin, histamine, or leukotriene release as well as other agonists.

The initial phase involves *neutrophil rolling,* a process by which PMN bind loosely but reversibly to nonactivated endothelial cells (Fig IV-1). Involved are molecules on both cell types belonging to at least three sets of CAM families:

□ The *selectins,* especially L-, P- and E-selectin

□ The *integrins,* especially LFA-1 and MAC-1

□ Molecules in the immunoglobulin (Ig) superfamily, especially ICAM-1 and -2

The primary events are mediated largely by members of the selectin family and occur within minutes of stimulation. The ligands for selectin molecules are as yet poorly characterized oligosaccharides found in the cell membranes. Nonactivated PMN express L-selectin, which mediates a weak bond to endothelial cells. Upon exposure to activating factors mentioned above, endothelial cells become activated, expressing in turn at least two other selectins (E and P) by which they can bind to the PMN and help stabilize the interaction by a process called *adhesion.* Subsequently, other factors such as PAF, various cytokines, and bacterial products can induce the upregulation of the β integrin family. As integrins are expressed, the L-selectins are shed, and PMN then bind firmly to endothelial cells through the Ig superfamily molecules.

Subsequent to adhesion, various chemotactic factors are required to induce *transmigration* of PMN across the endothelial barrier and extracellular matrix into the tissue site. Chemotactic factors are short-range signaling molecules that diffuse in a declining concentration gradient from the source of production within a tissue to the vessel itself. PMN have receptors for these molecules, and they are induced

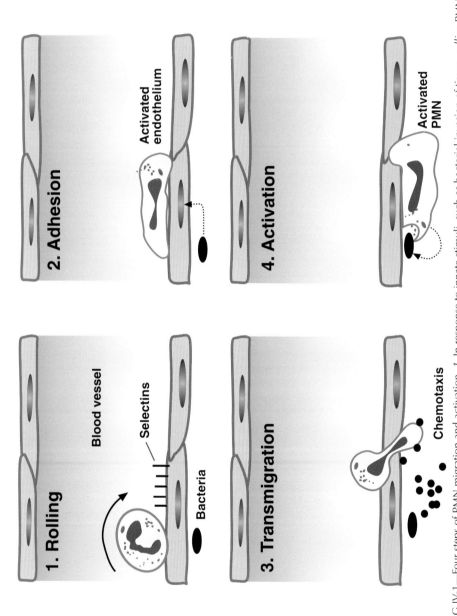

FIG IV-1—Four steps of PMN migration and activation. *1.* In response to innate stimuli, such as bacterial invasion of tissue, *rolling* PMN within blood vessel bind loosely but reversibly to nonactivated endothelial cells by selectins. *2.* Exposure to innate activating factors activates endothelial cells, which in turn express E and P selectins, β integrins, and Ig superfamily molecules to enhance and stabilize the interaction by a process called *adhesion. 3.* Chemotactic factors triggered by the infection induce *transmigration* of PMN across the endothelial barrier into the extracellular matrix of the tissue. *4.* Finally, PMN are fully *activated* into functional effector cells upon stimulation by bacterial toxins and phagocytosis. (Illustration by Barb Cousins, modified by Joyce Zavarro.)

to undergo membrane changes so they can migrate in the direction of highest concentration. A large number of such factors have been identified:

□ Complement products (C5a)

□ Fibrin split products

□ Certain neuropeptides, such as substance P

□ Bacteria-derived formyl tripeptides, such as FMLP

□ Leukotrienes

□ Alpha chemokines, such as IL-8

□ Many others

Another function of certain chemotactic factors is that they may also enhance endothelial cell activation to upregulate CAM and to synthesize additional chemotactic factors.

Activation of PMN into functional effector cells begins during adhesion and transmigration but is fully exploited upon interaction with specific signals within the injured or infected site. Perhaps the most effective triggers of activation are bacteria and their toxins, especially LPS. Other innate or adaptive mechanisms, especially complement, and chemical mediators such as leukotrienes and PAF can also contribute to PMN activation. Unlike monocytes or lymphocytes, PMN do not leave a tissue to recirculate but remain and die.

Phagocytosis   Phagocytosis of bacteria and other pathogens is a selective receptor-mediated process, and the two most important receptors are the *antibody Fc receptors* and the *complement receptors*. Thus, those pathogens in complexes with antibody or activated complement components are specifically bound to the cell surface membrane–expressed Fc or complement (C) receptors and are effectively ingested. Other less well characterized receptors may also mediate attachment to phagocytes. The actual process of particle ingestion is an energy-requiring process that is modulated by several biochemical events within the cells. Concomitant processes that occur in the cells during ingestion include

□ Membrane synthesis

□ Lysosomal enzyme synthesis

□ Generation of metabolic products of oxygen and nitrogen

□ Migration of the various types of granules toward the phagosome

Ultimately, several granules fuse with the phagosomes, a process that may occur prior to complete invagination, spilling certain granule contents outside of the phagocyte. Phagocytes are endowed with multiple means of destroying microorganisms, especially antimicrobial polypeptides that reside within cytoplasmic granules, reactive oxygen radicals generated from oxygen during the respiratory burst, and reactive nitrogen radicals, which are discussed later in this chapter. Although these mechanisms are primarily designed to destroy pathogens, released contents such as lysosomal enzymes may contribute to amplification of inflammation and tissue damage.

Innate Mechanisms for the Recruitment and Activation of Macrophages

Monocyte-derived macrophages are the second important type of effector cell for the innate immune response following trauma or acute infection. The various molecules involved in monocyte adhesion and transmigration from blood into tissues are probably similar to those discussed with PMN, although they have not been studied so thoroughly. However, the functional activation of macrophages is more complex. Macrophages exist in different levels or stages of metabolic and functional activity, each representing different "programs" of gene activation and synthesis of macrophage-derived cytokines or mediators:

□ Resting (immature or quiescent)

□ Primed

□ Activated

A fourth category of macrophages, often called *stimulated, reparative,* or *inflammatory,* is used by some authorities to refer to those macrophages that are not quite fully activated. This multilevel model is clearly oversimplified, but it does provide a framework for conceptualizing different levels of macrophage activation in terms of acute inflammation (Fig IV-2).

Resting and scavenging macrophages   Host cell debris is cleared from a tissue site by phagocytosis in a process called *scavenging.* Resting macrophages are the classic scavenging cell, capable of phagocytosis and uptake of the following:

□ Dead cell membranes by recognition of phosphatidyl serine

□ Chemically modified extracellular protein through acetylated or oxidized lipoproteins

□ Sugar ligands through mannose receptors

□ Naked nucleic acids as well as bacterial pathogens

Resting monocytes express scavenging receptors of at least three types but synthesize very low levels of proinflammatory cytokines. In general, scavenging can occur in the absence of inflammation.

CLINICAL EXAMPLE

Phacolytic glaucoma   Mild infiltration of scavenging macrophages centered around retained lens cortex or nucleus fragments occurs in nearly all eyes with lens injury, including those subjected to routine cataract surgery. This infiltrate is notable for the *absence* of prominent neutrophil infiltration or significant nongranulomatous inflammation. An occasional giant cell may be present, but extensive granulomatous changes do not occur.

Phacolytic glaucoma is a variant of scavenging macrophage infiltration in which glaucoma occurs in the setting of a hypermature cataract that leaks lens protein through an *intact* capsule. Lens protein–engorged scavenging macrophages are present in the anterior chamber, and glaucoma develops as these cells block the trabecular meshwork outflow channels. Other signs of typical lens-associated uveitis are conspicuously absent. Experimental studies suggest that lens proteins may be chemotactic stimuli for monocytes.

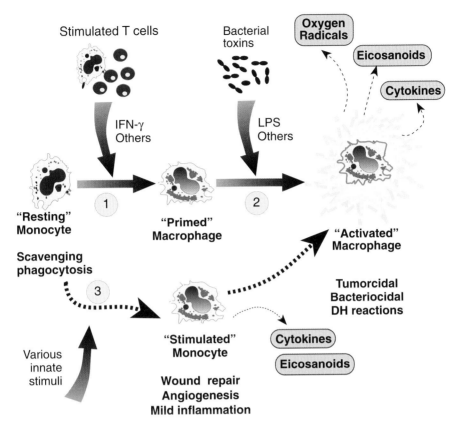

FIG IV-2—Schematic representation of macrophage activation pathway. Classically, *resting monocytes* are thought to be the principal noninflammatory scavenging phagocyte. *1,* Upon exposure to low levels of INF-γ from T cells, monocytes become primed, upregulating class II MHC molecules and other functions. *Primed monocytes* function in antigen presentation. *2, Fully activated macrophages,* after exposure to LPS and interferon, are tumorcidal and bactericidal and mediate severe inflammation. *3, Stimulated monocytes* are incompletely activated, producing low levels of cytokines and eicosanoids, but not reactive oxygen intermediates. These cells participate in wound healing, angiogenesis, and low-level inflammatory reactions. (Illustration by Barb Cousins, modified by Joyce Zavarro.)

Primed macrophages Resting macrophages become primed by exposure to certain cytokines. Upon priming, these cells become MHC class II antigen positive and capable of functioning as APC to T cells. Priming implies activation of specialized lysosomal enzymes such as cathepsins D and E for degrading proteins into peptide fragments, upregulation of certain specific genes such as class II MHC and costimulatory molecules such as B7.1, and increased cycling of proteins between endosomes and surface membrane. Prototypically, primed macrophages resemble dendritic cells. They can exit tissue sites by the afferent lymphatics to reenter the lymph node. Classically, T cell–derived INF-γ was believed to be the most important priming signal. It is now known, however, that many cytokines not necessarily of T cell origin can also prime macrophages, and the cellular response to the priming stimulus has tissue-specific variations.

Activated and stimulated macrophages Activated macrophages are classically defined as macrophages producing the full spectrum of proinflammatory and cytotoxic cytokines; thus, they are the cells that mediate and amplify acute inflammation (delayed hypersensitivity), tumor killing, and major antibacterial activity. *Epithelioid cells* and *giant cells* represent the terminal differentiation of the activated macrophage. Activated macrophages synthesize numerous mediators to amplify inflammation:

☐ Inflammatory or cytotoxic cytokines such as IL-1, IL-6, TNF-α

☐ Reactive oxygen or nitrogen intermediates

☐ Lipid mediators

☐ Other products

Traditionally, full activation was observed to require stimulation by two signals: INF-γ from DH T cells plus LPS from gram-negative bacteria. Nevertheless, the level of macrophage activation can vary tremendously and can be regulated much more precisely than is implied by the monolithic term *activated*.

It is now believed that macrophages can be partially activated by many different "innate" stimuli, such as

☐ Non–T cell–derived cytokines such as the chemokines

☐ Bacterial cell walls or toxins from gram-positive or acid-fast organisms

☐ Complement activated through the alternative pathway

☐ Foreign bodies composed of potentially toxic substances such as talc or beryllium

☐ Exposure to certain surfaces such as some plastics

Thus, macrophages that are partially activated to produce some inflammatory cytokines, but perhaps not fully activated to antimicrobial or tumorcidal function, are sometimes termed *stimulated* or *reparative* macrophages. Such partially activated macrophages also contribute to fibrosis and wound healing through synthesis of mitogens such as platelet-derived growth factors, metalloproteinases, and other matrix degradation factors and angiogenesis through synthesis of angiogenic factors such as vascular endothelial growth factor (VEGF).

Effector Reactivities of Adaptive Immunity

Although most adaptive (or innate) immune responses are protective and occur subclinically, when adaptive immune responses do cause inflammation, these responses have classically been called *immune hypersensitivity reactions*. The traditional classification for describing the four mechanisms of adaptive immune-triggered inflammatory responses was elaborated by Coombs and Gell in 1962, and a fifth category, *stimulatory hypersensitivity,* was added later (Table IV-2). Although this system is still useful, it was developed before T cells had been discovered, in a time when understanding was limited to antibody-triggered mechanisms. In addition, it is unlikely that any effector mechanism in a disease process is purely one type. For example, all antibody-dependent mechanisms require a processing phase using

P acnes *endophthalmitis* Infection of the capsular bag and residual lens material with the anaerobic organism *Propionibacterium acnes* has been found to cause some cases of chronic postoperative uveitis after cataract surgery and IOL implantation. This bacterium, presumably introduced at the time of surgery, replicates very slowly and fails to produce a significant purulent infection. Thus, the initial infection is noninflammatory and clinically inapparent. However, some clinical event, such as additional surgery with the Nd:YAG laser or other unknown trigger, results in inflammation apparently related to enhanced replication or release of the bacterium. Granulomatous inflammation ultimately develops that spreads to involve the residual lens and vitreous.

No clear explanation for the pattern of inflammation in the *P acnes* syndrome is presently known. Some investigators speculate that the infective plaque of organisms is growing, initially, within an anaerobic environment formed by a sequestered pocket of capsular flap and IOL, and the bacteria are thus isolated from the immune response. After release of the toxins, especially cell wall components, macrophages are directly activated through innate immunity to initiate a subacute inflammatory reaction. Activated macrophages then produce mediators and cytokines that amplify the inflammation.

---

helper T cells, which may also contribute to effector responses. Finally, the term *hypersensitivity* may obscure the concept that many of these same mechanisms are often protective and noninflammatory. Thus, in some ways, this traditional classification is inadequate. This discussion introduces an expanded classification system that incorporates modern concepts for immune effector reactivities and, when appropriate, points out where the classic Coombs and Gell system applies (Table IV-3).

Male DK, Cooke A, Owen M, et al. *Advanced Immunology.* 3rd ed. St Louis: Mosby; 1996.

Roitt IM. *Essential Immunology.* 9th ed. Malden, MA: Blackwell Science; 1997.

TABLE IV-2

TYPES OF HYPERSENSITIVITY (COOMBS AND GELL)

Type I	Anaphylactoid
Type II	Cytotoxic antibodies
Type III	Immune complex reactions
Type IV	Cell-mediated
Type V	Stimulatory

TABLE IV-3

EFFECTOR REACTIVITIES OF THE ADAPTIVE IMMUNE RESPONSE IN THE EYE

Predominantly antibody-mediated soluble effectors

Intravascular circulating antibodies that form circulating immune complexes with bloodborne antigen (Type III)

Passive leakage of antibody into a tissue followed by complex formation with tissue-bound antigen causing
    Complement-mediated cell lysis (Type II)
    Complement activation with inflammation (a variant of Type III)
    Novel cytotoxic mechanisms
    Stimulation of cell activities (Type V)

Local infiltration of circulating B cells into a tissue with local secretion of antibody and other cell activities (a variant of Type III)

Predominantly lymphocyte-mediated (cellular) effectors

Delayed hypersensitivity T cells (Type IV)
    Th1 type of delayed hypersensitivity
    Th2 type of delayed hypersensitivity

Cytotoxic lymphocytes
    Cytotoxic T lymphocytes
    Natural killer cells
    Lymphokine-activated killer cells

Combined antibody and cellular effector mechanisms

Antibody-dependent cellular cytotoxicity (ADCC) with killer cells or macrophages

Acute IgE-mediated mast cell degranulation (Type I)

Chronic mast cell degranulation and Th2 delayed hypersensitivity

Antibody-Mediated Immune Effector Responses

Structural and functional properties of antibody molecules *Structural features of immunoglobulins.* Five major classes (M, G, A, E, and D) of immunoglobulin exist in nine different subclasses, or *isotypes* (IgG1, IgG2, IgG3, IgG4, IgM, IgA1, IgA2, IgE, and IgD). The basic immunoglobulin structure is composed of four covalently bonded glycoprotein chains forming a monomer of approximately 150,000–180,000 daltons (Fig IV-3). This monomer is about two and a half to three times the size of albumin. Each antibody monomer contains two identical *light chains,* either kappa (κ) or lambda (λ), and two identical *heavy chains* from one of the nine structurally distinct subclasses of immunoglobulins. Thus, the heavy chain type defines

52

the specific isotype (Table IV-4). IgM can form pentamers or hexamers in vivo, and IgA can form dimers in secretions, so that the molecular size of these two classes in vivo is much larger than the others.

Each monomer has analogous regions called *domains*. Certain domains carry out specific functions of the antibody molecule. In particular, the *Fab region* on each molecule contains the antigen recognition/combining domain, called the *hypervariable region*. The opposite end of the molecule, on the heavy chain portion, contains the attachment site for effector cells *(Fc portion)* as well as the site of other effector functions, such as complement activation (e.g., as for IgG3) or binding to secretory component so it can transported through epithelia and secreted into tears (e.g., as for IgA). Table IV-4 summarizes important structural differences of immunoglobulin isotypes.

Functional properties of immunoglobulins. All immunoglobulin isotypes do not mediate the effector functions of antibody activity equally. For example, human IgM and IgG3 are good complement activators, but IgG4 is not. Only IgA1 or IgA2 can bind secretory component and thus be actively passed into mucosal secretions after transport through the epithelial cell from the subepithelial location where it is synthesized by B cells. Other isotypes must remain in the subepithelial tissue. A partial list of isotype-specific functions is included in Table IV-4. The importance of these differences is that two antibodies with identical capacity to bind to an antigen, but of different isotype, will have different effector and inflammatory outcomes.

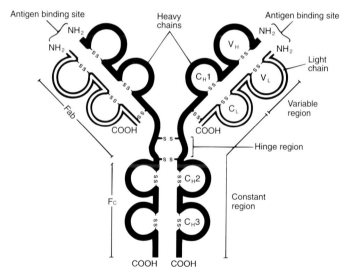

FIG IV-3—Schematic representation of an immunoglobulin molecule. The solid line indicates the identical two heavy chains; the open lines indicate the identical light chains. -s-s- indicates intra- and interchain covalent disulfide bonds. (Reprinted from *Dorland's Illustrated Medical Dictionary.* 28th ed. Philadelphia: Saunders; 1994:824.)

TABLE IV-4

STRUCTURAL AND FUNCTIONAL PROPERTIES OF IMMUNOGLOBULIN ISOTYPES

IMMUNO-GLOBULIN ISOTYPE (HEAVY CHAIN)	STRUCTURAL PROPERTIES			FUNCTIONAL PROPERTIES		
	% OF TOTAL SERUM Igs	RELATIVE SIZE	OTHER STRUCTURAL FEATURES	ACTIVATES COMPLEMENT	Fc RECEPTOR BINDING PREFERENCES	OTHER FUNCTIONS
IgD δ	<1%	Monomer	Mostly on surface of B cells	No		B-cell antigen receptor
IgM μ	5%	Pentamer or hexamer	Mostly on B cells or intravascular	Strong (classic pathway)		B-cell antigen receptor; agglutinization; neutralization; intravascular cytolysis
IgG1 γ	50%	Monomer	Intravascular, in tissues, crosses placenta	Moderate (classic pathway)	Monocytes	Cytolysis
IgG2 γ	18%	Monomer	Same as IgG1	Weak (classic pathway)	PMN monocytes, killer lymphocytes	ADCC
IgG3 γ	6%	Monomer	Same as IgG1	Strong (classic pathway)	PMN monocytes, killer lymphocytes	ADCC, agglutinization, cytolysis
IgG4 γ	3%	Monomer	Same as IgG1	No		Neutralization
IgE ε	<<1%	Monomer	Mostly in skin or mucosa, bound to mast cells	No	Mast cells	Mast cell degranulation
IgA1 α	15%	Mostly monomer in serum, dimer in secretions	In mucosal secretions, binds secretory component in subepithelial tissues for transepithelial transport and protection from proteolysis	Moderate (alternative pathway)		Mucosal immunity, neutralization
IgA2 α	3%	Same as IgA1	Same as IgA1	Same as IgA1		

Terminology   Variable regions of an antibody can themselves be antigenic. These antigenic sites are called *idiotopes* to be distinguished from *epitopes,* the antigenic sites on foreign molecules. Antibodies to idiotopes are called *idiotypes.* Anti-idiotypic antibodies might be important feedback mechanisms for immune regulation.

The concept of *monoclonal antibodies* has become very important in research and diagnostic medicine. After immunization with a particular antigen, a high frequency of B cells producing antibodies specific for that antigen will be present in the spleen or lymph nodes. Although one B cell synthesizes antibody of one antigenic specificity, different B cells responding to different epitopes of the same antigen will produce specific antibodies to each different epitope. The population of all antigen-specific antibodies to the various epitopes is termed *polyclonal*, as these antibodies derive from different B cell clones or progeny from one initial parental B cell, each producing antibodies of different specificities.

For example, myeloma cells are immortal tumor cells that have the cellular machinery for making unlimited production of one antibody without additional helper stimulation by T cells, antigen, or cytokines. If activated B cells from an immunized host and myeloma cells are fused by various laboratory manipulations, then a population of "hybridomas" is formed. Each hybridoma makes an unlimited amount of the original B cell's single antibody, yet it is immortal and therefore easy to grow and care for in the laboratory. Thus, the antibody is *monoclonal,* since it represents the product of one specific parental B cell fused to the myeloma tumor. The population of hybridomas produced by this fusion can be screened for selection of the one(s) that may be synthesizing the monoclonal antibody of interest.

Intravascular circulating antibodies that form circulating immune complexes with bloodborne antigen   Systemic release of antibody into the circulation or into external secretions occurs frequently after immunization, and antibody interactions with antigen solubilized in plasma or secretions are important effector mechanisms in this setting (Fig IV-4).

Neutralization, opsonization, and agglutinization. When antibody combines with a live pathogen such as virus or bacteria, it can block or *neutralize* the ability of the pathogen to bind to host cell receptors, thereby preventing infection of host cells. This process can occur in the blood or in external secretions such as tears. The role of this process in preventing reinfection with adenovirus has been discussed (see p 33). When antibody coats a soluble pathogen or antigen in blood, it can enhance phagocytosis or reticuloendothelial clearance by macrophage-like cells in the spleen or liver in a process called *opsonization.* Opsonization is usually facilitated by Fc receptor recognition by the phagocyte. In some cases, such as certain bacterial cell wall antigens, an antigen contains multiple identical antigenic sites on one molecule so that more than one antibody can bind each molecule. In these cases the antibody/antigen complex may *agglutinize,* causing the complex to precipitate out of solution.

Deposition of circulating soluble immune complexes. Usually, when antigen is soluble within blood, as during viremia or bacteremia, soluble immune complexes formed between antigen and antibody are efficiently removed from the circulation by binding to erythrocytes, then cleared by the reticuloendothelial system. However, in some cases soluble immune complexes can passively deposit within the blood vessels, kidney, and other vascular structures, usually facilitated by predisposing stimuli that cause altered vascular permeability (e.g., mast cell degranulation). This mechanism must be differentiated from the in situ formation of immune complexes

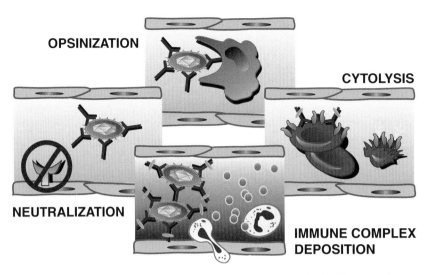

OPSINIZATION

CYTOLYSIS

NEUTRALIZATION

IMMUNE COMPLEX DEPOSITION

FIG IV-4—Schematic representation of the four most important antibody effector mechanisms in the blood. (Illustration by Barb Cousins, modified by Joyce Zavarro.)

within a tissue, which is discussed below. Tissue deposition of circulating immune complexes can trigger an inflammatory response by activating complement, one variant of Coombs and Gell Type III.

The classic clinical setting in which circulating immune complexes caused a systemic disease was *serum sickness,* a disease occurring in the preantibiotic and presteroid era that was caused by a late primary or secondary immune response following intravenous treatment with animal serum for a patient suffering from infection or inflammation. Massive intravascular immune complex formation caused severe systemic vasculitis and chronic inflammation in many organs. Now, serum sickness occurs rarely after certain infections such as Lyme disease or in rare individuals treated with certain drugs, such as antibiotics. In these cases the drug binds to self proteins to form a drug/protein "neo-antigen," or *hapten,* that inadvertently initiates an immune response. Deposition of circulating immune complexes may occur in some forms of systemic vasculitis, but their causative role has been deemphasized recently.

Passive leakage of antibody into peripheral tissues followed by complex formation with tissue-bound antigen Antibody in serum, especially of the IgG subclasses, can passively leak into peripheral tissues, particularly those with fenestrated capillaries, leading to formation of a local complex of antibody with tissue-associated antigens. Figure IV-5 illustrates the antibody effector mechanisms discussed below.

Complement-mediated cell lysis, or immune cytolysis. If an antigen is associated with the external surface of the plasma membrane, antibody binding might activate the complement cascade to induce cell lysis through formation of specialized porelike structures called the *membrane attack complex (MAC)* (i.e., Coombs and

56

Anterior uveitis is probably **not** *caused by circulating immune complexes*
Following observations that uveitis developed in some animal models of
serum sickness, investigators in the 1970s and 1980s sought to confirm
a role for circulating immune complexes as a cause of anterior uveitis.
Although elevated levels of immune complexes were detected in many
patients, a convincing correlation with disease activity was never established. Now, most immunologists and clinicians believe that the ocular
deposition of circulating immune complexes is *not* an important pathogenic
mechanism for uveitis in humans.

Gell Type II). Hemolytic anemia of a newborn as a result of Rh incompatibility is the
classic example of this process. Others include Hashimoto thyroiditis, glomerulonephritis of Goodpasture syndrome, and autoimmune thrombocytopenia. This mechanism does not appear to be very important in uveitis or ocular inflammation, although it may play a role in killing virus-infected cells during viral conjunctivitis.

Tissue-bound immune complexes and the acute Arthus reaction. When free
antibody passively leaks from the serum into a tissue, it can combine with tissue-
bound antigens trapped in the extracellular matrix or with cell-associated antigens
such as a viral protein expressed on the surface of an infected cell. These in situ, or
locally formed, complexes sometimes activate the complement pathway to produce
complement fragments called *anaphylatoxins* (a second variant of Coombs and Gell
Type III). This mechanism should be differentiated from the deposition of circulating
immune complexes, which are preformed in the blood. Typically, the histology is
dominated by neutrophils and monocytes. The resultant lesion, called the *acute
Arthus reaction,* can be produced experimentally by injection of antigen into a tissue site of an animal previously immunized in a way to optimize antibody rather
than T-cell production. In general, many types of glomerulonephritis and vasculitis
are thought to represent this mechanism. See Clinical Example: Retinal vasculitis in
systemic lupus erythematosus, p 59.

Novel cytotoxic mechanisms. Circulating antibodies can cause tissue injury by
mechanisms different from cytolysis or complement activation, using pathogenic
mechanisms not yet elucidated. For example, some autoantibodies in SLE appear to
be taken up by renal cells, leading to loss of function, and these may cause some
cases of nephritis in the absence of immune complex activation. In paraneoplastic syndromes autoantibodies to various tissues can develop and mediate *cellular
degeneration* or other manifestations. See Clinical Example: Cancer-associated
retinopathy, p 59.

Stimulatory antibodies. Tissue- or cell-bound immune complexes that stimulate
receptors on target cells are known as *stimulatory antibodies.* In some cases antibody leaking into tissues or binding to cells in the blood can cross-react with and
bind to a receptor or molecule expressed on the surface of normal parenchymal
cells, thereby activating the receptor as if the antibody were the natural ligand for
that receptor (Coombs and Gell Type V). For example, in Graves disease antibodies
to the thyroid-stimulating hormone (TSH) receptor activate the thyroid gland as if the
patient had taken an overdose of TSH. Immunologists have used this information to

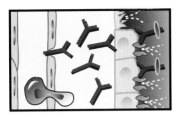

CYTOLYSIS

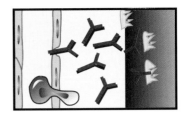

CELL DEGENERATION

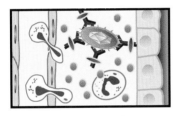

STIMULATORY

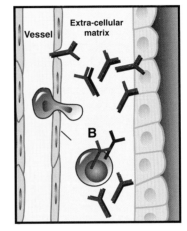

Vessel

Extra-cellular matrix

B

ANTIBODY DEPOSITION

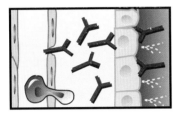

ARTHUS REACTION

FIG IV-5—Schematic representation of the most important antibody effector mechanisms caused by passive leakage of antibody into tissues. (Illustration by Barb Cousins, modified by Joyce Zavarro.)

develop many antibodies to activate cell receptors in the absence of the natural ligand and to develop antibodies with enzymatic or other metabolic functions. In other cases the autoantibody can block function of the receptor, as in myasthenia gravis, where antiacetylcholine antibodies cause internalization of the normal receptor without activation, thereby depleting functional receptors from the nerve ending. Many other examples of stimulatory, or metabolically active, antibodies have been identified. See Clinical Example: Scleritis or retinal vasculitis in Wegener granulomatosis, p 60.

Retinal vasculitis in systemic lupus erythematosus   Although rare, retinal vasculitis can develop in patients with systemic lupus erythematosus (SLE) (see p 163). Observation of the probable mechanism for vasculitis elsewhere in SLE suggests that local immune complex formation plays a role in this development. DNA and histones released from injured cells can become trapped in the basement membrane of the blood vessel wall, perhaps as a result of electrostatic binding by matrix proteins. Circulating cationic anti-DNA IgG autoantibodies permeate into the vessel wall, bind the auto-antigen, and activate complement. These cationic IgG antibodies are believed to have a stronger affinity for anionic extracellular matrix and therefore permeate tissues efficiently.

Complement fragments, or anaphylatoxins, initiate an Arthus reaction. The observed vascular sheathing in the retinal vessels is presumed to be caused by infiltration of neutrophils and macrophages in response to complement activation. However, helper T-cell responses and innate mechanisms may also contribute. In addition to DNA, other potential autoantigens in SLE include collagen and phospholipids.

Alternatively, molecular mimicry between basement membrane components and DNA may occur. The mechanism for the initiation of afferent events causing the induction of aberrant autoimmunity to DNA and other antigens is unknown. A similar effector mechanism has been postulated for scleritis in rheumatoid arthritis.

Cancer-associated retinopathy (CAR)   CAR is a paraneoplastic syndrome in which some patients with carcinoma, especially small cell carcinoma of the lung or occasionally cutaneous melanoma, develop antibodies against a tumor-associated antigen that happens to cross-react with an ocular auto-antigen. For example, some small cell carcinomas aberrantly synthesize recoverin, a normal protein in photoreceptors. The immune system inappropriately recognizes and processes recoverin and produces an antibody effector response, releasing antirecoverin antibodies into the circulation. These antibodies passively permeate into the retina, are taken up by photoreceptors, and cause slowly progressive photoreceptor degeneration by a novel, poorly understood cytotoxic mechanism. Current research speculates that induction of programmed cell death may be caused by intracellular antibody/antigen complex formation after photoreceptor uptake of antirecoverin antibodies.

Scleritis or retinal vasculitis in Wegener granulomatosis   Necrotizing scleritis is a common feature in Wegener granulomatosis, and retinal vasculitis can, rarely, develop in some of these patients as well (see pp 165–166). Although the mechanism for scleritis and retinal vasculitis in Wegener granulomatosis is unknown, the primary pathogenesis can be inferred from experimental studies of systemic disease to be a vasculitis mediated in part by stimulatory autoantibodies. The autoantigen is thought to be the PMN-derived serine protease *proteinase-3*. The initial effector process is believed to require the translocation of proteinase-3 from cytoplasmic granules to the cell surface after PMN exposure to various innate activational stimuli, such as a predisposing infection or systemic cytokine release. Then, antineutrophil cytoplasmic antibodies (ANCA) can bind surface proteinase-3, further activating and stimulating the PMN. This process, in turn, causes the PMN to bind to endothelium and to release granules and other mediators that injure the vessel wall. The endothelial cells then synthesize cytokines to recruit additional inflammatory cells, especially T cells, which amplify the process. The mechanism for the initiation of afferent events causing the induction of aberrant autoimmunity to proteinase-3 is unknown. However, the processing phase must also include proteinase-specific helper T cells, which are responsible for providing cytokine help to B cells; and DH effector cells presumably contribute to granuloma formation in tissue sites.

Kallenberg CG, Brouwer E, Mulder AH, et al. ANCA—pathophysiology revisited. *Clin Exp Immunol.* 1995;100:1–3.

Infiltration of B cells into tissues and local production of antibody   *B-cell infiltration.* B cells can infiltrate into the site of an immunologic reaction in response to persistent antigenic stimulus, leading to a clinical picture of moderate to severe inflammation. If the process becomes chronic, plasma cell formation occurs, representing fully differentiated B cells that have become dedicated to antibody synthesis. In both of these cases local production of antibody specific for the inciting antigen(s) occurs within the site. If the antigen is known, as for certain presumed infections, local antibody formation can be used as a diagnostic test.

Differentiation between local production of antibody and passive leakage from the blood involves calculation of the *Goldmann-Witmer coefficient,* which is generated by comparison of the ratio of intraocular fluid–serum antibody concentration for the specific antibody in question to the intraocular fluid–serum ratio of total immunoglobulin levels. Theoretically, a coefficient above 1.0 would indicate local production of antibodies within the eye. In practice, multiple positive quotients above 1.0 can be identified in a single eye, confusing interpretation. See Clinical Example: Diagnosis of atypical necrotizing retinitis, p 61.

Diagnosis of atypical necrotizing retinitis   The sensitivity, specificity, and accuracy of aqueous humor antibody levels (intraocular antibody synthesis) were compared in the diagnoses of atypical retinitis ultimately caused by *Toxoplasma gondii,* varicella-zoster virus, herpes simplex virus, cytomegalovirus (CMV), and noninfectious etiologies. In general, the authors found the best results (78% diagnostic accuracy) were obtained when the highest quotient >1.0 was used for diagnosis even in the face of multiple positive quotients. False-positive quotients for CMV were the most frequent confounding finding, causing four of six false diagnoses.

Davis JL, Feuer W, Culbertson WW, et al. Interpretation of intraocular and serum antibody levels in necrotizing retinitis. *Retina.* 1995;15:233–240.

Local antibody production within a tissue and chronic inflammation. Persistence of antigen within a site coupled with infiltration of specific B cells and local antibody formation can produce a chronic inflammatory reaction with a complicated histologic pattern, often demonstrating lymphocytic infiltration, plasma cell infiltration, and granulomatous features (a third variant of Coombs and Gell Type III). This process is sometimes called the *chronic Arthus reaction.* This mechanism may contribute to the pathophysiology of certain chronic autoimmune disorders, such as rheumatoid arthritis, which feature formation of pathogenic antibody. See Clinical Example: Phacoantigenic endophthalmitis on the next page.

Lymphocyte-Mediated Effector Responses

Delayed hypersensitivity T lymphocytes   Delayed hypersensitivity (DH, or Coombs and Gell Type IV) represents the prototypical adaptive immune mechanism for lymphocyte-triggered inflammation. It is especially powerful in secondary immune responses. Previously primed DH CD4 T cells leave the lymph node, home into local tissues where antigen persists, and become activated by further restimulation with the specific priming antigen and class II MHC–expressing APC. Fully activated DH T cells secrete mediators and cytokines, leading to the recruitment and activation of macrophages or other nonspecific leukocytes (Fig IV-6, p 63). The term *delayed* for this type of hypersensitivity refers to the fact that this reaction becomes maximal 12–48 hours after antigen exposure.

Analysis of experimental animal models and the histopathologic changes of human inflammation suggests that different subtypes of delayed hypersensitivity might exist. One of the most important determinants of the pattern of DH reaction is the subtype of DH CD4 T effector cells that mediate the reaction. Just as helper T cells can be differentiated into two groups—Th1 and Th2 subsets—according to the spectrum of cytokines secreted, DH T cells can also be grouped by the same criteria. Experimentally, the Th1 subset of cytokines, especially INF-γ, also known as

Phacoantigenic endophthalmitis This condition is a form of lens-associated uveitis with three distinct zones of inflammation centered around the lens:

- An inner zone of neutrophils invading the lens substance

- A secondary zone of macrophages, epithelioid cells, and/or giant cells surrounding the capsule injury site

- An outer zone of fibrotic reparative or granulation tissue infiltrated with nongranulomatous inflammation and plasma cells, presumably secreting specific antibodies into ocular fluids

Antibody-mediated autoimmunity has been well demonstrated in rats immunized against whole lens proteins. The mechanism for the initiation of afferent events causing the induction of aberrant autoimmunity to lens crystallins is unknown. The adaptive immune system of unaffected patients has already been exposed to crystallins in a "tolerizing" manner (see chapter V).

Since lens-associated uveitis almost always occurs in a severely traumatized or congenitally abnormal eye, it has been suggested that the disease is initiated in eyes with an atypical immunologic microenvironment that allows a secondary afferent response to override tolerance. The effector phase appears to be dominated by complement-fixing antibodies specific for lens crystallins, which are either produced locally by B cells or plasma cells within the eye or leaked passively from the blood. Presumably, generation of the anaphylatoxin C5a by complement-activating immune complexes *within the lens substance* explains the neutrophil infiltration into the lens. Diffusion of anaphylatoxins into the anterior chamber probably results in a chemotactic gradient, yielding a zonal pattern. Activated macrophages must also contribute, since epithelioid and giant cells that are subsets of activated, differentiated macrophages are classic features. The mechanism for giant cell formation has not been totally resolved, but phagocytosis of immune complexes coated with complement can contribute to macrophage activation and induce giant cell formation. Injury to retina or other tissues is probably exacerbated by toxic oxygen radicals. It has been suggested that T-cell and innate effector mechanisms may also be involved.

---

macrophage-activating factor, and TNF-β, activates macrophages to secrete inflammatory mediators and kill pathogens, amplifying inflammation. Thus, Th1-mediated DH mechanisms are thought to produce the following:

- The classic delayed hypersensitivity reaction (i.e., the PPD skin reaction)

- Immunity to intracellular infections (i.e., to mycobacteria or pneumocystis)

- Immunity to fungi

- Most forms of severe T cell–mediated autoimmune diseases

- Chronic transplant rejection

The Th2 subset of DH cells secretes IL-4 and IL-5 and other cytokines. IL-4 can induce B cells to synthesize IgE, and IL-5 can recruit and activate eosinophils within a site. IL-4 can also induce macrophage granulomas in response to parasite-

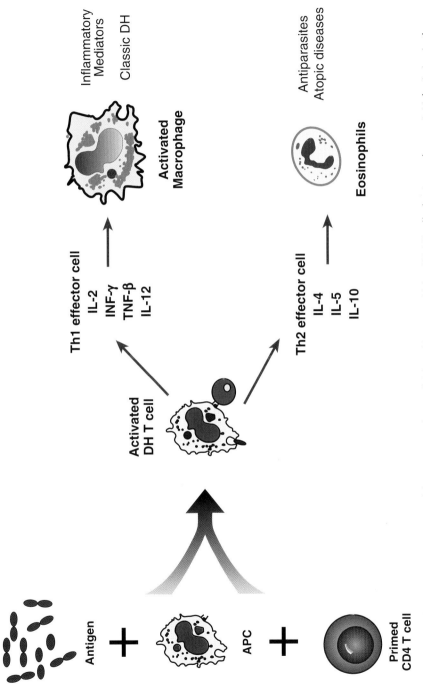

FIG IV-6.—Schematic representation of the two major forms of delayed hypersensitivity. CD4 T cells, having undergone initial priming in the lymph node, enter the tissue site where they again encounter APC and antigen. Upon restimulation, they become activated into either Th1 or Th2 effector cells. Th1 are the classic DH effector cells associated with most severe forms of inflammation. Th2 cells are thought to be less intensively inflammatory, but they have been associated with parasite-induced granulomas and atopic diseases. (Illustration by Barb Cousins, modified by Joyce Zavarro.)

derived antigens. Thus, Th2-mediated DH mechanisms are thought to play a major role in the following:

□ Response to parasite infections

□ Late phase responses of allergic reactions

□ Asthma

□ Atopic dermatitis or other manifestations of atopic diseases

The inciting antigen and the immunologic microenvironment of the tissue site are other important variables in determining the pattern of DH, affecting the afferent and efferent phases, respectively. Some of these variables probably influence the development of a Th1 versus Th2 pattern of cytokine production as well. Some soluble antigens, especially in mucosal sites, can induce a type of DH with features of immediate hypersensitivity and basophil infiltration called *cutaneous basophil hypersensitivity.* Most epidermal toxins, especially heavy metals, plant toxins, or chemical toxins, cause monocyte infiltration and epidermal desquamation of the skin, the *contact hypersensitivity* type of Th1 DH. Deposition of certain insoluble antigens (bacterial or fungal debris) or immunization with soluble proteins using adjuvants causes the classic *tuberculin* type of Th1 DH that is characterized by fibrin deposition and monocyte and lymphocyte infiltration.

Persistence of certain infectious agents, especially bacteria within intracellular compartments of APC or certain extracellular parasites, can cause destructive induration with granuloma formation and giant cells, the *granulomatous* form of DH. However, immune complex deposition (see lens-associated uveitis) or innate immune mechanisms in response to heavy metal or foreign body reactions can also cause granulomatous inflammation in which the inflammatory cascade resulting in DH is triggered in the absence of specific T cells. Unfortunately, for most clinical entities in which T-cell responses are suspected, especially autoimmune disorders such as multiple sclerosis or arthritis, the precise immunologic mechanism remains highly speculative.

Cytotoxic lymphocytes *Cytotoxic T lymphocytes (CTL).* CTL are a subset of antigen-specific T cells, usually bearing the CD8 marker, that are especially good at killing tumor cells and virus-infected cells. They can also mediate graft rejection and some cases of autoimmunity. In most cases the ideal antigen for CTL represents an intracellular protein that either occurs naturally or is produced as result of viral infection. CTL appear to require help from CD4 helper T-cell signals to fully differentiate. Primed *precursor* CTL leave the lymph node and migrate to the target tissue where they are restimulated by the interaction of the CTL antigen receptor and foreign antigens within the antigen pocket of class I molecules (HLA-A, -B, or -C) on the target cell. Additional CD4 T cells help at the site, and expression of other accessory costimulatory molecules on the target is often required to obtain maximal killing.

CTL kill cells in one of two ways: by assassination or suicide induction (Fig IV-7, p 67). *Assassination* refers to CTL-mediated *lysis* of targets, using a specialized pore-forming protein called *perforin,* which puts pores, or holes, into cell membranes, causing osmotic lysis of the cell. *Suicide induction* refers to the capacity of CTL to stimulate *programmed cell death* of target cells, called *apoptosis,* using the CD95 ligand, the *FasL,* to activate its receptor on targets. Alternatively, CTL can release cytotoxic cytokines like tumor necrosis factor (TNF) to induce apoptosis. Activation of the apoptosis pathway induces the release of target cell enzymes and nucleases that cause fragmentation of chromosomal DNA and blebbing of the cell membrane, ultimately killing the cell. CTL produce low-grade lymphocytic infiltrate within tumors or infected tissues and usually kill without causing significant inflammation.

Toxocara granuloma (Th2 DH)   *Toxocara canis* is a nematode parasite that infects up to 2% of all children and may occasionally produce vitreoretinal inflammatory manifestations. Although the ocular immunology of this disorder is not clearly delineated, animal models and study of the immunopathogenesis of human nematode infections at other sites suggest the following scenario. The primary immune response begins in the gut after ingestion of viable eggs, which mature into larvae within the intestine. The primary processing phase produces a strong Th2 response, leading to a primary effector response that includes production of IgM, IgG, and IgE antibodies as well as Th2-mediated DH T cells. Hematogenous dissemination of a few larvae may result from accidental avoidance of immune effector mechanisms, leading to choroidal or retinal dissemination followed by invasion into the retina and vitreous. There, a Th2-mediated T-cell effector response recognizes larva antigens and releases Th2-derived cytokines to induce eosinophil and macrophage infiltration, causing the characteristic eosinophilic granuloma seen in the eye. In addition, antilarval B cells can infiltrate into the eye and are induced to secrete various immunoglobulins, especially IgE. Finally, eosinophils, in part by attachment through Fc receptors, can recognize IgE or IgG bound to parasites and release cytotoxic granules containing the antiparasitic cationic protein directly in the vicinity of the larvae using a mechanism similar to antibody-dependent cellular cytotoxicity (ADCC), which is discussed below.

> Grencis RK. Th2-mediated host protective immunity to intestinal nematode infections. *Philos Trans R Soc Lond Biol Sci.* 1997;352:1377–1384.

Sympathetic ophthalmia (Th1 DH)   Sympathetic ophthalmia (SO) is a bilateral panuveitis that follows penetrating trauma to one eye (see chapter X for a more detailed discussion). This disorder represents one of the few human diseases in which autoimmunity can be directly linked to an initiating event. In most cases penetrating injury activates the afferent phase. It is unclear whether the injury causes a de novo primary immunization to self antigens, perhaps because of externalization of "sequestered" uveal antigens through the wound and exposure to the afferent immune response arc of the conjunctiva/extraocular sites, or if it instead somehow changes the immunologic microenvironment of the retina, RPE, and uvea so that a secondary afferent response is initiated that serves to alter preexisting tolerance to retinal and uveal self antigens.

It is generally believed that the inflammatory effector response is dominated by a Th1-mediated DH mechanism generated in response to uveal or retinal antigens. CD4 T cells predominate early in the disease course, although CD8, or suppressor, T cells can be numerous in chronic cases. Activated macrophages are also numerous in granulomas, and Th1 cytokines have been identified in the vitreous or produced by T cells recovered from the eyes of affected patients. Although the target antigen for SO is unknown, cutaneous immunization in experimental animals with certain retinal antigens (arrestin, rhodopsin, interphotoreceptor retinol–binding protein), RPE-associated antigens, and melanocyte-associated tyrosinase can induce autoimmune uveitis with physiology or features suggestive of sympathetic ophthalmia. Th1-mediated DH is thought to mediate many forms of ocular inflammation. Table IV-5 lists other examples.

Rao NA. Mechanisms of inflammatory response in sympathetic ophthalmia and VKH syndrome. *Eye.* 1997;11:213–216.

TABLE IV-5

OCULAR INFLAMMATORY DISEASES THOUGHT TO REQUIRE A MAJOR
CONTRIBUTION OF TH1-MEDIATED DH EFFECTOR MECHANISMS

SITE	DISEASE	PRESUMED ANTIGEN
Conjunctiva	Contact hypersensitivity to contact lens solutions	Thimerosal or other chemicals
	Giant papillary conjunctivitis	Unknown
	Phlyctenulosis	Bacterial antigens
Cornea and sclera	Chronic allograft rejection	Histocompatibility antigens
	Marginal infiltrates of blepharitis	Bacterial antigens
	Disciform keratitis after viral infection	Viral antigens
Anterior uvea	Acute anterior uveitis	Uveal autoantigens, bacterial antigens
	Sarcoid-associated uveitis	Unknown
	Intermediate uveitis	Unknown
Retina and choroid	Sympathetic ophthalmia	Retinal or uveal autoantigens
	Vogt-Koyanagi-Harada syndrome	Retinal or uveal autoantigens
	Birdshot choroiditis	Unknown
Orbit	Acute thyroid orbitopathy	Unknown
	Giant cell arteritis	Unknown

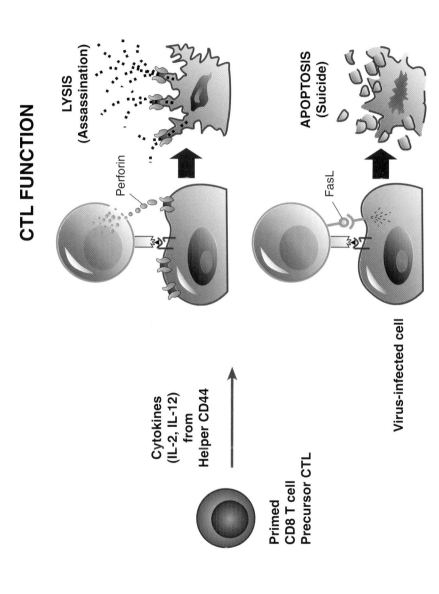

CTL FUNCTION

LYSIS (Assassination)

Perforin

APOPTOSIS (Suicide)

FasL

Cytokines (IL-2, IL-12) from Helper CD44

Primed CD8 T cell Precursor CTL

Virus-infected cell

FIG IV-7—Schematic representation of the two major mechanisms of CD8 T-cell cytotoxicity. CD8 T cells, having undergone initial priming in the lymph node, enter the tissue site where they again encounter antigen in the form of infected target cells. Upon restimulation, usually requiring CD4 helper T-cell factors, they become activated into fully cytolytic T cells. CD8 T cells can kill by lysing the infected cell, using a pore-forming protein called *perforin*. Or CTL can kill by inducing *programmed cell death*, or *apoptosis*, using either FasL or cytokine-mediated mechanisms. (Illustration by Barb Cousins, modified by Joyce Zavarro.)

Antiviral immunity in cytomegalovirus (CMV) retinitis CMV retinitis is the most frequent opportunistic ocular infection in patients with AIDS. The majority of most populations have serologic evidence of prior CMV infection, which is typically thought to occur during childhood or after contact with infected children. The pathophysiology of CMV infection is not entirely understood, but it can be inferred from analysis of animal experiments and human epidemiological studies. The primary afferent phase is usually initiated after upper respiratory tract infection, not uncommonly associated with viremia. The site of processing is unknown. Innate effectors, such as macrophages, natural killer cells, and neutrophils provide some antiviral activity. However, most investigators believe virus-specific CD8 T cells are the best antiviral effector for controlling active infection. Some evidence also suggests a role for DH T cells. Antibodies are also generated, but they do not seem to play a major role in controlling virus infection, spread, or clearance. Antibodies may, however, limit reinfection.

During the primary infection, virus is not completely cleared from the infected host but remains in a chronic state. It was originally thought that virus disseminated to various target tissues such as eye, gut, or kidney and became latent. More recent research suggests that the virus chronically infects the bone marrow and lung, probably persisting in certain macrophage precursor cells. Alternatively, CMV might infect the salivary gland where it remains in epithelial cells. CMV appears to persist in these sites in a chronic but nonproductive state, and the existence of true latency is debated. However, as long as the host immune response is intact, the virus does not replicate effectively to infect the eye or other target organs.

Immunosuppression allows the virus to reactivate into a productive infection. Virus infects neutrophils, macrophages, and other leukocytes and spreads through the blood to susceptible target sites such as the retina. Alternatively, viremia during a primary CMV infection that occurs in previously uninfected immunosuppressed persons, especially after organ transplantation, can cause virus spread by a similar mechanism. It is believed that virus-specific CD8 T cells are the most important effector cell in preventing spread, but natural killer cells might also be effective. CD4 T cells play a role primarily by providing helper cytokines to fully activate CD8 T cells. Thus in AIDS, CMV retinitis presumably occurs late in the disease because CD8 effectors become diminished later in the course of infection than do CD4 T cells. Transfusion of virus-specific CD8 T cells in organ transplant patients and replacement of helper cytokines to activate CD8 T cells in a mouse model of AIDS have both been shown to prevent CMV. Highly active antiretroviral therapy to suppress the HIV viral load has dramatically decreased the incidence of new cases of CMV retinitis in AIDS. The role of intravenous immune globulins, polyclonal antibodies enriched from human sera, in prophylaxis or treatment is controversial, but they may help prevent CMV disease after organ transplantation.

Riddell SR. Pathogenesis of cytomegalovirus pneumonia in immunocompromised hosts. *Semin Respir Infect.* 1995;10:199–208.

Natural killer (NK) cells. NK cells—a subset of non-T, non-B lymphocytes—were originally called *null cells,* or large granular lymphocytes. They also kill tumor cells and virally infected cells but, unlike CTL, NK do not have a specific antigen receptor. Instead, they are triggered by a less well characterized "NK" cell receptor. Once triggered, however, NK cells kill target cells using the same molecular mechanisms as CTL. Since NK cells are not antigen specific, they theoretically have the advantage of not requiring the time delay caused by induction of the adaptive, antigen-specific CTL immune response. However, NK cells do seem to require some of the same effector activational signals at the tissue site, especially cytokine stimulation. Thus, NK cells are probably most effective in combination with adaptive effector responses.

In some ways NK and CTL are complementary in that they are inversely regulated, that is, cell processes such as diminished class I molecule expression that inhibit CTL function often enhance activation of NK cells, and vice versa. NK thereby provide another layer of protection against pathogens that interfere with class I expression, as do many viruses, especially CMV. Experimental evidence suggests that NK cells may contribute to antiviral protection in CMV and herpes simplex virus infections of the eye.

Lymphokine-activated killer (LAK) cells. LAK cells are T cells that have become nonspecifically activated by iatrogenic administration of immune cytokines such as IL-2 and others. LAK cells kill by various mechanisms, including those described above. Once it was learned that T cells are produced and become activated upon exposure to immune cytokines, or *lymphokines,* clinicians began to evaluate the clinical efficacy of treatment with cytokine immunotherapy. Originally, it was discovered that patients with certain tumors, especially metastatic malignant melanoma, who were treated with large doses of intravenous IL-2 sometimes responded with immune-mediated rejection of the tumor. Efficacy was subsequently improved when CTL were removed from the blood or even from within metastatic tumor foci (i.e., tumor-infiltrating lymphocytes) and treated with cytokines extracorporeally, then reinfused. Currently, numerous biotechnological approaches are being developed to enhance immunotherapy of LAK function for treatment of tumors and viral infections.

Combined Antibody and Cellular Effector Mechanisms

Antibody-dependent cellular cytotoxicity Antibody can combine with a cell-associated antigen such as a tumor or viral antigen, but if the antibody is not a subclass that activates complement, it may not induce any apparent cytotoxicity. However, because the Fc tail of the antibody is externally exposed, various leukocytes can recognize the Fc domain of the antibody molecule and be directed to the cell through the antibody. When this happens, binding to the antibody activates various leukocyte cytotoxic mechanisms, including degranulation and cytokine production.

Since human leukocytes can express various types of Fc receptors—IgG subclasses have three different Fcγ receptors, IgE has two different Fcε receptors, and so on—leukocyte subsets will differ in their capacity to recognize and bind different antibody isotypes. Classically, ADCC was observed to be mediated by a special subset of large granular (non-T, non-B) lymphocytes, called *killer cells,* that induce cell

Immune responses to malignant melanoma Several investigators have recently evaluated the immune response to human uveal melanomas. Although controversial, recent data suggest that most primary or metastatic uveal melanomas demonstrate *melanoma antigen genes (MAGE)* and that these growing tumors express at least one family of tumor-asociated antigens that should be recognized by CD8 cytolytic adaptive immune responses. Tumor-infiltrating lymphocytes were isolated from eyes undergoing enucleation because of large, growing melanomas. Numerous CD8 T cells could be isolated from all tumors, including tumor-specific T cells (indicating that afferent and processing phases had been initiated).

In cell culture the cytolytic T cells failed to effectively kill melanoma cells. After treatment with the cytokine (or lymphokine) IL-2, however, the CD8 T cells became fully cytolytic and did effectively kill the melanoma cells. The investigators conclude that uveal melanomas might create an immunologic microenvironment that prevents activation of the antitumor effector responses even though sensitized CTL may be present in the tumor. Lymphokine activation may be a method to overcome this suppressive microenvironment and to upregulate the host's antitumor response to melanoma in order to prevent or control metastases.

Chen PW, Murray TG, Uno T, et al. Expression of MAGE genes in ocular melanoma during progression from primary to metastatic disease. *Clin Exp Metastasis.* 1997;15:509–518.

Niederkorn JY. Immunoregulation of intraocular tumours. *Eye.* 1997;11:249–254.

death in a manner similar to CTL. The killer cell itself is nonspecific but gains antigen specificity through interaction with specific antibody. Macrophages, NK cells, certain T cells, and neutrophils can also participate in ADCC using other Fc receptor types. An IgE-dependent form of ADCC might also exist for eosinophils.

ADCC is presumed to be important in tumor surveillance, antimicrobial host protection, graft rejection, and certain autoimmune diseases such as cutaneous SLE. Nevertheless, this effector mechanism probably does not play an important role in uveitis, although it might contribute to corneal graft rejection and antiparasitic immunity.

Acute IgE-mediated mast cell degranulation Mast cells can bind IgE antibodies to their surface through a high-affinity Fc receptor specific for IgE molecules, positioning the antigen-combining site of the bound IgE externally (Fig IV-8). Combination of the antibody with a specific allergen (see Clinical Example: Allergic conjunctivitis, p 72) causes degranulation of the mast cell and release of mediators within minutes, producing an acute inflammatory reaction called *immediate hypersensitivity* (Coombs and Gell Type I), which is characterized by local plasma leakage and itching. When severe, this response can produce a systemic reaction called *anaphylaxis,* which ranges in severity from generalized skin lesions such as erythema, urticaria, or angioedema to severe altered vascular permeability with plasma leakage into tissues that causes airway obstruction or hypotensive shock. Mast cells and vasoactive amines are discussed in greater detail below.

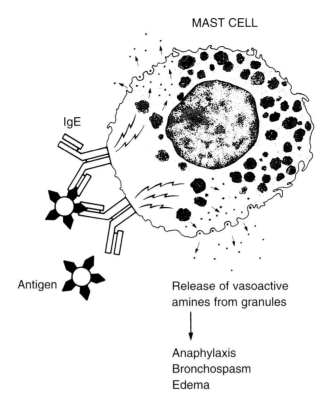

MAST CELL

IgE

Antigen

Release of vasoactive
amines from granules

Anaphylaxis
Bronchospasm
Edema

FIG IV-8—Schematic representation of IgE-mediated mast cell degranulation.

Chronic mast cell degranulation plus Th2 DH   Recent research has suggested that mast cells, B lymphocytes, and T lymphocytes can cooperate in atopic diseases to mediate chronic inflammatory reactions with a pattern that represents a mixture of acute allergy and delayed hypersensitivity. As discussed above, a Th2 subset of CD4+ DH cells not only releases inflammatory mediators but also secretes certain cytokines (IL-4) that induce B cells to synthesize IgE and to recruit and activate eosinophils within a site (IL-5). Since mast cells can degranulate in response to stimuli other than IgE, the precise contributions of IgE-mediated mast cell degranulation in these chronic reactions have not been clarified. This pathogenic mechanism is believed to be especially important in the skin and at mucosal sites.

Allergic conjunctivitis   Allergic conjunctivitis represents a secondary adaptive immune response to a family of antigens called *allergens* that induce predominately an acute IgE–mast cell effector response. The primary response presumably has occurred during a prior exposure to the allergen, often within the nasopharynx, in which afferent and processing phases were initiated. During this primary response, allergen-specific B cells were distributed to specialized areas in various MALT sites. At these sites the B cells, with T-cell help, switch from IgM-antiallergen production to IgE-antiallergen production. IgE released at the site then combines with Fc receptors of surrounding mast cells, thereby arming the mast cell with a specific allergen receptor (i.e., the antigen-recognizing Fab portion of the immunoglobulin). Thus, one mast cell may have bound antibodies specific for numerous different allergens.

When reexposure to allergen occurs in a secondary response at a different site from the initial encounter, allergen must permeate beyond the superficial conjunctival epithelium to the subepithelial region, where the antigen binds allergen-specific IgE on the surface of mast cells. Within 60 minutes degranulation occurs, leading to the release of mediators causing chemosis and itching. A late response, within 4–24 hours, is characterized by the recruitment of lymphocytes, eosinophils, and neutrophils. The role of Th2 DH or helper T cells in the effector response has not been confirmed for allergic conjunctivitis, but presumably both play a role, especially in B-cell differentiation, since the IgE is thought to be produced locally within the conjunctiva.

Atopic keratoconjunctivitis   Atopic keratoconjunctivitis is a chronic inflammatory condition of the palpebral and bulbar conjunctiva with features of allergic and cell-mediated inflammation (see BSCS Section 8, *External Disease and Cornea*). Analysis of biopsy specimens reveals the inflammatory infiltration to consist of mast cells and eosinophils, as well as activated CD4 T cells and B cells. Although immunopathogenesis is not clearly defined, a mechanism similar to that of atopic dermatitis can be inferred, combining poorly understood genetic mechanisms, chronic mast cell degranulation, and features of Th2-type delayed hypersensitivity. Immunopathogenesis of vernal conjunctivitis and giant papillary conjunctivitis is probably also similar.

TABLE IV-6

Plasma-derived enzyme systems: complement, kinins, and fibrin

Vasoactive amines: seratonin and histamine

Lipid mediators: eicosanoids and platelet-activating factors

Cytokines

Reactive oxygen intermediates

Reactive nitrogen products

Neutrophil-derived granules and products

Mediator Systems That Amplify Innate and Adaptive Immune Responses

Although innate or adaptive effector responses may directly induce inflammation, in most cases these effectors instead initiate a process that must be amplified to produce overt clinical manifestations. Molecules generated within the host that induce and amplify inflammation are termed *inflammatory mediators,* and mediator systems include several categories of these molecules (Table IV-6). Most act on target cells through receptor-mediated processes, although some act in enzymatic cascades that interact in a complex fashion.

Plasma-Derived Enzyme Systems

Complement factors Complement is an important inflammatory mediator in the eye. Components and fragments of the complement cascade, which account for approximately 5% of plasma protein and more than 20 different proteins, represent important endogenous amplifiers of innate and adaptive immunity as well as mediators of inflammatory responses. Both adaptive and innate immune responses can initiate complement activation pathways, which generate products that contribute to the inflammatory process (Fig IV-9). Adaptive immunity typically activates complement by the classic pathway with antigen-antibody (immune) complexes, especially those formed by IgM, IgG1, and IgG3. Innate immunity typically activates complement by the alternative pathway using certain carbohydrate moieties or LPS on the cell wall of microorganisms.

Complement serves the following three basic functions during inflammation:

☐ Coating of antigenic or pathogenic surfaces by C3b to enhance phagocytosis

☐ Promotion of lysis of cell membranes through pore formation by membrane attack complexes (MAC)

☐ Recruitment of PMN and induction of inflammation through generation of the anaphylatoxins C3a, C4a, and C5a

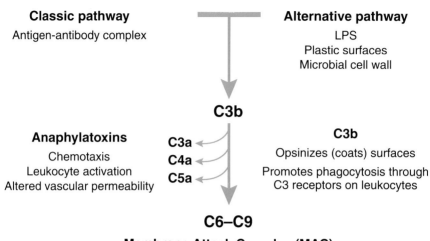

Classic pathway
Antigen-antibody complex

Alternative pathway
LPS
Plastic surfaces
Microbial cell wall

C3b

Anaphylatoxins
Chemotaxis
Leukocyte activation
Altered vascular permeability

C3a
C4a
C5a

C3b
Opsinizes (coats) surfaces
Promotes phagocytosis through
C3 receptors on leukocytes

C6–C9
Membrane Attack Complex (MAC)
Forms pores in cell membranes
Osmotic lysis

FIG IV-9—Overview of the essential intermediates of the complement pathway.

The anaphylatoxins, so named because they cause anaphylaxis upon systemic administration into animals, are the principal complement-derived mediators. The effects of these anaphylatoxins include chemotaxis and changes in cell adhesiveness, mediated principally by C5a, and degranulation and release of mediators from mast cells and platelets, mediated by all three (these effects are described below in discussions of vasoactive amines, arachidonic acid metabolites, and platelet-activating factors). The proinflammatory complement mediator C5a also stimulates oxidative metabolism and the production and release of toxic oxygen radicals from leukocytes as well as the extracellular discharge of leukocyte granule contents.

Kinin-forming system   *Kinins* are low-molecular-weight polypeptides derived from precursors, or *kininogens,* in plasma and tissue fluids. They mediate numerous inflammatory effects, including vasodilation, pain, constriction of smooth muscle, increased vascular permeability, and stimulation of arachidonic acid metabolism. The generation of kinins proceeds in the multiple steps typical of cascade reactions, and more than one pathway is known. In one pathway innate triggers such as LPS activate Hageman factor, which in turn converts inactive proenzymes (prekallikrein) into active forms, or *kallikrein.* Substrates for the kallikrein enzymes are kininogens that are converted into kinins. The best-known kinin product of the Hageman factor–dependent pathway is *bradykinin.* Interestingly, the four cascade systems that play major or minor roles during inflammation (kinin, fibrinolytic, clotting, and complement) may all interact with Hageman factor, a plasma protein that can be activated by numerous stimuli, including negatively charged surfaces, collagen, trypsin, plasmin, kallikrein, coagulation factor XI, and LPS.

Fibrin and other plasma factors   *Fibrin* is the final deposition product of another important plasma-derived enzyme system, and its deposition during inflammation promotes hemostasis, fibrosis, angiogenesis, and leukocyte adhesion. Fibrin is released from its circulating zymogen precursor, *fibrinogen,* upon cleavage by thrombin, also a zymogen, or proenzyme. In situ polymerization of smaller units gives rise to the characteristic fibrin plugs or clots. Fibrin dissolution is mediated by plasmin, which is activated from its zymogen precursor, plasminogen, by plasminogen activators such as tissue plasminogen activator (t-PA). Thrombin, which is derived principally from platelet granules, is released after any vascular injury that causes platelet aggregation and release.

Fibrin deposition has long been considered a clinical sign of DH, since fibrin deposits in skin lesions of DH reactions give the skin a "hardened" or indurated feeling upon palpation, and extracellular fibrin deposits are visible by histology. However, significant fibrin deposits occur in forms of inflammation triggered by innate mechanisms as well. The role of fibrin deposition in the eye during uveitis is unknown, but it is thought to promote complications such as synechiae, cyclitic membranes, and tractional retinal detachment.

Vasoactive Amines

Histamine and *serotonin* are small preformed molecules released early during inflammatory responses that cause smooth muscle contraction and strongly influence vascular permeability and blood flow. In addition, histamine can influence cytokine production and receptor expression by leukocytes. Both of these amines subserve other functions as well. For example, serotonin also acts as a neurotransmitter. Vasoactive amines are important mediators for certain types of ocular inflammation, especially allergic reactions on the ocular surface such as vernal conjunctivitis.

Serotonin   Platelets probably provide the principal source of serotonin, which like histamine participates in regulating the initial increased blood flow and vascular permeability responses of inflammation. Platelets release serotonin from the granules following activation or aggregation. Since platelet plasma membranes are easily activated and respond rapidly to a wide variety of injuries and inflammatory stimuli, serotonin probably acts synergistically with other platelet-derived inflammatory mediators such as platelet-activating factors and thromboxanes. Further platelet aggregation and activation then ensues (see below).

Histamine   Histamine is present in the granules of mast cells and basophils, and it is actively secreted from this source following exposure of cells to a wide range of stimuli. Histamine acts by binding to one of at least three known types of receptors present differentially on target cells. The best-studied pathway for degranulation is antigen cross-linking of IgE bound to mast-cell Fc IgE receptors, but many other inflammatory stimuli can stimulate secretion, including complement, direct membrane injury, certain drugs, and others. Classically, histamine release has been associated with allergy. The contribution of histamine to intraocular inflammation remains equivocal.

Lipid Mediators

Two groups of lipid molecules synthesized by stimulated cells act as powerful mediators and regulators of inflammatory responses: the acetylated triglycerides, usually called *platelet-activating factors (PAF)*, and the arachidonic acid metabolites, or *eicosanoids*. Both groups of molecules may be rapidly generated from the same lysophospholipid precursors by the enzymatic action of cellular phospholipases such as phospholipase A_2 (Fig IV-10).

Eicosanoids All eicosanoids are derived from *arachidonic acid (AA)*. AA is liberated from membrane phospholipids by phospholipase A_2, which is activated by various agonists. AA is oxidized by two major pathways to generate the various mediators:

◻ The *cyclo-oxygenase (COX) pathway*, which produces prostaglandins (PG), thromboxanes, and prostacyclins; cyclo-oxygenase is also known as *prostaglandin G/H synthase (PG/H synthase)*

◻ The 5-lipoxygenase pathway, which produces hydroxyeicosatetraenoic acid (HETE), lipoxins, and leukotrienes

Many other important enzymes also function in eicosanoid metabolism.

The COX-derived mediators are evanescent compounds induced in virtually all cells by a variety of stimuli. In general, they act in the immediate environment of their release to directly mediate many inflammatory activities, including effects on vascular permeability, cell recruitment, platelet function, and smooth muscle contraction. Perhaps of even greater importance, COX-derived products act on cells to regulate other functions, and they have very complicated effects on immune responses. Depending on conditions, COX-derived products can either upregulate or downregulate the production of cytokines, enzyme systems, and oxygen metabolites. Two forms of cyclo-oxygenase exist: COX-1 and COX-2. COX-1 is thought to be constitutively expressed in many cells, especially in cells that use PG for basal metabolic functions, such as the gastric mucosa or the renal tubular epithelium. COX-2 is inducible by many proinflammatory stimuli, including other inflammatory mediators (e.g., PAF and some cytokines) and innate stimuli (e.g., LPS).

Of the COX-derived mediators, *prostaglandins* probably play the most important role in ocular inflammation. PG have long been associated with regulation of vascular permeability in the eye, although their part in mediating cellular infiltration is not completely clear. Among the best characterized PG are PGE_1 and PGE_2, but their ultimate role in the eye, whether harmful or protective, is unclear. For instance, increased levels of PGE_2 have been associated with uveitis, yet this PG can suppress effector cell function in vitro. The role of PG in miosis of the pupil during inflammation has generated great interest, yet most PG have minimal or no significant miotic activity on nonhuman primates or in human eyes. Some PG have been hypothesized to cause corneal neovascularization.

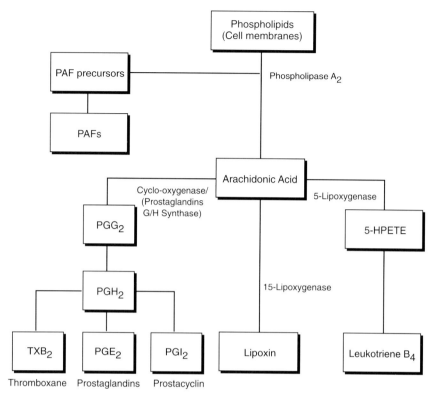

FIG IV-10—Overview of the essential intermediates of the eicosanoid and PAF pathways. (Modified from Pepose JS, Holland GN, Wilhelmus KR, eds. *Ocular Infection and Immunity.* St Louis: Mosby; 1996.)

Finally, PG may be the cause of cystoid macular edema (CME) in association with anterior segment surgery or inflammation. Posterior diffusion of one or more of the eicosanoids through the vitreous is assumed to alter capillary permeability of the perifoveal network, leading to the characteristic pattern of intraretinal fluid accumulation and cyst formation. Clinical trials in humans have indicated that topical treatment with COX inhibitors does diminish the onset of mild CME after cataract surgery and might be efficacious in the treatment of severe, persistent CME.

Prostaglandins and other eicosanoids indisputably play a major role in the physiology of the eye, reaching far beyond their putative participation as mediators of inflammation. For example, PGE_1 regulates the alternative (uveoscleral) outflow pathway for aqueous humor, perhaps explaining why IOP is diminished in some inflamed eyes. Latanoprost, a PGF_2 alpha analogue, may act with a similar mechanism.

The products of the other major pathway of AA metabolism, the 5-lipoxygenase pathway, are also numerous, and some of them are extremely potent mediators of the inflammatory response. Derivatives of 5-lipoxygenase, an enzyme found mainly in granulocytes and some mast cells, have been also detected in the brain and retina. In contrast to prostaglandins, *leukotrienes* probably contribute significantly to inflammatory infiltration. One of the best characterized is leukotriene B_4 (LTB_4), a potent chemotactic factor that also causes lysosomal enzyme release and reactive oxygen radical production by granulocytes. Some leukotrienes may have 1000 times the effect of histamine on vascular permeability. Another lipoxygenase product, lipoxin, is a potent stimulator of superoxide anion.

Platelet-activating factors Platelet-activating factors are a family of phospholipid-derived mediators that appear to be important stimuli in the early stage of inflammation. PAF also serve physiologic functions unrelated to inflammation, especially in reproductive biology, physiology of secretory epithelium, and neurobiology. In these physiologic roles of PAF, a de novo biosynthetic pathway has been identified. However, the *remodeling pathway* is the one implicated with PAF inflammatory actions.

Phospholipase A_2 metabolizes phosphocholine precursors in cell membranes, releasing AA and PAF precursors, which are then acetylated into multiple species of PAF. PAF release can be stimulated by various innate triggers such as bacterial toxins or trauma and cytokines. PAF not only activates platelets but also activates most leukocytes as well, which in turn produce and release additional PAF. The PAF function by binding to one or more guanosine triphospate protein–associated receptors on target cells.

In vitro, PAF induce an impressive repertoire of responses including phagocytosis, exocytosis, superoxide production, chemotaxis, aggregation, proliferation, adhesion, eicosanoid generation, degranulation, and calcium mobilization as well as diverse morphological changes. PAF seem to be a major regulator of cell adhesion and vascular permeability in many forms of acute inflammation, trauma, shock, and ischemia. PAF antagonists are being developed and tested in clinical trials. Synergistic interactions probably exist between PAF, nitric oxide, eicosanoids, and cytokines. PAF have been associated with ocular inflammation, but their precise role is under investigation.

Cytokines

Cytokine is a generic term for any soluble polypeptide mediator that is synthesized and released by cells for the purposes of intercellular signaling and communication. Table IV-7 lists some examples of cytokines that are most likely to be associated with ocular inflammation. Cytokines can be released to signal neighboring cells at the site (paracrine action), to stimulate a receptor on its own surface (autocrine action), or in some cases to act upon a distant site through being released into the blood (hormonal action). Traditionally, investigators have subdivided cytokines into families with related activities, sources, and targets, using terms such as *growth factors, interleukins, lymphokines, interferons, monokines,* and *chemokines.* Thus, growth factor traditionally refers to cytokines mediating cell proliferation and differentiation. Interleukin or lymphokine identifies cytokines thought to mediate intercellular communication among lymphocytes or other leukocytes. Interferons would be cytokines that limited or "interfered with" virus infection of a cell. Chemokines, originally called *intercrines,* are chemotactic cytokines. However, research has demonstrated that although some cytokines are cell-type specific, most cytokines have such multiplicity and redundancy of source, function, and target that this focus on specific terminology is not particularly useful for the clinician. For example, activated macrophages in an inflammatory site synthesize growth factors, interleukins, interferons, and chemokines.

Both innate and adaptive responses result in the production of cytokines. T lymphocytes are the classic cytokine-producing cell of adaptive immunity, but macrophages, mast cells, and even PMN can also synthesize a wide range of cytokines upon stimulation. Nevertheless, the exact role of individual molecules during the inflammatory response is not clear. Cytokine interactions can be additive, combinatorial (two factors combining for greater effect than the sum of their individual activities), or synergistic (two factors enabling a new activity not manifest by either alone). Further complicating the issue, cytokines usually have multiple functions that overlap and counteract; as a consequence, elimination of the action of a single molecule may have an unpredictable outcome. Moreover, the function of various cytokines might change during the course of an inflammatory response. Finally, not only do innate and adaptive immune responses use cytokines as mediators and amplifiers of inflammation, but cytokines also modulate the initiation of immune responses; the function of most leukocytes is altered by preexposure to various cytokines. Thus, for many cytokines, their regulatory role may be as important as their actions as mediators of inflammation.

TABLE IV-7

CYTOKINES OF RELEVANCE TO OCULAR IMMUNOLOGY

FAMILY	EXAMPLE	MAJOR CELL SOURCE	MAJOR TARGET CELLS	MAJOR GENERAL ACTIONS	SPECIFIC OCULAR ACTIONS
Interleukins	IL-1α	Macrophages Many others	Most leukocytes Various ocular cells	Many actions on T and B cells Systemic toxicity (fever, shock)	Altered vascular permeability PMN and macrophage infiltration Langerhans migration to central cornea
	IL-6	Macrophages T cells Mast cells Most ocular epithelium	Most leukocytes Various ocular cells	Many actions on B cells Systemic toxicity (fever, shock)	Altered vascular permeability PMN infiltration High levels in many forms of uveitis and nonuveitic diseases
	IL-2	Th0 or Th1 CD4 T cells	T cells, B cells, NK cells	Activates CD4 and CD8 T cells, induces Th1	Detectable levels in some forms of uveitis
	IL-4	Th2 CD4 T cells Basophils, mast cells	T cells, B cells	Induces Th2, blocks Th1 Induces B cells to make IgE	?Role in atopic and vernal conjunctivitis
	IL-5	Th2 CD4 T cells		Recruits eosinophils	?Role in atopic and vernal conjunctivitis
Alpha chemokines	IL-8	Many cell types	Endothelial cells PMN Many others	Recruits and activates PMN Upregulates CAM on endothelium	Altered vascular permeability PMN infiltration
Beta chemokines	Macrophage chemotactic protein-1 (MCP-1)	Macrophages Endothelium RPE	Endothelial cells Macrophages T cells	Recruits and activates macrophages, some T cells	Recruits macrophages and T cells to eye
Tumor necrosis factors	TNF-α or -β	Macrophages (TNF-α) T cells (TNF-β)		Tumor apoptosis Macrophage and PMN activation Cell adhesion and chemotaxis Fibrin deposition and vascular injury Systemic toxicity (fever, shock)	Altered vascular permeability Mononuclear cell infiltration

TABLE IV-7

CYTOKINES OF RELEVANCE TO OCULAR IMMUNOLOGY (Continued)

FAMILY	EXAMPLE	MAJOR CELL SOURCE	MAJOR TARGET CELLS	MAJOR GENERAL ACTIONS	SPECIFIC OCULAR ACTIONS
Interferons	Interferon gamma (IFN-γ)	Th1 T cells NK cells		Activates macrophages	PMN and macrophage infiltration
	IFN-α	Most leukocytes	Most parenchymal cells	Prevents viral infection of many cells. Inhibits hemangioma, conjunctival intraepithelial neoplasia, and other tumors	Innate protection of ocular surface from viral infection, treatment of ocular surface neoplasms
Growth Factors	Transforming growth factor–β (TGF-β)	Many cells Leukocytes, T cells RPE and NPE of ciliary body Pericytes Fibroblasts	Macrophages T cells RPE Glia Fibroblasts	Suppresses T-cell and macrophage inflammatory functions. Fibrosis of wounds	Regulator of immune privilege and ACAID
	Platelet-derived growth factors (PDGF)	Platelets Macrophages RPE	Fibroblasts Glia Many others	Fibroblast proliferation	Role in inflammatory membranes, subretinal fibrosis
Neuropeptides	Substance P	Ocular nerves Mast cells	Leukocytes Others	Pain. Altered vascular permeability	Altered vascular permeability. Leukocyte infiltration, photophobia
	Vasoactive intestinal peptide	Ocular nerves	Leukocytes Others	Suppresses macrophage and T cell inflammatory function	Role in ACAID and immune privilege

Reactive Oxygen Intermediates

Under certain conditions, oxygen can undergo chemical modification to transform into highly reactive substances with the potential to damage cellular molecules and inhibit functional properties in pathogens or host cells. BCSC Section 2, *Fundamentals and Principles of Ophthalmology,* discusses the processes involved in greater detail in Part 4, Biochemistry and Metabolism. See especially chapter XVIII, Free Radicals and Antioxidants.

Three of the most important oxygen intermediates are superoxide anion, hydrogen peroxide, and the hydroxyl radical:

$$O_2 + e^- \rightarrow O_2^- \qquad \text{superoxide anion}$$

$$O_2^- + O_2^- + 2H^+ \rightarrow O_2 + H_2O_2 \qquad \begin{array}{l}\text{superoxide dismutase catalyzes} \\ \text{anions to form hydrogen peroxide}\end{array}$$

$$H_2O_2 + e^- \rightarrow OH^- + OH\cdot \qquad \text{hydroxyl anion and hydroxyl radical}$$

Oxygen metabolites generated by leukocytes, especially PMN and macrophages, triggered by immune responses are the most important source during inflammation. A wide variety of stimuli can trigger leukocyte oxygen metabolism, including

□ Innate triggers such as LPS or formyl methionine-leucine-proline (fMLP)

□ Adaptive effectors such as complement-fixing antibodies or certain cytokines produced by DH T cells

□ Other chemical mediator systems such as C5a, PAF, or leukotrienes

Reactive oxygen intermediates can also be generated as part of noninflammatory cellular biochemical processes, especially by electron transport in the mitochondria, detoxification of certain chemicals, or interactions with environmental light or radiation.

The principal mechanism by which oxygen metabolites are activated during inflammation is by the induction of various oxidases in PMN or macrophage cell membranes, especially NADPH oxidase, but also NADH oxidase, xanthine oxidase, and aldehyde oxidase. NADPH oxidase catalyses the transfer of electrons from NADPH, the reduced form of nicotinamide-adenine dinucleotide phosphate, or from NADH, the reduced form of nicotinamide-adenine dinucleotide, to oxygen or hydrogen peroxide (H_2O_2) to form intermediates such as the reactive oxygen radical superoxide anion. As shown in the formulas above, the transfer of a single electron to oxygen forms superoxide anion, an unstable radical that may dismutate spontaneously; that is, one of the molecules gains an electron and the other loses one. Otherwise, the reaction can be catalyzed by the enzyme superoxide dismutase (SOD) to form H_2O_2 and oxygen.

Alternatively, two electrons can be transferred to molecular oxygen, a process that normally occurs in the peroxisomes. This process also results in formation of H_2O_2, a molecule that by itself has feeble inflammatory and microbicidal activity. Moreover, H_2O_2 can be readily "neutralized" into water and oxygen by enzymes such as catalase in peroxisomes and glutathione peroxidase in the cytosol, as shown in Fig IV-11.

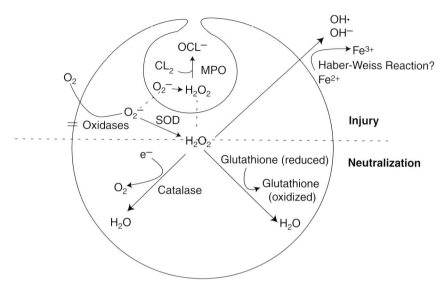

FIG IV-11—Overview of the essential intracellular and extracellular pathways in the generation of reactive oxygen intermediates. Activation of oxidases catalyzes the production of superoxide anion (O_2-), which can be converted into H_2O_2 by superoxide dismutase (SOD). Catalase (in the peroxisome) and glutathione can neutralize H_2O_2. However, H_2O_2 can be converted into hydroxyl ion ($OH+$) or hydroxyl radical ($OH\cdot$) by the Haber-Weiss reaction. Alternatively, H_2O_2 can be catalyzed by myeloperoxidase (MPO) into hypochlorous anion and other reactive intermediates. (Reproduced from Pepose JS, Holland GN, Wilhelmus KR, eds. *Ocular Infection and Immunity.* St Louis: Mosby; 1996.)

H_2O_2 can, however, be converted into molecules with potential inflammatory and antimicrobial activity by at least three chemical processes:

- The Fenton or Haber-Weiss reactions can add one electron to form the hydroxyl anion ($OH-$) along with the highly reactive hydroxyl radical ($OH\cdot$). However, the existence of this pathway in vivo has been disputed.

- In a second, recently discovered, process H_2O_2 may be catalyzed by myeloperoxidase, an abundant protein found in PMN, to react with halide or pseudohalide (thiocyanate) substrates to form extremely toxic products that are highly damaging to bacteria and tissues. These include hypohalous acids, halogens, chloramines, and hydroxyl radicals. Hydroxyl radicals interact with several potential cellular targets to cause enzyme and protein damage as a result of cross-linking of sulfhydryl groups; cell membrane injury caused by lipid peroxidation of the lipid bilayers; loss of energization and cellular stores of adenosine triphosphate (ATP) as a result of loss of integrity of the inner membrane of the mitochondria; and breaks or cross-links in DNA from chemical alterations of nucleotides

- A third inflammatory process involves the formation of peroxynitrite after chemical interaction between superoxide and nitric oxide (see below)

Role of oxygen-mediated damage in experimental uveitis Reactive oxygen intermediates are likely mediators in many forms of ocular inflammation, especially those forms involving the retina. In a series of studies examining a model of autoimmune uveoretinitis, investigators demonstrated that the generation of toxic oxygen intermediates was associated with PMN and monocyte infiltration. The formation of superoxide anion and hydroxyl radicals was an early event, and peroxidation of photoreceptor membranes, especially the depletion of polyunsaturated fatty acids, occurred simultaneously with the onset of free radical formation and electrophysiologic loss of photoreceptor function. Interestingly, the peroxidation products were chemotactic for PMN, thereby providing a possible mechanism for amplifying the cycle of inflammatory tissue destruction. Some antioxidants were partially protective.

Rao NA. Role of oxygen free radicals in retinal damage associated with experimental uveitis. *Trans Am Ophthalmol Soc.* 1990;88:797–850.

Reactive Nitrogen Products

Another important pathway of host defenses and inflammation involves the toxic products of nitrogen, especially *nitric oxide (NO)*. NO is a highly reactive chemical species that, like reactive oxygen intermediates, can react with various important biochemical functions in microorganisms and host cells. This pathway was first observed in patients with a deficiency of the respiratory burst enzymes. Because of this deficiency, their PMN and macrophages were unable to generate reactive oxygen intermediates, but they were still able to mount effective antimicrobial function through a toxic nitrogen product, nitric oxide.

The formation of NO is dependent on the enzyme nitric oxide synthetase (NOS), which is located in the cytosol and is NADPH-dependent. NO is formed from the terminal guanidino-nitrogen atoms of L-arginine. Several forms of nitric oxide synthetase are known, including several constitutive forms of NOS (cNOS) and an inducible NOS (iNOS). Many normal cells produce basal levels of NO, which is considered secondary to the calcium-dependent, constitutive form of the enzyme. Activation *induces* enhanced production of NO in certain cells, especially macrophages. This enhanced production appears to be secondary to the induced synthesis of a second, calcium-independent form of NO synthetase (iNOS). Many innate and adaptive stimuli modulate induction of iNOS, especially cytokines and bacterial toxins.

How NO functions to kill microorganisms is not known with certainty. Likely possibilities include interaction with the Fe-S groups of aconitase, an enzyme important for the control of DNA synthesis and RNA production, or complex I and complex II of the mitochondrial electron transport system. During inflammation, NO may also interact with O_2 to form the toxic hydroxyl radical and peroxynitrite ($ONOO^-$). Peroxynitrite displays high chemical reactivity, including great capacity to peroxidate lipids in cell membranes, modify cellular proteins, and damage DNA. NO biology in the eye during uveitis is under active investigation.

Neutrophil-Derived Granule Products

PMN are also a source of specialized products that can amplify innate or adaptive immune responses. A large number of biochemically defined antimicrobial polypeptides are present in many types of granules found in PMN. The principal well-characterized antimicrobial polypeptides found in human PMN granules are BPI, defensins, lysozyme, lactoferrin, and the serine proteases (or their homologues).

In addition to antimicrobial polypeptides, the PMN contain numerous other molecules that may contribute to inflammation. These include hydrolytic enzymes, elastase, metalloproteinases, gelatinase, myeloperoxidase, vitamin B_{12}–binding protein, cytochrome b_{558}, and others. Granule contents are considered to remain inert and membrane-bound when the granules are intact, but they become active and soluble when granules fuse to the phagocytic vesicles or plasma membrane.

Exactly how the various granulocyte products enhance inflammation is not clear. Originally, it was thought that the release of proteases and other enzymes directly degraded the extracellular matrix of inflamed sites, thereby enabling the recruitment of additional leukocytes, damaging the integrity of microvessels, and injuring the attachment substrate of the parenchymal cells. However, recent evidence suggests that hypochlorous acid, derived from reactive oxygen byproducts, must interact with proteases and protease inhibitors in a complex fashion to enhance the tissue-destructive effects of PMN granule products. The role of PMN-derived proteases in ocular inflammation remains unclear. Collagenases are believed to contribute to corneal injury and liquefaction during bacterial keratitis and scleritis, especially in *Pseudomonas* infections. Collagenases also contribute to peripheral corneal melting syndromes secondary to rheumatoid arthritis–associated peripheral keratitis.

CHAPTER V

Special Topics in Ocular Immunology

Immunoregulation of the Adaptive Immune Response

T- and B-cell Antigen Receptor Repertoire

The biology of B-cell and T-cell antigen receptors has become a major area of research. The specificities of B-cell antigen receptors such as surface IgM and IgD and of T-cell antigen receptors must account for tens of thousands (if not millions) of possible antigens in nature. Since antigen receptor specificities are originally generated randomly, before the initial encounter with antigen, this wide range of potential specificities requires that the adaptive immune system generate a huge number of different antibody and T-cell receptor molecules from relatively few associated genes. This diversity requires a very elegant form of molecular *recombination,* or the mixing and matching of genetic segments of immunoglobulin or T-cell receptor germline genes during maturation of T cells and B cells. For B cells additional recombination and mutation of the receptor genes take place during the immune response. These genetic manipulations do not occur for other types of receptors. Nevertheless, the random formation of antigen receptors implies that the generation of many receptors that recognize self antigens is possible, leading to the potential for autoimmunity. BCSC Section 2, *Fundamentals and Principles of Ophthalmology,* discusses recombination in Part 3, Genetics.

Tolerance and Immunoregulation

A central theme in immunology is the ability of the adaptive immune response to differentiate between *self* and *nonself,* or foreign. The paradox involved was eloquently recognized by Erlich, who coined the term *horror autotoxicus,* or fear of self-poisoning, to convey the idea that a sophisticated mechanism must exist to prevent the immune system from attacking normal tissues. Medawar subsequently enunciated the formal concept of self tolerance.

In modern immunology, *tolerance* is usually defined as the sum total of the mechanisms by which the immune system differentiates self from foreign to prevent *inflammation-triggering* immune responses against self antigens. Recent advances in immunology have clarified various mechanisms of immunologic tolerance that prevent widespread autoimmune inflammation. Although a detailed description of these mechanisms is beyond the scope of this book, a brief overview is included below. See also chapter II for a discussion of *T-cell cross-regulation,* the concept that Th1 cells can regulate Th2 activation, and vice versa.

Clonal deletion   The thymus has the ability to destroy self-reactive T cells during T-cell maturation, resulting in clonal deletion. Perhaps 99% of all T cells that enter the thymus are deleted from the host by this mechanism, suggesting that at least some of the deleted T cells were autoreactive. Thus, clonal deletion provides a mechanism for immunologic unresponsiveness that creates a gap in the repertoire of potential antigens, presumably self antigens, against which the immune response can mobilize. Clonal deletion has been demonstrated in principle in mice through several different experimental approaches.

The precise role of clonal deletion in immunologic tolerance to ocular auto-antigens remains uncertain. Intriguingly, α crystallin protein and S antigen have been detected within the thymus, suggesting the possibility of crystallin-specific and S antigen–specific deletion of T cells. However, actual clonal deletion of autoreactive T cells has not yet been demonstrated for ocular autoantigens. If clonal deletion were complete, lens- or retinal-responsive T cells would be absent during uveitis. Because such T cells can indeed be demonstrated under certain experimental conditions, clonal deletion, if present, must be incomplete.

Anergy   *Anergy* and *clonal inactivation* are terms that have been used to describe the situation in which antigen-specific T cells or B cells are rendered incapable of mounting a normal inflammation-triggering response to that antigen. For example, when B cells of mice are exposed to antigen early in the developmental process, they are rendered unresponsive to that antigen after maturation. Similarly, several different mechanisms that "tolerize" T cells have been demonstrated. When T cells are presented antigen by nonprofessional APC such as corneal endothelium or Müller cells, they become inactivated from further differentiation into inflammatory effector cells. Although these T cells survive, they are incapable of initiating inflammatory immune responses. Anergy therefore provides an additional mechanism for immunologic unresponsiveness.

Suppression   Suppression, the third classic mechanism for tolerance, postulates that a population of *downregulatory T cells* exists to balance the population of helper and inflammation-enhancing T cells. These downregulatory T cells modulate and diminish the level of activation by the effector or helper T cell. Whereas clonal deletion or anergy supports immunologic unresponsiveness, suppression indicates an active but tolerizing immune response to a specific antigen. The best-characterized mechanism involves the release of immunosuppressive cytokines such as TGF-β by CD8 suppressor T cells, but several other mechanisms have also been supported by experimental data. Although the physiologic importance and mechanism(s) by which suppression is induced and regulated have been challenged, suppression is clearly an important regulatory mechanism for the immune system in general, and for ocular immune responses in particular. See chapter III for discussion of suppression induced during ACAID.

Potential role of antibody isotype   An interesting paradox can be demonstrated in many healthy people: antiself antibodies to many major autoantigens can be demonstrated in sera, but these autoantibodies do not seem to cause inflammation. One explanation may be related to the different effector functions of various antibody isotypes (see Table IV-4). The major inflammation-inducing mechanism of antibody is brought about by complement activation, which in turn is a function of the isotype of the antibody molecule itself. As discussed in chapter IV, isotypes vary in their capacity to activate complement. Preferential activation of B cells that produce

Tolerance to lens crystallins Why does violation of the lens capsule and release of lens proteins during cataract surgery almost always produce only minimal immunologic sequelae? Intuitively, cataract surgery or any type of lens injury and the ensuing release of lens protein would seem likely to initiate an autoimmune attack. Yet even though serum titers of antilens antibodies often rise in patients after cataract surgery, effector T cells, pathogenic antibodies, and true autoimmune uveitis rarely develop. Most investigators believe that the protection of the lens is caused by the presence of active immunologic tolerance and that the lens is *not* sequestered from the immune system. Thus, the relative rarity of true autoimmune uveitis directed against the lens indicates the power of protective tolerance to self.

The nature of the T-cell tolerance to the lens, and whether it involves clonal deletion, anergy, suppression, and/or cross-regulation, is not known. Clonal deletion of antilens T cells is suggested by the detection of α crystallin protein and mRNA within the thymus. Anergy is also suggested by some other animal experiments. Ocular immune privilege (ACAID) may provide an additional mechanism for tolerance by the generation of suppressor T cells. However, tolerance is not complete, since responses of antilens helper T cells can be demonstrated under certain experimental conditions, although DH effector cells rarely develop.

B-cell tolerance to lens protein is probably indirect, controlled at the level of the helper T cell. Thus, functional lens-specific B cells certainly exist, since antilens antibody can be identified in serum of many normal individuals and in most individuals after cataract surgery. In addition, antibody titers can be stimulated in all animals by cutaneous immunization. An increase in the titer of antilens antibody after immunization or surgery, however, does not necessarily indicate loss of tolerance as long as the antibody titers are predominated by non–complement-fixing isotypes.

Pepose JS, Holland GN, Wilhelmus KR, eds. *Ocular Infection and Immunity.* St Louis: Mosby; 1996.

complement-fixing antibodies will result in inflammation-inducing immunity, since complement activation will be initiated following immune complex formation. Conversely, preferential activation of non–complement-fixing antibodies will result in high antibody titers but not severe inflammation. Immune complexes will opsonize or agglutinate the antigen, but complement will not be activated. Therefore, one key to B-cell effector function is determined by the regulation of the class switch from an IgM-synthesizing B cell to one producing an antibody of the other isotypes. This switch is controlled by different T cell–derived cytokines. By inference, the regulation of this form of B-cell tolerance is passive and under the control of helper T-cell signals.

Male DK, Cooke A, Owen M, et al. *Advanced Immunology.* 3rd ed. St Louis: Mosby; 1996.

Roitt IM. *Essential Immunology.* 9th ed. Malden, MA: Blackwell Science; 1997.

Molecular mimicry and autoimmune uveitis   Molecular mimicry has been suggested as a mechanism for uveitis after finding that the primary amino acid sequence of a variety of foreign antigens (including those of baker's yeast histone, *E coli*, hepatitis B virus, and certain murine and primate retroviruses) showed sequence homology to a pathogenic epitope of the ocular autoantigen S antigen. Immunization of rats with crude extracts prepared from these organisms or synthetic peptides corresponding to the homologous epitopes induced retinal inflammation. In addition, T cells isolated from rats immunized with foreign substances cross-reacted with retinal autoantigens, providing evidence of molecular mimicry between self and nonself proteins. Currently, no definitive clinical evidence suggests that molecular mimicry contributes to autoimmune diseases of the human eye.

Molecular Mimicry

Autoimmunity may play an important role in the pathogenesis of inflammatory ocular diseases, and one mechanism through which autoimmunity to self antigens in the eye may be triggered is *molecular mimicry,* the immunologic cross-reaction between epitopes of an unrelated foreign antigen and self epitopes with similar structures. Theoretically, these epitopes would be similar enough to stimulate an immune response yet different enough to cause a breakdown of immunologic tolerance.

For example, a foreign antigen such as those present within yeast, viruses, or bacteria can induce an appropriate afferent, processing, and effector immune response. A self antigen with similar epitopes may induce antimicrobial antibodies or effector lymphocytes to inappropriately cross-react. A dynamic process would then be initiated, causing tissue injury by an autoimmune response that would induce additional lymphocyte responses directed at other self antigens. Thus, the process would not require the ongoing replication of a pathogen or the continuous presence of the inciting antigen.

HLA Associations and Disease

Normal Function of HLA Molecules

All animals with white blood cells express a family of cell surface glycoproteins called *major histocompatibility complex (MHC)* proteins. In humans the MHC proteins are called *human leukocyte antigen (HLA)* molecules. As discussed in chapter II, six different families of HLA molecules have been identified:

□ Three class I MHC: HLA-A, -B, -C

□ Three class II MHC: HLA-DR, –DP, -DQ

A seventh category, HLA-D, does not exist as a specific molecule but instead represents a functional classification as determined by an in vitro assay. Class III MHC molecules and minor MHC antigens have also been identified, but they will not be discussed here.

The important role MHC molecules play in immunologic function was discussed in chapter II, and Table V-1 on p 92 gives a historical perspective linking MHC molecules and transplantation biology with immune response genes. HLA antigens are also considered to be human immune response genes, since the HLA type determines the capacity of the APC to bind peptide fragments and thus determines T-cell immune responsiveness.

Allelic Variation

Many different alleles or polymorphic variants of each of the six HLA types exist within the population: more than 25 alleles for HLA-A, 50 for -B, 10 for -C, 100 for -DR, and so on. Since there are six major HLA types, and each individual has a pair of each HLA type, or one *haplotype* from each parent, an APC will express six pairs of MHC molecules. Thus, with the exception of identical twins, it is rare that two individuals will match all 12 potential haplotypes. Alleles and genetic variations are discussed in greater detail in BCSC Section 2, *Fundamentals and Principles of Ophthalmology,* Part 3, Genetics.

Allelic diversity may be designed to provide protection through "population-wide" immunity. Each HLA haplotype theoretically covers a set of antigens to which a particular individual can respond adaptively. Thus, in theory, the presence of many different HLA alleles within a population should ensure that the adaptive immune system in at least some individuals in the whole group will be able to respond to a wide range of potential pathogens. The converse will also be true: some individuals may be at increased risk for immunologic diseases.

Clinical detection and classification of different alleles   Currently, the different alleles of HLA-A, -B, -C, -DR, and -DQ are detected by reacting lymphocytes with special antisera that have been standardized by international HLA Workshops sponsored by the World Health Organization (WHO). HLA-DP and HLA-D typing requires performance of specialized T-cell culture assays. Traditionally, provisional serotypes pending official recognition were often designated *workshop* (i.e., DRw53). More recently, molecular techniques have been developed to characterize the nucleic acid sequence of various MHC alleles. HLA molecules are composed of two chains: α and β chains for class II, an α chain and the β_2-microglobulin chain for class I. Since subtle differences in molecular structure can be easily missed using antisera, molecular genotyping is a more precise method to determine MHC types. Thus, the genotype specifies the chain, the major genetic type, and the specific minor molecular variant subtype. For example, genotype DRB1*0408 refers to the HLA-DR4 molecule β chain with the "—08" minor variant subtype.

New serotypes now must correspond to a specific genotype and the provisional "w" label is rarely used. Nonetheless, haplotypes currently recognized as a single group will continue to be subdivided into new categories or new subtypes. For example, at least two different A29 subtypes and eight different HLA-B27 subtypes have been recognized. Finally, some investigators have proposed that HLA classification based on similarities of peptide binding, rather than on serotyping or genetic typing, may reveal other disease associations.

MHC and Transplantation

As indicated in Table V-1, failure of *allogeneic* transplanted tissue, from a genetically nonidentical donor, to remain viable was first recognized as an adaptive immune response in the 1940s. The association between transplantation antigens (i.e., MHC antigens) and immune response genes was not recognized until decades later. The mechanism for immune system recognition of HLA haplotype differences as foreign antigens is not entirely clear. Intuitively, it seems that T cells from the recipient individual should simply ignore APC from a donor individual bearing a different HLA haplotype. Short-term cell culture experiments (i.e., 1–3 days) accordingly show that the recipient's T cells do fail to recognize exogenous foreign antigens presented by the donor APC, even if the T cells had been previously sensitized. However, if the T-cell cultures and donor APC are left to react over a longer term (i.e., 5–7 days), a significant fraction of the recipient T cells will unexpectedly become activated in response to the donor APC HLA molecules, especially class II differences. What remains unknown is whether this *mixed lymphocyte reaction*–induced activation process represents a direct interaction between the foreign HLA and the recipient's T-cell receptor, or if instead the foreign HLA molecule is processed as a foreign protein and presented by host APC to host T cells. Both DH and CTL effector responses are activated by this process, and both appear crucial in transplant rejection, including corneal allograft rejection.

Although antibodies to class I transplantation antigens can also occur in some cases of hyperacute rejection, this mechanism does not appear to be important in corneal graft rejection. In general, HLA matching, especially at DR loci, followed by A and B loci, greatly reduces rejection for many types of organ allografts. Similar observations have not been confirmed for high-risk corneal allograft rejection.

Disease Associations

In 1973 the first association between HLA haplotype and ankylosing spondylitis was identified. Since then, more than 100 other disease associations have been made, including several for ocular inflammatory diseases (Table V-2). In general, an HLA disease association is defined as the statistically increased frequency of an HLA haplotype in individuals with that disease as compared to the frequency in a disease-free population. The ratio of these two frequencies is called *relative risk (RR),* which

Table V-1

The Major Histocompatibility Complex Locus and the HLA System:
A Short History

1940s	Skin autografts succeed, but allografts are rejected unless from a twin
1950s	Transfusion reactions noted against white blood cells among patients matched to RBC antigens, called *human leukocyte antigens (HLA)*
	Antibodies to disparate fetal HLA types noted among multiparous mothers
1960s	Immune response genes in mice control ability to respond to one antigen but not another
	Immune response genes probably code for mouse equivalent of HLA (immune antigen, or Ia)
	Allograft rejection is genetically determined by the Major Histocompatibility Complex (MHC) locus
1970s	Ia in mice and HLA types in humans correlate with transplant rejection, giving rise to the concept that immune response genes are part of the MHC
	Prediction that Ia type in mice and HLA type in humans will correlate with propensity to autoimmunity on basis of immune responsiveness to environmental pathogens
	First HLA association with inflammatory disease (HLA-B27 and ankylosing spondylitis)
1980s	Mechanism of MHC function: HLA required on antigen-presenting cells to activate T cells—class I molecules present to CD8 T cells; class II molecules present to CD4 T cells
	T cells and B cells see antigen differently; B cells see the whole, natural antigen; T cells "see" antigens after they are chopped up into peptides
	Function of class I and II molecules confirmed—antigen fragments are placed within a groove formed by the tertiary structure of the molecule to allow presentation to the T cell receptor
	Different HLA molecules have different capacity to bind different fragments, explaining role as immune response gene
	Mutations in the binding site within the groove of class I and II molecules may allow some individuals to bind and present certain environmental or self peptides, thereby predisposing to autoimmunity
1990s	Molecular typing of HLA becoming more available and better than serotyping
	Molecular mechanism of antigen processing well characterized

TABLE V-2

HLA ASSOCIATIONS AND OCULAR INFLAMMATORY DISEASE

DISEASE	HLA ASSOCIATION	SPECIFIC RELATIVE RISK (RR) FOR ASSOCIATED SUBGROUP
Acute anterior uveitis	HLA-B27	RR=8
Reiter syndrome	HLA-B27	RR=60
Juvenile rheumatoid arthritis	HLA-DR4, -Dw2	Acute systemic disease
Behçet syndrome	HLA-B51	Japanese and Middle Eastern descent RR=4–6
Birdshot chorioretinitis	HLA-A29, -A29.2	RR=80–100, for North Americans and Europeans
Intermediate uveitis	HLA-B8, -B51, -DR2 HLA-DR15	RR=6, possibly the DRB1*1501 genotype
Sympathetic ophthalmia	HLA-DR4	
VKH syndrome	HLA-DR4	Japanese and North Americans
Sarcoidosis	HLA-B8	Acute systemic disease
	HLA-B13	Chronic systemic disease but not for eye
Multiple sclerosis	HLA-B7, -DR2	
Ocular histoplasmosis syndrome (OHS)	HLA-B7, -DR2	RR=12
Retinal vasculitis	HLA-B44	Britons

is the simplest method for expressing the magnitude of an HLA disease association. Nevertheless, several caveats must be kept in mind:

☐ The association is only as strong as the clinical diagnosis. Diseases that are difficult to diagnose on clinical features may obscure real associations.

☐ The association depends on the validity of the haplotyping. Older literature often reflects associations based on HLA classifications (some provisional) that might have changed.

☐ The HLA association identifies individuals at risk and is not a diagnostic marker. The associated haplotype is not necessarily present in all persons affected with the specific disease, and its presence in a person does not assure the correct diagnosis.

☐ The concept of linkage disequilibrium proposes that if two genes are physically near on the chromosome, they may be inherited together rather than undergo genetic randomization in a population. Thus, HLA may be coinherited with an unrelated disease gene, and sometimes two HLA haplotypes can occur together more frequently than predicted by their independent frequencies in the population.

HLA-B27–associated acute anterior uveitis Approximately 50% of patients with acute anterior uveitis (AAU) express the HLA-B27 haplotype, and many of these patients also experience other immunologic disorders such as Reiter syndrome, ankylosing spondylitis, and psoriatic arthritis (see chapter VII). Although the immunopathogenesis remains unknown, various animal models permit some informed speculation. Many cases of uveitis or Reiter syndrome follow gram-negative bacillary dysentery or chlamydial infection. The possible role of LPS and innate mechanisms was discussed in chapter IV. Experiments in rats and mice genetically altered to express human HLA-B27 molecules seem to suggest that bacterial infection of the gut predisposes rats to arthritis and a Reiter-like syndrome, although uveitis is uncommon.

It has been suggested that chronic intracellular chlamydial infection of a joint, and presumably the eye, might stimulate an adaptive immune response using the endogenous (class I) antigen-processing pathway of the B27 molecule, invoking a CD8 T-cell effector mechanism activated to kill the infection but indirectly injuring the eye. Others have suggested that B27 haplotype might present *Klebsiella* peptide antigens to CD8 T cells, but how a presumed exogenous bacterial antigen would be presented through the class I pathway is unknown. Another hypothesis posits that molecular mimicry may exist between bacterial antigens and an epitope of HLA-B27. Analysis of human AAU fluids and various animal models of AAU and arthritis suggests that anterior uveitis might be a CD4 Th1–mediated DH response, possibly in response to bacteria-derived antigens such as bacterial cell wall antigens or heat shock proteins trapped in the uvea or to endogenous autoantigens of the anterior uvea, possibly melanin-associated antigens, type II collagen, or myelin-associated proteins. How a CD4-predominant mechanism would relate to a class I immunogenetic association is unclear.

At least four theoretical explanations have been offered for HLA disease associations. The most direct theory postulates that HLA molecules act as peptide-binding molecules for etiologic antigens or infectious agents. Thus, individuals bearing a specific HLA molecule might be predisposed to processing certain antigens, such as an infectious agent that cross-reacts with a self antigen, and other individuals lacking that haplotype would not be so predisposed. Specific variations or mutations in the peptide-binding region would greatly influence this mechanism, and these variations can be detected only by molecular typing. Preliminary data in support of this theory have been provided for type I diabetes.

A second theory proposes molecular mimicry between bacterial antigens and an epitope of an HLA molecule (i.e., an antigenic site on the molecule itself). An appropriate antibacterial effector response might inappropriately initate a cross-react effector response with an epitope of the HLA molecule. The third theory suggests that the T-cell antigen receptor (gene) is really the true susceptibility factor. Since a specific T-cell receptor uses a specific HLA haplotype, a strong correlation would exist between HLA and T-cell antigen receptor repertoire. A fourth theory implicates an innate etiology unrelated to the role of HLA in adaptive immunity. For example, transgenic mice genetically altered to express the HLA-B51 molecule, which is associated with Behçet syndrome, develop PMN with enhanced activation and perhaps exaggerated innate effector function.

Immunotherapeutics

BCSC Section 2, *Fundamentals and Principles of Ophthalmology,* includes chapters on pharmacologic principles and ocular pharmacotherapeutics in Part 5, Ocular Pharmacology. See also chapter VI of this volume, under "Medical Management of Uveitis," p 112.

Nonsteroidal Anti-Inflammatory Drugs (NSAIDs)

NSAIDs are a family of aspirin-like drugs that inhibit the production of prostaglandins by acting on cyclo-oxygenase. COX itself has a complex structure that includes a helical channel at the enzymatically active site that oxidizes arachidonic acid. Aspirin and most NSAIDs act by various mechanisms to reversibly or irreversibly inhibit the arachidonic acid–binding site in the channel of both COX-1 and COX-2. New experimental drugs are being designed to specifically inhibit COX-2, and these will likely become the NSAIDs of choice for anti-inflammatory treatment, since they will be able to selectively block the inflammation mediated by COX-2 without the adverse effects of stomach lesions and renal toxicity that often arise from COX-1 inhibition. Topical or systemic NSAIDs are moderately effective at inhibiting COX in the eye but appear to have only mild anti-inflammatory efficacy for most types of acute ocular inflammation. Nevertheless, some authorities believe that they can play an important supplementary role in the treatment of uveitis.

Glucocorticosteroids

The mainstay of uveitis therapy is topical, periocular, or systemic administration of glucocorticosteroids. Corticosteroids bind intracellular receptors that translocate into the nucleus, where the drug acts to alter DNA transcription into mRNA. Systemically administered, corticosteroids can alter the homing pattern of T cells and other effector cells to prevent recruitment into sites of inflammation. Local corticosteroids suppress inflammation through many cellular mechanisms, but the most potent is direct inhibition of most types of inflammatory mediator synthesis or release by effector cells, especially macrophages and neutrophils as well as T cells.

Cytotoxic Chemotherapy

Systemic immunosuppression with cytotoxic chemotherapy includes a wide variety of unrelated compounds often used in treating cancer (see further discussion in chapter VI):

□ Alkylating agents such as cyclophosphamide (Cytoxan), chlorambucil (Leukeran)

□ Antimetabolites such as methotrexate

Alkylating agents are presumed to cross-link DNA, thereby preventing cell division. These agents presumably function to prevent the bone marrow from replenishing lymphocytes and other effector subpopulations that mediate inflammation. Methotrexate is a folate analogue that inhibits folate metabolism to block purine ring biosythesis, ultimately affecting pathways that require nucleotide precursors, such as

DNA and mRNA synthesis. Thus, this drug will theoretically inhibit protein synthesis in nondividing effector cells, limit activation and differentiation of T cells within lymphoid tissue, and suppress effector cell expansion within bone marrow. The ability of any of these drugs to target effector cells within the eye is unknown, but experimental data in animals suggest that local delivery of some cytotoxic agents may be efficacious.

Cyclosporine

Systemic immunosuppression with the T-cell inhibitor cyclosporine is often an effective therapy for severe uveitis. Cyclosporine is a lipid-soluble fungus-derived cyclic polypeptide that binds an intracellular receptor. It acts to block helper T-cell activation and differentiation by various mechanisms, as well as by blocking some functions of APC. Cyclosporine appears to have limited actions on other effector cell subsets, presumably acting primarily within lymphoid tissue to inhibit immune processing. However, clinical experience with topical cyclosporine and experimental data with a device for intraocular drug delivery of cyclosporine during uveitis indicate that it can also function to inhibit T-cell effector responses locally within the eye.

Oral Tolerance

When the immune response arc of the gut is immunized with orally administered soluble antigens, it produces tolerizing rather than inflammatory effector responses to that antigen. This form of acquired tolerance is known as *oral tolerance*. In animals feeding on a variety of autoantigens, including retinal S antigen, a tolerizing immune response is initiated that probably depends on the induction of suppressor T cells and demonstrates other components of noninflammatory immunity. If an orally tolerized experimental animal is subsequently immunized with the same autoantigen through a cutaneous site, autoimmune disease fails to develop in the relevant target organ. Clinical trials with oral tolerance are under way for uveitis and for corneal transplantation, although several studies of oral tolerance for arthritis and multiple sclerosis have been contradictory.

PART 2

INTRAOCULAR INFLAMMATION AND UVEITIS

CHAPTER VI

Clinical Approach to Uveitis

Introduction

The uvea of the eye consists of the iris, ciliary body, and choroid, which is the eye's major blood supply. *Uveitis* is broadly defined as inflammation (i.e., *itis*) of the uvea (from the Greek *uva,* meaning "grape"). The study of uveitis is complicated by the fact that the causes of inflammatory reaction of the inner eye can be infectious, traumatic, neoplastic, or autoimmune. In addition, processes that may only secondarily involve the uvea, such as ocular toxoplasmosis, a disease that primarily affects the retina, may cause a marked inflammatory spillover into the choroid and vitreous.

This chapter uses an anatomic flowchart approach to uveitis diagnosis to untangle the myriad types of inflammation of the inner eye and introduce a systematic classification of these many manifestations. One simple approach is, first, to determine the *symptoms* of uveitis that are causing the patient to seek help and, next, to complete the basic examination evaluating the *signs* pertinent to uveitis. Since uveitis is frequently associated with systemic disease, a careful history and review of systems is an important first step in elucidating the etiology of the patient's inflammatory disease. Next, a thorough examination is done to determine the type of inflammation present.

Each patient will demonstrate only a portion of the possible symptoms and signs of uveitis. After the physician has used the information obtained from the history and physical examination to determine the *anatomic classification* of uveitis, several *associated factors* can be used to further subcategorize, leading in turn to the choice of *laboratory studies* and *therapeutic options.*

Albert DM, Jakobiec FA, eds. *Principles and Practice of Ophthalmology.* 2nd ed. Philadelphia: Saunders; 1994. (See chapter on uveitis by JH Elliott.)

Michelson JB. *A Color Atlas of Uveitis Diagnosis.* 2nd ed. St Louis: Mosby; 1991.

Nussenblatt RB, Whitcup SM, Palestine AG. *Uveitis: Fundamentals and Clinical Practice.* 2nd ed. St Louis: Mosby; 1996.

Rao NA, Augsburgher JJ, Forster DJ. *The Uvea: Uveitis and Intraocular Neoplasms.* New York: Gower; 1992.

Symptoms of Uveitis

The most common symptoms of uveitis are blurred vision, floaters, pain, photophobia, and redness (Table VI-1). These symptoms vary depending on the type of inflammation (e.g., acute or chronic) as well as the specific ocular structures involved. Blurred vision may be a result of refractive error such as a myopic or hyperopic shift

TABLE VI-1

SYMPTOMS OF UVEITIS

Redness
Pain
Photophobia
Epiphora
Visual disturbances
    Diffuse blur—caused by:
        Myopic or hyperopic shift
        Inflammatory cells
        Cataract
    Scotoma (central or peripheral)
    Floaters

associated with macular edema, hypotony, or change in lens position. Other possible causes of blurred vision include opacities in the visual axis from inflammatory cells, fibrin, or protein in the anterior chamber; keratic precipitates; secondary cataract; vitreous debris; macular edema; or retinal atrophy.

The pain of uveitis usually results from acute onset of inflammation in the region of the iris, as in acute iritis, or from secondary glaucoma. The pain associated with ciliary spasm in iritis may be a referred pain that seems to radiate over a larger area served by cranial nerve V (trigeminal nerve). Epiphora and photophobia are usually present when inflammation involves the iris, cornea, or iris–ciliary body. Occasionally, uveitis is discovered on a routine ophthalmic examination in an asymptomatic patient.

Signs of Uveitis

Part 1 of this volume reviews the basic concepts of immunology, which can be used to understand the symptoms and signs of inflammation in uveitis. An inflammatory response to infectious, traumatic, neoplastic, or autoimmune processes produces the signs of uveitis (Table VI-2). Chemical mediators of the acute stage of inflammation include serotonin, complement, and plasmin. Leukotrienes, kinins, and prostaglandins modify the second phase of the acute response through antagonism of vasoconstrictors. Activated complement is a leukotactic agent. Polymorphonuclear leukocytes (PMN), eosinophils, and mast cells may all contribute to signs of inflammation. But the lymphocyte is, by far, the predominant inflammatory cell in the inner eye in uveitis. These chemical mediators result in vascular dilatation (ciliary flush), increased vascular permeability (aqueous flare), and chemotaxis of inflammatory cells into the eye (aqueous and vitreous cellular reaction).

TABLE VI-2

Eyelid and skin
Vitiligo
Nodules

Conjunctiva
Perilimbal or diffuse injection
Nodules

Corneal endothelium
Keratic (cellular) precipitates (diffuse
  or gravitational)
Fibrin
Pigment (nonspecific)

Anterior/posterior chamber
Inflammatory cells
Flare (proteinaceous influx)
Pigment (nonspecific)

Iris
Nodules
Posterior synechiae
Atrophy
Heterochromia

Angle
Peripheral anterior synechiae
Nodules
Vascularization

Intraocular pressure
Hypotony
Secondary glaucoma

Vitreous
Inflammatory cells (single/clumped)
Traction bands

Pars plana
Snowbanking

Retina
Inflammatory cells
Inflammatory cuffing of blood vessels
Edema
Cystoid macular edema
RPE: hypertrophy/clumping/loss
Epiretinal membranes

Choroid
Inflammatory infiltrate
Atrophy
Neovascularization

Optic nerve
Edema (nonspecific)
Neovascularization

Anterior Segment

Signs of uveitis in the anterior portion of the eye include

☐ Keratic precipitates (KP) (Figs VI-1, VI-2)

☐ Cells

☐ Flare (Fig VI-3)

☐ Fibrin

☐ Hypopyon

☐ Pigment dispersion

☐ Pupillary miosis

☐ Iris nodules (Fig VI-4)

☐ Synechiae, both anterior and posterior (Fig VI-5)

Band keratopathy may also be seen in the cornea with long-standing uveitis.

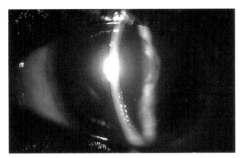

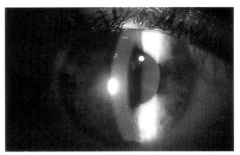

FIG VI-1—Keratic precipitates (medium and small) with broken posterior synechiae. (Photograph courtesy of H. Jane Blackman, MD.)

FIG VI-2—Small, nonpigmented keratic precipitates in Fuchs heterochromic iridocyclitis. (Photograph courtesy of H. Jane Blackman, MD.)

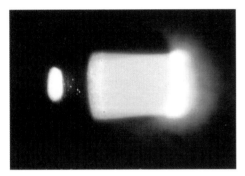

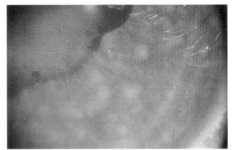

FIG VI-3—Aqueous flare (4+) in acute iritis.

FIG VI-4—Koeppe and Busacca iris nodules and posterior synechiae.

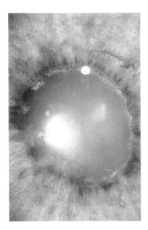

FIG VI-5—Extensive posterior synechiae in juvenile rheumatoid arthritis–associated iridocyclitis. (Photograph courtesy of H. Jane Blackman, MD.)

Perilimbal vascular engorgement (ciliary flush) or diffuse injection of the conjunctiva and/or episclera is typically seen with acute anterior uveitis. With increased capillary permeability, the anterior chamber reaction can be described as

□ Serous (aqueous flare caused by protein influx)

□ Purulent (PMN and necrotic debris causing hypopyon)

□ Fibrinous ("plastic," or intense fibrinous exudate)

□ Sanguinoid (inflammatory cells with erythrocytes manifested by hypopyon mixed with hyphema)

The intensity of the cellular reaction in the anterior chamber is graded according to the number of inflammatory cells seen in a 1×3-mm high-powered beam at full intensity at a 45°–60° angle:

0	no inflammatory cells
trace	<5 cells
1+	5–10 cells
2+	10–20 cells
3+	20–30 cells
4+	cells too numerous to count

Keratic precipitates are collections of inflammatory cells on the corneal endothelium. When newly formed, they tend to be white and smoothly rounded, but they then become crenated (shrunken), pigmented, or glassy. Large yellowish KP are described as "mutton-fat" keratic precipitates; these are usually associated with granulomatous types of inflammation.

Uveitis is sometimes classified as either granulomatous or nongranulomatous. However, this classification system is limited because different experimental doses of the same antigen can produce either appearance; and sarcoidosis, often considered the classic example of granulomatous uveitis, can also present with a nongranulomatous appearance within the eye.

Iris involvement may manifest as either anterior or posterior synechiae, iris nodules (Koeppe nodules at the pupillary border and Busacca nodules within the iris stroma), iris granulomas, heterochromia (e.g., Fuchs heterochromic iridocyclitis), or stromal atrophy (e.g., herpetic uveitis).

With uveitic involvement of the ciliary body and trabecular meshwork, intraocular pressure (IOP) often is low secondary to decreased aqueous production or increased alternative outflow, but it may increase precipitously if the meshwork becomes clogged by inflammatory cells or debris, or if the trabecular meshwork itself is the site of inflammation (trabeculitis). Pupillary block with iris bombé and secondary angle closure may also lead to an acute rise in IOP.

Intermediate Segment

Signs in the intermediate anatomic area of the eye include

□ Vitreal inflammatory cells, which are graded from 0 to 4+ in density

□ "Snowball opacities," which are frequently seen with sarcoidosis or intermediate uveitis

□ Exudates over the pars plana ("snowbanking")

□ Vitreal strands

Chronic uveitis may be associated with cyclitic membrane formation with secondary ciliary body detachment and hypotony.

Posterior Segment

Signs seen in the posterior segment of the eye include

- Retinal or choroidal inflammatory infiltrates
- Perivascular inflammatory cuffing
- Retinal pigment epithelial hypertrophy or atrophy
- Atrophy or swelling of the retina, choroid, or optic nerve head

Retinal and choroidal signs may be unifocal, multifocal, or diffuse. The uveitis can be diffuse throughout the eye (panuveitis) or appear dispersed with spillover from one area to another, as with toxoplasmosis primarily involving the retina but showing anterior chamber inflammation as well.

Classification of Uveitis

One thoughtful stepwise approach to uveitis by Sheppard and Nozik (1989) includes the following:

- Descriptive naming
- Meshing
- Office testing
- Specific and nonspecific clinical laboratory tests
- Specialty consultation
- Therapeutic intervention

Another logical approach to uveitis is categorization of diseases anatomically and then further subdivision by means of modifying factors. The International Uveitis Study Group has proposed an anatomic classification of uveitis divided into four categories with associated specific etiologies. Discussion in this book follows this basic classification into four groups:

- Anterior uveitis
- Intermediate uveitis
- Posterior uveitis
- Panuveitis

Bloch-Michel E, Nussenblatt RB. International Uveitis Study Group recommendations for the evaluation of intraocular inflammatory disease. *Am J Ophthalmol.* 1987; 103:234–235.

Sheppard JD, Nozik RA. Practical diagnostic approach to uveitis. In: Tasman W, Jaeger EA, eds. *Duane's Clinical Ophthalmology.* Philadelphia: Lippincott; 1989.

Anterior Uveitis

Anterior uveitis can have a range of presentations from a quiet white eye with low-grade inflammatory reaction apparent only on close examination to a painful red eye with moderate or severe inflammation. Inflammation confined to the anterior chamber is called *iritis;* if it spills over into the retrolental space, it is called *iridocyclitis;* if it spills over onto the cornea, it is called *keratouveitis;* and if the inflammatory reaction involves the sclera and iris, it is called *sclerouveitis.*

By far, most types of anterior uveitis are sterile inflammatory reactions, whereas many of the posterior uveitic syndromes are infectious in origin. In contrast to endophthalmitis from an infectious source, only two noninfectious etiologies—typically the HLA-B27–associated diseases and Behçet syndrome—are associated with hypopyon. Many cases of anterior uveitis are isolated instances of unknown etiology that often resolve within 6 weeks; for example, idiopathic iritis. Glaucomatocyclitic crisis causes a moderately inflamed eye with elevated IOP that subsides quickly over a few weeks. Blunt trauma is a fairly common cause of a generally self-limited uveitis.

The anterior uveitis associated with juvenile rheumatoid arthritis (JRA) can be deceptive, because even though the conjunctiva appears quiet externally, the anterior segment may be severely involved in a child without any symptomatic complaints. Another low-grade inflammation of the anterior portion of the eye is seen in Fuchs heterochromic iridocyclitis. Here the damage to the anterior segment is apparently minimal, but the eye needs continued observation because of the commonly occurring secondary complications of cataract and glaucoma. Chapter VII discusses anterior uveitis in greater detail.

Intermediate Uveitis

Inflammation of the middle portion of the eye manifests primarily as floaters affecting the vision, while the eye frequently appears quiet externally. Visual loss is primarily a result of chronic cystoid macular edema or, less commonly, cataract formation. See chapter VIII of this volume for discussion.

Posterior Uveitis

Posterior uveitis may present either with a quiet-appearing eye or with inflammation spilling over to the anterior segment. Inflammation may affect the retina alone *(retinitis),* the choroid alone *(choroiditis),* or both layers *(retinochoroiditis or chorioretinitis).* The inflammation can be focal, diffuse, or multifocal. Visual symptoms of posterior uveitis may be caused by involvement of the macula or a reduction in peripheral vision. When inflammatory processes involving the retina spill over into the vitreous (i.e., retinitis with vitritis), floaters are a common symptom.

Infectious involvement is seen more commonly in the retina and choroid than in the anterior segment of the eye. Infections may be viral, bacterial, protozoal, or fungal and have various presentations. Associated systemic findings thus take on particular importance in providing diagnostic clues. Clinical appearance guides the diagnostic work-up, with laboratory evaluations frequently required for corroboration. See chapter IX for discussion, as well as Table VI-4 later in this chapter.

TABLE VI-3

ASSOCIATED FACTORS IN DIAGNOSIS OF UVEITIS

MODIFYING FACTORS	ASSOCIATED FACTORS SUGGESTING SYSTEMIC CONDITIONS

Time course of disease
    Acute
    Relapsing
    Chronic
Severity
    Severe
    Quiescent
Distribution of uveitis
    Unilateral
    Bilateral
    Alternating
    Focal
    Multifocal
    Diffuse
Patient's sex
Patient's age
Patient's race
	Immune system status
	Systemic medications
	Trauma history
	Travel history
	Social history
	    Eating habits
	    Pets
	    Sexual practices
	    Occupation
	    Drug use

Panuveitis

Uveitis can affect the entire inner eye. Some patients follow a stormy course, while others have a quiet-appearing eye that nonetheless experiences a slowly debilitating course. Sarcoidosis and syphilis commonly cause a bilateral panuveitis, whereas endophthalmitis generally is a unilateral process. Chapter X discusses panuveitis in greater depth, and chapter XI covers endophthalmitis.

Review of the Patient's Health and Other Associated Factors

Many factors other than ocular symptoms and signs can aid in the classification or identification of uveitis (Table VI-3). These factors include

- ☐ Onset
- ☐ Duration
- ☐ Severity
- ☐ Unilaterality or bilaterality
- ☐ Distribution and location of ocular involvement
- ☐ The patient's age, sex, and racial background

Determining whether the onset was sudden or slow and insidious may help the clinician to narrow the range of diagnostic possibilities. Uveitis may be subcategorized as acute or chronic: *acute* is generally the term used to describe episodes of sudden onset that usually resolve within a few weeks to months, whereas *chronic* uveitis persists for several months to years.

Whether the inflammation is severe or low grade can influence categorization and prognosis. The inflammatory process may occur in one or both eyes, or it may alternate between them. The distribution of ocular involvement—focal, multifocal, or diffuse—is also a helpful feature to note when classifying uveitis. The age, sex, sexual practices, and racial background of the patient are important findings to ascertain in some uveitic syndromes.

Chronic uveitis can be further characterized histopathologically as being either *granulomatous* or *nongranulomatous*. Nongranulomatous inflammation typically has a lymphocytic and plasma cell infiltrate, whereas granulomatous reactions also include epithelioid and giant cells. Discrete granulomas are characteristic of sarcoidosis, while diffuse granulomatous inflammation appears in Vogt-Koyanagi-Harada syndrome and sympathetic ophthalmia. Zonal granulomatous disease is seen with phacoantigenic endophthalmitis. However, the physician should be aware that the *clinical* appearance of uveitis as granulomatous or nongranulomatous may not necessarily correlate with the *histopathologic* description and may instead be related to the stage in which the disease is first seen, the amount of presenting antigen, or the host's state of immunocompromise (for example, in a patient being treated with corticosteroids).

Although ocular inflammation may be an isolated process involving only the eye, it can also be associated with a systemic condition. However, the ocular inflammation frequently does not correlate with the inflammatory activity elsewhere in the body, so it is important for the clinician to take a careful review of systems. In some cases the uveitis may actually precede the development of inflammation at other body sites. The presence of immunocompromise, use of intravenous drugs, hyperalimentation, or occupation of the patient are just a few risk factors that can direct the investigation of uveitis. Neoplastic disease can masquerade as inflammatory disease. Large cell lymphoma, retinoblastoma, leukemia, and malignant melanoma may all be mistaken for uveitis. In addition, juvenile xanthogranuloma, pigment dispersion syndrome, retinal detachment, retinitis pigmentosa, and ischemia all must be considered in the differential diagnosis of uveitis.

Chapters that follow in this volume describe discrete uveitis entities. However, many patients do not present with the classic symptoms and signs of a particular disease. Some of these patients will require monitoring through follow-up visits, and laboratory tests may need to be repeated at a later date, as the clinical appearance may be unclear or change with time and treatment. The presentation of disease can also be modified by prior therapy or by a delay in seeing the physician.

Differential Diagnosis and Prevalence of Uveitic Entities

Once a comprehensive history and physical examination have been performed, the most likely etiologies are ranked in a list based on how well the individual patient's type of uveitis "fits" with the various known uveitic entities. This *naming-meshing system,* described by Smith and Nozik, first names the type of uveitis based on anatomic criteria as well as other associated factors (acute versus chronic, unilateral versus bilateral, and so on), and then matches the pattern of uveitis exhibited by the patient with a list of potential uveitic entities that share similar characteristics. One such system for helping to identify a possible etiology for a particular patient's uveitis is outlined in Table VI-4.

TABLE VI-4

FLOWCHART FOR EVALUATION OF UVEITIS PATIENTS

TYPE OF INFLAMMATION	ASSOCIATED FACTORS	SUSPECTED DISEASE	LABORATORY TESTS
		PANUVEITIS	
	See entities described below: sarcoidosis, toxoplasmosis, toxocariasis, endophthalmitis, VKH syndrome, sympathetic ophthalmia, syphilis, cysticercosis		
		ANTERIOR UVEITIS	
Acute/sudden onset, severe with or without fibrin membrane or hypopyon	Arthritis, back pain, GI/GU symptoms	Seronegative spondyloarthropathies	HLA-B27, sacroiliac films
	Aphthous ulcers	Behçet syndrome	HLA-B5, B51
	Postsurgical, posttraumatic	Infectious endophthalmitis	Vitreous culture, vitrectomy
	None	Idiopathic	Possibly HLA-B27
Moderate severity (red, painful)	Shortness of breath, African descent	Sarcoidosis	Serum ACE, lysozyme; chest x-ray; gallium scan; biopsy
	Posttraumatic	Traumatic iritis	
	Increased IOP	Glaucomatocyclitic crisis, herpetic iritis	
	Poor response to steroids	Syphilis	RPR, VDRL (screening); FTA-ABS (confirmatory)
	Post–cataract extraction	Low-grade endophthalmitis, IOL-related iritis	Consider vitrectomy, culture
	None	Idiopathic	
Chronic; minimal redness, pain	Child, especially with arthritis	JRA-related iridocyclitis	ANA, ESR
	Heterochromia, diffuse KP, unilateral	Fuchs heterochromic iridocyclitis	None
	Postsurgical	Low-grade endophthalmitis (e.g., *P acnes*); IOL-related	Consider vitrectomy, capsulectomy with culture
	None	Idiopathic	
		INTERMEDIATE UVEITIS	
Mild to moderate	Shortness of breath, African descent	Sarcoidosis	As above
	Tick exposure, erythema chronicum migrans rash	Lyme disease	ELISA
	Neurologic symptoms	Multiple sclerosis	MRI of brain
	Over age 50	Intraocular lymphoma	Vitrectomy, cytology
	None	Pars planitis	

POSTERIOR UVEITIS

TYPE OF INFLAMMATION	ASSOCIATED FACTORS	SUSPECTED DISEASE	LABORATORY TESTS
Chorioretinitis *with* vitritis			
Focal	Adjacent scar; raw meat ingestion	Toxoplasmosis	ELISA
	Child; history of geophagia	Toxocariasis	ELISA
	HIV infection	CMV retinitis	As above
Multifocal	Shortness of breath	Sarcoidosis	PPD, chest x-ray
		Tuberculosis	
	Peripheral retinal necrosis	Acute retinal necrosis (ARN) Progressive outer retinal necrosis (PORN, if immunocompromised)	VZV, HSV titers (ELISA), possibly vitrectomy/retinal biopsy
	AIDS	Syphilis, toxoplasmosis	As above
		Candida, Aspergillus	Blood, vitreous cultures
	Visible intraocular parasite; from Africa or Central or South America	Cysticercosis Onchocerciasis	As above
	Over age 50	Intraocular lymphoma Birdshot choroidopathy	HLA-A29, fluorescein angiography (FA)
	None	Multifocal choroiditis with panuveitis	Rule out TB, sarcoidosis, syphilis
Diffuse	Dermatologic/CNS symptoms; serous RD	Vogt-Koyanagi-Harada syndrome (VKH)	FA, lumbar puncture to document CSF pleocytosis
	Postsurgical/traumatic, bilateral	Sympathetic ophthalmia	FA
	Postsurgical/traumatic, unilateral	Infectious endophthalmitis	As above
	Child, history of geophagia	Toxocariasis	As above
Chorioretinitis *without* vitritis			
Focal	None; history of carcinoma	Neoplastic	Metastatic work-up
Multifocal	Ohio/Mississippi Valley	Ocular histoplasmosis	FA if macula involved
	Lesions confined to posterior pole	White dot syndromes (e.g., APMPPE, MEWDS, PIC)	FA
Diffuse	Geographic (maplike) pattern of scars	Serpiginous choroidopathy	FA
	From Africa, Central/South America	Onchocerciasis	
Vasculitis			
	Aphthous ulcers, hypopyon	Behçet syndrome	As above
	Malar rash, female, arthralgias	Systemic lupus erythematosus (SLE)	ANA

A knowledge of the prevalence of the various etiologies seen in uveitis survey populations is also helpful in determining the most probable cause of the uveitis. Numerous studies have been performed to determine the prevalence of various types of uveitis, but the data often vary from one study to another depending on whether the study was performed at a tertiary referral center or was community based. The location of the study population also produces differing results. For example, the prevalence of CMV retinitis would be expected to be much higher in large urban areas with higher rates of AIDS, whereas ocular histoplasmosis would be higher in rural areas in the midwestern United States. Large worldwide variations also occur in certain types of uveitis: entities such as Behçet syndrome and Vogt-Koyanagi-Harada syndrome are much more common in Japan than in Europe or the United States, for example.

Table VI-5 summarizes the data from three surveys, comparing the prevalence of various types of uveitis in both referral-based and community-based populations. In general, the data demonstrate that idiopathic causes are frequently found in anterior uveitis and that infectious causes are more commonly seen in posterior uveitis. Also, most university/referral–based studies probably overestimate the prevalence of intermediate and posterior uveitis compared to those cases that are seen in the community.

Henderly DE, Genstler AJ, Smith RE, et al. Changing patterns of uveitis. *Am J Ophthalmol.* 1987;103:131–136.

McCannel CA, Holland GN, Helm CJ, et al. Causes of uveitis in the general practice of ophthalmology. UCLA Community-Based Uveitis Study Group. *Am J Ophthalmol.* 1996;121:35–46.

Rodriguez A, Calonge M, Pedroza-Seres M, et al. Referral patterns of uveitis in a tertiary eye care center. *Arch Ophthalmol.* 1996;114:593–599.

Smith RE, Nozik RA. *Uveitis: A Clinical Approach to Diagnosis and Management.* 2nd ed. Baltimore: Williams & Wilkins; 1989.

Laboratory and Medical Evaluation

The diagnosis may require laboratory and medical evaluation guided by the history and physical examination. It should be stressed that there is no one standardized battery of tests that needs to be ordered for all uveitis patients. Rather, a tailored approach should be taken based on the most likely etiologic possibilities for each individual patient. Once a rank-ordered list of potential uveitic entities is compiled, appropriate laboratory tests can then be ordered, if necessary. Many patients may only require one or a few diagnostic tests. Table VI-4 summarizes which laboratory tests may be useful for a particular presentation of uveitis. These laboratory tests are discussed further in the chapters that follow covering the various types of uveitis.

TABLE VI-5

MOST COMMON CAUSES OF UVEITIS

	UNIVERSITY/REFERRAL–BASED			COMMUNITY-BASED
	HENDERLY (1987)	RODRIGUEZ (1996)	McCANNEL (1996)	McCANNEL (1996)
Anterior	27.8%	51.5%	60.6%	90.6%
Idiopathic	12.1	19.5	30.5	52.1
HLA-B27+/seronegative spondyloarthropathies	5.8	11.2	10.8	17.4
Juvenile rheumatoid arthritis associated	2.8	5.6	2.3	1.4
Herpes simplex/zoster	2.5	5.0	11.3	7.5
Fuchs heterochromic	1.8	2.6	1.4	0.9
Intraocular lens related	1.0	0.6	0.9	0.9
Sarcoidosis	0	3.0	0.5	0.9
Traumatic	0	0	0	5.2
Intermediate	15.4%	13.0%	12.2%	1.4%
Idiopathic	–	9.1	12.2	0.9
Sarcoidosis	–	2.9	–	–
Multiple sclerosis	–	1.1	–	0.5
Posterior	38.4%	19.4%	14.6%	4.7%
Toxoplasmosis	7.0	4.8	3.5	4.2
Retinal vasculitis	6.8	1.3	1.4	0.5
Idiopathic	3.7	1.3	2.3	0
Ocular histoplasmosis	3.5	0.2	0.5	0
Toxocariasis	2.6	0.5	0.5	0
Cytomegalovirus retinitis	2.5	2.3	*	*
Serpiginous choroidopathy	2.0	0.3	0.5	0
Acute multifocal placoid pigment epitheliopathy	1.8	0.4	0	0
Necrotizing herpetic retinopathy (ARN/PORN)	1.3	1.1	2.8	0
Birdshot choroidopathy	1.2	1.5	0.9	0
Sarcoidosis	0	1.5	0	0
Panuveitis	18.4%	16.0%	9.4%	1.4%
Idiopathic	8.2	3.6	2.5	0.5
Sarcoidosis	3.9	2.3	0.3	0
Vogt-Koyanagi-Harada	3.3	0.9	1.6	0.5
Multifocal choroiditis with panuveitis	–	1.9	0.6	0
Behçet syndrome	1.8	1.9	0.6	0

* Cases of CMV retinitis were excluded from the causes of *general* uveitis in this study. When included in all cases of uveitis, CMV retinitis accounted for 32.6% of university/referred patients and 7.0% of community-based patients.

In the evaluation of patients with certain types of uveitis, ancillary testing can be extremely helpful:

□ *Fluorescein angiography* may show the presence of cystoid macular edema, choroiditis, vascular involvement, serous retinal detachment, and choroidal neovascularization.

□ *Ultrasonography* can be useful in demonstrating vitreous opacities, choroidal thickening, retinal detachment, or cyclitic membrane formation, particularly if media opacities preclude a view of the posterior segment.

□ *Vitreous biopsy* may be necessary for a diagnostic evaluation in suspected cases of large cell lymphoma (formerly called *reticulum cell sarcoma*) or bacterial or fungal endophthalmitis.

□ *Chorioretinal biopsy* may be useful in situations where the diagnosis cannot be definitively made on the basis of clinical appearance or other laboratory investigations (e.g., certain cases of necrotizing retinitis in patients with AIDS or suspected cases of intraocular lymphoma).

Many patients with mild, self-limited uveitis need no referral to a uveitis specialist. However, in uveitis with a chronic or downwardly spiraling course, referring the patient to a uveitis specialist may be helpful not only in eliciting the cause and determining the therapeutic regimen but also in reassuring the patient that all avenues are being explored. Evaluation of vision-threatening uveitis may require coordination with other medical or surgical consultants, (e.g., in pursuing the diagnosis of HIV-related diseases or in kidney transplant patients on immunosuppressive therapy). Discussion with the patient and other specialists about the prognosis and complications of uveitis will be helpful in determining the appropriate therapy. Therapy for uveitis ranges from simple observation to medical or surgical intervention (Table VI-6).

Medical Management of Uveitis

Generally, medical therapy includes topical or systemic corticosteroids and may also include topical cycloplegics. Immunosuppressive therapy may be required in patients with severe uveitis unresponsive to corticosteroid therapy or in patients with severe corticosteroid-induced complications. The choice of therapeutic approach depends on the relative risk of complications of uveitis, of which the most common are cataracts, cystoid macular edema, hypotony, and glaucoma. Treatment should be tailored as specifically as possible to the individual patient and adjusted according to response. The physician should consider the patient's systemic involvement and other factors such as age, immune status, and tolerance for side effects. See also the discussion, "Immunotherapeutics," in chapter V, pp 95–96.

Cycloplegics

Topical cycloplegic agents are beneficial for breaking or preventing the formation of posterior synechiae and for providing relief of photophobia secondary to ciliary spasm. The stronger the inflammatory reaction, the stronger or more frequent is the dosage of cycloplegic. Short-acting drops such as cyclopentolate hydrochloride (Cyclogyl) or long-acting drops such as atropine may be used. Most cases of acute anterior uveitis require only short-acting cycloplegics; these allow the pupil to

Table VI-6

Observation
  For development of complications
  For change in the appearance/severity/progression

Medical therapy
Cycloplegics
  To relieve pain
  To break posterior synechiae/pupillary block
Corticosteroids
  Topical drops/ointment
  Sub-Tenon's injection
  Oral or intravenous injection
Immunosuppressives
  Alkylating agents
  Antimetabolites
  T-cell suppressors

Surgical therapy
Diagnostic procedures
  Anterior chamber aspiration
  Vitreous biopsy
Reparative procedures
  Cataract extraction
  Pupillary reconstruction
  Glaucoma surgery
  Epiretinal membrane peeling
  Scleral buckle
  Vitrectomy

remain mobile and permit rapid recovery upon discontinuation. Patients with chronic uveitis and moderate flare in the anterior chamber (e.g., JRA-associated iritis) may need to be maintained on short-acting agents (e.g., tropicamide) on a long-term basis to prevent the development of posterior synechiae.

Corticosteroids

Corticosteroids are the mainstay of uveitis therapy (Table VI-7). Because of their potential side effects, however, they should be reserved for specific indications:

☐ Treatment of active inflammation in the eye

☐ Prevention or treatment of complications such as cystoid macular edema

☐ Reduction of inflammatory infiltration of the retina, choroid, or optic nerve

Complications of corticosteroid therapy are numerous and can be seen with any mode of administration. Therefore, these agents should be used only in cases where the benefits of therapy outweigh the risks of the medications themselves.

  The amount and duration of corticosteroid therapy must be determined on an individual basis. The minimum amount needed to control inflammation should be

TABLE VI-7

CORTICOSTEROIDS FREQUENTLY USED IN UVEITIS THERAPY AND THEIR COMPLICATIONS

ROUTE OF ADMINISTRATION	COMPLICATIONS
Topical Prednisolone acetate Prednisolone sodium phosphate Fluorometholone Dexamethasone phosphate Rimexalone	Cataract formation Elevation of IOP Worsening of external infection Corneal/scleral thinning or perforation
Periocular Methylprednisolone acetate (Depo-Medrol) Triamcinolone acetonide (Kenalog) Hydrocortisone sodium succinate (Solu-Cortef) Betamethasone (Celestone)	Same complications as topical above Ptosis Scarring of conjunctiva/Tenon's capsule Worsening of infectious uveitis Scleral perforation Hemorrhage
Systemic Prednisone Triamcinolone Dexamethasone Methylprednisolone	Same complications as topical above Increased appetite Weight gain Peptic ulcers Sodium and fluid retention Osteoporosis/bone fractures Aseptic necrosis of hip Hypertension Diabetes mellitus Menstrual irregularities Mental status changes Exacerbation of systemic infections Impaired wound healing Acne Others

prescribed to reduce complications of the treatment. If the steroid therapy is needed longer than 2–3 weeks, the dosage should be tapered before discontinuation. The dosage may need to be increased when surgical intervention is required to prevent exacerbation of the uveitis postoperatively.

Topical administration   Topical corticosteroid drops are effective primarily for anterior uveitis, although they may have beneficial effects on vitritis or macular edema in patients who are pseudophakic or aphakic. Topical corticosteroid drops are given in dosages ranging from once daily to hourly. They can also be given in an ointment form for nighttime use or if preservatives in the eyedrops are not well tolerated. Of the topical preparations, rimexolone and fluorometholone have been shown to have less of an ocular hypertensive effect than the other medications and may be particularly useful in patients who are steroid responders. It is unclear whether these agents are as effective as prednisolone in controlling inflammation, however.

Corticosteroids do not reduce chronic flare in the anterior chamber, hyalinized KP, or pigment in the aqueous caused by dilatation. They are not always indicated in the therapy of specific diseases such as Fuchs heterochromic iridocyclitis or pars planitis without macular edema, or to treat a peripheral lesion of toxoplasmosis (i.e., a lesion that does not threaten the papillomacular bundle).

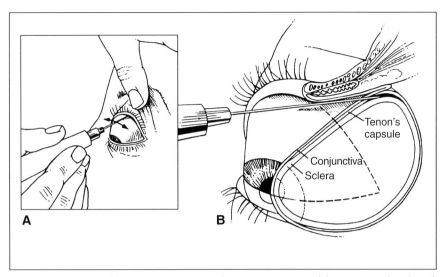

FIG VI-6—Posterior sub-Tenon's injection. *A,* The correct position of the operator's hands and the needle. The arrows indicate the direction of the side-to-side circumferential motion (here exaggerated for emphasis). *B,* The positioning of the tip of the needle in its ideal location between Tenon's capsule and the sclera. (Reproduced with permission from Smith RE, Nozik RA. *Uveitis: A Clinical Approach to Diagnosis and Management.* 2nd ed. Baltimore: Williams & Wilkins; 1989.)

Periocular administration Periocular corticosteroids are generally given as depot injections when a more posterior effect is needed or when a patient is noncompliant or poorly responsive to topical or systemic administration. Periocular injections can be performed using either a transseptal or sub-Tenon's approach (Fig VI-6). With a sub-Tenon's injection, a 25-gauge 5/8″ needle is used. If the injection is given in the superotemporal quadrant (the preferred location), the upper eyelid is retracted and the patient is instructed to look down and nasally. After anesthesia is applied with a cotton swab soaked in proparacaine or tetracaine, the needle is placed bevel-down against the sclera and advanced through the conjunctiva and Tenon's capsule using a side-to-side movement, which allows the physician to determine whether the needle has entered the sclera or not. As long as the globe does not torque with the side-to-side movement of the needle, the physician can be reasonably sure that the needle has not penetrated the sclera. Once the needle has been advanced to the hub, the steroid is injected into the sub-Tenon's space.

Periocular injections should not be used in cases of infectious uveitis (e.g., toxoplasmosis) and should also be avoided in patients with scleritis since scleral thinning and possible perforation may result. The physician should be aware that periocular corticosteroid injections have the potential to raise the IOP precipitously.

Systemic administration *Oral* or *intravenous* therapy may supplement or replace other routes of administration. Systemic corticosteroids are used for chronic bilateral uveitis that threatens vision when topical steroids are insufficient or when the systemic disease also requires therapy. The many side effects of both short- and long-term corticosteroids must be discussed with the patient and his or her general health must be closely monitored, often with the assistance of an internist. High-dose intravenous corticosteroids may be indicated in a few situations—for example, in the acute phase of Vogt-Koyanagi-Harada syndrome or posterior scleritis—and these patients may require monitoring in a hospital setting.

Immunomodulating and Immunosuppressive Agents

Other medications that modulate the immune system are the nonsteroidal anti-inflammatory agents (NSAIDs) and immunosuppressive agents. Oral desensitization with retinal S antigen is in the experimental stage and may hold promise for treatment of uveitis patients who are reactive to this antigen.

NSAIDs Topical NSAIDs may be useful in the treatment of postoperative inflammation and cystoid macular edema, but their usefulness in treating endogenous anterior uveitis has not been proven. Several studies have shown a benefit from the use of systemic NSAIDs in patients with chronic iridocyclitis (e.g., JRA-associated iridocyclitis); their use may allow the practitioner to maintain the patient on a lower dose of topical corticosteroids.

Cytotoxic agents and antimetabolites Cytotoxic agents such as the alkylating agents cyclophosphamide and chlorambucil as well as antimetabolites such as azathioprine and methotrexate and the T-cell suppressor cyclosporine have all had reported successes in the therapy of vision-threatening, frequently bilateral, uveitis. Some indications for immunotherapy include Behçet syndrome, sympathetic ophthalmia, and Wegener granulomatosis.

Cytotoxic agents are believed to work by killing the rapidly dividing clones of lymphocytes that are responsible for the inflammation (see Part 1, Inmmunology). In many cases the benefits from these agents outweigh the potential risks associated with their use, and they are considered the first line of therapy in certain entities. However, because of their potentially serious complications, patients must be monitored closely by a practitioner who is experienced in their use. The most serious complications include the future development of malignancies such as leukemia, lymphoma, or soft-tissue tumors, as well as teratogenesis (for example, chromosomal damage and azoospermia). Whenever these agents are used, the patient should be advised fully of the potential complications, including the development of opportunistic bacterial, fungal, and viral infections. The physician should consider obtaining informed consent prior to beginning therapy.

Indications. The following indications generally apply to the therapeutic use of immunosuppressive agents in uveitis:

□ Vision-threatening intraocular inflammation

□ Reversibility of the disease process

□ Lack of response to corticosteroid treatment

□ Contraindication of corticosteroid treatment because of systemic problems or intolerable side effects

Certain specific uveitis entities also warrant cytotoxic agents for suppression of the intraocular inflammation, including Behçet syndrome and rheumatoid necrotizing sclerouveitis. Even though these disorders may initially respond well to cortico-steroids, the long-term prognosis and morbidity are unacceptable. Initial treatment of these entities with cytotoxic agents has been shown to improve the long-term prognosis and to lessen the visual morbidity. Vogt-Koyanagi-Harada syndrome is an entity where cytotoxic agents have been found to be particularly helpful.

Relative indications for the cytotoxic agents include those conditions that are initially treated with corticosteroids. If the corticosteroids fail to control the inflammation, then cytotoxic agents can be tried. Clinical entities in this category include intermediate uveitis (pars planitis), retinal vasculitis, and chronic iridocyclitis. With some of these conditions, however—for example, intermediate uveitis in children—the use of cytotoxic agents is controversial. In these patients the newer immunosuppressive agents such as cyclosporine and related drugs may be helpful.

Recently, more attention has been given to the use of weekly low-dose methotrexate in patients with chronic uveitis unresponsive to corticosteroid therapy or in patients who are intolerant of it, such as patients with JRA-associated iridocyclitis. Such treatment, often in combination with low-dose corticosteroids, has been shown to be effective in treating refractory uveitis in these patients, often sparing them the complications of chronic corticosteroid therapy. This combined therapy appears to have minimal side effects in the short term (6 months).

Treatment. Before initiating therapy with any cytotoxic agent, the physician should consider these guidelines:

□ Absence of infection

□ Absence of hematologic contraindications

□ Meticulous follow-up by an ophthalmologist or internist or by a medical oncologist, if necessary

□ Objective evaluation of the disease process

□ Informed consent

Cyclophosphamide treatment is begun at 1–2 mg/kg/day, while chlorambucil is started at 2 mg/day and slowly increased to a dosage of 8–12 mg/day. The patient's blood count must be monitored closely; the goal is a reduction in white blood cell count to no lower than 3000 cells/mm. The dose is tapered as the inflammation subsides or if the white cell or platelet count falls too drastically.

Azathioprine and methotrexate are examples of antimetabolites. Azathioprine is usually given in a dose of 50–150 mg/day, while methotrexate can be given as a weekly oral or intramuscular dose of 7.5–25.0 mg. Methotrexate at a dose of 12.5 mg/week has been shown to be effective therapy for corticosteroid-resistant uveitis.

Cyclosporine Cyclosporine (Cyclosporin A) is a naturally occurring compound produced by soil fungi. It has a much more specific effect on immune function than do either corticosteroids or cytotoxic agents. While cyclosporine's exact mechanism of action remains controversial, the primary effects appear to be related to inhibition of T-cell activation and recruitment, most likely through its suppressive effect on IL-1 function and indirect inhibition of IL-2 production, both of which are necessary for activation of T lymphocytes.

Cyclosporine has been shown to be effective in treating various types of uveitis, such as Behçet syndrome and Vogt-Koyanagi-Harada syndrome. Therapy is usually begun at a dose of 2.5–5.0 mg/kg/day, and it may be combined with 20–40 mg of prednisone for a more potent anti-inflammatory effect. It should be noted that cyclosporine is not cytolytic—it does not kill the lymphocytes responsible for the inflammation. Thus, the beneficial effects usually disappear when the medication is discontinued, making long-term treatment necessary in many patients.

The major side effects of cyclosporine are nephrotoxicity and hypertension. The renal impairment is often reversible if the dose is decreased, but irreversible damage to the tubules has occurred in patients on prolonged therapy. Additional side effects include paraesthesia; gastrointestinal upset; fatigue; hypertrichosis; gingival hyperplasia; elevated sedimentation rate; and a normochromic, normocytic anemia. Clearly, patients receiving cyclosporine should be followed closely by an internist to monitor their renal function as well as blood pressure and hematologic status. It is recommended that the dosage be reduced if serum creatinine increases by more than 20%–30% above the pretreatment baseline value. Although cyclosporine is probably not carcinogenic, in contrast to the cytotoxic agents, its teratogenic effects are unknown. Thus, it should not be used in pregnant patients unless absolutely necessary and then only after consultation with the patient's obstetrician or internist, or both.

Another promising approach to the treatment of chronic uveitis is the implantation of a sustained-release device containing cyclosporine through the pars plana. Preliminary results in animal studies have shown this technique to be successful in the treatment of intraocular inflammation. FK506, a potent immunosuppressive agent similar to cyclosporine, is undergoing trials for the management of severe uveitis. Initial results indicate a potential beneficial effect from this agent, but further studies are required to evaluate its indications, contraindications, and effectiveness.

Vitale AT, Rodriguez A, Foster CS. Low-dose cyclosporin A therapy in treating chronic, noninfectious uveitis. *Ophthalmology.* 1996; 103:365–378.

Surgery

Surgical therapy may include diagnostic evaluation such as paracentesis or vitreous and/or chorioretinal biopsy to rule out neoplastic or acute infectious processes. Other surgical approaches are restorative and addressed to the particular complication such as cataract extraction, glaucoma control, and vitrectomy. See chapter XII, Complications of Uveitis, for further discussion of surgery. See also the volumes of BCSC that deal with these conditions in detail: Section 10, *Glaucoma;* Section 11, *Lens and Cataract;* and Section 12, *Retina and Vitreous.*

CHAPTER VII

Anterior Uveitis

Because uveitis may occur secondarily to inflammation of the cornea and sclera, the physician should evaluate these structures to rule out a primary keratitis or scleritis. Inflammation of the sclera and the cornea is covered in depth in BCSC Section 8, *External Disease and Cornea,* and not in this chapter.

Acute Anterior Nongranulomatous Iritis and Iridocyclitis

The classic presentation of acute anterior uveitis is a triad of pain, redness, and photophobia. Fine keratic precipitates and fibrin dust the corneal endothelium in most cases. Endothelial dysfunction may cause the cornea to become acutely edematous. The anterior chamber shows an intense cellular response and variable flare. Severe cases may show a protein coagulum in the aqueous or, less commonly, a hypopyon (Fig VII-1). Occasionally, a fibrin net will form across the pupillary margin (Fig VII-2), potentially producing a seclusion membrane and iris bombé. Dilated iris vessels may be seen, and rarely, a spontaneous hyphema occurs. Cells may also be present in the anterior vitreous, and on rare occasions patients may develop severe, diffuse vitritis. Fundus lesions are not characteristic, although cystoid macular edema, disc edema, pars plana exudates, or small areas of peripheral localized choroiditis may be noted. Occasionally, IOP may be elevated because of blockage of the trabecular meshwork by debris and cells or by pupillary block.

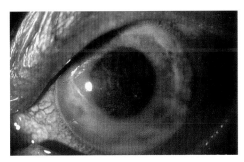

FIG VII-1—Acute HLA-B27–positive anterior uveitis with pain, photophobia, marked injection, fixed pupil, loss of iris detail from corneal edema, and hypopyon.

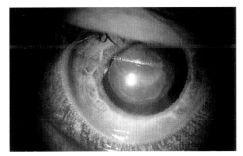

FIG VII-2—Ankylosing spondylitis, acute unilateral iridocyclitis, severe anterior chamber reaction with central fibrinous exudate contracting anterior to the lens capsule and posterior synechiae from 10 o'clock to 12 o'clock.

The attack of inflammation usually lasts several days to weeks. Typically, an attack is acute and unilateral, with a history of episodes alternating between the two eyes. Recurrences are common. Either eye may be affected, but recurrence is rarely bilateral. If damage to the vascular endothelium can be minimized, no silent, ongoing damage or low-grade inflammation should occur between attacks.

D'Alessandro LP, Forster DJ, Rao NA. Anterior uveitis and hypopyon. *Am J Ophthalmol.* 1991;112:317–321.

Rodriguez A, Akova YA, Pedroza-Seres M, et al. Posterior segment ocular manifestations in patients with HLA-B27–associated uveitis. *Ophthalmology.* 1994;101:1267–1274.

Corticosteroids are the mainstay of treatment to reduce inflammation, prevent cicatrization, and minimize damage to the uveal vasculature. Topical corticosteroids are the first line of treatment, and they often need to be given every 1–2 hours. If necessary, periocular or oral steroids may be used for severe episodes. Initial attacks may require all three routes of treatment, particularly in the severe cases found mostly in younger patients.

Severely damaged vessels may leak continuously, transforming the typical course from acute and intermittent to chronic and recalcitrant. This chronic course must be avoided at all costs by timely diagnosis, aggressive initial therapy, and patient compliance. Maintenance therapy is not indicated in well-controlled cases where permanent damage has not taken place, because continued simmering inflammation generally does not occur.

Cycloplegia is used both to relieve pain and to break and prevent synechiae formation. Cycloplegic agents may be given topically or with conjunctival cotton pledgets soaked in tropicamide (Mydriacyl), cyclopentolate (Cyclogyl), and phenylephrine hydrochloride (NeoSynephrine) (Fig VII-3).

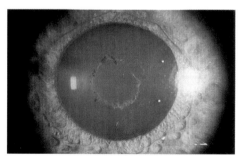

FIG VII-3—Acute iridocyclitis after intensive topical steroids and perilimbal subconjunctival dilating agents, leaving an anterior capsular ring of pigment following posterior synechiolysis. (Photograph courtesy of John D. Sheppard Jr., MD.)

HLA-B27–Related Diseases

HLA-B27 denotes a genotype located on the short arm of chromosome 6. Although it is present in only 1.4%–8.0% of the general population, 50%–60% of patients with acute iritis may be HLA-B27 positive. Racial background and national origin both affect the rate of incidence. The precise trigger for acute iritis in genetically susceptible individuals is not clear. The HLA-B27 test should be performed on patients with recurrent anterior nongranulomatous uveitis, but the test does not provide an absolute diagnosis.

Power WJ, Rodriguez A, Pedroza-Seres M, et al. Outcomes in anterior uveitis associated with the HLA-B27 haplotype. *Ophthalmology.* 1998;105:1646–1651.

Several autoimmune diseases known as the *seronegative spondyloarthropathies* are strongly associated with both acute anterior uveitis and a positive HLA-B27. Patients with these diseases, by definition, do not have a positive rheumatoid factor. The seronegative spondyloarthropathies include

- Ankylosing spondylitis
- Reiter syndrome
- Inflammatory bowel disease
- Psoriatic arthritis
- Postinfectious, or reactive, arthritis

These entities are sometimes clinically indistinguishable, and all may be associated with spondylitis and sacroiliitis. Women tend to have more atypical spondyloarthropathies than men.

Wakefield D, Stahlberg TH, Toivanen A, et al. Serologic evidence of *Yersinia* infection in patients with anterior uveitis. *Arch Ophthalmol.* 1990;108:219–221.

Ankylosing spondylitis This disorder varies from asymptomatic to severe and crippling. Symptoms of ankylosing spondylitis include lower back pain and stiffness after inactivity. Sacroiliac x-ray films may be difficult to interpret but should show sclerosis and eventual narrowing of the joint space. Ligamentous ossification is frequent. These films are best obtained by ordering a sacroiliac view that tunnels down the joint rather than a lumbosacral spine film, which is obtained by direct anteroposterior imaging and is less likely to clearly reveal sacroiliitis (Figs VII-4, VII-5). Similar pathology is found in the pubic symphysis, where localized mineral loss and sclerosis erodes the subchondral bone.

HLA-B27 is found in 88% of patients with ankylosing spondylitis. The chance that an HLA-B27–positive patient will develop spondyloarthritis or eye disease is one in four, and family members may also have ankylosing spondylitis and/or iritis. Often, symptoms of back disease are lacking in individuals with iritis who test positive. Certainly, not all HLA-B27–positive patients develop disease; most do not develop any form of autoimmune disease.

The ophthalmologist may be the first physician to suspect ankylosing spondylitis. Symptoms or family history of back problems together with a positive HLA-B27 suggest a diagnosis. Sacroiliac x-ray films should be obtained when indicated by a suggestive history in a patient with ocular disease consistent with HLA-B27 syndrome. Patients with ankylosing spondylitis should be informed of the risk of deformity and referred to an internist or a rheumatologist. Pulmonary apical fibrosis may

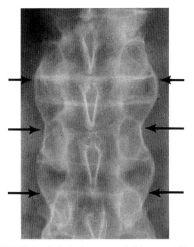

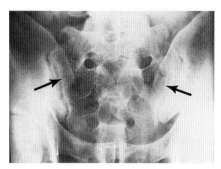

FIG VII-4—Ankylosing spondylitis x-ray film showing total fusion of vertebrae (arrows) and marked decalcification. (Photograph courtesy of John D. Sheppard Jr., MD.)

FIG VII-5—Ankylosing spondylitis with moderately severe sacroiliitis shown by tunnel view, with blurring of sacroiliac joint (arrows). (Photograph courtesy of John D. Sheppard Jr., MD.)

FIG VII-6—Ankylosing spondylitis and aortitis with arterial wall destruction by fibrosis, thickening, and elastic fragmentation. (Photograph courtesy of John D. Sheppard Jr., MD.)

develop; aortitis occurs in about 5% of cases and may be associated with aortic valvular insufficiency (Fig VII-6).

Tay-Kearney M, Schwam BL, Lowder C, et al. Clinical features and associated systemic diseases of HLA-B27 uveitis. *Am J Ophthalmol.* 1996;121:47–56.

Wakefield D, Montanaro A, McCluskey P. Acute anterior uveitis and HLA-B27. *Surv Ophthalmol.* 1991;36:223–232.

Reiter syndrome   A classic triad of symptoms is diagnostic of Reiter sydrome:

☐ Nonspecific urethritis

☐ Polyarthritis

☐ Conjunctival inflammation, often accompanied by iritis

HLA-B27 is found in 85%–95% of patients, and prostatic fluid culture is negative. The condition occurs most frequently in young adult males, although 10% of patients are female.

Reiter syndrome may be triggered by episodes of diarrhea or dysentery without urethritis. *Chlamydia, Ureaplasma ureolyticum, Shigella, Salmonella,* and *Yersinia* have all been implicated as triggering infections. Arthritis begins within 30 days of infection in 80% of patients. The knees, ankles, feet, and wrists are affected asymmetrically and in an oligoarticular distribution. Sacroiliitis is present in as many as 70% of patients.

Two conditions in addition to the classic triad are considered to be major diagnostic criteria:

☐ *Keratoderma blennorrhagicum:* a scaly, erythematous, irritating disorder of the palms and soles of the feet (Figs VII-7, VII-8)

☐ *Circinate balanitis:* a persistent, scaly, erythematous, circumferential rash of the distal penis

The keratoderma blennorrhagicum may resemble a pustular psoriasis; this resemblance demonstrates the difficulty of distinguishing among the various seronegative spondyloarthropathies.

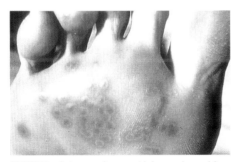

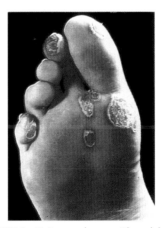

FIG VII-7—Reiter syndrome with keratoderma blennorrhagicum on the sole. (Photograph courtesy of John D. Sheppard Jr., MD.)

FIG VII-8—Reiter syndrome with pedal discoid keratoderma blennorrhagicum. (Photograph courtesy of John D. Sheppard Jr., MD.)

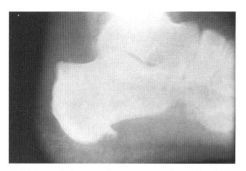 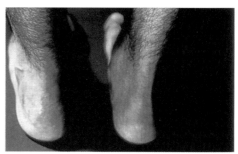

FIG VII-9—Reiter syndrome, x-ray view of calcific plantar fasciitis. (Photograph courtesy of John D. Sheppard Jr., MD.)

FIG VII-10—Reiter syndrome with chronic Achilles tendinitis. (Photograph courtesy of John D. Sheppard Jr., MD.)

Numerous minor criteria are also useful in establishing a diagnosis of Reiter syndrome, according to the American Rheumatologic Association (ARA) guidelines. These include plantar fasciitis (Fig VII-9), Achilles tendinitis (Fig VII-10), sacroiliitis, nail-bed pitting, palate ulcers, and tongue ulcers.

Conjunctivitis is the most common eye lesion associated with Reiter syndrome. It is usually mucopurulent and papillary. Punctate and subepithelial keratitis may also occur, occasionally leaving permanent corneal scars. Acute nongranulomatous iritis recurs frequently. In some cases, the iritis becomes bilateral and chronic because of a permanent breakdown of the blood–aqueous barrier.

Inflammatory bowel disease   *Ulcerative colitis* and *Crohn disease (granulomatous ileocolitis)* are both associated with acute iritis. Between 5% and 12% of patients with ulcerative colitis and 2.4% of patients with Crohn disease develop acute anterior uveitis. Occasionally, bowel disease is asymptomatic and follows the onset of iritis. Of patients with inflammatory bowel disease, 20% may have sacroiliitis, and of these patients, 60% are HLA-B27 positive. Patients with both acute iritis and inflammatory bowel disease tend to have HLA-B27 as well as sacroiliitis. In contrast, patients with inflammatory bowel disease who develop sclerouveitis tend to be HLA-B27 negative, have symptoms resembling rheumatoid arthritis, and usually do not develop sacroiliitis.

Salmon JF, Wright JP, Murray AD. Ocular inflammation in Crohn's disease. *Ophthalmology.* 1991;98:480–484.

FIG VII-11—Psoriatic arthritis with classic erythematous, hyperkeratotic rash. (Photograph courtesy of John D. Sheppard Jr., MD.)

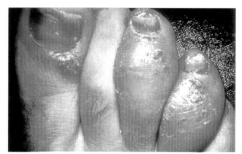

FIG VII-12—Psoriatic arthritis with sausage digits resulting from tissue swelling and distal interphalangeal joint inflammation. (Photograph courtesy of John D. Sheppard Jr., MD.)

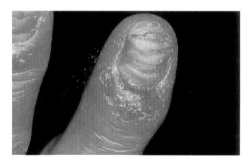

FIG VII-13—Psoriatic arthritis with typical destructive nail changes of subungual hyperkeratosis and onycholysis. (Photograph courtesy of John D. Sheppard Jr., MD.)

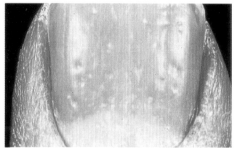

FIG VII-14—Psoriatic arthritis with typical nail-bed pitting changes. (Photograph courtesy of John D. Sheppard Jr., MD.)

Psoriatic arthritis   Acute iritis may occur in conjunction with psoriatic arthritis. Iritis is not associated with psoriasis without arthritis. Twenty percent of patients with psoriatic arthritis may have sacroiliitis, and inflammatory bowel disease occurs more frequently than would be expected by chance with psoriatic arthritis. Diagnosis is based upon the findings of the typical cutaneous changes (Fig VII-11), terminal phalangeal joint inflammation (Fig VII-12), and ungual involvement (Figs VII-13, VII-14).

Derhaag PJ, Linssen A, Broekema N, et al. A familial study of the inheritance of HLA-B27–positive acute anterior uveitis. *Am J Ophthalmol.* 1988;105:603–606.

Rothova A, van Veenedaal WG, Linssen A, et al. Clinical features of acute anterior uveitis. *Am J Ophthalmol.* 1987;103:137–145.

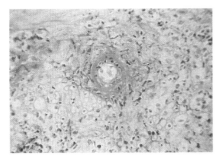

FIG VII-15—Behçet syndrome, histopathology, perivascular inflammation.

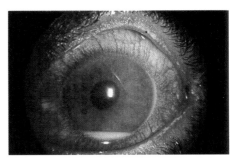

FIG VII-16—Behçet syndrome, hypopyon.

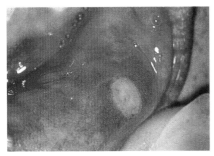

FIG VII-17—Behçet syndrome, mucous membrane ulcers.

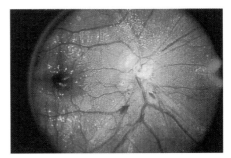

FIG VII-18—Behçet syndrome, retinal vasculitis.

Behçet Syndrome

Behçet syndrome is a generalized occlusive vasculitis of unknown cause (Fig VII-15). Its classic presentation is a triad consisting of

□ Acute iritis with hypopyon (Fig VII-16)

□ Aphthous stomatitis (cankerlike mouth ulcers) (Fig VII-17)

□ Genital ulceration

Although Behçet syndrome may actually cause a panuveitis, it is discussed with acute anterior uveitis because of the classic acute hypopyon iritis seen in Figure VII-16. Behçet syndrome is rare in the United States; 1.8% of patients had the syndrome at one referral uveitis clinic. It is more common in countries stretching eastward from the eastern Mediterranean to Japan. At one Japanese uveitis clinic 20% of patients had Behçet syndrome. The disease occurs most frequently in young adults.

A characteristic ocular feature of Behçet syndrome is recurrent acute iritis or chronic iridocyclitis that is often bilateral and associated with a transient hypopyon. More common than anterior involvement in men is a posterior involvement that includes retinal vasculitis (Fig VII-18) (occlusive arteritis and periphlebitis), retinal hemorrhages, macular edema, focal areas of retinal necrosis, ischemic optic neuropathy, and vitritis.

The characteristic mucous membrane lesions are orogenital ulcerations. Lesions elsewhere on the skin are the fourth typical feature of Behçet syndrome. The most common skin lesion is erythema nodosum on the legs, ankles, and elsewhere. Nondestructive recurrent arthritis-arthralgia may affect the wrists and ankles in 60% of patients. Ulcerative hemorrhages that can mimic inflammatory bowel disease may occur in the gastrointestinal tract. Central nervous system symptoms such as strokes, palsies, and confusional state may develop in 25% of patients. Superficial thrombophlebitis is common.

The diagnosis is based on finding some or all of the four main signs: oral aphthous lesions, skin lesions, ocular lesions, and genital lesions. The complete type of Behçet syndrome will display all four main signs, while the incomplete type will display either three main signs or typical ocular findings along with one main sign. The suspect group of patients will display two main (nonocular) signs, while the possible group shows only one main sign.

Incidence of HLA-B5 or subset B51 is increased among Behçet patients. The Behçetine skin test may be useful: the skin is punctured intradermally with a sterile hypodermic needle, and the formation of a pustule within a few minutes indicates a positive test. Treatment of Behçet syndrome includes the use of oral corticosteroids, chlorambucil, or other immunosuppressive drugs. Colchicine and azathioprine have been found useful, as has cyclosporine. Behçet syndrome is a chronic disorder that tends to recur over a 2–4–year period and may lead to blindness if ischemic optic neuropathy and retinopathy are not adequately treated.

Hashimoto T, Takeuchi A. Treatment of Behçet's disease. *Current Opinions in Rheumatology.* 1992;4:31–34.

Michaelson JB, Friedlaender MH. Behçet's disease. *Int Ophthalmol Clin.* 1990;30: 271–278.

Nussenblatt JB, Palestine AG, Chan CC, et al. Effectiveness of cyclosporine therapy for Behçet's disease. *Arthritis Rheum.* 1985;28:671–679.

Tabbara KF. Chlorambucil in Behçet's disease: a reappraisal. *Ophthalmology.* 1983;90: 906–908.

Yazici H, Pazarli H, Barnes CG, et al. A controlled trial of azathioprine in Behçet's syndrome. *N Engl J Med.* 1990;322:281–285.

Glaucomatocyclitic Crisis (Posner-Schlossman Syndrome)

Glaucomatocyclitic crisis (Posner-Schlossman syndrome) usually manifests as a unilateral mild acute iritis. Symptoms are vague, such as discomfort, blurred vision, or haloes. Signs include markedly elevated IOP, corneal edema, fine KP, low-grade cell and flare, and a slightly dilated pupil. Episodes last from several hours to several days, and recurrences are common over many years. Treatment is with topical corticosteroids and antiglaucoma medication including, if necessary, carbonic anhydrase inhibitors. Pilocarpine probably should be avoided because it may exacerbate ciliary spasm.

Glaucomatocyclitic crisis, like VKH syndrome, which is discussed later under panuveitis, may be associated with the HLA-B54 gene locus. Because Posner-Schlossman syndrome is rare, it should be a diagnosis of exclusion, established only after other more common syndromes, which may respond to specific antibiotic or antiviral therapy, have been ruled out.

Lens-Associated Uveitis

Several entities are included in the category of lens-associated uveitis. They are divided based on histopathologic features into phacoantigenic endophthalmitis, phacotoxic uveitis, and phacolytic glaucoma. Clinically, however, these three entities are not necessarily mutually exclusive but may show considerable overlap in terms of their presentation.

Phacoantigenic endophthalmitis   This entity is an immune response to lens protein released after injury to the lens capsule or after extracapsular surgery (Figs VII-19 through VII-22). In rare instances spontaneous lens capsule rupture may cause the disease. Although this ocular inflammation appears to result from autoimmunity to lens protein, the precise immune mechanism is not known. Experimental animal studies suggest that altered tolerance to lens protein leads to the inflammation, which usually has an abrupt onset but may occasionally occur insidiously. Patients previously sensitized to lens protein (e.g., after cataract extraction in the fellow eye) can experience inflammation within 24 hours after capsular rupture.

Mutton-fat KP may appear on the cornea, and the iris may have congested vessels. Posterior synechiae and dense flare and cells are present. Fundus lesions do not occur. Histopathologic studies reveal a zonal granulomatous inflammation centered at the site of lens injury. Neutrophils are present about the lens material with surrounding epithelioid cells and occasional giant cells. Lymphocytes, plasma cells, and granulation tissue wall off the site. Some cases have attendant sympathetic ophthalmia.

Treatment of phacoantigenic endophthalmitis is with corticosteroids and cycloplegics. Surgical removal of lens material is indicated.

Phacotoxic uveitis   The term *phacotoxic uveitis* has been used to refer to the supposedly toxic effect of lens proteins that enter the anterior chamber, but this effect is in dispute. Many physicians believe that lens protein is not toxic and that so-called phacotoxic uveitis is really a less severe form of phacoantigenic endophthalmitis. Perhaps the term *phacoallergic uveitis* would be more appropriate. An example of this condition might be a mild to moderate inflammatory response following cataract surgery. Histopathologically, phacotoxic uveitis is said to lack the epithelioid cell response around lens protein that occurs in phacoantigenic endophthalmitis.

Treatment is with corticosteroids. If the inflammation persists, the ophthalmologist should consider surgical removal of lens material. Nuclear fragments dropped into the vitreous cavity, unless they are small, should likewise be removed, as they may incite a severe inflammatory response.

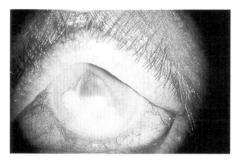

FIG VII-19—Phacoantigenic reaction following phacoemulsification.

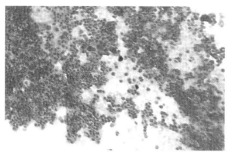

FIG VII-20—Phacoantigenic reaction, histopathology (aqueous tap). Note neutrophils (blue) around lens (gray).

FIG VII-21—Retained cortex following complicated phacoemulsification, anterior vitrectomy, and anterior chamber lens implant. Low-grade uveitis was readily controllable with chronic topical steroids. (Photograph courtesy of John D. Sheppard Jr., MD.)

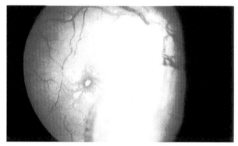

FIG VII-22—Traumatically dislocated nucleus atop the optic nerve produced progressively severe phacoantigenic uveitis and glaucoma, necessitating pars plana lensectomy and vitrectomy. (Photograph courtesy of John D. Sheppard Jr., MD.)

Phacolytic glaucoma   This condition involves an acute increase in IOP caused by clogging of the trabecular meshwork by lens protein and engorged macrophages. It occurs with hypermature cataracts. Elevated IOP, lack of KP, refractile bodies in the aqueous, and lack of synechiae all suggest this diagnosis.

Therapy includes pressure reduction, often with osmotic agents as well as topical medications, and prompt cataract extraction. Aqueous tap may reveal swollen macrophages.

Apple DJ, Mamalis N, Steinmetz RL, et al. Phacoanaphylactic endophthalmitis associated with extracapsular cataract extraction and posterior chamber intraocular lens. *Arch Ophthalmol.* 1984;102:1528–1532.

Meisler DM. Intraocular inflammation and extracapsular cataract surgery. In: *Focal Points: Clinical Modules for Ophthalmologists.* San Francisco: American Academy of Ophthalmology; 1990;8:7.

Rao NA, Calandra AJ, Sevanian A, et al. Modulation of lens-induced uveitis by super-oxide dismutase. *Ophthalmic Res.* 1986;18:41–46.

Wohl LG, Kline OR Jr, Lucier AC, et al. Pseudophakic phacoanaphylactic endophthalmitis. *Ophthalmic Surg.* 1986;17:234–237.

Pseudophakia

Uveitis may be associated with pseudophakia. The problem is more likely to occur with rigid closed-loop anterior chamber intraocular lenses. Surgical manipulation breaks down the blood–aqueous barrier, leading to vulnerability in the early postoperative period. Infectious endophthalmitis must be included in the differential diagnosis of postoperative inflammation and hypopyon. *Propionibacterium acnes* is a cause of delayed or late-onset endophthalmitis following placement of a posterior or anterior chamber IOL. Infectious endophthalmitis is discussed in more detail in chapter XI.

Iris chafing caused by the edges or loops of IOLs on either the anterior or posterior surface of the iris can result in mechanical irritation and inflammation. Metal-loop lenses and poorly polished lenses, in particular, can cause this reaction. The incidence of this type of complication with modern lenses is 1% or less of cases. The motion of an iris-supported or an anterior chamber IOL may cause intermittent corneal touch and lead to corneal endothelial damage, low-grade iritis, and cystoid macular edema.

The *uveitis-glaucoma-hyphema (UGH) syndrome* can still be seen today, although it has become much less common. The syndrome was caused in the past through irritation of the iris root by the warped footplates of poorly made rigid anterior chamber IOLs. Flexible anterior chamber IOLs are less likely to cause UGH syndrome. Various polymers used in the manufacture of IOLs may activate complement and cause PMN chemotaxis and resultant inflammation. Retained lens material from extracapsular cataract extraction may exacerbate the usual transient postoperative inflammation.

Phacoantigenic endophthalmitis may also occur. If the surgeon does not recognize this entity early, the eye may be lost. Removal of the IOL alone is of no benefit in these cases; all lens protein must be eliminated. If cataract extraction is performed in the fellow eye, the patient is at risk of developing phacoantigenic endophthalmitis in that eye as well.

Until recently, pseudophakic bullous keratopathy following cataract extraction was the leading indication for corneal transplantation in the United States. Poorly designed anterior chamber IOLs, as well as complicated surgical techniques, were responsible for most postoperative corneal edema and chronic anterior segment inflammation (Figs VII-23, VII-24). The most notorious IOLs associated with pseudophakic uveitis are the closed-loop designs, which are no longer implanted in the United States. Patients with these lenses can develop chronic uveitis as well as extensive peripheral anterior synechiae, recalcitrant glaucoma, chronic or irreversible cystoid macular edema, and endothelial decompensation. These lenses should be removed and exchanged when penetrating keratoplasty is performed.

Auffarth GU, Wesendahl TA, Brown SJ, et al. Are there acceptable anterior chamber intraocular lenses for clinical use in the 1990s? An analysis of 4104 explanted anterior chamber intraocular lenses. *Ophthalmology.* 1994;101:1913–1922.

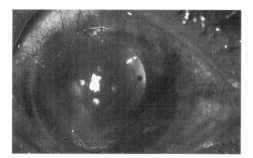

FIG VII-23—Pseudophakic bullous keratopathy and chronic iridocyclitis caused by iris-fixated anterior chamber IOL, with corneal touch, iris stromal erosion, and chronic recalcitrant cystoid macular edema. (Photograph courtesy of John D. Sheppard Jr., MD.)

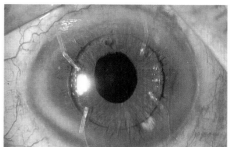

FIG VII-24—Fixed-haptic anterior chamber IOL (Azar 91Z) associated with peripheral and superior corneal edema, chronic low-grade iridocyclitis, peripheral anterior synechiae, global tenderness, and intermittent microhyphema. (Photograph courtesy of John D. Sheppard Jr., MD.)

Although silicone IOLs have been associated with iritis in the past, the data at this time are not sufficient to determine whether they are directly associated with intraocular inflammation. Nevertheless, several attempts have been made to modify the IOL surface to decrease the intraocular inflammation following cataract surgery, particularly in patients with preexisting inflammatory conditions. These modifications include molecular bonding of viscoelastic or heparin to the surface of the IOL material, as well as molecular surface passivation to minimize bacterial and leukocyte adherence. No adequately controlled prospective studies have evaluated the efficacy of such surface modifications in limiting postoperative inflammation among uveitis patients undergoing cataract surgery.

Irregular or damaged IOL surfaces as well as polypropylene haptics have been associated with enhanced bacterial and leukocyte binding and probably should be avoided in patients with uveitis. Adhesion of bacteria to IOLs, particularly those with polypropylene haptics, may be associated with an increased risk of postoperative endophthalmitis. For further discussion and illustrations, see BCSC Section 11, *Lens and Cataract.*

Raskin EM, Speaker MG, McCormick SA, et al. Influence of haptic materials on the adherence of staphylococci to intraocular lenses. *Arch Ophthalmol.* 1993;111: 250–253.

Kawasaki Syndrome

Also known as *mucocutaneous lymph node syndrome* or *infantile periarteritis nodosa*, Kawasaki syndrome is an acute exanthematous disease of childhood (85% of patients are less than 5 years old). This disease occurs worldwide, and its etiology is unknown. It is characterized by the following:

- Fever lasting 5 days or longer
- Bilateral conjunctival congestion
- Oral mucous membrane congestion
- Desquamation of the palms and soles
- Polymorphous exanthem
- Acute nonsuppurative swelling of the cervical lymph nodes

A systemic vasculitis can lead to coronary arteritis. Sudden death from coronary aneurysm and thrombosis occurs in 1%–2% of cases.

Ocular features include bulbar conjunctival injection that spares the limbus. No discharge is present. Transient anterior bilateral acute iritis occurs frequently. However, the uveitis is mild, and synechiae have not been reported.

Topical corticosteroids and a short-acting cycloplegic are the only treatment necessary for the ophthalmic manifestations; aspirin is considered the drug of choice for systemic manifestations. Systemic steroids are contraindicated. See also BCSC Section 6, *Pediatric Ophthalmology and Strabismus.*

> Googe JM Jr, Brady SE, Argyle JC, et al. Choroiditis in infantile periarteritis nodosa. *Arch Ophthalmol.* 1985;103:81–83.
>
> Ohno S, Miyajima T, Higuchi M, et al. Ocular manifestations of Kawasaki's disease (mucocutaneous lymph node syndrome). *Am J Ophthalmol.* 1982;93:713–717.
>
> Puglise JV, Rao NA, Weiss RA, et al. Ocular features of Kawasaki's disease. *Arch Ophthalmol.* 1982;100:1101–1103.

Herpetic Disease

Acute anterior uveitis is often associated with herpetic viral disease. BCSC Section 8, *External Disease and Cornea,* discusses extensively herpes simplex virus and herpes zoster virus (Figs VII-25, VII-26, VII-27). Usually, the uveal inflammation associated with these herpesviruses is a keratoiritis secondary to corneal disease. On occasion, the iritis may occur without noticeable keratitis. In many cases the inflammation becomes chronic. Herpes zoster virus may be considered in the differential diagnosis of chronic unilateral iridocyclitis, even if the cutaneous component of the condition occurred in the past or was minimal even when present.

Varicella (chickenpox), which is caused by the same virus responsible for secondary varicella-zoster virus reactivation, is frequently associated with an acute, mild, nongranulomatous, self-limited, bilateral iritis or iridocyclitis. Cutaneous vesicles at the side of the tip of the nose (Hutchinson's sign) indicate nasociliary nerve involvement and a greater likelihood that the eye will be affected. Most patients are asymptomatic, but as many as 40% of patients with primary herpes zoster virus infection may develop iritis when examined in prospective fashion.

Patients with intraocular viral infections, particularly the herpes group infections, which also includes cytomegalovirus, may occasionally develop stellate KP.

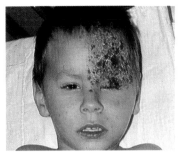

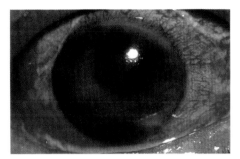

FIG VII-25—Herpes zoster virus, skin lesions.

FIG VII-26—Herpes zoster virus, hyphema and hypopyon.

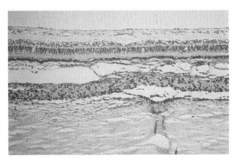

FIG VII-27—Herpes zoster virus, necrosis of long ciliary nerve.

This morphology is also seen in Fuchs heterochromic iridocyclitis and toxoplasmosis. These stellate KP usually assume a diffuse distribution, as opposed to the usual distribution in the inferior third of the cornea known as Arlt's triangle. In addition, the KP are fine and fibrillar, often with a distinctly stellate pattern on high magnification by biomicroscopic examination. The identification of diffuse or stellate KP is useful in the differential diagnosis of anterior segment inflammation, although not diagnostic of any particular condition. In patients with herpetic disease and concomitant keratopathy, however mild, anterior segment inflammation may also be associated with diffuse or localized decreased corneal sensation and neurotrophic keratitis.

Glaucoma is a frequent complication of herpetic uveitis and is thus a helpful diagnostic hallmark. Most inflammatory syndromes are usually associated with decreased IOP as a result of ciliary body hyposecretion. However, just as the herpesvirus can localize to corneal, cutaneous, or conjunctival tissues, herpetic reactivation may directly cause trabeculitis and thus increase IOP, often to as high as 50–60 mm Hg. In addition, inflammatory cells may contribute to trabecular obstruction and congestion. Hyphema may occur in herpetic uveitis.

Iris atrophy is also characteristic of herpetic inflammation, particularly herpes zoster. With herpes simplex virus the atrophy tends to occur closer to the pupillary sphincter, whereas with herpes zoster the atrophy is more basal. Segmental iris atrophy is characteristic of herpes zoster, which produces an iris stromal occlusive vasculitis responsible for this distinctive pattern.

Viral retinitis may occur with these entities, particularly in immunocompromised hosts. Vasculitis commonly occurs with herpes zoster ophthalmicus, and it may lead to anterior segment ischemia, retinal artery occlusion, and scleritis. Vasculitis in the orbit may lead to cranial nerve palsies.

Treatment for viral iritis is controversial but usually includes cycloplegia. The effectiveness of available topical antiviral agents in treating uveitis is poor. Systemic antivirals such as acyclovir, famcyclovir, or valcyclovir are often beneficial in cases of severe uveitis. Initiation of oral antiviral therapy within the first few days after herpes zoster onset is now recommended. The use of corticosteroids is controversial, although topical corticosteroid drops may be used in selected cases. Corneal problems from topical corticosteroid use are less likely to occur in herpes zoster uveitis than in herpes simplex. However, once a patient with herpes zoster uveitis is started on corticosteroids, it is often difficult to discontinue the regimen because of severe rebound inflammation. In fact, some patients with herpes zoster require chronic, albeit extremely low, doses of topical corticosteroids (as infrequent as 1 drop per week) to remain quiescent. Systemic corticosteroids are at times necessary. Consultation with an infectious disease specialist may be appropriate.

Barron BA, Gee L, Hauck WW, et al. Herpetic Eye Disease Study: a controlled trial of oral acyclovir for herpes simplex stromal keratitis. *Ophthalmology*. 1994;101: 1871–1882.

Hirsch M, Schooley RT. Drug therapy: treatment of herpes virus infections. *N Engl J Med*. 1983;309:1034–1039.

Parrish CM. Herpes simplex virus eye disease. In: *Focal Points: Clinical Modules for Ophthalmologists*. San Francisco: American Academy of Ophthalmology; 1997;15:2.

Sandor EV, Millman A, Croxson TS, et al. Herpes zoster ophthalmicus in patients at risk for the acquired immune deficiency syndrome (AIDS). *Am J Ophthalmol*. 1986; 101:153–155.

Wilhelmus KR, Gee L, Hauck WW, et al. Herpetic Eye Disease Study: a controlled trial of topical corticosteroids for herpes simplex stromal keratitis. *Ophthalmology*. 1994;101:1883–1895.

Other Viral Diseases

Acute iritis may occur in other infectious entities. The iritis in influenza, adenovirus, and infectious mononucleosis is mild and transient. Synechiae and ocular damage seldom occur. Iritis with adenovirus is usually secondary to corneal disease; see BCSC Section 8, *External Disease and Cornea*. Rarely, retinal periphlebitis may be seen in mononucleosis. Treatment beyond cycloplegia may not be necessary, although topical corticosteroids can be used. Iritis is unusual in mumps, although it may occur 4–14 days after onset. Papillitis or neuroretinitis appears 2–4 weeks after onset and lasts 2–3 weeks.

Drug-Induced Uveitis

Treatment with certain medications has been associated with the development of intraocular inflammation. Examples include rifabutin and cidofovir, both of which can cause an acute anterior uveitis. Treatment is generally with topical cortico-steroids and cycloplegic agents if necessary. Recalcitrant cases may require cessation or tapering of the offending systemic medication.

Chronic Iridocyclitis

Inflammation of the anterior segment that lasts longer than 2–3 months is termed *chronic iridocyclitis,* and it may persist for years. This type of inflammation usually starts insidiously, with variable amounts of redness, discomfort, and photophobia. Some patients have no symptoms. The disease can be unilateral or bilateral, and the amount of inflammatory activity is variable. Cystoid macular edema is a common feature.

Juvenile Rheumatoid Arthritis

Juvenile rheumatoid arthritis (JRA) is the most common systemic disorder associated with iridocyclitis in the pediatric age group. JRA is subdivided into three types:

□ *Systemic onset (Still disease).* This type, usually seen in children under age 5, is characterized by fever, rash, lymphadenopathy, and hepatosplenomegaly. Joint involvement may be minimal or absent initially. This type accounts for approximately 20% of all patients with JRA, but ocular involvement is rare: fewer than 6% of the JRA patients who have uveitis.

□ *Polyarticular onset.* This group shows involvement of five or more joints in the first 6 weeks of the disease. It constitutes 40% of JRA cases overall but only 7%–14% of cases of JRA-associated iridocyclitis.

□ *Pauciarticular onset.* This group includes the vast majority (80%–90%) of JRA patients who have uveitis. Patients have involvement of four or fewer joints during the first 6 weeks of disease and may have no joint symptoms. This type is subdivided into two subsets. *Type 1* disease is seen primarily in girls under age 5 who are typically antinuclear antibody (ANA) positive; chronic iridocyclitis is seen in up to 25% of these patients. *Type 2* disease is seen in older boys, many of whom go on to develop evidence of a seronegative spondyloarthropathy (75% are HLA-B27 positive). The uveitis in these patients tends to be acute and recurrent rather than chronic as in type 1.

Ocular involvement in JRA   The average age of onset of uveitis in JRA patients is 6 years. It generally develops within 5–7 years of the onset of joint disease but may occur as long as 28 years after the development of arthritis. There is usually little or no correlation between ocular and joint inflammation. Risk factors for the development of chronic iridocyclitis in JRA patients include female sex, pauciarticular onset, and the presence of circulating ANA. Most patients are rheumatoid factor (RF) negative.

The eye is often white and uninflamed in appearance. Symptoms include moderate pain, photophobia, and blurring, although some patients do not have pain.

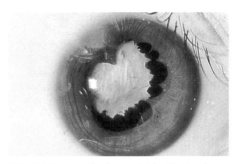

FIG VII-28—Juvenile rheumatoid arthritis, chronic iridocyclitis, cataract.

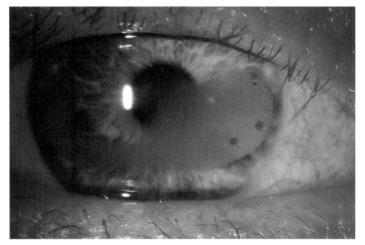

FIG VII-29—Chronic calcific band keratopathy.

Often, the eye disease is found incidentally during a routine school physical. The signs of inflammation include fine KP, band keratopathy, flare and cells, posterior synechiae, and cataract (Figs VII-28, VII-29). Patients in whom JRA is suspected should have ANA testing and should be evaluated by a pediatric rheumatologist, since the joint disease may be minimal or absent at the time the uveitis is diagnosed. The differential diagnosis in these patients includes sarcoidosis, the seronegative spondyloarthropathies, herpetic uveitis, and Lyme disease.

Prognosis The prognosis is often poor, in part because of delay in diagnosis and treatment. Profound silent ocular damage can occur, and the long-term prognosis often depends on the extent of damage present at the time of first diagnosis. Complications are frequent and often severe. One recent series of patients with JRA-associated iridocyclitis referred to a tertiary care center showed the following complication rates:

□ Cataract (84% of patients)

□ Band keratopathy (70%)

□ Macular edema (42%)

□ Vitreous debris (37%)

□ Glaucoma (26%)

□ Chronic hypotony or phthisis (21%)

Although these numbers are probably not representative of the population at large, they illustrate the potential severity of the disease.

Children with JRA, especially of the pauciarticular variety, should have regular slit-lamp examinations. Table VII-1 outlines the recommended schedule for screening JRA patients for uveitis, as developed by the American Academy of Pediatrics.

Management The initial treatment consists of topical corticosteroids. More severe cases may require systemic or periocular corticosteroids. Steroid therapy is not indicated in patients with chronic aqueous flare in the absence of active cellular reaction. Short-acting mydriatic agents are useful in patients with chronic flare to keep the pupil mobile and to prevent posterior synechiae formation. Use of systemic NSAIDs may permit a lower dose of corticosteroids.

TABLE VII-1

RECOMMENDED SCREENING SCHEDULE FOR
JRA PATIENTS WITHOUT KNOWN IRIDOCYCLITIS

	AGE OF ONSET	
JRA SUBTYPE AT ONSET	<7 YEARS[1]	≥7 YEARS[2]
Pauciarticular		
+ANA	Every 3–4 months[3]	Every 6 months
−ANA	Every 6 months	Every 6 months
Polyarticular		
+ANA	Every 3–4 months[3]	Every 6 months
−ANA	Every 6 months	Every 6 months
Systemic	Every 12 months	Every 12 months

[1] All patients are considered at low risk 7 years after the onset of their arthritis and should have yearly ophthalmologic examinations indefinitely.

[2] All patients are considered at low risk 4 years after the onset of their arthritis and should have yearly ophthalmologic examinations indefinitely.

[3] If no uveitis 4 years after onset of arthritis, should have ophthalmologic examination every 6 months.

Adapted from: Guidelines for ophthalmologic examinations in children with juvenile rheumatoid arthritis. *Pediatrics.* 1993;92:295–296.

Because of the chronic nature of the inflammation, steroid-induced complications are frequently seen. In general, a trend has been emerging to no longer accept even a minimal level of inflammation in these patients on a long-term basis, given the complications that often arise in patients with chronic "low-grade" inflammation. Studies have shown that such patients can benefit from treatment with low-dose methotrexate, with relatively few side effects.

Patients with JRA-associated iridocyclitis present some of the most difficult management problems of all uveitis patients with respect to cataract removal. Conventional cataract extraction is associated with a high rate of complications in these patients. Great care must be taken, including the following steps:

□ Control the inflammation adequately for at least 3 months prior to surgery

□ Evaluate the angle and synechiae preoperatively

□ Treat with adequate anti-inflammatory medications, including immunosuppressive therapy if indicated, in the perioperative period

IOL implantation is generally contraindicated in children with JRA-associated iridocyclitis, although it may be successful in selected adults with JRA in whom the inflammation has been adequately controlled. Combined lensectomy-vitrectomy may improve the prognosis. Patients with band keratopathy should be treated (e.g., scraping or chelation with sodium EDTA) and allowed to heal well before cataract surgery is attempted. See also chapter XII, Complications of Uveitis; and BCSC Section 6, *Pediatric Ophthalmology and Strabismus,* chapter XXIII.

Glaucoma should be treated with medical therapy initially, although surgical intervention is often necessary in severe cases. Standard filtering procedures are usually unsuccessful, and the use of antifibrotic agents or aqueous drainage devices is usually required for successful control of the glaucoma.

Dana MR, Merayo-Lloves J, Schaumberg DA, et al. Visual outcomes prognosticators in juvenile rheumatoid arthritis–associated uveitis. *Ophthalmology.* 1997;104:236–244.

Dinning WJ. Uveitis and juvenile chronic arthritis. In: *Focal Points: Clinical Modules for Ophthalmologists.* San Francisco: American Academy of Ophthalmology, 1990;8:5.

Flynn HW Jr, Davis JL, Culbertson WW. Pars plana lensectomy and vitrectomy for complicated cataracts in juvenile rheumatoid arthritis. *Ophthalmology.* 1988;95: 1114–1119.

Giannini EH, Brewer EJ, Kuzmina N, et al. Methotrexate in resistant juvenile rheumatoid arthritis. Results of the U.S.A.–U.S.S.R. double-blind placebo-controlled trial. The Pediatric Rheumatology Collaborative Study Group and The Co-operative Children's Study Group. *N Engl J Med.* 1992;326:1043–1049.

Kanski JJ. Juvenile arthritis and uveitis. *Surv Ophthalmol.* 1990;34:253–267.

Olson NY, Lindsley CB, Godfrey WA. Nonsteroidal anti-inflammatory drug therapy in chronic childhood iridocyclitis. *Am J Dis Child.* 1988;142:1289–1292.

Probst LE, Holland EJ. Intraocular lens implantation in patients with juvenile rheumatoid arthritis. *Am J Ophthalmol.* 1996;122:161–170.

Weiss AH, Wallace CA, Sherry DD. Methotrexate for resistant chronic uveitis in children with juvenile rheumatoid arthritis. *J Pediatr.* 1998;133:266–268.

Chronic Iridocyclitis in Young Girls

The name *chronic iridocyclitis in young girls* may be misleading, as the disease does affect boys as well, although it occurs up to 12 times more frequently in girls. The course, prognosis, and therapy are similar to those of chronic iridocyclitis associated with bona fide JRA; however, no concomitant arthritis has ever been documented in these patients. Some of these children eventually develop true arthritis. The ANA test is frequently but not always positive. In young men, particularly, a negative ANA test suggests an HLA-B27 syndrome rather than a JRA-like syndrome.

Fuchs Heterochromic Iridocyclitis

Fuchs heterochromic iridocyclitis is an entity that is frequently overlooked. Between 2% and 3% of patients referred to various uveitis clinics have Fuchs heterochromic iridocyclitis. This condition is usually unilateral, and its symptoms vary from none to mild blurring and discomfort. Signs include

□ Diffuse iris stromal atrophy with variable pigment epithelial layer atrophy

□ Small white stellate KP scattered diffusely over the entire endothelium (the differential diagnosis of diffuse KP also includes sarcoidosis, syphilis, keratouveitis, herpetic uveitis, and, rarely, toxoplasmosis)

□ Minimal aqueous cells and flare

□ Cells and opacities in the anterior vitreous

Synechiae almost never form, but glaucoma and cataracts occur frequently (Fig VII-30). Generally, fundus lesions are absent, but fundus scars and retinal periphlebitis have been reported on rare occasions. Macular edema seldom occurs.

The diagnosis is made based on the distribution of KP, lack of synechiae, lack of symptoms, and heterochromia. Often, the inflammation is discovered on a routine

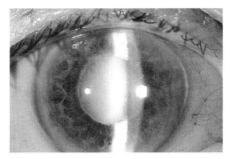

FIG VII-30—Fuchs heterochromic iridocyclitis, cataract.

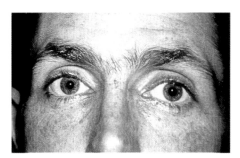 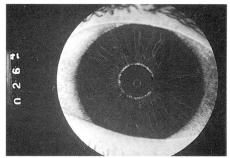

FIG VII-31—Heterochromia in Fuchs hetero-chromic iridocyclitis in a brown-eyed patient.

FIG VII-32—Fuchs heterochromic iridocyclitis, iris fluorescein angiography.

examination as, for example, when a unilateral cataract develops. Usually, but not invariably, the lighter-colored iris indicates the involved eye (Fig VII-31). In blue-eyed individuals, however, the affected eye may become darker as the stromal atrophy progresses and the darker iris pigment epithelium shows through. Iris fluorescein angiography demonstrates poor perfusion of some segments (Fig VII-32).

Patients generally do well with cataract surgery, and IOLs can usually be implanted successfully. However, some patients may suffer significant visual disability as a result of extensive vitreous opacification, even after uncomplicated cataract surgery with IOL implantation in the capsular bag. Pars plana vitrectomy should be carefully considered in such patients. Glaucoma control can be difficult. Abnormal (neovascular) or prominent (nonneovascular) angle vessels may be present.

Few cases of Fuchs heterochromic iridocyclitis require therapy. The prognosis is good in most cases even though the inflammation persists for decades. Since topical corticosteroids can lessen the inflammation but typically do not resolve it, aggressive treatment to eradicate the cellular reaction is not indicated. Cycloplegia is seldom necessary. Histopathology shows plasma cells in the ciliary body indicating that true inflammation occurs.

Jones NP. Fuchs' heterochromic uveitis: a reappraisal of the clinical spectrum. *Eye.* 1991;5:649–661.

Liesegang TJ. Clinical features and prognosis in Fuchs' heterochromic uveitis syndrome. *Arch Ophthalmol.* 1982;100:1622–1626.

Unknown Etiology

In many patients with chronic iridocyclitis the etiology is unknown. Therapy, including cycloplegia, may be necessary before a specific diagnosis is obtained. In many cases observation and subsequent testing may yield a specific uveitis diagnosis.

CHAPTER VIII

Intermediate Uveitis and Pars Planitis

Intermediate uveitis is characterized by ocular inflammation concentrated in the anterior vitreous and the vitreous base overlying the ciliary body and peripheral retina–pars plana complex. Anterior vitreous cellular reaction is apparent. Inflammatory cells may aggregate in the vitreous *(snowballs)* where some coalesce *(snowmen)*. In some patients inflammatory exudative accumulation on the inferior pars plana *(snowbanking)* seems to correlate with a more severe disease process. There may be associated retinal phlebitis. Anterior chamber reaction may occur, but in adults it is usually mild and attributed to "spillover" from the vitreous.

Intermediate uveitis is associated with various conditions, including sarcoidosis, multiple sclerosis, Lyme disease, peripheral toxocariasis, syphilis, tuberculosis, and connective tissue disease. Intermediate uveitis of unknown etiology, *pars planitis,* is the most common form, constituting approximately 85%–90% of cases.

Pars planitis, also known as *chronic cyclitis* and *peripheral uveitis,* most commonly affects persons under the age of 40, and approximately 80% of cases are bilateral. In children the initial presentation may consist of significant anterior chamber inflammation accompanied by redness, photophobia, and discomfort. The onset in teenagers and young adults may be more insidious, with the presenting complaint generally being floaters.

Fluorescein angiography may show diffuse peripheral venular leaking. Histopathologic examination shows vitreous condensation and cellular infiltration in the vitreous base. The inflammatory cells consist mostly of macrophages, lymphocytes, and few plasma cells. Pars planitis is characterized by peripheral lymphocytic cuffing of venules and a loose fibrovascular membrane over the pars plana.

Pars planitis may remain active for many years and has occasionally been documented at more than 30 years. With chronicity, posterior synechiae and band keratopathy may also develop. Cystoid macular edema may occur, and this is the major cause of visual loss in pars planitis. Other possible causes for visual loss associated with chronic inflammation include posterior subcapsular cataracts, epiretinal membrane, retinal detachment, vitreous cellular opacification, and peripheral neovascularization that may give rise to vitreous hemorrhage.

Therapy should be directed toward treating the underlying cause of the inflammation, if possible. For example, infective etiologies such as Lyme disease, tuberculosis, and syphilis should be treated with appropriate antimicrobial agents. If an underlying condition is not identified, as in pars planitis, or if therapy of an associated condition consists of nonspecific control of inflammation, as with sarcoidosis, anti-inflammatory therapy should be implemented.

Therapy also varies with the severity of visual loss. Mild cases may require no treatment. However, if vision-threatening vitreous cellular accumulation or macular edema is present, corticosteroids are usually the first line of therapy. Therapy may be administered by local injection of depot corticosteroids, using the posterior sub-Tenon's route (see Figure VI-6, p 115). Systemic steroid therapy may be implemented if local therapy is not effective. Systemic immunomodulating agents such as methotrexate, cyclosporine, or cyclophosphamide may also be tried.

Cryoablation of the pars plana may be indicated, particularly if neovascularization is present. Peripheral scattered photocoagulation seems to be as effective as cryotherapy in treating inflammation and peripheral neovascularization and does not seem to increase the risk of rhegmatogenous retinal detachment. Vitrectomy may be necessary to treat severe visual loss caused by dense vitreous cellular accumulation and veils, vitreal hemorrhage or traction, retinal detachment, and cystoid macular edema.

Böke WRF, Manthey KF, Nussenblatt RB. *Intermediate Uveitis. Developments in Ophthalmology 23*. Basel: Karger; 1992.

Hooper PL. Pars Planitis. In: *Focal Points: Clinical Modules for Ophthalmologists.* San Francisco: American Academy of Ophthalmology; 1993;9:11.

Malinowski, SM, Pulido JS, Folk JC. Long-term visual outcome and complications associated with pars planitis. *Ophthalmology.* 1993;100:818–824.

Park SE, Mieler WF, Pulido JS. Peripheral scatter photocoagulation for neovascularization associated with pars planitis. *Arch Ophthalmol.* 1995;113:1277–1280.

Pederson JE, Kenyon KR, Green WR, et al. Pathology of pars planitis. *Am J Ophthalmol.* 1978;86:762–774.

CHAPTER IX

Posterior Uveitis

Entities included in this chapter may have some common symptoms. Typically, the onset of ocular problems is gradual, with blurred vision, floating spots, and scotomata. Because many of the conditions included in this chapter have vitreous cells with focal or multifocal retinal and choroidal involvement, their clinical pictures may appear similar. The differential diagnosis is quite long and includes both infectious and noninfectious conditions. Among the infectious conditions are viral, bacterial, fungal, protozoal, and helminthic causes. The noninfectious group includes conditions of possible immunologic or allergic origin and unknown etiology and masquerade conditions such as endophthalmitis and neoplasms.

The approach to the diagnosis of posterior uveitis should include an accurate and complete medical history and review of systems designed to detect any associated systemic disorders that may be responsible for the uveitis. A history of underlying systemic disease such as acquired immunodeficiency syndrome (AIDS), corticosteroid or other immunosuppressive therapy, antibiotic therapy, intravenous drug use, or hyperalimentation is frequently seen in patients with endogenous bacterial, fungal, or viral ocular disease. Patients with systemic collagen vascular diseases may have dermatologic, joint, pulmonary, gastrointestinal, or genitourinary complaints that are associated with the ocular inflammation.

Ancillary laboratory testing and diagnostic procedures are often indicated in patients with posterior uveitis. These tests have been discussed in chapter VI. Perhaps the most useful test in evaluating posterior forms of uveitis is fluorescein angiography, which can provide critical information not available from biomicroscopic or fundus examination that can greatly assist in the diagnosis and management. Cystoid macular edema, retinal vasculitis, secondary choroidal or retinal neovascularization, and areas of retinal or choroidal inflammation can all be detected using angiography. Diagnostic vitrectomy may provide information to clarify the etiology by antibody titer, culture, and cytology. Individual tests should be ordered only when the patient's clinical presentation suggests the particular diagnosis.

Posterior uveitis entities are grouped by the most common anatomic features into two major categories: *retinitis* and *choroiditis*. Within these two groups, conditions may present with focal, multifocal, or diffuse involvement. Contiguous inflammation of the overlying or underlying tissue layers may result in vitritis, retinochoroiditis, or chorioretinitis. This differentiation may help diagnostically.

Syndromes with primarily posterior segment involvement are included in this chapter on posterior uveitis, while diagnoses routinely producing both anterior and posterior segment involvement are addressed in the following chapter on panuveitis. The astute diagnostician must realize, however, that these categories exist for convenience only and that many uveitis syndromes may present with a wide variety of clinical manifestations.

Infectious Diseases

Viral Disease

Herpetic diseases Anterior uveal inflammation frequently accompanies the keratitis associated with herpes simplex virus and herpes zoster keratitis. Posterior uveitis (retinal necrosis) occurs rarely with herpes zoster, and it is treated with IV acyclovir. See chapter VII for a discussion of ocular inflammation caused by herpesviruses.

Yoser SL, Forster DJ, Rao NA. Systemic viral infections and their retinal and choroidal manifestations. *Surv Ophthalmol.* 1993;37:313–352.

Acute retinal necrosis (ARN) syndrome ARN is a fulminant, necrotizing viral infection of the retina. The disease is bilateral (BARN) in 33% of patients, and onset of contralateral involvement may be delayed up to 26 years after initial presentation. ARN/BARN is not an etiologic diagnosis. Varicella-zoster virus, herpes simplex virus type 2, and cytomegalovirus have all been associated with this syndrome. It affects adolescents to older adults. Patients are typically healthy and not debilitated, although ARN may occur in patients with AIDS.

ARN is diagnosed by clinical appearance. Patients present with an acute loss of vision. Anterior segment inflammation may range from minor to severe, and vitreous cellular exudation is heavy. Within 2 weeks the classic triad develops of occlusive retinal arteriolitis, vitritis, and a multifocal yellow-white peripheral retinitis (Figs IX-1, IX-2). Scattered retinal hemorrhages may be present but are not characteristic or extensive in nature. The peripheral retinal lesions progress rapidly and coalesce to form a confluent 360° "creamy" retinitis. The posterior pole tends to be spared, and no sharp demarcation appears between involved and uninvolved retina.

Unlike other forms of viral retinitis, most patients with ARN are not immunosuppressed, and systemic antiviral agents may be useful. Intravenous acyclovir (1500 mg/m^2 per day in three divided doses over 10–14 days) is the treatment of choice to inhibit further viral replication. After 24–48 hours of antiviral therapy, corticosteroids can be introduced to treat the active vitritis. Aspirin or other anticoagulation agents may be used to treat an associated hypercoaguable state, and intravitreal ganciclovir

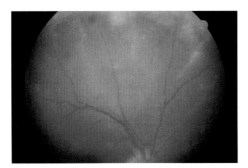

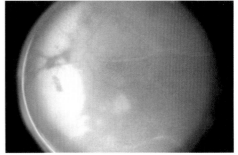

FIG IX-1—Acute retinal necrosis, vitritis, arteriolitis, and multiple peripheral "thumbprint" areas of retinitis.

FIG IX-2—Acute retinal necrosis, confluent peripheral retinitis.

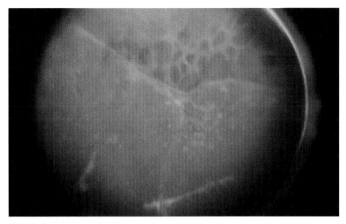

FIG IX-3—Acute retinal necrosis, retinal detachment with multiple, posterior retinal breaks.

(200 µg/0.1 ml) can assist in the induction phase of therapy in certain patients (see chapter XIII).

Multiple posterior retinal breaks and combined traction-rhegmatogenous retinal detachments occur in up to 75% of patients (Fig IX-3). Prophylactic laser demarcation applied to areas of healthy retina may prevent retinal detachment. Internal repair through vitrectomy techniques and use of silicone oil may be more successful at reattaching the retina than standard scleral buckle procedures because of the extensive vitreous scarring and multiple posterior retinal tears. Although the condition tends to resolve slowly over 1–2 months, the visual prognosis is poor; 65% of patients have worse than 20/200 acuity as a result of the extensive retinal necrosis and retinal detachment. See also BCSC Section 12, *Retina and Vitreous*.

Blumenkranz M, Clarkson J, Culbertson WW, et al. Visual results and complications after retinal reattachment in the acute retinal necrosis syndrome. The influence of operative technique. *Retina*. 1989;9:170–174.

Matsuo T, Nakayama T, Koyama T, et al. A proposed mild type of acute retinal necrosis syndrome. *Am J Ophthalmol*. 1988;105:579–583.

Cytomegalovirus The exact incidence of ocular inflammatory disease induced by cytomegalovirus (CMV) is not known. Undoubtedly, a significant number of cases are congenital, but the absence of dependable serologic data precludes an accurate assessment of the importance of the congenital disease in the production of any but the typical lesions in adults. Signs and symptoms include fever, thrombocytopenia, anemia, pneumonitis, and hepatosplenomegaly as a result of the systemic inflammatory process. Multiple peripheral retinal lesions with minimal tissue destruction are seen, frequently in association with total cataract formation. Both pigmented and atrophic lesions are present, and optic nerve atrophy may also occur.

Signs and symptoms of acquired disease include yellow-white areas of retinal necrosis, hemorrhages, vascular sheathing, and attenuation. The ophthalmic appearance most closely approximates that of multiple branch vein occlusions. Microaneurysms of the retinal vessels have also been described. Precipitates are found on the back of the detached vitreous, and mild to moderate anterior segment inflammation may occur. Ocular infections in a previously healthy individual may be atypical, with exudative retinal detachment and minimal retinitis. Rhegmatogenous retinal detachments with holes in the areas of necrosis may be present. Massive periretinal proliferation and late development of new holes can occur.

Diagnosis of congenital disease is suggested by the clinical appearance of the lesions coupled with the findings of viral inclusion bodies in urine, saliva, and subretinal fluid and the associated systemic disease findings. The complement fixation test for cytomegalic inclusion disease is of value 5–24 months after the loss of the maternal antibodies transferred during pregnancy. Diagnosis of acquired disease is suggested by the clinical picture noted in immunocompromised patients receiving chemotherapy for leukemia, lymphoma, malignant neoplasms, and kidney transplantation or those with AIDS.

The disease frequently causes significant retinal destruction and rhegmatogenous retinal detachment (Fig IX-4). The histopathologic features of both the congenital and acquired disease are primary coagulative necrotizing retinitis and secondary diffuse choroiditis. Infected retinal cells show large eosinophilic intranuclear inclusions and small multiple basophilic cytoplasmic inclusions (Fig IX-5). Viral inclusions may also be seen in the RPE and vascular endothelium. Electron microscopy of infected retinal tissue reveals viral particles with typical morphology of the herpes family of viruses. Chapter XIII, Ocular Involvement in AIDS, gives a more extensive discussion of CMV, including its management.

Epstein-Barr virus   Epstein-Barr virus (EBV) is an encapsulated, double-stranded DNA virus in the herpes family that is ubiquitous: 90% of the population has acquired antibodies by the third decade of life. EBV has a tropism for B lymphocytes resulting in B-cell activation and mononuclear proliferation. Specific antibodies develop directed toward viral capsid antigens during the course of infection, and these antibodies are diagnostically helpful. EBV nuclear antigens (EBNA) and other

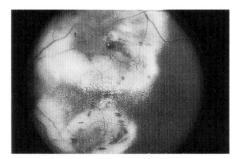

FIG IX-4—Cytomegalovirus retinitis.

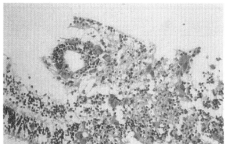

FIG IX-5—Cytomegalovirus histopathology of retinitis. Note giant *(megalo)* cells with inclusions in necrotic retina.

viral proteins stimulate anti-EBNA antibodies as well as antibodies against early diffuse (EA-D) and restricted (EA-R) antigens.

EBV infection has been associated with asymptomatic childhood illnesses, infectious mononucleosis (IM), nasopharyngeal carcinoma, Burkitt lymphoma, Hodgkin disease, and Sjögren syndrome. Macular edema, retinal hemorrhages, chorioretinitis, punctate outer retinitis, and a multifocal choroiditis and panuveitis (MCP) have been reported during the course of infectious mononucleosis and other Epstein-Barr virus infections.

The diagnosis is suggested by fundus lesions developing during IM or serologic testing supporting active or persistent EBV infection. The differential diagnosis for the various retinal findings is quite extensive, and other etiologies for posterior uveitis should be considered.

Therapy for EBV infection is supportive, and oral acylovir may limit viral replication. As with all herpesviruses, a latent infection is established following initial exposure, introducing the possibility of recurrent or chronic illness.

Raymond LA, Wilson CA, Linnemann CC Jr. Punctate outer retinitis in acute Epstein-Barr virus infection. *Am J Ophthalmol.* 1987;104:424–426.

Rubella Rubella virus, an enveloped, single-stranded RNA virus, is the etiologic agent for German measles. Rubella may involve the retina in both congenital and acquired forms of the disease. German measles presents with a viral prodrome of malaise and fever and evolves into a characteristic maculopapular skin rash that begins on the trunk and spreads to the extremities over a 3–5 day period. Acquired rubella has been reported to cause conjunctivitis, keratitis, iritis, and, rarely, a bilateral retinitis and exudative retinal detachment. Retinitis is more frequently seen in infants with maternal rubella syndrome contracted during the first trimester of pregnancy (approximately 25%–50%). Although cataract (15%), glaucoma (10%), and anterior segment inflammatory signs with atrophy of the iris and posterior synechiae may be present, the most prominent findings occur in the posterior pole.

Histopathologic studies of the lens reveal retention of cell nuclei in the embryonic nucleus, as well as anterior and posterior cortical degeneration. Poor development of the dilator muscle, necrosis of the iris pigment epithelium, and chronic nongranulomatous inflammation are present in the iris. The RPE displays alternating areas of atrophy and hypertrophy. The anterior chamber angle appears similar to that noted in congenital glaucoma.

Vitreous haze seen on ocular examination seldom prevents a view of the retina, where unilateral or bilateral pigmentary changes result in a "salt-and-pepper fundus." Pigmentation is generally fine and powdery in character (Fig IX-6); however, rather large, more discrete areas of pigmentation may be seen as well. The blood vessels are normal, and the optic nerve may be slightly pale. Despite a loss of the foveal light reflex and the prominent RPE changes, neither vision nor electrophysiologic testing (i.e., electroretinogram) are typically affected. In rare instances subretinal neovascularization with significant visual loss may complicate the usually benign course.

The pathognomonic retinal appearance and the history of maternal exposure to rubella suggest the diagnosis. Other stigmata of congenital rubella syndrome may also be present (Fig IX-7). Viral antibody studies may be confirmatory. Although usually present at birth, the process may develop postnatally.

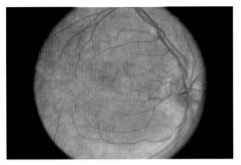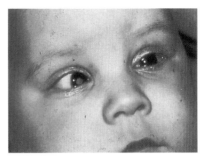

FIG IX-6—Congenital rubella syndrome with fine salt-and-pepper pigmentation.

FIG IX-7—Congenital rubella syndrome patient with cataract, esotropia, mental retardation, congenital heart disease, and deafness. (Photograph courtesy of John D. Sheppard Jr., MD.)

Measles (rubeola)   Measles virus is an enveloped, extremely contagious RNA virus that causes worldwide pandemics every 2–3 years. Immunization has reduced the frequency of the disease in the United States, and incidence is now quite rare. Measles virus can cause both congenital and acquired disease. Fundus changes similar to congenital rubella retinopathy have been reported in children whose mothers developed measles (rubeola) during pregnancy. The virus is transmitted from the pregnant woman to her fetus through the placenta. Measles retinitis has also been reported to occur following an acquired infection. Macular edema, neuroretinitis, attenuated retinal vessels, and macular star formation occur. No effective treatment is known, and the visual prognosis is variable.

Subacute sclerosing panencephalitis virus (SSPE)   This slow viral infection of the central nervous system can cause a distinct maculopathy. SSPE is caused by a variant of the measles virus with a mutation of the viral envelope M protein. It affects school-age children 6–7 years after the measleslike infection. The slow virus infection of the cerebrum, the cerebellum, and the eye causes an encephalitis with behavioral changes, mental deterioration, progressive neurologic deficits, and a cortical blindness. Disc edema, papillitis, and optic atrophy can be found in 30%–75% of cases. The most consistent finding is a maculopathy that begins as a focal area of macular edema and evolves into a localized white retinal infiltrate that may be associated with macular hemorrhage. Late in the course of the disease the retinitis resolves, leaving focal gliosis of the macula.

SSPE should be considered in any school-age child with slowly progressive deterioration of mental function, behavioral changes, and visual dysfunction. The optic nerve and macular findings do not coincide with the other CNS symptoms and may precede other neurologic signs. Extremely high titers of measles antibodies and brain biopsy confirm the diagnosis. Treatment is supportive and visual prognosis is grave.

Robb RM, Watters GV. Ophthalmic manifestations of subacute sclerosing panencephalitis. *Arch Ophthalmol.* 1970;83:426–435.

Fungal Diseases

Ocular histoplasmosis syndrome (OHS)   This multifocal chorioretinitis is epidemiologically linked to *Histoplasma capsulatum,* a dimorphic fungus with both yeast and filamentous forms. The yeast form is the cause of systemic and ocular disease. OHS is frequently diagnosed in endemic areas of the United States such as the Ohio–Mississippi River valleys. However, sporadic cases are seen in other areas as well. Primary infection occurs after inhalation of the fungal spores into the lungs. Dissemination to the spleen, liver, and choroid follows the initial pulmonary infection. Acquired histoplasmosis is usually asymptomatic or may result in a benign illness, typically during childhood.

"Histo spots" first appear in the eye during adolescence, but maculopathy does not usually develop until 20–50 years of age with an average of 41 years. Pathologically, the first lesion seems to be a granuloma in the choroid. This choroiditis may subside and leave a scar with depigmentation of the pigment epithelium, or it may result in breaks in Bruch's membrane and the pigment epithelium with an associated lymphocytic infiltration. Focal areas of choroiditis result in RPE proliferation and secondary subretinal neovascularization originating from the choroid. Lacking tight junctions, these neovascular complexes may leak fluid, lipid, and blood, resulting in loss of macular function.

The diagnosis of OHS is based on the clinical triad of disseminated atrophic histo spots, peripapillary pigment changes, and a maculopathy characterized by a pigment ring with detachment of the overlying sensory retina, usually with hemorrhage (Figs IX-8, IX-9, IX-10). The maculopathy typically begins at the site of a histo scar in the disc–macula area. Vitreous cells are *not* seen in OHS, and symptoms seldom accompany the peripheral, atrophic histo spots. These spots represent focal, healed, "punched-out" lesions resulting from a variable amount of scarring in the choroid and adjacent outer layers of retina. The visual distortion and profound reduction in central vision following macular involvement bring the patient to the ophthalmologist.

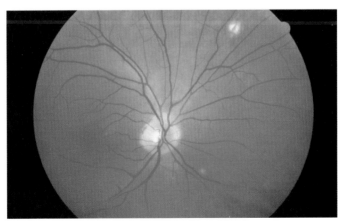

FIG IX-8—Ocular histoplasmosis: atrophic histo spots.

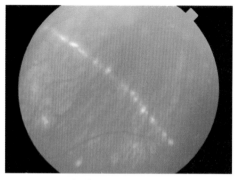

FIG IX-9—Ocular histoplasmosis: linear equatorial streaks.

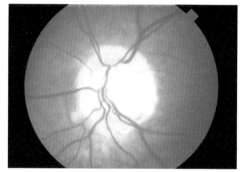

FIG IX-10—Ocular histoplasmosis: peripapillary pigment change.

Symptomatic areas of choroiditis may be treated with oral or regional cortico-steroids (Figs IX-11, IX-12). In the early stages of the fluorescein angiogram, active choroiditis will block the dye and appear hypofluorescent. In later frames, the choroidal lesions will stain and become hyperfluorescent. In contrast, areas of active subretinal neovascular membrane (SRNVM) will be hyperfluorescent early in the angiogram and intensify throughout the study. The neovascular membrane is important only if it lies in the disc–macula area; if it is outside the superotemporal and inferotemporal vascular arcades, it does not reduce vision and therefore requires no treatment. However, if this membrane is located 1–200 μm from the center of the foveal avascular zone (FAZ) (juxtafoveal location) or 20–2500 μm from the center (extrafoveal location), laser photocoagulation is indicated to prevent further loss of vision (Figs IX-13, IX-14, IX-15).

The Macular Photocoagulation Study Group in a collaborative multicenter study has shown a beneficial effect with argon blue-green photocoagulation. Untreated

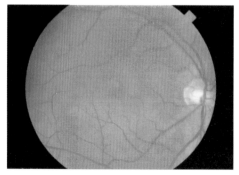

FIG IX-11—Ocular histoplasmosis: macular choroiditis with multiple yellow elevated lesions.

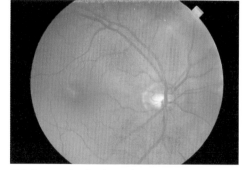

FIG IX-12—Ocular histoplasmosis: macular choroiditis with resolution and mild pigmentation of the lesions following periocular steroid injection.

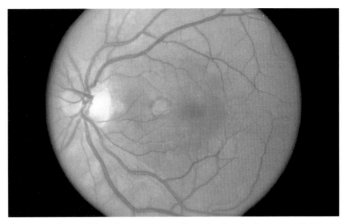

FIG IX-13—Ocular histoplasmosis: extrafoveal subretinal neovascularization.

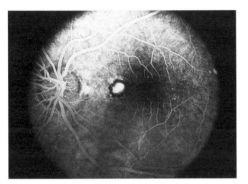

FIG IX-14—Ocular histoplasmosis: fluorescein angiogram of an extrafoveal subretinal neovascular
membrane.

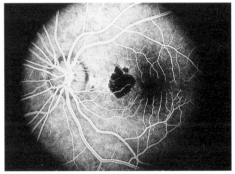

FIG IX-15—Ocular histoplasmosis: fluorescein angiogram of subretinal neovascular membrane following laser photocoagulation.

patients showed a higher percentage (50%) of a six-line loss of vision compared to
laser-treated patients (22%) over a 24-month period. Krypton red or argon green
wavelengths may give better visual results with less retinal injury than argon blue-
green photocoagulation. Patients with SRNVM located under the FAZ may benefit
from submacular surgery and removal of the membrane (Figs IX-16, IX-17).

Without treatment 59% of the patients with maculopathy end up with visual
acuity of 20/200 or worse. Massive subretinal exudation and hemorrhagic retinal
detachments may occur and result in permanent loss of macular function (Fig IX-18).
If histo spots appear in the macular area, the patient has a 25% chance of developing maculopathy within 3 years. If no histo spots are present, the chances fall to 2%.
Macular disease is highly variable; some cases resolve spontaneously with a return
to normal vision.

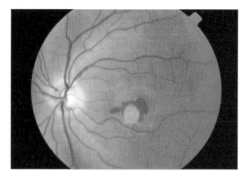

FIG IX-16—Ocular histoplasmosis: subfoveal neovascularization.

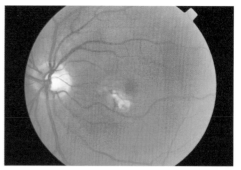

FIG IX-17—Ocular histoplasmosis: subfoveal neovascular membrane following submacular surgical
removal.

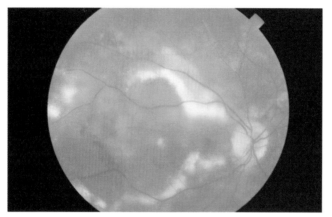

FIG IX-18—Ocular histoplasmosis: massive exudative and hemorrhagic macular detachment.

The differential diagnosis of OHS includes angioid streaks, choroidal rupture, and idiopathic choroidal neovascularization. The atrophic spots and maculopathy of myopic degeneration and the maculopathy of age-related macular disease may also be confused with OHS.

Campochiaro PA, Morgan KM, Conway BP, et al. Spontaneous involution of subfoveal neovascularization. *Am J Ophthalmol.* 1990;109:668–675.

Macular Photocoagulation Study Group. Argon laser photocoagulation for ocular histoplasmosis: results of a randomized clinical trial. *Arch Ophthalmol.* 1983;101: 1347–1357.

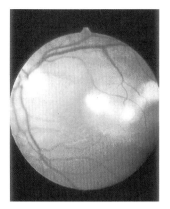

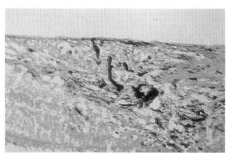

FIG IX-19—*Candida* retinitis.

FIG IX-20—Pathology of *Candida* retinitis. Note fungi (black) in Gomori's methenamine silver stain of retina.

Sabates FN, Lee KY, Ziemianski MC. A comparative study of argon and krypton laser: photocoagulation in the treatment of presumed ocular histoplasmosis syndrome. *Ophthalmology.* 1982;89:729–734.

Thomas MA, Kaplan HJ. Surgical removal of subfoveal neovascularization in the presumed ocular histoplasmosis syndrome. *Am J Ophthalmol.* 1991;111:1–7.

Candidiasis **(Candida albicans)**   Although still uncommon, incidence of ocular inflammatory disease caused by *Candida albicans* has increased notably as a result of the widespread use of immunosuppressive therapy, hyperalimentation, and intravenous drugs. Rarely, *Candida* retinitis is seen in AIDS following intravenous drug use (Figs IX-19, IX-20). *Candida* endophthalmitis occurs in 10%–37% of patients with candidemia if they are not receiving antifungal therapy. Ocular involvement drops to 3% in patients who are receiving treatment for their disease.

The organism spreads through metastasis to the choroid. Fungal replication results in secondary retinal and vitreous involvement. Symptoms of ocular candidiasis include decreased vision or perception of floaters, depending on the location of the lesions. Mimicking toxoplasmic choroiditis, posterior pole lesions appear yellow white with fluffy borders, ranging in size from small cotton-wool spots to several disc diameters wide. The lesions originate in the retina and result in exudation into the vitreous. Peripheral lesions may resemble pars planitis.

Diagnosis of ocular candidiasis can be made by positive blood cultures obtained during candidemia. The physician should be alert to the possible diagnosis of candidiasis in hospitalized patients with indwelling intravenous catheters or those receiving hyperalimentation or systemic therapy with antibiotics, steroids, and antimetabolites. Symptomatic or newly diagnosed untreated patients with candidemia should be examined for ocular involvement. These patients should have two dilated fundus examinations 1–2 weeks apart to detect metastatic ocular disease.

Treatment of ocular candidiasis includes intravenous, periocular, and intraocular administration of antifungal agents such as amphotericin B and ketoconazole. Oral flucytosine, fluconazole, or rifampin may be administered in addition to intravenous amphotericin B. If the infectious process breaks through the retina into the vitreous cavity, intravitreal antifungal agents and vitrectomy should be considered. Prompt treatment of peripherally located lesions promotes a favorable prognosis. However, early treatment of central lesions seldom salvages useful vision because of damage to central photoreceptors. Consultation with an infectious disease specialist may be extremely helpful.

Protozoal Diseases

Toxoplasmosis   *Toxoplasma gondii* is an obligate intracellular parasitic protozoon that causes a necrotizing retinochoroiditis (Fig IX-21). It exists in three forms:

□ Oocyst, or soil form (10–12 μm)

□ Tachyzoite, or active infectious form (4–8 μm) (Fig IX-22)

□ Tissue cyst, or latent form (10–200 μm), containing as many as 3000 bradyzoites

T gondii is an intestinal parasite found in cats. The oocysts of the organism are shed in cat feces that may then be ingested by rodents or birds that can in turn serve as reservoirs or intermediate hosts for the parasite. Insect vectors may also transmit *T gondii* from cat feces to human food sources, including plants and herbivorous animals.

Humans probably acquire the infection most frequently by eating raw or undercooked meat that contains tissue cysts, and avoidance of steak tartare and similar foods could probably prevent many infections. Women who acquire toxoplasmosis during pregnancy may transmit tachyzoites to the fetus with severe potential ocular, CNS, and systemic complications. BCSC Section 6, *Pediatric Ophthalmology and Strabismus,* discusses maternal transmission of toxoplasmosis in greater detail. Nonimmune pregnant women without serologic evidence of prior exposure to toxo-

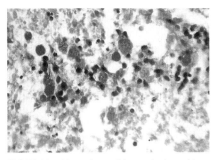

FIG IX-21—*Toxoplasma* histopathology. Note cysts in necrotic retina.

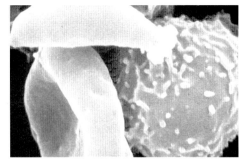

FIG IX-22—Scanning electron microscope view of toxoplasmal tachyzoite parasitizing a macrophage while a red blood cell looks on. (Photograph courtesy of John D. Sheppard Jr., MD.)

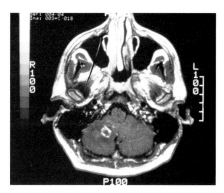

FIG IX-23—CNS toxoplasmosis in AIDS patient presenting with ataxia: cerebellar lesion in enhanced CT scan. (Photograph courtesy of John D. Sheppard Jr., MD.)

plasmosis should take sanitary precautions when cleaning up after cats and avoid undercooked meats. Patients with AIDS are also particularly vulnerable (Fig IX-23); see discussion in chapter XIII.

Toxoplasmosis may account for 7%–15% of all uveitis. Because the disease can destroy visually important structures of the eye, it is important for the ophthalmologist to recognize its lesions and to appreciate its potential for morbidity. Timely diagnosis is important, as toxoplasmosis responds to antimicrobial therapy and is thus a potentially treatable form of posterior uveitis.

Depending largely on the location of the lesion, the patient's complaints are unilateral floating spots or blurred vision. Generally, the anterior segment is not inflamed at the onset of the disease, and the patient shows a white, comfortable-looking eye. Occasionally, however, a granulomatous inflammation with elevated IOP can occur, especially in recurrent disease.

Vitreous opacities are generally obvious on ocular examination by both direct and indirect ophthalmoscopic examination. A whitish yellow, slightly raised, fuzzy lesion can usually be seen in the fundus, often next to a chorioretinal scar (Figs IX-24, IX-25). These lesions occur more commonly in the posterior pole than elsewhere in the fundus and are occasionally seen immediately adjacent to the optic nerve head. They may sometimes be mistaken for an optic papillitis. Retinal vessels in the vicinity of an active lesion may show perivasculitis with diffuse venous sheathing and segmental arterial sheathing. This is the classic clinical complex of ocular toxoplasmosis.

The characteristic lesion is an exudative focal retinitis. The anterior layers of the retina are often singled out as the preferred site for proliferation of *T gondii;* however, a deep retinal form of ocular toxoplasmosis also exists. This lesion does not cloud the vitreous early in the course of the disease, and the patient fails to notice floating spots until the anterior layers of the retina and the posterior hyaloid membrane become involved. Toxoplasmal retinitis may be manifested only by small, punctate, peripheral retinal lesions, often called *punctate outer retinal toxoplasmosis (PORT)* (Fig IX-26).

 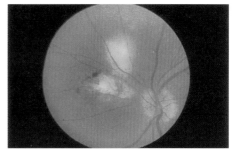

FIG IX-24—*Toxoplasma* retinochoroiditis, "headlight in the fog."

FIG IX-25—*Toxoplasma*, satellite retinitis around old scar.

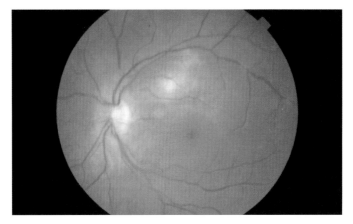

FIG IX-26—Punctate outer retinal toxoplasmosis.

Diagnosis. The diagnosis of ocular toxoplasmosis is made by the following:

☐ Observation of characteristic fundus lesion (focal necrotizing retinochoroiditis)

☐ Detection of the presence of anti-*Toxoplasma* antibodies in the patient's serum

☐ Reasonable exclusion of other infectious diseases that might cause necrotizing lesions of the fundus, principally syphilis, cytomegalovirus, and fungus

The *Toxoplasma* dye test of Sabin and Feldman, the hemagglutination test, or the indirect immunofluorescent antibody test all provide approximately the same information. However, the enzyme-linked immunosorbent assay (ELISA) may offer more sensitivity and specificity.

It should be remembered that the serum titers of any of these tests may be extremely low in patients with ocular toxoplasmosis and no other manifest systemic signs of toxoplasmal disease. Any titer of serum antibodies is significant if the patient has a fundus lesion that is compatible with ocular toxoplasmosis. Tests on the aqueous humor have been used to confirm the presence of toxoplasmal disease in doubtful cases. Such tests are most significant when the titer of antibodies is higher in the aqueous humor than in the serum.

Although the diagnosis of ocular toxoplasmosis is based primarily upon the physical examination, negative antitoxoplasmal antibodies must alert the ophthalmologist to another diagnosis. The clinician interpreting the standard IgG antibody test must remember that laboratories generally perform the test at a dilution of 1:8 or greater, even though a positive antibody reaction may be found at dilutions of 1:4 or less. These extremely low antibody titers may still indicate a previous exposure to toxoplasmosis but are also more likely to be falsely positive as a result of nonspecific reactions.

Most patients with toxoplasmal infections in the United States are presumed to have contracted the disease in utero and to have a congenital infection (Figs IX-27, IX-28). In countries where patients are more likely to have consumed toxoplasmal cysts as adults, acquired toxoplasmosis may be found as well. An acquired infection may often be more fulminating than a congenital infection in which established maternal antibody titers may play a greater role. An acquired toxoplasmal infection is diagnosed by a positive IgM antibody titer. The IgM antibody titer will no longer be detectable 2–6 months following initial infection, even during a relapse of acquired toxoplasmosis.

Treatment. Small lesions in the retinal periphery not associated with significant decrease in vision or vitritis may not require treatment. These lesions can be observed for 3 weeks to 6 months for spontaneous resolution in patients with mild symptoms. The anterior uveitis associated with toxoplasmosis may be treated with topical corticosteroids and cycloplegic agents. Patients with a prominent vitritis or vision-threatening lesions in the posterior pole or adjacent to the optic nerve should be treated with antiprotozoal agents.

The standard treatment for ocular toxoplasmosis consists of pyrimethamine (Daraprim) and sulfonamide therapy. A loading dose of 150 mg of pyrimethamine followed by 25 mg daily for 6 weeks is used, with a loading dose of 4 g of triple sulfa

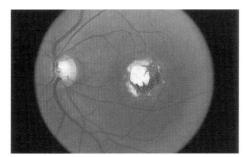

FIG IX-27—Congenital quiescent, mature, hyperpigmented toxoplasmal macular scar. Patient has 20/400 acuity. (Photograph courtesy of John D. Sheppard Jr., MD.)

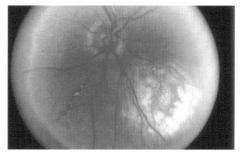

FIG IX-28—Recently acquired large, nonpigmented, inactive toxoplasmal retinal scar. (Photograph courtesy of John D. Sheppard Jr., MD.)

or sulfadiazine, followed by 1 g of the same medication four times a day for 6 weeks. Therapy with pyrimethamine and sulfonamides produces disappointing or unreliable results in older, massive lesions of the fundus that have been present for several months. Potential side effects of sulfa compounds include skin rash, kidney stones, and Stevens-Johnson syndrome.

Many ophthalmologists currently use trimethoprim/sulfamethoxazole (Bactrim, Septra) as an alternative to sulfadiazine because sulfadiazine is more expensive and very difficult to obtain. Folinic acid generally prevents the leukopenia and thrombocytopenia that may result from pyrimethamine therapy. Leukocyte and platelet counts should be monitored weekly. Folinic acid is now available in an oral preparation and administered as a 5 mg tablet (leucovorin calcium) once daily. Clindamycin, 300 mg four times a day, has been effective in the management of acute lesions when used alone or in combination with other agents. However, pseudomembranous colitis has been reported with clindamycin therapy.

Newer agents are becoming available for the treatment of toxoplasmosis. Atovaquone is a cysticidal agent with the potential to eradicate even the encysted form of the parasite. This medication is highly fat soluble and is extremely well tolerated, even in systemically ill, immunocompromised patients. Recurrences have been observed in patients treated with this agent, however, and it has not been proven in the clinical setting to prevent subsequent attacks of toxoplasmosis. Further investigation is required before it is established as a front-line treatment for ocular toxoplasmosis.

Many ophthalmologists believe that maintenance suppression of toxoplasmal disease lowers the incidence of recurrent retinitis, particularly in immunocompromised patients. Agents that are candidates for chronic suppressive therapy include trimethoprim/sulfamethoxazole or doxycycline. No adequate clinical trials have proven the effectiveness of prophylactic suppressive regimens, however.

Corticosteroids must be used with great caution and only with concomitant administration of antimicrobial agents. Oral corticosteroids to quell acute inflammatory lesions that threaten the destruction of the macula or the optic nerve may be given in doses of 60–100 mg prednisone per day 24–48 hours after initiating antibiotic therapy. Periocular injections of depot corticosteroids should be avoided: corticosteroids administered by this route may be immunosuppressive, resulting in an uncontrolled proliferation of the organism, acute retinal necrosis, and disastrous clinical results (Figs IX-29, IX-30).

Photocoagulation therapy and cryotherapy have enjoyed limited success, although overly vigorous treatment with these modalities has resulted in ophthalmic disasters and neither has completely prevented recurrences. Retinal neovascularization may be seen with toxoplasmosis, and photocoagulation of neovascular lesions may prevent loss of vision secondary to vitreous hemorrhages. Pars plana vitrectomy may be helpful when inflammatory vitreous membranes, epiretinal membranes, or traction retinal detachments produce significant visual symptoms and perpetuate the inflammatory process.

Engstrom RE Jr, Holland GN, Nussenblatt RB, et al. Current practices in the management of ocular toxoplasmosis. *Am J Ophthalmol.* 1991;111:601–610.

Lam S, Tessler HH. Quadruple therapy for ocular toxoplasmosis. *Can J Ophthalmol.* 1993;28:58–61.

Lopez JS, de Smet MD, Masur H, et al. Orally administered 566C80 for treatment of ocular toxoplasmosis in a patient with the acquired immunodeficiency syndrome. *Am J Ophthalmol.* 1992;113:331–333.

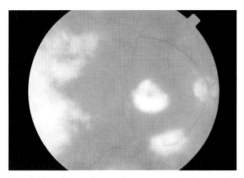

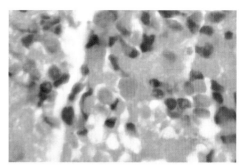

FIG IX-29—Toxoplasmosis, acute retinal necrosis following periocular corticosteroid injection.

FIG IX-30—Retinal biopsy from same patient showing toxoplasmosis organisms.

Opremcak EM, Scales DK, Sharpe MR. Trimethoprim-sulfamethoxazole therapy for ocular toxoplasmosis. *Ophthalmology.* 1992;99:920–925.

Rothova A. Ocular involvement in toxoplasmosis. *Br J Ophthalmol.* 1993;77:371–377.

Rutzen AR, Smith RE, Rao NA. Recent advances in the understanding of ocular toxoplasmosis. *Curr Opinion Ophthalmol.* 1994;5:3–9.

Helminthic Diseases

Toxocariasis   Ocular toxocariasis is a rare but well-known cause of unilateral ocular disease in children and young adults caused by *Toxocara canis*. One series found antibody testing in a kindergarten population as high as 30%. Clinically, however, toxocariasis is seen only occasionally. A study of enucleated globes showed that 2% of 1100 globes of children under 15 years of age harbored the causative organism.

Toxocara canis, a common canine intestinal parasite found in up to 50% of healthy dogs, may invade humans through the ingestion of ova-contaminated soil or vegetables. The ova reach the human intestine and produce larvae, which then invade the intestinal wall, penetrate the blood vessels and lymphatic system, and reach the liver and lungs. Once in the liver and lungs, the larvae can be disseminated to many organs, including the eye.

The disease is usually unilateral. Toxocariasis produces three recognizable ocular syndromes:

☐ Leukocoria from chronic endophthalmitis (Fig IX-31)

☐ Localized granuloma (Fig IX-32)

☐ Peripheral granuloma (Fig IX-33)

Table IX-1 on p 161 lists characteristics for each. In all forms, the eye may be asymptomatic or may present with minimal redness and photophobia. Strabismus from reduced vision in the affected eye may be the presenting complaint.

Aqueous cytology may show eosinophils (Fig IX-34). Because of the specificity of the serum ELISA, this test is helpful in identifying patients with ocular toxocariasis. The presence of any antibody titer (even in undiluted serum) may be significant.

FIG IX-31—*Toxocara,* leukocoria.

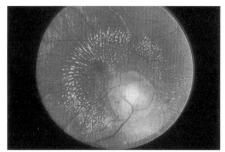

FIG IX-32—*Toxocara,* macular granuloma.

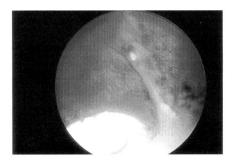

FIG IX-33—*Toxocara,* peripheral granuloma.

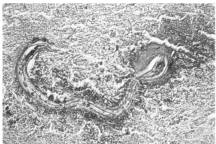

FIG IX-34—*Toxocara,* eosinophilic vitreous abscess, organism in center of abscess.

The antibody titer in intraocular fluids of patients with this disorder is higher than that found in the serum. Ova and parasites in stool specimens are negative in ocular toxocariasis.

Chronic endophthalmitis may result in loss of vision and subsequent enucleation. The location of the granuloma determines the visual deficit. Peripheral granulomas usually cause heterotropia of the macula and some loss of central vision, but the globe remains intact. Corticosteroids, both systemic and periocular, can be used in the active inflammatory phase of the syndrome. Thiabendazole, while useful for systemic toxocariasis, has not been effective in treating the ocular disease and may make the ocular disease worse. Vitrectomy surgery may reduce vitreous traction and clear the media.

Biglan AW, Glickman LT, Lobes LA Jr. Serum and vitreous *Toxocara* antibody in nematode endophthalmitis. *Am J Ophthalmol.* 1979;88:898–901.

Cysticercosis This condition is a common cause of ocular inflammation in Mexico, Central and South America, and Africa. *Cysticercus cellulosae,* the larva of

TABLE IX-1

SYNDROME	AGE OF ONSET	CHARACTERISTIC LESION
Chronic endophthalmitis	2–9	Chronic unilateral uveitis, cloudy vitreous cyclitic membrane
Localized granuloma	6–14	Present in the macula and peripapillary region Solitary, white, elevated in the retina: minimal reaction; 1–2 disc diameters in size
Peripheral granuloma	6–40	Peripheral hemispheric masses with dense connective tissue strands in the vitreous cavity that may connect to the disc Rarely bilateral

Taenia solium, is the most common tapeworm to invade the eye. The eggs of the *Taenia solium* mature, and the larvae penetrate the intestinal mucosa and are spread hematogenously to the eye. Larvae may be seen in the vitreous or subretinal space in 13%–46% of infected patients. A viable larva with the protoscolex can often be seen undulating in these spaces. Death of the larvae produces a severe inflammatory reaction. Pathologic studies show a zonal granulomatous inflammation surrounding the necrotic larva.

Diagnosis is by the observation of a *Cysticercus* organism within the eye (Figs IX-35, IX-36); an ELISA for antibodies to types of *Taenia* may be helpful. Eosinophils are in evidence. Surgical removal of larvae from the vitreous and subretinal space can be performed through vitrectomy and subretinal surgical techniques. Praziquantel (50 mg/kg/day) and laser photocoagulation can kill the larvae, but these treatments may be associated with worsening ocular disease and a panuveitis.

Kraus-Mackiw E, O'Connor GR, eds. *Uveitis, Pathophysiology and Therapy.* 2nd ed. New York: Thieme; 1986.

Smith RD, Nozik RA. *Uveitis: A Clinical Approach to Diagnosis and Management.* 2nd ed. Baltimore: Williams & Wilkins; 1989:125–128.

Diffuse unilateral subacute neuroretinitis (DUSN)   This condition, also called *unilateral wipe-out syndrome,* is caused by a motile nematode, probably the raccoon ascarid *Baylisascaris procyonis.* An immunologic or toxic reaction to the worm or worm by-products appears to cause the DUSN. The average age of patients is 14 years with a range of 11 to 65 years.

DUSN is a biphasic condition. Patients first note a unilateral decrease in acuity. Early in the course of the disease the fundus develops multiple, postequatorial, evanescent crops of grayish white dots (400–1500 µm) with a mild vitritis and reti-

FIG IX-35—Intraocular cysticercus.

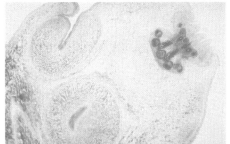

FIG IX-36—Pathology of cysticercus, showing protoscolex, or head of larva.

nal vasculitis (Fig IX-37). Careful ophthalmoscopy will reveal a motile 400–2000 μm nematode. In the second phase of the disease the RPE, retina, and optic nerve develop a "unilateral wipe-out" with optic atrophy, extensive pigmentary disruption, and arteriolar attenuation (Fig IX-38). Rarely, a small retinal granuloma may be seen associated with the worm's demise.

The diagnosis is made on clinical findings. Laser photocoagulation in the early phases of the disease can prevent disease progression and is not associated with worsening ocular disease following the death of the worm (Fig IX-39).

Goldberg MA, Kazacos KR, Boyce WM. Diffuse unilateral subacute neuroretinitis. Morphometric, serologic, and epidemiologic support for *Baylisascaris* as a causative agent. *Ophthalmology.* 1993;100:1695–1701.

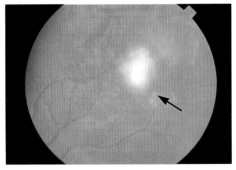

FIG IX-37—Diffuse unilateral subacute neuroretinitis. Note the multiple white retinal lesions and the S-shaped subretinal nematode (arrow).

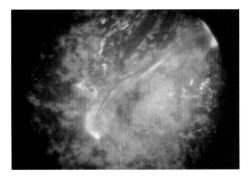

FIG IX-38—DUSN, or unilateral wipe-out.

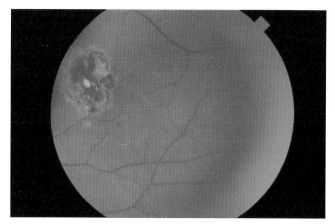

FIG IX-39—Retinal scar following laser photocoagulation of a nematode in DUSN.

Immunologic Diseases

Collagen Vascular Diseases

Systemic lupus erythematosus Systemic lupus erythematosus (SLE) is a collagen vascular disease with multisystemic and protean manifestations. Most patients (90%) are women of child-bearing age. While the pathogenesis of SLE is not completely understood, it is thought to be an autoimmune disorder resulting in the formation of autoantibodies including the antinuclear antibodies (ANA) and immune complexes. Systemic symptoms include malaise, fever, arthritis, rash, pleurisy, and oral ulcers. Renal disease and neurologic complications occur commonly.

The eye is involved in 50% of SLE patients through keratitis, scleritis, and rarely uveitis. The most common ocular manifestations are in the retina:

□ Cotton-wool spots form as a result of the microvascular disease (Fig IX-40)

□ Retinal arteriolitis and vascular occlusion may occur, resulting in ischemic retina and secondary retinal neovascularization and vitreous hemorrhage (Figs IX-41, IX-42)

□ The choroid can develop choroidal infarction, choroiditis, subretinal exudation, and choroidal neovascularization (Figs IX-43, IX-44)

It is important to separate these findings from the effects on the retina of SLE-induced hypertension and nephritis, which may result in arteriolar narrowing, retinal hemorrhage, and disc edema.

The diagnosis is made clinically by establishing the presence of 4 of 14 major symptoms, signs, and laboratory tests. A positive ANA, anemia, proteinuria, and urinary casts support the diagnosis. Treatment involves control of the underlying SLE through use of NSAIDs, corticosteroids, and immunosuppressive agents. The ischemic retina and proliferative changes that occur in SLE can be treated with panretinal photocoagulation. The presence of retinal vasculitis and neovascularization may indicate CNS involvement and an occult cerebral vasculitis.

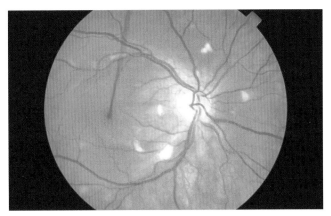

FIG IX-40—Systemic lupus erythematosus, multiple cotton-wool spots.

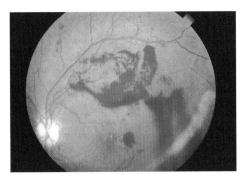

FIG IX-41—Ischemic retinal vasculitis and neovascularization in systemic lupus erythematosus.

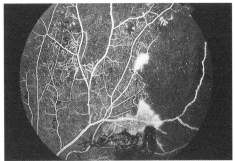

FIG IX-42—Fluorescein angiogram of the same patient showing capillary nonperfusion.

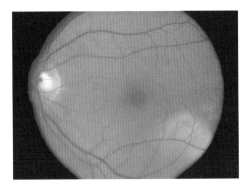

FIG IX-43—Multifocal choroiditis in SLE.

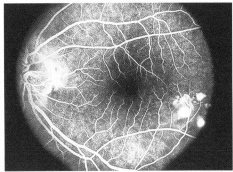

FIG IX-44—Fluorescein angiogram showing multifocal areas of hyperfluorescence.

Jabs DA, Hanneken AM, Schachat AP, et al. Choroidopathy in systemic lupus erythematosus. *Arch Ophthalmol.* 1988;106:230–234.

Vine AK, Barr CC. Proliferative lupus retinopathy. *Arch Ophthalmol.* 1984;102: 852–854.

Polyarteritis nodosa (PAN) This multisystemic disease is associated with a necrotizing vasculitis. The disease affects adults in the age 40–60 range. Immune complexes are found deposited within the walls of medium to small-sized arterioles, and an autoimmune response is the postulated disease mechanism. Patients with PAN note fatigue, fever, weight loss, and arthralgia. The heart, kidneys, liver, GI tract, and CNS are affected by the multifocal necrotizing vasculitis. The disease has serious and potentially fatal complications related to renal and CNS injury.

The eye is involved in 20% of cases. Scleritis, iritis, and vitritis can be present, and the most common findings are retinal vasculitis, cotton-wool spots, and retinal hemorrhages (Fig IX-45). Central retinal artery occlusion and optic atrophy may also be noted.

PAN should be considered in the differential diagnosis of any patient presenting with multiple systemic complaints and retinal vasculitis, specifically a necrotizing arteriolitis. Tissue biopsy confirms the diagnosis. Without treatment the disease has a 5-year mortality rate of 90%. Corticosteroids reduce this rate to 50%. Appropriate systemic immunosuppression with cyclophosphamide results in a 5-year survival rate of 80% and resolution of the retinal vasculitis.

Akova YA, Jabbur NS, Foster CS. Ocular presentation of polyarteritis nodosa: clinical course and management with steroid and cytotoxic therapy. *Ophthalmology.* 1993; 100:1775–1781.

Wegener granulomatosis This multisystemic autoimmune disorder results in a granulomatous necrotizing vasculitis. The disease is uncommon and may occur between the ages of 8 and 80 years. It characteristically affects the upper and lower

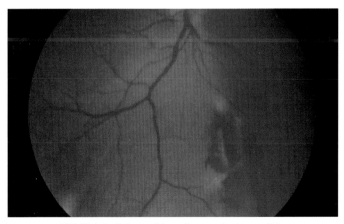

FIG IX-45—Polyarteritis nodosa, retinal vasculitis.

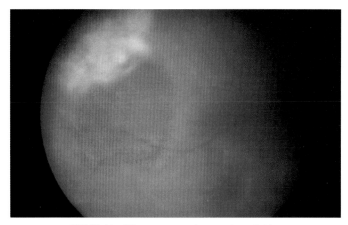

FIG IX-46—Wegener granulomatosis, retinitis.

respiratory tract: sinusitis, epistaxis, cough, saddle-nose deformity, and renal disease are systemic manifestations.

The eye is involved in 50% of cases with proptosis, orbital pseudotumor, and scleritis. Posterior scleritis may cause visual loss and ocular pain with exudative retinal detachment. Retinal vasculitis and true retinitis have been reported in 8%–18% of patients with Wegener granulomatosis (Fig IX-46).

Tissue biopsy establishes the histologic diagnosis. Antineutrophilic cytoplasmic antibodies (ANCA) are detected in this disease, and this test is useful in patients presenting with retinal vasculitis and respiratory complaints. Treatment includes oral corticosteroid and immunosuppressive regimens. Without therapy the 1-year mortality rate is 80%. With cyclophosphamide and corticosteroid treatment 90% of patients attain complete remission and resolution of the ocular manifestations.

Bullen CL, Liesegang TJ, McDonald TJ, et al. Ocular complications of Wegener's granulomatosis. *Ophthalmology.* 1983;90:279–290.

Retinochoroidopathies

Retinochoroidopathies are conditions of unknown etiology that have a common presentation and characteristic clinical picture including inflammation of the RPE, choroid, and choriocapillaris. Common symptoms include blurred vision and scotomata. Anterior segment inflammation is usually absent, and vitreous cellular reaction is usually minimal. During the early stages, single or multiple white, yellow, or gray areas appear deep to the retina. Later, pigment may be deposited at the periphery of the lesions (Table IX-2). The diagnosis is one of exclusion, ruling out infectious causes of multifocal choroiditis. Fluorescein angiography may be helpful in the diagnosis, showing early blockage of fluorescence as well as late leakage in the areas of choroiditis.

TABLE IX-2

WHITE DOT SYNDROMES

	AGE	SEX	PATH-OLOGY	LATER-ALITY	SIZE	MORPHO-LOGY	LOCATION	COLOR	A/C	VIT	FA	EOG	ERG	PROG-NOSIS	ETIOLOGY	TREATMENT
ARPE	29 (16–40)	=	RPE	75% Uni	Small	⊙	Macula	Black Halo	–	–	No leak ⊙	→	↑	Good	Virus?	None
MEWDS	26 (14–47)	F>M (4:1)	RPE Retina	80% Uni	100–200 μm	Granular Macula	Perifoveal	White	–	+	Early "Wreath"	→	→	Recover	Virus 50%	None
OHS	41 (20–50)	=	C-R	62% Bi	200–700 μm	Punched out	Triad	White Green	–	–	Stain SRNVM	OK	OK	Variable	Histoplasmosis	Laser Steroids
PIC	27	F	Choroid	Bi	100–300 μm	Discrete	Posterior pole	Yellow pigment scar	–	–/+	Block Stain	OK	OK	Poor if SRNVM	? Myopia	Steroids
MCP	33	F>M (3:1)	Choroid RPE	80% Bi	50–350 μm	Punched out	Multifocal	Yellow pigment ring	52%	98%	Early Stain		↑↓	Poor	EBV?	Steroids Acyclovir?
SFU	(14–34)	F 100%	Subret	Bi	Large Small	Stellate Fibrous	Multifocal	White Yellow	–/+	+	Black Stain	→	→	Poor	B Cell	Immuno-suppressives/steroids Acyclovir
Birdshot	50 (35–70)	M:F (1:2)	Choroid RPE	Bi	100–300 μm	Ovoid	Posterior equator	Creamy, no pigment	30%	100%	Vessel Leak Mac/ON		→	Chronic	S-Ag CMI	CSA
APMPPE	29	=	RPE Choroid	Bi	Large	Placoid	Posterior pole	White Scar	+	50%	Block Stain	→	→	80% Good	50% Viral	None Steroids
Serpig-inous	45	=	Choroid RPE	Bi	Large	Serpig-inous	Disc Macula	Yellow Gravy	–	30%	Loss of chorio-capillaris	→		Poor	?	None Immuno-suppressives

⊙ = bull's-eye lesion

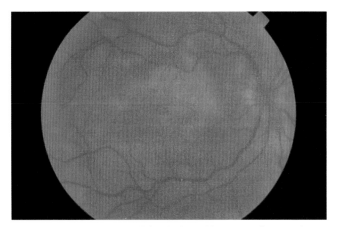

FIG IX-47—APMPPE, multifocal placoid lesions in the macula.

Acute posterior multifocal placoid pigment epitheliopathy (APMPPE) This uncommon condition is believed to follow a prodromal influenza-like illness in adolescents and young adults. Controversy exists whether APMPPE is a result of primary disease of pigment epithelium or is caused by obstruction of choroidal circulation with secondary pigment epithelial reaction. Patients complain of decreased vision. Characteristically, there is minimal anterior segment inflammation. Vitreous cells and disc edema may occur along with multiple cream-colored, plaquelike, homogeneous lesions beneath the retina, probably at the level of the pigment epithelium or choriocapillaris. These lesions are usually 1 disc diameter or less in size but may be confluent, and the margins are slightly blurred (Fig IX-47). Over 2–6 weeks, the lesions fade, leaving a permanent geographic-shaped alteration in the pigment epithelium, which consists of alternate depigmentation and pigment clumping. Rarely, cerebral vasculitis may cause associated life-threatening complications.

Diagnosis of APMPPE is made by the characteristic clinical presentation, especially if preceded by a viral-like systemic illness. In the acute state fluorescein angiography shows initial blockage of choroidal flush by the placoid lesions and a late hyperfluorescent staining (Figs IX-48, IX-49). The differential diagnosis includes serpiginous (geographic) choroidopathy. APMPPE is an acute, usually nonrecurrent, disease; serpiginous choroidopathy is insidious and relentlessly progressive. A variant of APMPPE may have features of both diseases, being chronic or recurrent with progressive destruction of the retina and loss of central acuity.

There is no evidence that corticosteroids or any other medications are beneficial. Most patients recover normal visual acuity of 20/40 or better over a period of weeks to months. However, if the fovea is involved, visual acuity may remain at the 20/200 level.

Williams DF, Mieler WF. Long-term follow-up of acute multifocal posterior placoid pigment epitheliopathy. *Br J Ophthalmol.* 1989;73:985–990.

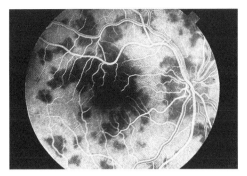

FIG IX-48—APMPPE, fluorescein angiogram showing early blocking of the choroidal circulation.

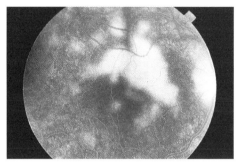

FIG IX-49—APMPPE, late-phase angiogram showing staining.

Acute retinal pigment epitheliitis (ARPE) ARPE, or Krill disease, is an acute self-limiting inflammation of the RPE. The etiology is unknown. ARPE generally occurs between the ages of 16 and 40 years. Patients are otherwise healthy and complain of a sudden unilateral loss of central acuity. Fundus examination shows subtle small hyperpigmented lesions at the level of the RPE (Figs IX-50, IX-51). Two to four clusters of two to six "dots" appear in the posterior pole. Fluorescein angiography demonstrates a "target" or "honeycomb" pattern with hyperpigmented centers and a halo of hyperfluorescence around each lesion. No treatment is required, as the visual symptoms and retinal lesions subside over 6–12 weeks.

Lewis H, Lozano-Rechy D. Retinal pigment epithelial inflammations. In: Nozik RA, Michelson JB. *Ophthalmol Clin North Am.* 1993;6(1):97–108.

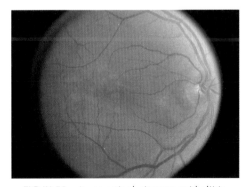

FIG IX-50—Acute retinal pigment epitheliitis.

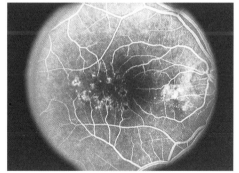

FIG IX-51—Fluorescein angiogram in ARPE showing "honeycomb" lesions at the level of the RPE.

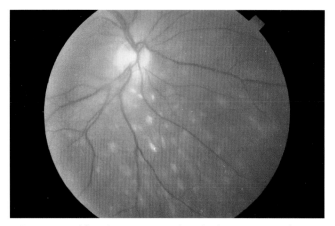

FIG IX-52—Birdshot chorioretinitis with multiple postequatorial cream-colored, ovoid lesions.

Birdshot retinochoroidopathy (vitiliginous chorioretinitis) This uncommon condition occurs in adults past the fourth decade of life, females more than males. Decreased vision, nyctalopia, and disturbance of color vision are the primary symptoms. Anterior segment inflammation may be minimal or lacking. Cells and strands are present in the vitreous. Multifocal postequatorial cream-colored or depigmented spots scattered throughout the fundus, as if the fundus had been hit by "birdshot from a shotgun," are characteristic (Fig IX-52). The spots appear to be at the level of the pigment epithelium. Attenuated and sheathed retinal vessels are present in some patients. Disc edema, optic atrophy, narrowing of retinal vasculature, cystoid macular edema, and surface-wrinkling retinopathy may be present.

The diagnosis is suggested by retinal vascular leakage on fluorescein angiography with pronounced perifoveal capillary leakage and cystoid macular edema (Figs IX-53, IX-54). The electroretinogram (ERG) is reduced or extinguished. Optic

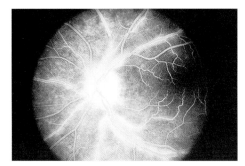

FIG IX-53—Fluorescein angiogram showing diffuse retinal phlebitis.

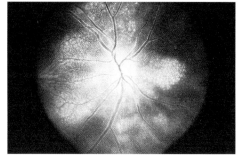

FIG IX-54—Fluorescein angiogram showing cystoid retinal edema in birdshot chorioretinitis.

nerve edema is present in some cases, and subretinal choroidal neovascularization may occur. HLA-A29 has been detected in 80%–96% of patients, in contrast to the incidence of HLA-A29 in the unafffected population, which is approximately 7%.

Birdshot retinochoroidopathy characteristically responds poorly or incompletely to oral NSAIDs, corticosteroids, and second-generation immunosuppressive agents. Periocular steroids can assist in controlling CME, and the disease appears to respond favorably to cyclosporine preparations. Dosages ranging from 2 to 5 mg/kg/day are associated with resolution of the vitreous inflammatory cells and retinal edema and can stabilize the development of new retinal lesions. Birdshot retinochoroidopathy is a chronic disease with exacerbations and remissions. Some patients experience eventual optic atrophy or cystoid macular degeneration; others maintain or recover good vision. Epiretinal membranes are not uncommon.

Bloch-Michel E, Frau E. Birdshot retinochoroidopathy and HLA-A29+ and HLA-A29– idiopathic retinal vasculitis: comparative study of 56 cases. *Can J Ophthalmol.* 1991; 26:361–366.

Brucker AJ, Deglin EA, Bene C, et al. Subretinal choroidal neovascularization in birdshot retinochoroidopathy. *Am J Ophthalmol.* 1985;99:40–44.

Nussenblatt RB, Mittal KK, Ryan S, et al. Birdshot retinochoroidopathy associated with HLA-A29 antigen and immune responsiveness to retinal S-antigen. *Am J Ophthalmol.* 1982;94:147–158.

Multiple evanescent white dot syndrome (MEWDS) This idiopathic inflammatory condition of the retina occurs in women (90%) between the ages of 14 and 47 years. Patients typically complain of a unilateral (80%) decrease in visual acuity. Fundus examination shows multiple small (100–200 μm) outer retinal white dots in the posterior pole (Fig IX-55). A pathognomonic "granular" appearance is noted in the macula in the acute phase of the disease. Fluorescein angiography demonstrates late staining of the lesions in a "wreathlike" distribution in the posterior pole (Fig IX-56). Rarely, MEWDS can be recurrent.

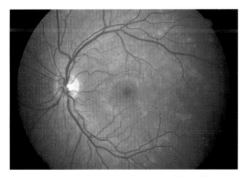

FIG IX-55—Multiple evanescent white dot syndrome (MEWDS).

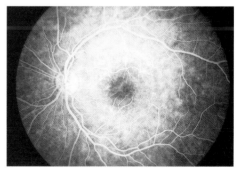

FIG IX-56—Fluorescein angiogram showing "wreath sign."

MEWDS has been associated with *acute macular neuroretinopathy (AMN)* and the prolonged enlargement of the blind spot syndrome. AMN is a rare disorder causing paracentral scotomata and a characteristic reddish brown, wedge-shaped lesion in the macula. In the syndrome of prolonged enlargement of the blind spot, patients note a scotoma and on visual field testing show an enlargement of the physiologic blind spot. Treatment is not required, as recovery occurs over a 7-week period.

Gass JD, Hamed LM. Acute macular neuroretinopathy and multiple evanescent white dot syndrome occurring in the same patients. *Arch Ophthalmol.* 1989;107:189–193.

Jampol LM, Sieving PA, Pugh D, et al. Multiple evanescent white dot syndrome. I. Clinical findings. *Arch Ophthalmol.* 1984;102:671–674.

Punctate inner choroiditis (PIC)   PIC is an idiopathic inflammatory disorder of the choroid that typically occurs in myopic women between the ages of 18 and 37. Patients with PIC note a bilateral loss of central acuity. Cells are absent in the vitreous, but small (100–300 μm) punctate yellow inner choroidal lesions are found in the posterior pole (Fig IX-57). The lesions block early and stain late on the fluorescein angiogram (Figs IX-58, IX-59). Mild cases can be observed, as the disease clears in 4–6 weeks. Oral and regional corticosteroids have been used without adverse effect in these patients. Subretinal neovascular membranes can develop in the areas of choroiditis.

Watzke RC, Packer AJ, Folk JC, et al. Punctate inner choroidopathy. *Am J Ophthalmol.* 1984;98:572–584.

Serpiginous choroidopathy   This geographic or helicoid choroidopathy is uncommon, affecting adults in the fourth to sixth decades of life. Blurred vision is the primary symptom. The vitreous varies from clear to mildly cellular. A serpiginous (pseudopodial) or geographic (maplike) pattern of scars may present in the posterior fundus. The edges of these lesions may be active, with yellow-gray and edematous appearance (Fig IX-60). As active areas become atrophic over weeks to months, new lesions can occur elsewhere or contiguously in a snakelike pattern. Occasionally,

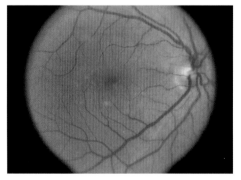

FIG IX-57—Punctate inner choroiditis.

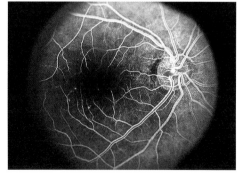

FIG IX-58—PIC, fluorescein angiogram showing blocked fluorescence early in the study.

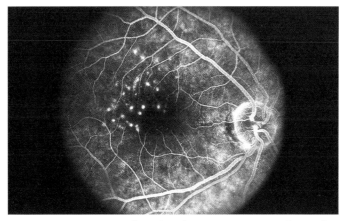

FIG IX-59—Punctate inner choroiditis, fluorescein angiogram showing late hyperfluorescence.

vascular sheathing is reported along with RPE detachment and neovascularization of the disc.

Diagnosis is suggested by the characteristic clinical picture and indolent course. Fluorescein angiography shows initial blockage of choroidal flush by the areas of active disease (Fig IX-61). When the disease is inactive, the affected pigmented areas transmit fluorescein but do not stain. Some cases appear inflammatory, while others appear atrophic.

Corticosteroids and even immunosuppressives have been advocated, but there is no good evidence that they alter the course of the disease. Sub-Tenon's corticosteroids, oral cyclosporine, and oral acyclovir have been advocated for macula-threatening disease. Relentless progression of the disease may occur despite aggressive therapies. Photocoagulation at the border of the lesions has been unsuccessful in halting the progression. If the macula is involved, central visual acuity will be

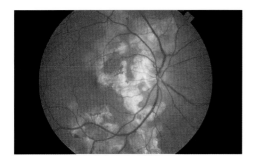

FIG IX-60—Serpiginous choroiditis.

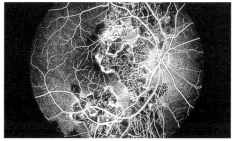

FIG IX-61—Fluorescein angiogram shows blocked fluorescence in the area of active disease.

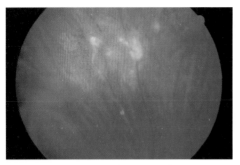

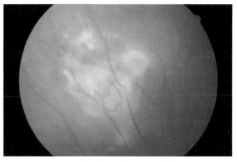

FIG IX-62—Subretinal fibrosis and uveitis syndrome, fundus photograph showing multifocal white subretinal lesions.

FIG IX-63—SFU, fundus photograph from the same patient showing progressive subretinal fibrosis.

impaired. If the usual centrifugal movement of the lesions from disc to periphery bypasses the macula, the prognosis tends to be good. Choroidal neovascularization may rarely occur.

> Wojno T, Meredith TA. Unusual findings in serpiginous choroiditis. *Am J Ophthalmol.* 1982;94:650–655.

Subretinal fibrosis and uveitis syndrome (SFU) This panuveitis affects predominantly women between the ages of 14 and 34 years. The etiology remains unknown. Histopathology from chorioretinal biopsy demonstrates primarily B cells and plasma cells. Patients are otherwise healthy and note a bilateral decrease of visual acuity. Early in the disease patients present with a bilateral vitritis and a multifocal choroiditis. Later in the course, the choroidal lesions evolve into large stellate subretinal fibrotic lesions (Figs IX-62, IX-63). SFU responds poorly to most forms of treatment, and the visual prognosis is poor. Steroids and immunosuppressive agents have been used with little success (Figs IX-64, IX-65).

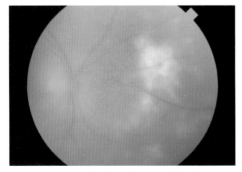

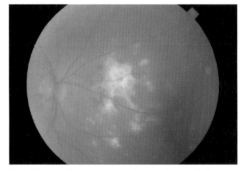

FIG IX-64—SFU, fundus photograph before treatment.

FIG IX-65—Same patient in remission following immunosupressive therapy.

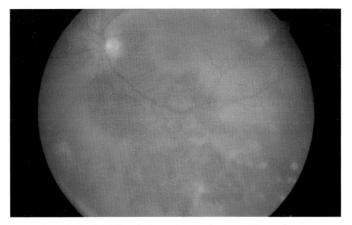

FIG IX-66—Multifocal choroiditis and panuveitis syndrome.

Kim MK, Chan CC, Belfort R Jr, et al. Histopathologic and immunohistopathologic features of the subretinal fibrosis and uveitis syndrome. *Am J Ophthalmol.* 1987; 104:15–23.

Multifocal choroiditis and panuveitis syndrome (MCP)   MCP is an idiopathic inflammation of the choroid, retina, and vitreous more often noted in women. The etiology is unknown. Patients present with a bilateral vitritis (82%) and a multifocal choroiditis. The lesions are small (50–350 μm) and yellowish when active (Fig IX-66). Peripapillary pigment scarring that resembles histoplasmosis scars appears. Macular lesions may be associated with subretinal neovascular membranes.

The diagnosis is one of exclusion, as many other conditions may cause a multifocal choroiditis and panuveitis. Sarcoidosis, syphilis, tuberculosis, and other white dot syndromes of the retina need to be considered (see Table IX-2, p 167). Oral or regional corticosteroids help control the choroidal and vitreous inflammation. The disease is often chronic, and macular function may be impaired by CME or subretinal neovascularization.

Dreyer RF, Gass JD. Multifocal choroiditis and panuveitis: a syndrome that mimics ocular histoplasmosis. *Arch Ophthalmol.* 1984;102:1776–1784.

Masquerade Conditions

Endophthalmitis

Nocardia asteroides   Although ocular involvement with *Nocardia asteroides* is rare, ocular disease may be the presenting complaint in this potentially lethal but treatable systemic disease characterized by pneumonia and disseminated abscesses. Ocular involvement occurs by hematogenous spread. Choroidal abscess in heart transplant patients has been described. The organism that is responsible is commonly found in soil, and initial infection is by ingestion or inhalation. Symptoms of ocular infection caused by *N asteroides* may vary from the mild pain and redness of iridocyclitis to severe pain and decreased vision or panophthalmitis. Findings range from an isolated unilateral chorioretinal mass with minimal vitritis to diffuse iridocyclitis with flare and cells, vitritis, and multiple choroidal abscesses with overlying retinal detachment.

Diagnosis of this condition can be established with a culture of the organism taken from tissue or fluid, vitreous aspiration for Gram stain and culture, or occasionally, by enucleation and identification of organisms microscopically. Treatment of systemic *N asteroides* infection is systemic sulfonamide for 6 weeks in immunologically competent patients and up to 1 year in immunosuppressed patients.

CHAPTER X

Panuveitis

Many systemic entities associated with uveitis are likely to cause diffuse inflammation, leading to concomitant iridocyclitis and posterior uveitis. These include tuberculosis, the "great imitator," and spirochetal diseases such as syphilis, the "great masquerader," as well as sarcoidosis, sympathetic ophthalmia, and Vogt-Koyanagi-Harada syndrome. Many cases of Behçet syndrome, JRA, lens-associated uveitis, and severe cases of toxoplasmosis or toxocariasis could also be considered panuveitides. These diseases have also been discussed in earlier chapters in the context of anterior or posterior uveitis; see chapters VII and IX. BCSC Section 1, *Update on General Medicine,* also discusses syphilis, tuberculosis, and Lyme disease.

Although *panuveitis,* or *diffuse uveitis,* may originate as an iritis or as a choroiditis, usually these syndromes eventually involve all of the uvea as well as other major ocular structures including the cornea, trabecular meshwork, sclera, or optic nerve. Generally, panuveitis is bilateral, although one eye may present first and the severity is not necessarily symmetric.

Infectious Diseases

Bacterial Disease

Syphilis   This sexually transmitted or bloodborne bacterial infection is associated with multiple ocular manifestations. The disease is caused by *Treponema pallidum,* a highly coiled, helical bacterium with a long, 30-hour replication cycle. The incidence of syphilis is increasing. Syphilis accounts for 1%–3% of all uveitis cases; 5%–10% of all patients with secondary syphilis develop uveitis. The disease is one of the great masqueraders in medicine and must be considered as a possible etiology in all cases of uveitis.

Syphilitic uveitis is one of the few types of uveitis that can be cured, even in patients with AIDS. Delay in diagnosis of syphilitic chorioretinitis can lead to permanent visual loss that might have been avoided with early treatment. Syphilis can affect individuals from any socioeconomic group, especially those with active sex lives with many different partners and patients with AIDS.

Congenital syphilis. Keratouveitis from acute interstitial keratitis occurs in congenital syphilis between the ages of 5 and 25 years (Fig X-1). It is believed to be an allergic response to *T pallidum* in the cornea. Symptoms are intense pain and photophobia, and signs include a diffusely opaque cornea with vision reduced, even to light perception. Blood vessels invade the cornea, and when they meet in the center of the cornea after several months, the inflammation subsides and the cornea partially clears. Late stages show deep ghost (nonperfused) stromal vessels and opacities. The iritis accompanying interstitial keratitis is difficult to observe because of corneal haze; however, evidence of it is seen in secondary guttata and hyaline strands projecting into the angle. Glaucoma may also occur.

Congenital syphilis may also result in a bilateral salt-and-pepper fundus, which may affect the peripheral retina, the posterior pole, or a single quadrant. The changes

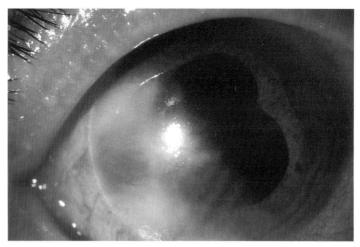

FIG X-1—Active syphilitic interstitial keratitis.

are not progressive and may be associated with normal vision. Less commonly described variant signs associated with congenital disease include a bilateral secondary degeneration of pigment epithelium, with narrowing of vessels of the choroid and retina, and a pale optic disc with sharp margins and morphologically variable deposits of pigment. These findings may mimic retinitis pigmentosa.

Secondary syphilis. Secondary syphilis, occurring 6 weeks to 6 months after primary disease, is characterized by skin rash involving the palms and soles, fever, weight loss, and arthralgias. Ocular involvement may present with pain, redness, and photophobia or with blurred vision and floaters. A granulomatous or nongranulomatous anterior uveitis may be present. The iritis can be associated with iris roseola, vascularized papules (iris papulosa), larger yellow-red nodules (iris nodosa), and gummata. Focal or multifocal choroiditis can be seen during this stage, and exudates may appear around the disc and along the retinal arterioles. Arteritis and a perivasculitis may occur along with ill-defined areas of retinitis and exudative retinal detachments (Fig X-2). In the later stages of secondary syphilis, extensive gliosis, atrophy, and pigment proliferation are present (Fig X-3). The clinical picture may resemble retinitis pigmentosa. Neuroretinitis with papillitis and periarterial sheathing also occur.

Syphilis patients with immunosuppression or AIDS often have atypical or more fulminant ocular disease patterns. Optic neuritis and neuroretinitis are more common as an initial presentation in these patients, and disease recurrences are noted even after appropriate antibacterial therapy.

Diagnosis. Syphilis is diagnosed on the basis of a positive serology. The nontreponemal tests such as the Venereal Disease Research Laboratory (VDRL) or rapid plasma reagin (RPR) alone are insufficient, and a treponemal test such as the fluorescent treponemal antibody absorption (FTA-ABS) or the microhemagglutination assay–*T pallidum* (MHA-TP) must be obtained. A positive VDRL or RPR indicates

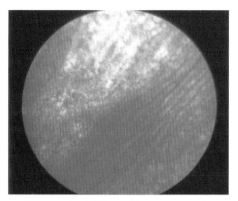

FIG X-2—Syphilitic uveitis, acute retinitis.

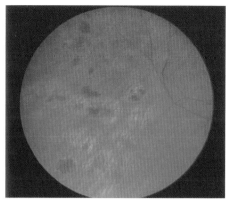

FIG X-3—Treated syphilitic uveitis. Note pigment proliferation.

active disease and exposure to the bacteria. Both the VDRL and RPR return to normal with effective therapy. In patients with uveitis and positive serology, asymptomatic neurosyphilis must be ruled out by a lumbar puncture. Any patient with syphilitic uveitis should have a spinal fluid examination.

In latent syphilis VDRL and FTA-ABS are positive; cerebrospinal fluid (CSF) is negative. In tertiary syphilis or in neurosyphilis the CSF serology and the serum FTA-ABS are positive, but the serum VDRL may be low or negative. The presenting ocular complaint is usually blurred vision. Gumma of the iris and Argyll Robertson pupil are both characteristic in this stage of the disease (see BCSC Section 5, *Neuro-Ophthalmology,* for description of this sign). Posterior pole lesions may develop in the late secondary stages of syphilis, but the presence of chorioretinitis usually indicates CSF involvement or neurosyphilis. Half of these lesions are bilateral, and the signs involve midzonal choroiditis. Vitreous haze, flame-shaped hemorrhages with fibrosis, and chorioretinal atrophy develop during the progress of inflammation (Fig X-4). Diffuse neuroretinitis with papillitis and periarterial sheathing may also occur.

Treatment. Once a diagnosis of syphilitic chorioretinitis has been established, systemic therapy is indicated. Different therapeutic regimens are used for ocular syphilis. Results of CSF serologic tests, protein, and cell count are important in determining the amount and duration of therapy. Ocular inflammation secondary to syphilis should be regarded and treated as neurosyphilis, because of its anatomic and embryologic development with the CNS and the analogous blood–ocular barrier. The only proven effective therapy for this form of syphilis in both normal and immunocompromised patients is

☐ Penicillin G, 2–5 million units IV every 4 hours for 10–14 days, or

☐ Penicillin G procaine, 2–4 million units given IM every day with probenicid, 500 mg every 4 hours for 10–14 days

Patients with penicillin allergy may be treated with doxycycline 200 mg PO b.i.d or erythromycin 500 mg PO q.i.d. for 15 days.

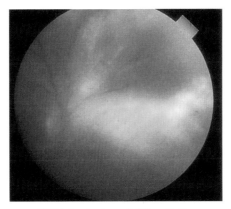

FIG X-4—Acute syphilitic retinitis.

Once effective antibiotic therapy has started, ocular inflammation typically subsides. Topical, regional, or oral corticosteroids may be used to quiet anterior or posterior segment inflammation. Follow-up for patients with chorioretinitis and abnormal CSF requires spinal fluid examination every 6 months until cell count, protein, and VDRL return to normal.

Gass JD, Braunstein RA, Chenoweth RG. Acute syphilitic posterior placoid chorioretinitis. *Ophthalmology.* 1990;97:1288–1297.

Hart G. Syphilis tests in diagnostic and therapeutic decision making. *Ann Intern Med.* 1986;104:368–376.

McLeish WM, Pulido JS, Holland S, et al. The ocular manifestations of syphilis in human immunodeficiency virus type 1–infected host. *Ophthalmology.* 1990;97:196–203.

Passo MS, Rosenbaum JT. Ocular syphilis in patients with human immunodeficiency virus infection. *Am J Ophthalmol.* 1988;106:1–6.

Tamesis RR, Foster CS. Ocular syphilis. *Ophthalmology.* 1990;97:1281–1287.

Lyme disease   Lyme disease is a tick-borne spirochetal illness caused by *Borrelia burgdorferi.* Animal reservoirs for *B burgdorferi* include rodents, deer, birds, cats, and dogs. The spirochete is transmitted to humans through the bite of a tick, *Ixodes dammini* (eastern United States) or *Ixodes pacificus* (western United States). Spirochetemia follows the tick bite. Lyme disease is the most prevalent vector-borne illness in the United States, with seasonal outbreaks, especially in early summer and midautumn.

The clinical manifestations of Lyme disease have been divided into three stages:

□ *Stage I,* occurring during the first month after infection, is characterized by skin, eye, and constitutional symptoms. Erythema chronicum migrans, an elevated annular erythematous skin lesion with central clearing, can occur at the site of the tick bite (Figs X-5, X-6). Follicular conjunctivitis may be present, and headache, stiff neck, malaise, myalgias, arthralgias, and fever may occur.

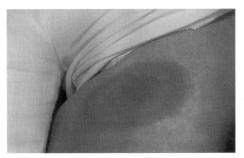

FIG X-5—Erythema chronicum migrans: a single dense erythematous lesion. (Photograph courtesy of Alan B. MacDonald, MD.)

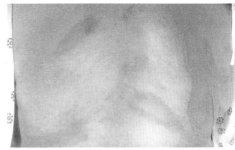

FIG X-6—Erythema chronicum migrans: multiple bull's-eye lesions. (Photograph courtesy of Alan B. MacDonald, MD.)

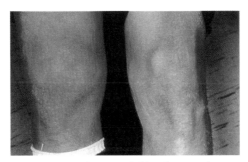

FIG X-7—Lyme disease arthritis. (Photograph courtesy of Alan B. MacDonald, MD.)

☐ *Stage II,* 1–4 months after infection, can be manifested by neurologic abnormalities and musculoskeletal disease, as well as by cardiac and ocular involvement. Neurologic disease, which occurs in 30%–40% of patients, can take the form of Bell's palsy, encephalitis, or meningitis. Musculoskeletal disease, arthritis, tendinitis, and joint effusions can be present at this stage (Fig X-7). Myocarditis or heart block appears in 8% of patients. Ocular manifestations in stage II Lyme disease include keratitis, iritis, intermediate uveitis, vitritis, panophthalmitis, and optic neuritis (Figs X-8, X-9).

☐ *Stage III,* with onset 5 months or more after infection, is characterized by chronic atrophic skin changes, keratitis, chronic meningitis, chronic arthritis, and adult respiratory distress syndrome.

Ocular involvement in Lyme disease occurs during all stages. An early sign is follicular conjunctivitis that is morphologically similar to that caused by other mechanisms (see BCSC Section 8, *External Disease and Cornea,* for further discussion and

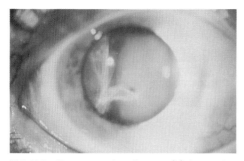 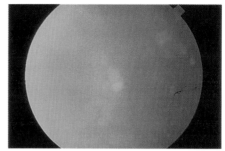

FIG X-8—Dense anterior vitreous debris causing floaters and blurring in ocular Lyme disease. (Photograph courtesy of William W. Culbertson, MD.)

FIG X-9—Grade III vitreous opacification in Lyme vitritis, as seen by indirect ophthalmoscopy, is reminiscent of severe pars planitis. (Photograph courtesy of John D. Sheppard Jr., MD.)

illustrations). The most characteristic intraocular manifestation of Lyme disease appears to be a chronic iridocyclitis and vitritis. Some cases of intermediate uveitis may be caused by *B burgdorferi.*

Laboratory diagnosis of Lyme disease is suboptimal with a high frequency of both false-positive and false-negative results. Lyme immunofluorescent antibody titer (IFA), ELISA for IgM and IgG, and Western blot testing should be ordered.

Because many cases of recalcitrant CNS Lyme disease have been well documented, antibiotic therapy of suspected Lyme disease should be aggressive. It is far easier to eradicate Lyme disease in its earlier stages with an oral course of antibiotic therapy alone than it is to eradicate established CNS disease even with long-term IV antibiotics such as ceftriaxone. A patient with intraocular involvement from Lyme disease must be considered to have CNS infection.

Recommended therapy for early Lyme disease consists of tetracycline, erythromycin, or penicillin. Duration of therapy is determined by clinical response. At present, IV ceftriaxone or penicillin is advised for neurologic or neuro-ophthalmologic Lyme disease.

Aaberg TM. The expanding ophthalmologic spectrum of Lyme disease. *Am J Ophthalmol.* 1989;107:77–80.

Winterkorn JM. Lyme disease: neurologic and ophthalmic manifestations. *Surv Ophthalmol.* 1990;35:191–204.

Winward KE, Smith JL, Culbertson WW, et al. Ocular Lyme borreliosis. *Am J Ophthalmol.* 1989;108:651–657.

Leptospirosis The spirochete responsible for leptospirosis is commonly found around sewer water, rats, and urine. There are 170 serotypes of pathogenic bacteria in this genus. The disease is a zoonosis that humans acquire through exposure to secretions from infected animals. Plumbers and sewer workers are at increased risk.

Leptospira gain access to humans through breaks in the skin or mucous membranes. The leptospiremia results in dissemination of the bacteria throughout the body, including the eye. Systemic manifestations include headache, chills, fever, and muscle ache. Kidney and liver disease are common, resulting in jaundice and azotemia. Ocular manifestations include both anterior and posterior uveitis.

A high degree of clinical suspicion assists in the diagnosis. Medically unresponsive uveitis in a patient with systemic illness and a history of exposure to contaminated water or sick animals should prompt laboratory testing for leptospirosis antibodies. Leptospirosis may cause a positive RPR or FTA-ABS. Penicillin, 2.4–3.6 million units/day given IV; and tetracyline, 2 g/day PO in four divided doses, have been used to treat this disease.

Rathinam SR, Rathnam S, Selvaraj S, et al. Uveitis associated with an epidemic outbreak of leptospirosis. *Am J Ophthalmol.* 1997;124:71–79.

Tuberculosis Once considered the most common cause of uveitis, tuberculous ocular disease is now rarely found in clinics in the United States. Recently, however, the incidence of pulmonary and extrapulmonary tuberculosis has increased, in part because of the spread of AIDS. The incidence of tuberculous uveitis may vary from one location to another, and certain populations are at greater risk:

- Health care professionals
- Recent immigrants from endemic areas
- Immunosuppressed patients
- Indigent populations

These demographics must be taken into consideration in establishing a differential diagnosis that includes ocular tuberculosis.

The tuberculosis bacillus is highly aerobic with an affinity for highly oxygenated tissues. Thus, tuberculous lesions frequently appear in the apices of the lungs as well as in the choroid, which has the highest blood flow rate in the body.

Both direct infection and delayed hypersensitivity reactions have been implicated in the pathogenesis of tuberculous uveitis. Mycobacterial cell wall components are potent immunoadjuvants, used experimentally, for instance, in Freund's complete adjuvant. Both granulomatous and nongranulomatous anterior uveitis with or without keratitis have been ascribed to tuberculosis. Yellow-white nodules in the choroid, ranging in size from 1/6 to 2 disc diameters with indistinct borders, may be present in association with miliary tuberculosis (Fig X-10). Other manifestations include

- Larger, solitary masses several disc diameters in size
- Retinal vasculitis, especially periphlebitis
- Vascular occlusion
- Dense vitritis
- Papillitis

Typically, patients with chronic ocular tuberculosis have chronic iridocyclitis, with or without posterior segment disease. These patients experience a waxing-and-waning course with long-term degradation in the blood–aqueous barrier, accumulation of vitreous opacities, and cystoid macular edema (Figs X-11, X-12). Patients who follow an adequate regimen of antituberculous agents often improve gradually until they cease to have chronic recurrent iritis or acute exacerbations of their disease.

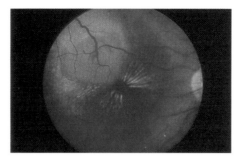

FIG X-10—Choroidal tubercle (miliary tuberculosis).

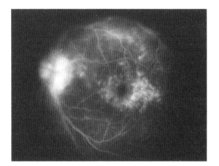

FIG X-11—Chronic tuberculous uveitis with disc edema, vasculitis, periphlebitis, and cystoid macular edema. (Photograph courtesy of John D. Sheppard Jr., MD.)

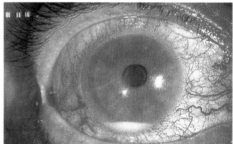

FIG X-12—Acute tuberculous uveitis with hypopyon, posterior synechiae, vitritis, retinal vasculitis, and cystoid macular edema. (Photograph courtesy of John D. Sheppard Jr., MD.)

A positive PPD or documented skin test conversion is useful in the diagnosis. Some patients have only second strength (250 TU, or tuberculin units) PPD positivity and yet are found histopathologically to have TB bacilli in their eyes. These patients may also have a normal chest x-ray. Thus, if the first strength (1 TU) and standard intermediate strength (5 TU) skin tests are negative, a second strength PPD may be important.

While interpreting positive tuberculin skin tests in standard or second strength, the clinician must also consider the possibility of atypical mycobacterial infection, which is particularly common among rural populations and patients who have lived on a farm. This possibility, of course, complicates the diagnosis of ocular tuberculosis. Moreover, false-positive PPDs may be seen in patients born overseas who might have received a BCG childhood vaccination and in patients with bladder carcinoma who have been treated with intraluminal BCG injections.

Antibiotic therapy is clearly called for in patients with uveitis, a recently converted TB skin test, a positive chest x-ray, and positive bacterial cultures. Multiple-agent therapy is suggested because of the increasing incidence of resistance to isoniazid as well as compliance problems associated with long-term therapy. The extremely slow growth rate of TB contributes to the acquisition of drug resistance. Populations at particularly high risk for resistant organisms, now known as *multidrug-resistant tuberculosis (MDRTB),* require three or more agents, such as isoniazid, rifampin, and pyrazinamide. MDRTB is found in previously noncompliant patients on single-agent therapy, migrant or indigent populations, immunocompromised patients, and recent immigrants from countries in which isoniazid and rifampin are available over the counter. The clinician may welcome the assistance of an infectious disease specialist or pulmonologist in treating these patients.

Less clear is the management approach to a patient with a diagnosis of possible or probable tuberculosis and uveitis. These patients are culture negative and have a normal chest x-ray. A diagnosis of extrapulmonary tuberculosis may be entertained in the setting of medically unresponsive uveitis and a recent TB skin test conversion. Serum lysozyme and angiotensin converting enzyme (ACE) levels may be elevated, supporting the clinical impression.

Corticosteroids are often necessary in conjunction with antimicrobial therapy. Because steroids administered without concomitant antituberculous agents may lead to progressive worsening of tuberculous ocular disease, any patient who may have tuberculous disease should be evaluated with skin testing before institution of intensive steroid therapy. Often, patients given topical steroids for what turns out to be tuberculous iritis may improve temporarily, only to worsen severely in the long run (Fig X-13).

Barnes PF, Bloch AB, Davidson PT, et al. Tuberculosis in patients with human immunodeficiency virus infection. *N Engl J Med.* 1991;324:1644–1650.

Psilas K, Aspiotis M, Petroutsos G, et al. Antituberculosis therapy in the treatment of peripheral uveitis. *Ann Ophthalmol.* 1991;23:254–258.

Rosenbaum JT, Wernick R. The utility of routine screening of patients with uveitis for systemic lupus erythematosus or tuberculosis. A Bayesian analysis. *Arch Ophthalmol.* 1990;108:1291–1293.

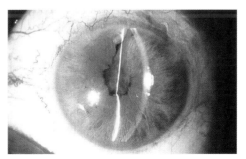

FIG X-13—Long-standing undiagnosed tuberculous uveitis with aphakia, dense pupillary membrane, posterior synechiae, CME, and chronic vitritis despite intensive steroid therapy. (Photograph courtesy of John D. Sheppard Jr., MD.)

Helminthic Diseases

Onchocerciasis   One of the leading causes of blindness in the world, onchocerciasis is endemic in many areas across Africa below the Sahara and in isolated foci in Central and South America. It is rarely seen or diagnosed in the United States. Worldwide, at least 18 million people are infected, and of these 1–2 million are blind. In hyperendemic areas everyone over the age of 15 will be infected and half will become blind before they die.

Humans are the only host for _Onchocerca volvulus,_ the filarial parasite that causes the disease. The infective larvae of _O volvulus_ are transmitted through the bite of female blackflies of the _Simulium_ genus. The flies breed in fast-flowing streams; hence the disease is commonly called _river blindness._ The larvae develop into mature adult worms that form subcutaneous nodules. The adult female releases millions of microfilariae that migrate throughout the body, particularly to the skin and the eye. Microfilariae probably reach the eye by multiple routes:

□ Direct invasion of the cornea from the conjunctiva

□ Penetration of the sclera both directly and through the vascular bundles

□ Possibly by hematogenous spread

Live microfilariae are usually well tolerated, but dead microfilariae initiate a focal inflammatory response.

Anterior segment signs of onchocerciasis are common. Microfilariae can be observed swimming freely in the anterior chamber. Live microfilariae can be seen in the cornea, while dead microfilariae cause a small stromal punctate inflammatory opacity that clears with time. Mild uveitis and limbitis are common, but severe anterior uveitis may occur and lead to synechiae, secondary glaucoma, and secondary cataract. Chorioretinal changes are common and vary widely in severity. Early disruption of the RPE is typical, with pigment dispersion and focal areas of atrophy. Later, severe chorioretinal atrophy occurs, predominantly in the posterior pole. Optic atrophy is common in advanced disease.

A diagnosis is made by the clinical appearance and history of exposure in an endemic area. The diagnosis is confirmed by finding microfilariae in small skin biopsies or in the eye. Ivermectin is the treatment of choice for onchocerciasis. Although not approved for sale in the United States, it is available on a compassionate basis for individual treatment. Ivermectin safely kills the microfilariae but does not have a permanent effect on the adult worms. A single oral dose of 150 µg/kg should be repeated annually, probably for 10 years or so. Topical corticosteroids can be used to control any anterior uveitis.

The former treatment, a course of diethylcarbamazine, was associated with many severe adverse reactions (Mazzotti reaction) caused by massive worm kill. It has now been totally replaced by ivermectin. Nodules containing adult worms can be removed surgically, but this approach will not usually cure the disease because many nodules are deeply buried and cannot be found.

Chan CC, Nussenblatt RB, Kim MK, et al. Immunopathology of ocular onchocerciasis. 2. Anti-retinal autoantibodies in serum and ocular fluids. _Ophthalmology._ 1987;94: 439–443.

Taylor HR, Trpis M, Cupp EW, et al. Ivermectin prophylaxis against experimental _Onchocerca volvulus_ infection in chimpanzees. _Am J Trop Med Hyg._ 1988;39:86–90.

FIG X-14—Sarcoidosis, histopathology of conjunctival biopsy. Note giant cells and granulomatous inflammation.

Immunologic and Granulomatous Diseases

Sarcoidosis

Sarcoidosis is a multisystem disease that primarily affects pulmonary function, although it is also capable of interfering with liver function and causing CNS disease. Sarcoidosis in the United States occurs 10 times more frequently among African Americans than among whites. While persons of all ages can be affected, occurrence is most common between the ages of 20 and 50 years. Between 25% and 50% of patients with systemic sarcoidosis exhibit ocular inflammatory disease. Uveitis is the most frequent ocular manifestation. In most series sarcoidosis accounts for 3%–10% of all uveitis.

The basic pathologic lesion of sarcoidosis is the noncaseating epithelioid cell granuloma, or tubercle (Fig X-14). The epithelioid cell is a polyhedral mononuclear histiocyte that is derived from the monocytes of the peripheral blood or the macrophage of the tissue. The tubercle of sarcoidosis is composed of

□ Epithelioid cells

□ Multinucleated giant cells of the Langhans type, with nuclei at the periphery of the cell arranged in an arc or incomplete circle

□ A thin rim of lymphocytes

Central areas of the tubercle seldom undergo fibrinoid degeneration or, in skin lesions (lupus pernio), micronecrosis. Various types of inclusion bodies may occur in the cytoplasm of the giant cells:

□ *Schaumann's, or lamellar, bodies:* ovoid, basophilic, calcific bodies measuring up to 100 μm in diameter and also containing iron

□ *Asteroid bodies:* star-shaped acidophilic bodies that measure up to 25 μm in diameter

A contagious etiologic agent has not been identified, although cell wall–modified or deficient mycobacteria have been implicated.

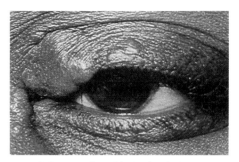

FIG X-15—Sarcoidosis, skin lesions.

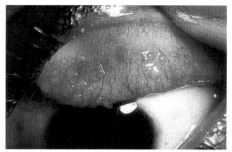

FIG X-16—Sarcoidosis, conjunctival nodules.

FIG X-17—Sarcoidosis, keratic precipitates and iridocyclitis.

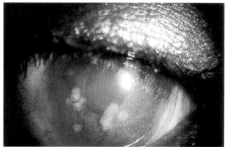

FIG X-18—Sarcoidosis, iris nodules.

Cutaneous involvement is frequent, and orbital and eyelid granulomas are common (Fig X-15). Palpebral and bulbar conjunctival nodules also occur (Fig X-16). Lacrimal gland infiltration may cause keratitis sicca. Symptoms of uveal involvement are variable and frequently include mild to moderate blurring of vision and aching about the eyes.

Sarcoidosis may involve all structures of the eye and present initially as a nongranulomatous process. More commonly, patients will have a chronic granulomatous iridocyclitis. Typical findings are

☐ Mutton-fat keratic precipitates (Fig X-17)

☐ Koeppe and Busacca iris nodules (Fig X-18)

☐ White clumps of cells (snowballs) in the inferior anterior vitreous

Nummular corneal infiltrates, inferior corneal endothelial opacification, and large iris granulomas also occur. Posterior synechiae can be extensive and may lead to iris bombé and angle-closure glaucoma. Peripheral anterior synechiae (PAS) may be extensive, encompassing the entire angle, for 360° in advanced cases. Secondary glaucoma can be severe, particularly when aggressive steroid therapy reverses ciliary body hyposecretion.

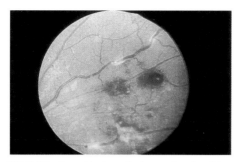

FIG X-19—Sarcoidosis, retinal vascular sheathing.

Posterior segment involvement is somewhat less frequent than anterior segment involvement. Nodular granulomas measuring 1/4 to 1 disc diameter in size occur in both the retina and choroid. Rarely, large granulomas several disc diameters in size may occur. Irregular nodular granulomas along venules have been termed *candlewax drippings*. Linear or patchy retinal periphlebitis presents as sheathing (Fig X-19). Cystoid macular edema is common, and retinal neovascularization, disc edema, and optic nerve granulomas also occur.

Diagnosis and management Because sarcoidosis is both variable in its presentation and known to be a frequent cause of uveitis, it must be considered as a possible etiology in every patient with ocular inflammation. If sarcoidosis is suspected, serum lysozyme and ACE with chest x-ray or chest CT are the tests most likely to indicate positive results. Frequently, a patient has a clinical picture compatible with sarcoidosis, yet laboratory data are inconclusive or negative. Additional testing may be useful, including a limited gallium scan of the head and neck. Gallium uptake is extremely sensitive to corticosteroids; a negative test in patients taking even small doses of prednisone is unreliable. Biopsy of suspicious skin, conjunctival, or lacrimal gland lesions may be considered (see Figure X-14). Transconjunctival lacrimal gland biopsy may be diagnostic, especially when the lacrimal gland is enlarged or nodular. This procedure may obviate the need for a more invasive transbronchial biopsy.

Topical, periocular, and systemic corticosteroids are the mainstay of therapy. Cycloplegia is required for comfort and for prevention of synechiae. When systemic disease is present, cooperation between the ophthalmologist and internist is required to devise an optimal therapeutic plan.

Aaberg TM. The role of the ophthalmologist in the management of sarcoidosis. *Am J Ophthalmol.* 1987;103:99–101.

Jabs DA, Johns CJ. Ocular involvement in chronic sarcoidosis. *Am J Ophthalmol.* 1986; 102:297–301.

Mayers M. Ocular sarcoidosis. *Int Ophthalmol Clin.* 1990;30:257–263.

Rothova A, Alberts C, Glasius E, et al. Risk factors for ocular sarcoidosis. *Doc Ophthalmol.* 1989;72:287–296.

Spaide RF, Ward DL. Conjunctival biopsy in the diagnosis of sarcoidosis. *Br J Ophthalmol.* 1990;74:469–471.

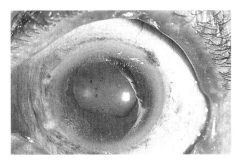

FIG X-20—Sympathetic ophthalmia, sympathizing eye with synechiae.

Weinreb RN, Tessler H. Laboratory diagnosis of ophthalmic sarcoidosis. *Surv Ophthalmol.* 1984;28:653–664.

Sympathetic Ophthalmia

Sympathetic ophthalmia (SO) is a rare bilateral, nonnecrotizing, granulomatous
panuveitis that occurs after injury to one eye, the *exciting eye,* followed by a latent
period and the development of uveitis in the uninjured globe, the *sympathizing eye*
(Fig X-20). Improved wound closure and early removal of severely damaged eyes
have significantly reduced the incidence of SO. With enucleation supplanting evisceration as the operation of choice in the removal of ocular contents, another potential
source for sympathetic disease has been largely eliminated. BCSC Section 7, *Orbit,
Eyelids, and Lacrimal System,* discusses the advantages and disadvantages of enucleation and evisceration in greater detail.

The etiology of sympathetic ophthalmia is not known, but theories include

- Hypersensitivity to pigment

- An infectious causal agent

- Sensitivity to retinal S antigen or other retinal or uveal proteins

Experimental animal studies suggest that these intraocular antigens require processing and presentation by the lymphatic system and that the antigens may gain access
to the system through penetrating ocular injury.

Histopathologic features include the following, some of which are shown in
Figures X-21 and X-22:

- Diffuse granulomatous uveal involvement, primarily with lymphocytes and epithelioid cells and occasionally with eosinophils

- Absence of reaction at the choriocapillaris

- Phagocytosis of uveal pigment by epithelioid cells

- Presence of Dalen-Fuchs nodules

- Extension of the granulomatous process into scleral canals and the optic disc

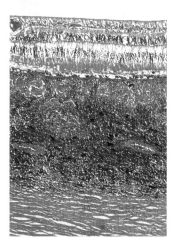

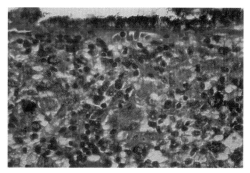

FIG X-21—Diffuse granulomatous inflammation in sympathetic ophthalmia.

FIG X-22—Sympathetic ophthalmia (histopathology). Note giant cells in choroid.

Clinical features appear at least 10 days after injury or operation: minimal problems in near vision, mild photophobia, and slight redness in the previously unaffected eye. Because the patient is already receiving treatment for the initially affected eye, these symptoms usually are brought quickly to the attention of the ophthalmologist. Severe panuveitis is found in the injured or operated eye. Thickening of the uveal tract, large mutton-fat KP, nodular infiltration in the iris, extensive PAS, and papillitis are seen in the sympathizing eye.

Diagnosis and management Bilateral uveitis following any ocular trauma or surgery should be suggestive of SO. The inflammation may occur as early as 10 days or as late as 50 years following the suspected triggering incident, but it usually occurs after 4–8 weeks. Table X-1 lists surgical procedures and injuries known to have provoked sympathetic ophthalmia.

The course of sympathetic ophthalmia is chronic, with frequent exacerbations. Local, systemic, and periocular corticosteroids may be effective therapy. Topical cycloplegic/mydriatic agents are also indicated to relieve symptoms. Frequently, treatment with antimetabolites is effective when corticosteroids have failed to reduce the inflammation. Cyclosporine has also been shown to be an effective treatment for selected patients with SO. The advent of multiple routes of corticosteroid therapy and antimetabolite treatment has greatly improved the prognosis, with partial or full recovery of vision possible.

Some evidence suggests that once SO has developed, the clinical course can be moderated by removing the inciting eye within 2 weeks of disease onset. With advances in microsurgical techniques, however, an inciting eye that may have potentially useful vision may turn out to be the eye with the best acuity and should not be removed.

TABLE X-1

SURGICAL PROCEDURES AND INJURIES
THAT MAY LEAD TO SYMPATHETIC OPHTHALMIA

Surgical procedures associated with sympathetic ophthalmia

Vitrectomy

Secondary IOL placement

Trabeculectomy

Iridencleisis

Contact and noncontact YAG laser cyclodestruction

Cyclocryotherapy

Proton beam and helium ion irradiation for choroidal melanoma

Cataract extraction, particularly when the iris is entrapped within the wound

Injuries associated with sympathetic ophthalmia

Perforating ulcers

Severe contusion

Subconjunctival scleral rupture

Any perforating injury, with or without direct uveal involvement or uveal prolapse

Kinyoun JL, Bensinger RE, Chuang EL. Thirty-year history of sympathetic ophthalmia. *Ophthalmology*. 1983;90:59–65.

Lam S, Tessler HH, Lam BL, et al. High incidence of sympathetic ophthalmia after contact and noncontact neodymium:YAG cyclotherapy. *Ophthalmology*. 1992;99:1818–1822.

Lubin JR, Albert DM, Weinstein M. Sixty-five years of sympathetic ophthalmia: a clinicopathologic review of 105 cases (1913–1978). *Ophthalmology*. 1980;87:109–121.

Marak GE Jr. Sympathetic ophthalmia. *Surv Ophthalmol*. 1982;89:1291–1292.

Rao NA, Robin J, Hartmann D, et al. The role of the penetrating wound in the development of sympathetic ophthalmia: experimental observations. *Arch Ophthalmol*. 1983;101:102–104.

Reynard M, Shulman IA, Azen SP, et al. Histocompatibility antigens in sympathetic ophthalmia. *Am J Ophthalmol*. 1983;95:216–221.

Sharp DC, Bell RA, Patterson E, et al. Sympathetic ophthalmia: histopathologic and fluorescein angiographic correlation. *Arch Ophthalmol*. 1984;102:232–235.

Sheppard JD. Sympathetic ophthalmia. In: Beatty RL, ed. *Seminars Ophthalmol*. 1994;9:177–184.

FIG X-23—Vogt-Koyanagi-Harada syndrome, choroiditis (histopathology).

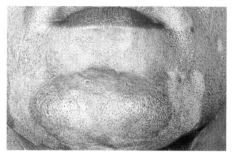

FIG X-24—VKH syndrome, skin lesion.

Vogt-Koyanagi-Harada (VKH) Syndrome

VKH syndrome is a rare cause of posterior or diffuse uveitis, even within the most commonly affected group of patients: individuals with Asian or American Indian ancestry between 30 and 50 years of age. However, any dark-skinned patients are considered to be at risk. An immune reaction to uveal melanin-associated protein, melanocytes, or pigment epithelium has been suggested as a mechanism, but the etiology remains unknown. A chronic, diffuse granulomatous uveitis resembling that of sympathetic ophthalmia is seen (Fig X-23). Unlike SO, however, patients with VKH syndrome do not have a history of antecedent ocular injury.

Symptoms of VKH syndrome can be both ocular and systemic. Systemic symptoms include headache, stiff neck, loss of consciousness, paralysis, and seizures. CNS signs include fever, nuchal rigidity, coma, seizures, monoparesis, hemiparesis, and focal neurologic signs. Optic neuropathy is present. Cerebrospinal fluid examination may show an increased number of lymphocytes, but this pleocytosis is transient. Skin and hair signs include alopecia, vitiligo, or poliosis in about 30% of patients (Figs X-24, X-25, X-26). Generally, these skin and hair signs occur several

FIG X-25—VKH syndrome, poliosis, vitiligo (skin and perilimbal).

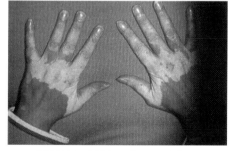

FIG X-26—VKH syndrome, vitiligo.

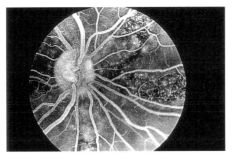

FIG X-27—VKH syndrome, serous detachment (fluorescein angiography).

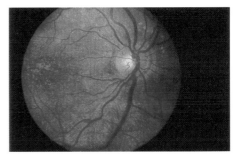

FIG X-28—VKH syndrome, retina following resolution of serous detachment.

weeks to months after the onset of ocular inflammation, but they may appear simultaneously. Perilimbal vitiligo occurs in more than 75% of cases. Temporary deafness or tinnitus occurs in about 30% of patients early in the course of the disease.

Ocular symptoms include bilateral decrease in vision, often associated with severe pain, redness, and photophobia. Ocular signs in the anterior segment include mild to extremely severe bilateral inflammation with seclusion of the pupil, formation of synechiae, and hypotony. Perilimbal vitiligo may occur. Keratic precipitates may range in size from very small to very large. Signs in the posterior segment include a swollen or hyperemic disc, an edematous exudative choroiditis, and vitreous opacities. Visual acuity may be greatly reduced. Exudative retinal detachment is often followed by spontaneous reattachment (Figs X-27, X-28).

During recovery from the uveal inflammation, depigmentation of the choroid occurs that is characterized by the orange-red fundus discoloration known as *sunset-glow fundus.* An RPE disturbance with focal areas of atrophy and hyperpigmentation may be observed in the healing phase of the inflammation (Figs X-29, X-30).

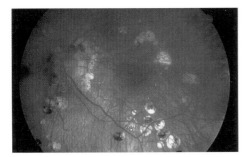

FIG X-29—VKH syndrome with peripapillary and posterior polar atrophic lesions and CME. (Photograph courtesy of John D. Sheppard Jr., MD.)

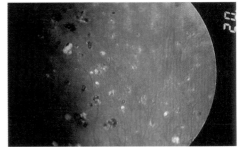

FIG X-30—VKH syndrome with numerous mature inactive, hyperpigmented atrophic choroidal lesions. (Photograph courtesy of John D. Sheppard Jr., MD.)

Diagnosis and management Diagnosis of VKH syndrome is suggested by the pathognomonic clinical picture. Sympathetic ophthalmia must be ruled out. Fluorescein angiography is helpful and may reveal multiple focal areas of subretinal leakage in the early phase of the angiogram. Ultrasonography has been useful in detecting diffuse choroidal thickening. Lumbar puncture showing lymphocytosis may be diagnostic in a patient with bilateral anterior and posterior segment inflammation. HLA-DR4 has a strong association with VKH syndrome.

Treatment includes the vigorous use of systemic, local, and periocular corticosteroids as well as cycloplegic/mydriatic agents. Many patients have a favorable response to treatment, with some recovering nearly normal vision; but PAS with secondary glaucoma, subretinal neovascularization, complicated cataract, and phthisis bulbi may occur. Occasionally, cyclosporine or other immunosuppressive therapy may be needed.

Beniz J, Forster DJ, Lean JS, et al. Variations in clinical features of the Vogt-Koyanagi-Harada syndrome. *Retina.* 1991;11:275–280.

Davis JL, Mittal KK, Friedlin V, et al. HLA associations and ancestry in Vogt-Koyanagi-Harada disease and sympathetic ophthalmia. *Ophthalmology.* 1990; 97:1137–1142.

Moorthy RS, Inomata H, Rao NA. Vogt-Koyanagi-Harada syndrome. *Surv Ophthalmol.* 1995;39:265–292.

Palestine AG. Medical therapy of uveitis. In: *Focal Points: Clinical Modules for Ophthalmologists.* San Francisco: American Academy of Ophthalmology; 1989;7:8.

Smith RD, Nozik RA. *Uveitis: A Clinical Approach to Diagnosis and Management.* 2nd ed. Baltimore: Williams & Wilkins; 1989:144–146.

Zhang XY, Wang XM, Hu TS. Profiling human leukocyte antigens in Vogt-Koyanagi-Harada syndrome. *Am J Ophthalmol.* 1992;113:567–572.

Masquerade Syndromes

Syphilis, which is known as the "great masquerader," has been discussed at the beginning of this chapter under infectious diseases.

Neoplasms

Intraocular lymphoma Intraocular lymphoma has been called *reticulum cell sarcoma, histiocytic lymphoma,* and *non-Hodgkin lymphoma of the CNS (NHL-CNS).* The disorder is a large cell, non-Hodgkin lymphoma that may originate in the eye or the CNS. The disorder is rare, with an average age of onset at 64 years and the youngest reported case being 27. Patients with NHL-CNS often present with CNS signs and symptoms (56%). Confusion, weakness, and deterioration in mental function are frequently noted, often by friends or family members. The disease causes bilateral (75%) decreased visual acuity and floaters. The vitreous has clumps and sheets of white cells, and the fundus shows characteristic multifocal, subretinal pigment epithelial infiltrates (Fig X-31).

A chronic, medically unresponsive uveitis, vitritis, and subretinal infiltrates in an elderly patient with CNS complaints should suggest the diagnosis. Radiologic testing including CT scanning or MRI can help establish the presence of CNS disease. CSF or vitreous biopsy can confirm the diagnosis (Fig X-32). Multiple vitreous biopsies may be required to establish the malignant nature of the vitreous cells.

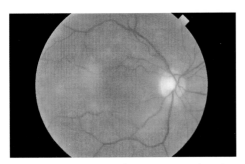 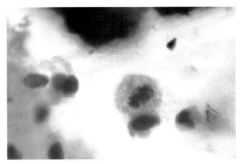

FIG X-31—Primary central nervous system lymphoma. Fundus photograph of multifocal, sub–retinal
pigment epithelial lesions.

FIG X-32—Vitreous aspirate showing mitotic figure
and cellular atypia in large cell lymphoma.

The disease may respond initially to corticosteroid therapy but eventually becomes resistant or recurrent. Hematology/oncology consultation is important once
the diagnosis is established to initiate appropriate therapy. Treatments include ocular irradiation (3000 rads), CNS irradiation, and intrathecal methotrexate when
indicated. Recurrent ocular disease may respond to intraocular methotrexate.
Systemic chemotherapy may improve the overall prognosis. Untreated, the disease
has a 5-year survival rate of 23%.

Valluri S, Moorthy RS, Khan A, et al. Combination treatment of intraocular lymphoma.
Retina. 1995: 15:125–129.

Whitcup SM, de Smet MD, Rubin BI, et al. Intraocular lymphoma: clinical and
histopathologic diagnosis. *Ophthalmology*. 1993:100:1399–1406.

CHAPTER XI

Endophthalmitis

The term *endophthalmitis* refers to intraocular inflammation predominantly involving the vitreous cavity and anterior chamber of the eye. Contiguous ocular structures such as the retina or the choroid may also be involved. *Infectious endophthalmitis,* inflammation associated with an infectious process, is the most common form and the focus of discussion in this chapter. Less often, a noninfectious stimulus such as retained lens material or a toxic substance introduced into the eye during trauma or intraocular surgery may be responsible for the inflammatory response, resulting in *sterile endophthalmitis.*

Signs and Symptoms

The most common signs of endophthalmitis are decreased vision, anterior chamber reaction (hypopyon), and vitritis. Immediate visual loss ranges from mild to more profound. Although patients may have endophthalmitis without significant pain, pain is often present. Conjunctival hyperemia and chemosis, eyelid edema, and corneal edema may also be observed.

Infectious Endophthalmitis

Infectious endophthalmitis can be classified according to the circumstances by which the infecting organism is introduced into the eye. *Exogenous endophthalmitis,* in which the organism enters the eye from the external environment, accounts for most cases, as in the following categories (Table XI-1):

□ Postoperative endophthalmitis: through a surgical incision (Fig XI-1)

□ Posttraumatic endophthalmitis: a traumatic laceration

□ Bleb-associated endophthalmitis: a conjunctival filtering bleb

A miscellaneous category includes cases associated with suture removal, wound infection, microbial keratitis, wound leaks, and infectious scleritis. The organism may also gain access to the eye from the internal environment or hematogenously, a classification known as *endogenous endophthalmitis* (Fig XI-2).

Overall, the incidence of postoperative endophthalmitis for cataract surgery by extracapsular cataract extraction or phacoemulsification ranges between 0.07% and 0.12%; for penetrating keratoplasty, 0.11%; and pars plana vitrectomy, 0.05%. The cumulative incidence of bleb-related endophthalmitis after glaucoma filtering surgery has been reported to range from 0.20% to 9.60%.

High rates of endophthalmitis follow trauma. The incidence of posttraumatic endophthalmitis ranges between 2.40% and 8.00%. In rural settings or in cases with a retained intraocular foreign body, the incidence has been reported to be as high as 30.00%.

TABLE XI-1

CHARACTERISTICS OF EXOGENOUS ENDOPHTHALMITIS

CATEGORY	INCIDENCE	MOST COMMON ORGANISMS	ONSET AFTER SURGERY OR TRAUMA	SYMPTOMS	CLINICAL FINDINGS
Acute postoperative (cataract surgery)	0.07%–0.12%				
Mild		Staphylococcus epidermidis Sterile	1–14 days	Photophobia, floaters	Slow progression, vision > 20/400, ± hypopyon, mild vitritis, fundus visible
Severe		Staphylococcus aureus Streptococcus species Gram-negative bacteria	1–4 days	Pain, decreased vision	Rapid progression, vision < 20/400, ± hypopyon, marked vitritis, fundus not visible
Chronic postoperative	?	Propionibacterium acnes Staphylococcus epidermidis Fungus	2 weeks to 2 years	Photophobia, hazy vision	Sometimes appearing with granulomatous keratic precipitates, ± hypopyon, mild to moderate vitritis, capsular plaque
Posttraumatic	2.4%–8.0% (as high as 30.0% in rural settings)	Staphylococcus epidermidis Bacillus species	1–5 days (fungi 1–4 weeks)	± increasing pain, decreasing vision	Increasing inflammation, hypopyon, increasing vitritis
Associated with filtering bleb	0.2%–9.6%	Streptococcus species Haemophilus influenzae	Anytime	Red eye, discharge, pain, decreasing vision	Infected bleb, hypopyon, vitritis

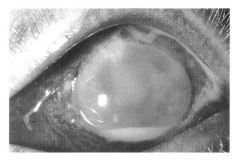

FIG XI-1—Exogenous postoperative endophthalmitis (bacterial).

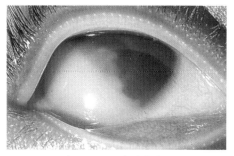

FIG XI-2—Endogenous endophthalmitis (meningococcal meningitis).

Postoperative Endophthalmitis

The eyelids and conjunctiva are the primary source of infection in postoperative endophthalmitis, and the organisms responsible may represent normal ocular surface flora such as *Staphylococcus* species and *Propionibacterium acnes.* The ocular microbiology of the eyelids and conjunctiva is discussed in detail in BCSC Section 8, *External Disease and Cornea.* Studies have demonstrated identical strains isolated from the ocular surface and from intraocular specimens taken from endophthalmitis cases. Other sources of contamination include

□ Secondary infection from other sites such as the lacrimal system

□ Blepharitis

□ Contaminated eyedrops

□ Contaminated surgical instruments, intraocular lenses, or irrigation fluids

□ Other agents introduced into the eye

□ Major breaches in sterile technique

In addition, IOLs may be the vector by which pathogens are introduced into the anterior chamber. Studies have suggested that bacteria bind to IOL components such as polypropylene.

In most cases of postoperative endophthalmitis the causative organism is introduced into the eye at the time of surgery. A sutureless cataract operation occasionally allows postoperative entry of bacteria into the eye. Fortunately, the anterior chamber has a clearing capacity for bacteria, which may account for the small number of endophthalmitis cases despite possible contamination at the time of surgery.

Aaberg TM Jr, Flynn HW Jr, Schiffman J, et al. Nosocomial acute-onset postoperative endophthalmitis survey: a 10-year review of incidence and outcomes. *Ophthalmology.* 1998;105:1004–1010.

Kattan HM, Flynn HW Jr, Pflugfelder SC, et al. Nosocomial endophthalmitis survey: current incidence of infection after intraocular surgery. *Ophthalmology.* 1991;98: 227–238.

Speaker MG, Menikoff JA. Postoperative endophthalmitis: pathogenesis, prophylaxis, and management. In: Smolin G, Friedlaender MH, eds. *Int Ophthalmol Clin: New and Evolving Ocular Infections.* 1993;33:51–70.

Winward KE, Pflugfelder SC, Flynn HW Jr, et al. Postoperative *Propionibacterium* endophthalmitis. Treatment strategies and long-term results. *Ophthalmology.* 1993; 100:447–451.

Acute-onset postoperative endophthalmitis Acute-onset postoperative endophthalmitis develops within 1–14 days following intraocular surgery. In general, the more prolonged and complicated the surgery, the greater the risk. Endophthalmitis may occur following any surgical procedure in which the intraocular space is entered or inadvertently violated:

- ☐ Cataract surgery
- ☐ Secondary IOL implantation
- ☐ Glaucoma procedures
- ☐ Penetrating keratoplasty
- ☐ Keratorefractive surgery
- ☐ Pterygium excision
- ☐ Strabismus surgery
- ☐ Scleral buckling surgery
- ☐ Retinal/vitreous surgery
- ☐ Anterior chamber paracentesis
- ☐ Intravitreal administration of antiviral agents

For prognostic and therapeutic purposes it is useful to distinguish between *mild* acute endophthalmitis cases with a slowly developing course and *severe* cases with a rapidly progressive course. The mild cases are less painful, have visual acuities on presentation of 20/400 or better, and may present as late as 7–14 days postoperatively. *Staphylococcus epidermidis* and other coagulase-negative *Staphylococcus* species are the organisms most commonly recovered in culture in these cases (Fig XI-3). When intraocular cultures are negative, the excessive intraocular inflammation is presumed to be caused by some unknown toxic or irritative factor or an infectious agent that cannot be cultured or identified.

Severe acute-onset postoperative endophthalmitis usually presents within 1–4 days after surgery. Vision is usually worse than 20/400, and the patients note having pain. Often there is marked vitritis and the fundus details are not visible. More virulent bacteria are often isolated in these cases, including *Staphylococcus aureus,* *Streptococcus* species, and gram-negative organisms such as *Serratia marcescens* (Fig XI-4), *Proteus,* and *Pseudomonas* species. Prompt recognition and treatment of severe acute-onset postoperative endophthalmitis are critical in limiting intraocular damage.

Chronic, or delayed-onset, postoperative endophthalmitis Chronic postoperative endophthalmitis develops 4 weeks or more after surgery and can even be seen months to years later. The onset of signs and symptoms is gradual, with good vision, minimal pain, and mild vitritis. A hypopyon is less commonly present. Chronic postoperative endophthalmitis can be caused by bacteria or fungi including *P acnes,* *S epidermidis,* or *Candida* species. *S epidermidis* infection presents within 6 weeks

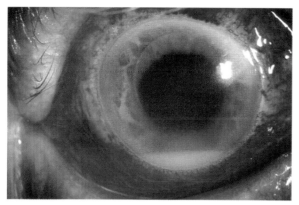

FIG XI-3—Mild acute postoperative endophthalmitis caused by *S epidermidis*.

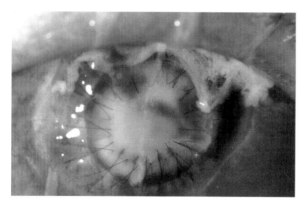

FIG XI-4—Severe acute postoperative endophthalmitis caused by *Serratia marcescens*, following penetrating keratoplasty.

of surgery with nongranulomatous inflammation. Fungal endophthalmitis usually begins within 3 months after surgery and is most commonly caused by *Candida* species. *P acnes* endophthalmitis may develop from 2 months to 2 years following cataract surgery and is characterized by granulomatous KP, a small hypopyon, vitritis, and a white plaque containing *P acnes* and residual lens material sequestered within the capsular bag (Fig XI-5).

Chronic postoperative endophthalmitis can rarely be precipitated by Nd:YAG laser capsulotomy. It is hypothesized that the laser allows the dissemination of sequestered pathogens from the capsular bag into the vitreous cavity and anterior chamber.

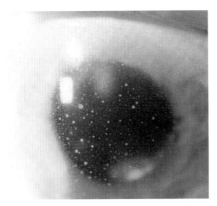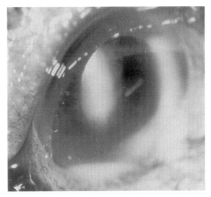

FIG XI-5—Chronic postoperative endophthalmitis caused by *P acnes.* Note granulomatous keratic precipitates and white plaque in the capsular bag.

Posttraumatic Endophthalmitis

Posttraumatic endophthalmitis can occur following any penetrating ocular injury; however, the incidence appears to be higher in rural settings and in cases where intraocular foreign bodies are retained. The most common organisms found are *S epidermidis, Bacillus* species, *Streptococcus* species, *S aureus,* and various fungi. *Bacillus* species such as *B cereus,* which are recovered in 26%–46% of culture-positive cases, cause a particularly fulminant endophthalmitis. In general, the larger and more contaminated the injury, the more likely endophthalmitis will develop. However, even small nonorganic materials such as a tiny hot metal shaving may occasionally cause endophthalmitis.

Removal of a retained intraocular foreign body within 24 hours of injury may reduce the risk of infectious endophthalmitis. Unfortunately, prompt recognition of the signs of possible endophthalmitis may be obscured by coexisting ocular injuries and the expected inflammatory response that normally follows a severe injury, resulting in treatment delay. Endophthalmitis should be suspected whenever a patient exhibits signs of increasing pain, intraocular inflammation (retinal periphlebitis), and/or a hypopyon after repair of a penetrating injury.

Boldt HC, Pulido JS, Blodi CF, et al. Rural endophthalmitis. *Ophthalmology.* 1989;96: 1722–1726.

Foster RE, Martinez JA, Murray TG, et al. Useful visual outcomes after treatment of *Bacillus cereus* endophthalmitis. *Ophthalmology.* 1996;103:390–397.

Thompson JT, Parver LM, Enger CL, et al. Infectious endophthalmitis after penetrating injuries with retained intraocular foreign bodies. National Eye Trauma System. *Ophthalmology.* 1993;100:1468–1474.

Endophthalmitis Associated with Filtering Blebs

Bacteria may enter the eye through either intact or leaking conjunctival filtering blebs. Thin-walled blebs, as seen with mitomycin-C therapy, and inferiorly placed blebs may put patients at an even greater risk. BCSC Section 10, *Glaucoma*, discusses filtering blebs and their complications in more detail. Infection may occur months to years after filtering surgery. It is important to differentiate between low-grade bleb infection, or *blebitis,* and bleb-associated endophthalmitis.

In endophthalmitis, patients present with an infected bleb, marked intraocular inflammation with hypopyon, and vitritis. The organisms responsible include *Streptococcus* species, *S epidermidis, H influenzae, Moraxella* species, and *Enterococcus* species. The prognosis is usually poor with profound visual loss.

In blebitis the organisms are usually of low virulence, the bleb appears thin and cystic, and there is no evidence of vitreous inflammation. These cases may be treated conservatively with good visual outcomes. However, the physician must be aware that bleb infection caused by more virulent organisms, such as *Streptococcus* species and *H influenzae*, may progress rapidly to endophthalmitis with pain and loss of vision and that prompt intervention may be necessary.

Brown RH, Yang LH, Walker SD, et al. Treatment of bleb infection after glaucoma surgery. *Arch Ophthalmol.* 1994;112:57–61.

Ciulla TA, Beck AD, Topping MT, et al. Blebitis, early endophthalmitis, and late endophthalmitis after glaucoma-filtering surgery. *Ophthalmology.* 1997;104:986–995.

Higginbotham EJ, Stevens RK, Musch DC, et al. Bleb-related endophthalmitis after trabeculectomy with mitomycin C. *Ophthalmology.* 1996;103:650–656.

Kangas TA, Greenfield DS, Flynn HW Jr, et al. Delayed-onset endophthalmitis associated with conjunctival filtering blebs. *Ophthalmology.* 1997;104:746–752.

Mandelbaum S, Forster RK, Gelender H, et al. Late onset endophthalmitis associated with filtering blebs. *Ophthalmology.* 1985;92:964–972.

Endogenous Endophthalmitis

Endogenous endophthalmitis results from the bloodborne spread of bacteria or fungi during generalized septicemia. A remote nonocular source—such as an infected intravenous line or an infected organ as in endocarditis, gastrointestinal disorders, pyelonephritis, meningitis, or osteomyelitis—may be the origin. Predisposed patients are chronically ill (i.e., diabetes or chronic renal failure) or immunosuppressed, use intravenous drugs, or have indwelling catheters, or they may be in the immediate postoperative or postpartum period.

Endogenous bacterial endophthalmitis is characterized by an acute onset with pain, decreased vision, hypopyon, and vitritis. Sometimes both eyes are affected simultaneously. A wide variety of bacteria have been reported. The most common gram-positive organisms are *Streptococcus* species (endocarditis), *S aureus* (cutaneous infections), and *Bacillus* species (intravenous drug use). The most common gram-negative organisms are *Neisseria meningitidis* and *H influenzae* and enteric organisms such as *Escherichia coli* and *Klebsiella.*

Endogenous fungal endophthalmitis develops slowly, as focal or multifocal areas of chorioretinitis. Granulomatous or nongranulomatous inflammation is observed with KP, hypopyon, and vitritis with cellular aggregates. The infection usually begins in the choroid, appearing as yellow-white lesions with indistinct borders,

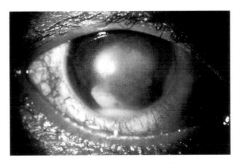

FIG XI-6—Fungal endophthalmitis.

ranging in size from small cotton-wool spots to several disc diameters (Fig XI-6). It subsequently can break through into the vitreous, producing localized cellular and fungal aggregates overlying the original site(s).

Candida is the most common causative organism (see Figures IX-19 and IX-20), with isolated cases of *Aspergillus* reported. *Candida albicans* endophthalmitis occurs in association with hyperalimentation; indwelling intravascular lines; and IV drug use, recent major surgery, or immunosuppression. *Candida* endophthalmitis will develop in a small percentage of patients with candidemia if not treated with antifungal therapies. In one study patients treated with antifungal agents after a single positive fungal culture had an incidence of endogenous endophthalmitis of 2.8%, which appears to be lower than previous reports of 10%–37% of untreated patients developing endophthalmitis.

Accurate diagnosis of the offending agent causing endogenous endophthalmitis is crucial for proper antibiotic treatment of both the ocular and systemic infections. Often, the cause may be presumed on the basis of existing positive cultures of blood or other suspected sites. If the agent is unknown, fungal and bacterial blood cultures should be obtained.

Donahue SP, Greven CM, Zuravleff JJ, et al. Intraocular candidiasis in patients with candidemia. Clinical implications derived from a prospective multicenter study. *Ophthalmology.* 1994;101:1302–1309.

Essman TF, Flynn HW Jr, Smiddy WE, et al. Treatment outcomes in a 10-year study of endogenous fungal endophthalmitis. *Ophthalmic Surg Lasers.* 1997;28:185–194.

Okada AA, Johnson RP, Liles WC, et al. Endogenous bacterial endophthalmitis: report of a ten-year retrospective study. *Ophthalmology.* 1994;101:832–838.

Scherer WJ, Lee K. Implications of early systemic therapy on the incidence of endogenous fungal endophthalmitis. *Ophthalmology.* 1997;104:1593–1598.

Prophylaxis

No study has established definitive standards for prophylaxis of endophthalmitis. Rather, an accumulation of data has led to trends, some of which remain subject to controversy.

Preoperative eyelid and conjunctival treatment with appropriate topical antibiotics may benefit patients who are at high risk for infection, such as those who have severe chronic blepharitis, lacrimal drainage abnormalities, cicatricial conjunctivitis, or a prosthesis in the other eye or who are diabetic or immunosuppressed. Preventive measures include preoperative topically applied broad-spectrum antibiotics, which can decrease the number of eyelid and conjunctival bacteria in comparison with no treatment. Preparation of the eyelids and conjunctiva with a 5% povidone solution just before surgery also substantially reduces the bacterial load of the external structures. Isolation of the eyelids and lashes from the surgical field with careful draping is also important.

The use of intraocular antibiotics either as a specific injection into the anterior chamber or as a concentration in irrigation fluids has also been advocated. Subconjunctival antibiotics may be given at the end of intraocular surgery. The effectiveness of these methods in preventing endophthalmitis is uncertain. The efficacy of systemic administration of antibiotics in the prevention of endophthalmitis is also uncertain. Yet IV antibiotics have been advocated by some for endophthalmitis prophylaxis in the setting of penetrating ocular injuries.

In general, the true effectiveness of any of these prophylactic strategies in the actual prevention of endophthalmitis is unknown. Moreover, routine antibiotic prophylaxis has raised concerns regarding costs, risk of toxicity, and the emergence of resistant organisms.

> Liesegang TJ. Prophylactic antibiotics in cataract operations. *Mayo Clin Proc.* 1997;72: 149–159.

Diagnosis

Differential Diagnosis

Infectious endophthalmitis caused by bacteria and fungi is often difficult to distinguish from other types of intraocular inflammation. Excessive inflammation without endophthalmitis is often encountered postoperatively in the setting of complicated surgery, preexisting uveitis and keratitis, diabetes, glaucoma therapy, and previous surgery. A vitreous and anterior chamber cellular reaction and a pseudohypopyon may be simulated by red blood cells, pigment, or debris. Retained lens material or other substances may cause sterile postoperative inflammation. Keratitis and post-surgical incision infections are often accompanied by a hypopyon without intraocular infection. It is important to avoid introducing a purely external infection (as in the case of bacterial keratitis) into the eye by performing an unnecessary paracentesis. Preexisting endogenous uveitis may flare up at any time following cataract surgery. Tumor cells from a lymphoma may accumulate in the vitreous, or retinoblastoma cells may accumulate in the anterior chamber, simulating intraocular inflammation.

The most helpful distinguishing characteristic of true infectious endophthalmitis is that the vitritis is progressive and out of proportion to other anterior segment findings. When in doubt, the clinician should manage the condition as an infectious process.

Obtaining Intraocular Specimens

Diagnosis is established by identifying an infective pathogen. Whenever possible, aqueous and vitreous specimens should be obtained for culture and microscopic study before antibiotic therapy is initiated. Obtaining vitreous specimens is important because postoperative infection might have disseminated to the vitreous without clinical evidence. Vitreous cultures are often positive even when aqueous cultures in the same case are negative, and the reverse may also be true.

Aqueous is obtained by passing a small-gauge needle through the limbus into the anterior chamber and withdrawing a 0.1 ml sample. Vitreous may be obtained by a vitreous tap using a needle or by a biopsy with an automated vitrector. For the tap, a 23-gauge 1-inch needle is passed through the pars plana 3.5 mm posterior to the limbus into the anterior vitreous cavity. If possible, the needle tip is visualized through the pupil to be in the proper position, and 0.2 ml of undiluted vitreous is withdrawn.

An alternative method is to perform the biopsy with a vitrector through the pars plana. Vitreous biopsy with a cutting instrument places less traction on a possibly inflamed and fragile retina as well as the vitreous base than does a vitreous tap performed with a needle.

Pars plana vitrectomy has been recommended in cases where rapidly progressive cellular infiltration of the vitreous obscures visualization of fundus details. The theoretical benefits of vitrectomy include

☐ Obtaining a larger sample of vitreous for culture and laboratory testing than is possible with a vitreous tap

☐ Removing potentially toxic bacterial byproducts, endotoxins, and inflammatory cells

☐ Removing the vitreous scaffolding

☐ Reducing the bacterial load

☐ Clearing the ocular media

The disadvantages of vitrectomy are its technical difficulty and the delay it may create in therapeutic intervention while the patient is referred to an experienced vitreous surgeon. Thus, any benefits of a pars plana vitrectomy must be weighed against the potential risks of surgery.

Cultures and Laboratory Evaluation of Intraocular Specimens

Regardless of how the intraocular specimens are obtained, the aqueous and vitreous specimens should promptly be inoculated directly onto culture media. Drops of the sample should be placed onto blood agar, Sabouraud's agar, chocolate agar, and thioglycollate broth, or similar media. In cases of chronic postoperative endophthalmitis, the lab should hold anaerobic cultures for 2 weeks, because it may take that long for *P acnes* to grow out.

One drop each of the aqueous and vitreous specimens should be placed on clean slides for Gram and Giemsa stains for bacteria and fungi. Additional slides should be prepared and available for special stains (e.g., calcofluor white) as indicated. If the responsible organism is definitively observed on these slides under the microscope, then treatment may be tailored accordingly before positive identification on cultures. However, stains of aqueous and vitreous are often negative in spite of florid bacterial and fungal endophthalmitis and, thus, may be of limited value in the selection of appropriate therapy.

Barza M, Pavan PR, Doft BH, et al. Evaluation of microbiological diagnostic techniques in postoperative endophthalmitis in the Endophthalmitis Vitrectomy Study. *Arch Ophthalmol.* 1997;115:1142–1150.

Brod RD, Flynn HW Jr. Advances in the diagnosis and treatment of infectious endophthalmitis. *Curr Opinion Ophthalmol.* 1991;2:306–314.

Treatment

Once infectious endophthalmitis is suspected, management should be tailored according to the course, severity, and extent of inflammation upon presentation. For example, mild cases of postoperative endophthalmitis may be treated by less aggressive means, while more severe cases often need vitrectomy.

Surgical Management

Vitrectomy is thought to debride the infected and inflamed vitreous cavity, allowing better antibiotic distribution in the vitreous cavity. It does not appear necessary to remove an IOL unless it hampers adequate visualization during vitrectomy. A national collaborative study, the Endophthalmitis Vitrectomy Study (EVS), investigated the management of postoperative endophthalmitis occurring within 6 weeks after cataract surgery with primary IOL or secondary IOL implantation. The study found that in eyes with vision better than light perception (defined as hand-motions acuity at 2 feet or more) at the time of presentation, visual results were not significantly different between eyes managed by immediate three-port pars plana vitrectomy and eyes managed by vitreous tap/biopsy. However, in eyes with light perception–only vision, the vitrectomy group had significantly better outcomes compared to the vitreous tap/biopsy group. The role of vitrectomy for other categories of endophthalmitis (i.e., posttraumatic, filtering bleb–associated, endogenous, and chronic postoperative cases) was not addressed in the EVS.

Medical Management

Antibacterial treatment of endophthalmitis should provide broad-spectrum coverage for both gram-positive and gram-negative organisms in cases where the organism is not known (Table XI-2). With the rising incidence of resistance to beta-lactam antibiotics, many physicians have turned to vancomycin for gram-positive coverage. Aminoglycosides, including gentamicin, tobramycin, and amikacin, are usually effective treatment for gram-negative infection and may also be synergistic with vancomycin against certain gram-positive organisms. However, concern regarding aminoglycoside retinal toxicity (i.e., macular infarction) has led many physicians to use third-generation cephalosporins such as ceftazidime to cover gram-negative bacilli. Recently, it has been suggested that fluoroquinolones may be used since they can be given orally, have intraocular penetration, and have a broad spectrum of activity. Unfortunately, they have limited effectiveness against anaerobic organisms, *Streptococcus* species, and other emerging resistant gram-positive bacteria.

Antibiotics may be administered by topical, subconjunctival, intraocular (usually intravitreal), and intravenous routes. The EVS employed intravitreal (vancomycin/amikacin), subconjunctival (vancomycin/ceftazidime), and topical (vancomycin/amikacin) antibiotics to treat acute postoperative endophthalmitis. Controversy

TABLE XI-2

MEDICATIONS USED IN EXOGENOUS ENDOPHTHALMITIS

		ROUTE AND DOSE		
	TOPICAL	SUBCONJUNCTIVAL	INTRAVITREAL	SYSTEMIC
Antibiotic				
Gentamicin	9 mg/ml	20 mg/0.5 ml	0.1 mg/0.1 ml	1 mg/kg IV q8hr
Vancomycin	50 mg/ml	25 mg/0.5 ml	1.0 mg/0.1 ml	1.0 g IV q12hr
Amikacin	—	—	0.4 mg/0.1 ml	—
Chloramphenicol	—	—	1.0 mg/0.1 ml	—
Amphotericin B	—	—	5.0 µg/0.1 ml	1.0 mg/kg IV daily
Ceftazidime	—	—	2.0–2.25 mg/0.1 ml	1.0–2.0 g IV q8hr
Nafcillin	—	—	—	1.0 g IV q12hr
Ceftriaxone	—	—	—	1.0 g IV q12hr
Ketoconazole	—	—	—	400 mg PO daily
Fluconazole	—	—	—	200 mg PO daily
Itraconazole	—	—	—	100–200 mg (PO q.d.)
Ciprofloxacin	—	—	—	250–750 mg (PO b.i.d.)
Corticosteroid Preparations				
Prednisolone acetate 1% drops	Every hour	—	—	—
Dexamethasone 0.1% drops	Every hour	—	—	—
Dexamethasone injection 4 mg/ml	—	1.0 ml (4.0 mg)	0.1 ml (0.4 mg)	—
Prednisone tablets	—	—	—	1 mg/kg/day PO

persists in the use of systemic antibiotics. The EVS showed that the use of the IV antibiotics (amikacin/ceftazidime) made no difference in visual acuity outcomes comparing treated and untreated groups. The efficacy of IV antibiotics for the other categories of endophthalmitis mentioned above has not been established through the use of randomized controlled trials.

Although corticosteroids may diminish the destructive intraocular inflammatory response to endophthalmitis, their timing and usage is controversial. It has been suggested that they should be withheld if a fungal pathogen is suspected.

General Considerations for Treatment

Mild acute-onset postoperative cases of infectious endophthalmitis are generally managed by injection of intraocular antibiotics alone, without vitrectomy, followed by topical antibiotics and steroids. In contrast, treatment of severe acute postoperative endophthalmitis includes

- Pars plana vitrectomy with vitreous and aqueous cultures
- Intravitreal, subconjunctival, and topical antibiotics
- Topical and periocular corticosteroids

The value of adjunctive intravitreal corticosteroids and systemic antibiotics is still under debate. As in postoperative endophthalmitis, the treatment of posttraumatic endophthalmitis should be guided by the severity of the clinical course.

Chronic postoperative endophthalmitis therapy depends on the organism isolated. *S epidermidis* responds to intraocular vancomycin injection alone. In *P acnes* cases intraocular vancomycin injection and local debridement or excision of the white intracapsular plaque and capsulectomy have been effective in eradicating the infection and reducing rates of recurrence.

Exogenous fungal endophthalmitis is treated by pars plana vitrectomy and intravitreal injection of amphotericin B. Topical, subconjunctival, and systemic antibiotics are given concomitantly, but their additional therapeutic value is unknown.

Treatment of endogenous bacterial and fungal endophthalmitis usually includes systemic antibiotic administration to treat not only the intraocular infection but also the systemic source of the pathogen. Treatment of endogenous bacterial endophthalmitis also usually includes intravitreal antibiotics. Systemic treatment of *Candida* chorioretinitis includes 5-flucytosine or oral fluconazole or, in more severe cases, IV amphotericin B. Intravenous amphotericin is nephrotoxic, and serum creatinine should be closely monitored during the course of treatment. When intravitreal involvement is present, intravitreal amphotericin B is usually used in combination with vitrectomy.

Blebitis usually responds to topical and subconjunctival antibiotic therapy. Infection in filtering blebs may, however, progress rapidly to endophthalmitis with pain and loss of vision. Vitreous inflammation dictates prompt intervention with vitreous cultures followed by intravitreal antibiotic injection, similar to the treatment of acute-onset postoperative cases.

Outcomes of Treatment

Visual loss in endophthalmitis results from the damage caused both by the toxins and proteases produced by the infectious organism and by the host's inflammatory response to the infection. The retina and anterior segment structures may be directly injured, which may lead to tractional or rhegmatogenous retinal detachments, ciliary body damage, hypotony, and phthisis bulbi.

In general, more virulent organisms capable of producing exotoxins, endotoxins, and/or proteases, such as *S aureus, Streptococcus* species, *Bacillus* species, and gram-negative organisms *(Pseudomonas, Serratia marcescens, Proteus),* cause the most rapidly progressive and fulminant disease and have the worst visual acuity outcomes. The less virulent organisms such as *S epidermidis* and *P acnes* are associated with more indolent clinical courses and better visual acuity outcomes.

The EVS reported the following findings:

□ At 3 months: 41% of patients achieved 20/40 or better visual acuity; 69% had 20/100 or better acuity

□ At 9–12 months: 53% of patients achieved visual acuity of 20/40 or better; 74% achieved 20/100 or better; 15% had worse than 5/200 vision

□ At the final follow-up visit: 5% of patients had no light perception

Chronic endophthalmitis cases usually have favorable visual prognosis, with one study showing visual acuity of 20/40 or better in 80% of cases. The incidence for achieving 20/400 or better visual acuity in endophthalmitis associated with infected filtering blebs was 47% in one recent study. Only 10% of patients who develop bacterial endophthalmitis after trauma obtain a visual acuity of 20/400 or better.

Aaberg TM Jr, Flynn HW Jr, Murray TG. Intraocular ceftazidime as an alternative to the aminoglycosides in the treatment of endophthalmitis. *Arch Ophthalmol.* 1994;112: 18–19.

Campochiaro PA, Lim JI. Aminoglycoside toxicity in the treatment of endophthalmitis. The Aminoglycoside Toxicity Study Group. *Arch Ophthalmol.* 1994;112:48–53.

Doft BH. The Endophthalmitis Vitrectomy Study. *Arch Ophthalmol.* 1991;109: 487–489.

Doft BH, Barza M. Ceftazidime or amikacin: choice of intravitreal antimicrobials in the treatment of postoperative endophthalmitis [letter]. *Arch Ophthalmol.* 1994;112:17–18.

Endophthalmitis Vitrectomy Study Group. Results of the Endophthalmitis Vitrectomy Study: a randomized trial of immediate vitrectomy and of intravenous antibiotics for the treatment of postoperative bacterial endophthalmitis. *Arch Ophthalmol.* 1995; 113:1479–1496.

This chapter was prepared with the assistance of Dennis P. Han, MD, and Peter K. Kaiser, MD. The author also wishes to acknowledge the contribution of Harry W. Flynn, Jr., MD.

Complications of Uveitis

Cataracts

Cataract may develop in any eye with chronic or recurrent uveitis as the result of both the inflammation itself and the corticosteroids used to treat it. Cataract surgery should be considered whenever the patient will benefit functionally. See also BCSC Section 11, *Lens and Cataract,* for further discussion of many of the issues covered in this section.

Careful evaluation is necessary to ascertain how much the cataract is actually contributing to visual dysfunction, since visual loss in uveitis may stem from a variety of other ocular problems such as macular edema or vitritis. Sometimes a cataract will preclude an adequate view of the posterior segment of the eye, and surgery can be justified to permit examination, diagnosis, and treatment of posterior segment abnormalities.

Studies have shown that extracapsular cataract extraction or phacoemulsification with posterior chamber IOL implantation effectively improves vision and is well tolerated in many eyes with uveitis even over long periods. For example, excellent surgical and visual results have been reported for eyes with Fuchs heterochromic cyclitis. Cataract surgery in other types of uveitis—including idiopathic and pars planitis and uveitis associated with sarcoidosis, herpes simplex virus, herpes zoster, syphilis, toxoplasmosis, and spondyloarthropathies—can be more problematic, although it may also have very good results.

Pars plana lensectomy/vitrectomy has been advocated for uveitis associated with JRA, although acceptable results have also been reported with combined phacoemulsification and vitrectomy. IOL implantation is in general contraindicated in children with JRA-associated iridocyclitis, but it may be successful in selected adults with JRA whose inflammation has been adequately controlled.

Extracapsular cataract extraction and phacoemulsification may be more challenging in uveitic eyes than in noninflamed eyes, and intraocular inflammation should be controlled before surgery is performed. Posterior synechiae may require synechialysis, and pupillary miosis may require pupil stretching, sphincterotomies, or use of iris retractors.

Nucleus extraction is performed in the usual manner. If logistically possible, phacoemulsification may be the preferred alternative for nucleus removal. Capsulorrhexis in conjunction with phacoemulsification may minimize the risk of postoperative posterior synechiae and may also facilitate implantation of the IOL haptics in the capsular bag. Cortical clean-up should be meticulous. Extracapsular cataract extraction or phacoemulsification can be done in conjunction with pars plana vitrectomy if clinical or ultrasonic examination suggests that substantial vision-limiting vitreous debris is present. Perioperative immunosuppressive agents such as topical, subconjunctival, and oral corticosteroids and/or other immunosuppressives should be administered.

Visual compromise following extracapsular cataract extraction with posterior chamber lens implantation in uveitis patients is usually attributed to posterior segment abnormalities, most commonly cystoid macular edema. The postoperative course may also be complicated by recurrence or exacerbation of uveitis. Posterior capsule opacification incidence rate is higher in uveitic eyes, leading to earlier use of Nd:YAG laser capsulotomy. In some uveitic conditions such as pars planitis, inflammatory debris may accumulate and membranes may form on the surface of the IOL, necessitating frequent Nd:YAG laser procedures. On occasion, posterior chamber IOLs have been removed from these eyes. The use of surface-modified IOLs has also been advocated to minimize deposit formation on the optics. Frequent follow-up examination, a high index of suspicion, and aggressive immunosuppressive treatment of these complications will optimize both the short- and the long-term visual results.

Flynn HW Jr, Davis JL, Culbertson WW. Pars plana lensectomy and vitrectomy for complicated cataracts in juvenile rheumatoid arthritis. *Ophthalmology.* 1988;95: 1114–1119.

Foster CS. Cataract surgery in the patient with uveitis. In: *Focal Points: Clinical Modules for Ophthalmologists.* San Francisco: American Academy of Ophthalmology; 1994; 12:4.

Foster CS, Barrett F. Cataract development and cataract surgery in patients with juvenile rheumatoid arthritis–associated iridocyclitis. *Ophthalmology.* 1993;100:809–817.

Foster CS, Fong LP, Singh G. Cataract surgery and intraocular lens implantation in patients with uveitis. *Ophthalmology.* 1989;96:281–288.

Foster RE, Lowder CY, Meisler DM, et al. Combined extracapsular cataract extraction, posterior chamber intraocular lens implantation, and pars plana vitrectomy. *Ophthalmic Surg.* 1993;24:446–452.

Foster RE, Lowder CY, Meisler DM, et al. Extracapsular cataract extraction and posterior chamber intraocular lens implantation in uveitis patients. *Ophthalmology.* 1992; 99:1234–1241.

Kaufman AH, Foster CS. Cataract extraction in patients with pars planitis. *Ophthalmology.* 1993;100:1210–1217.

Krishna R, Meisler DM, Lowder CY, et al. Long-term follow-up of extracapsular cataract extraction and posterior chamber intraocular lens implantation in patients with uveitis. *Ophthalmology.* 1998;105:1765–1769.

Probst LE, Holland EJ. Intraocular lens implantation in patients with juvenile rheumatoid arthritis. *Am J Ophthalmol.* 1996;122:161–170.

Glaucoma

Secondary glaucoma is a well-recognized complication of uveitis. Elevated IOP may be acute, chronic, or recurrent. In eyes with long-term ciliary body inflammation the IOP may fluctuate between abnormally high and low values. See also BCSC Section 10, *Glaucoma.*

Inflammatory open-angle glaucoma occurs when the trabecular meshwork is inflamed or blocked by inflammatory cells and debris as commonly occurs with infectious causes of uveitis, such as *Toxoplasma* retinitis, acute retinal necrosis, and herpes simplex and varicella-zoster iridocyclitis. This type of glaucoma usually responds to topical cycloplegics and corticosteroids and specific treatment of the infectious agent.

Chronic outflow obstruction in anterior chamber inflammation may be caused by peripheral anterior synechiae as well as by direct damage to the trabecular meshwork. Common examples of these mechanisms are chronic iridocyclitis associated with JRA, sarcoidosis, and Fuchs heterochromic iridocyclitis. Initial treatment is with topical and oral glaucoma medications such as carbonic anhydrase inhibitors, beta blockers, and alpha agonists. However, parasympathomimetic medications should be avoided. The beta blocker metipranolol (OptiPranolol) has been associated with intraocular inflammation, and it is possible that the new agent latanoprost (Xalatan) may also provoke inflammation.

When medical management fails, glaucoma filtering surgery is indicated, although standard trabeculectomy may have a greater risk of failure in these eyes. Results may be improved by using 5-fluorouracil or mitomycin-C with intensive topical corticosteroids. Trabeculodialysis, a modified goniotomy, and laser sclerostomy have also been suggested for treatment of uveitic glaucomas. Some eyes require aqueous drainage devices. Cyclodestructive procedures may worsen ocular inflammation and lead to hypotony and phthisis bulbi. Laser trabeculoplasty should be avoided in eyes with active intraocular inflammation or iris neovascularization.

Formation of posterior synechiae may result in pupillary block and iris bombé with acute secondary peripheral angle closure. This condition occasionally occurs in patients with chronic granulomatous iridocyclitis associated with sarcoidosis or VKH and in those with acute recurrent nongranulomatous iridocyclitis, as is seen with ankylosing spondylitis. Peripheral iridotomy with the Nd:YAG and/or argon laser results in resolution of the bombé and angle closure if performed before permanent peripheral synechiae form. Iridotomies should be multiple and as large as possible. Considerable inflammation can be anticipated following laser iridotomy procedures in these eyes. Intensive topical corticosteroid and cycloplegic therapy is given following the procedure. Surgical iridotomy may be indicated if laser iridotomy is not successful.

Topical periocular and oral corticosteroid therapy for uveitis may produce a steroid-induced elevation in IOP, which may be difficult to distinguish from other causes of glaucoma in uveitis. A less potent steroid preparation and/or less frequent administration schedule may avoid this IOP rise. Fluorometholone or rimexalone may be less likely to cause a corticosteroid-induced IOP elevation but may also be less effective in controlling intraocular inflammation than other topical ocular corticosteroid preparations.

Hill RA, Nguyen QH, Baerveldt G, et al. Trabeculectomy and Molteno implantation for glaucomas associated with uveitis. *Ophthalmology.* 1993;100:903–908.

Moorthy RS, Mermoud A, Baerveldt G, et al. Glaucoma associated with uveitis. *Surv Ophthalmol.* 1997;41:361–394.

Panek WC, Holland GN, Lee DA, et al. Glaucoma in patients with uveitis. *Br J Ophthalmol.* 1990;74:223–227.

Patel NP, Patel KH, Moster MR. Metipranolol-associated nongranulomatous anterior uveitis. *Am J Ophthalmol*. 1997;123:843–844.

Patitsas CJ, Rockwood EJ, Meisler DM, et al. Glaucoma filtering surgery with postoperative 5-fluorouracil in patients with intraocular inflammatory disease. *Ophthalmology*. 1992;99:594–599.

Watanabe TM, Hodes BL. Bilateral anterior uveitis associated with a brand of metipranolol. *Arch Ophthalmol*. 1997;115:421–422.

Hypotony

Hypotony in uveitis is usually caused by decreased aqueous production from the ciliary body, and it may follow intraocular surgery in patients with uveitis. Acute inflammation of the ciliary body may cause temporary hyposecretion, whereas chronic ciliary body damage results in permanent hypotony. Serous choroidal detachment often accompanies hypotony and complicates management.

Hypotony usually responds to intensive corticosteroid and cycloplegic therapy, although prolonged choroidal effusions may require surgical drainage. In eyes with ciliary body traction from a cyclitic membrane, pars plana membranectomy may restore normal pressure. In select cases vitrectomy and intraocular silicone oil may help maintain ocular anatomy and IOP.

Cystoid Macular Edema

Cystoid macular edema is a common cause of visual loss in eyes with uveitis. Therapy that reduces intraocular inflammation in general often has beneficial effects. Nonspecific therapy includes topical, periocular, and oral corticosteroids and oral and topical NSAIDs. Oral acetazolamide, 500 mg daily, has been effective in some patients. Eyes with chronic vitritis occasionally respond to pars plana vitrectomy and/or other systemic immunosuppressive therapy. See also BCSC Section 12, *Retina and Vitreous*.

Farber MD, Lam S, Tessler HH, et al. Reduction of macular oedema by acetazolamide in patients with chronic iridocyclitis: a randomised prospective crossover study. *Br J Ophthalmol*. 1994;78:4–7.

Jennings T, Rusin MM, Tessler HH, et al. Posterior sub-Tenon's injections of corticosteroids in uveitis patients with cystoid macular edema. *Jpn J Ophthalmol*. 1988;32: 385–391.

Vitreous Opacification and Vitritis

Permanent vitreous opacification affecting vision occasionally occurs in uveitis, particularly in eyes with toxoplasma retinitis and pars planitis. In other cases of vitritis the diagnosis is uncertain. Pars plana vitrectomy may be therapeutic and/or diagnostic in eyes with vitritis. It can be used both to debride vitreous and to obtain a vitreous sample that may be studied by culture, stains, and cytology to determine the etiology of the vitritis.

Retinal Detachment

Posterior uveitis occasionally causes a rhegmatogenous or tractional retinal detachment. Repair is often complicated by vitreous organization and poor visualization. Acute retinal necrosis and cytomegalovirus retinitis frequently lead to retinal detachments that are difficult to repair because of multiple, large, and posterior retinal breaks. Pars plana vitrectomy and endolaser treatment with internal gas or silicone oil tamponade may be required to repair the detachment and/or remove epiretinal membranes.

Freeman WR, Friedberg DN, Berry C, et al. Risk factors for development of rhegmatogenous retinal detachment in patients with cytomegalovirus retinitis. *Am J Ophthalmol.* 1993;116:713–720.

Kuppermann BD, Flores-Aguilar M, Quiceno JI, et al. A masked prospective evaluation of outcome parameters for cytomegalovirus-related retinal detachment surgery in patients with acquired immune deficiency syndrome. *Ophthalmology.* 1994;101: 46–55.

Nussenblatt RB, Whitcup SM, Palestine AG. *Uveitis: Fundamentals and Clinical Practice.* 2nd ed. St Louis: Mosby; 1996.

Sternberg P Jr, Han DP, Yeo JH, et al. Photocoagulation to prevent retinal detachment in acute retinal necrosis. *Ophthalmology.* 1988;95:1389–1393.

CHAPTER XIII

Ocular Involvement in AIDS

Acquired immunodeficiency syndrome (AIDS) is the first pandemic of the second half of the 20th century. This syndrome, first described in 1981 in Los Angeles, is now believed to be a new infection of human beings that originated in central Africa, perhaps in the 1950s. From there it probably spread to the Caribbean and then to the United States, Europe, and other parts of the world. This syndrome is caused by a retrovirus commonly known as *human immunodeficiency virus (HIV)*.

The HIV epidemic is about to enter its third decade, with new cases steadily being reported around the world. Although the infection was recognized initially in the United States, its spread continues to increase at an alarming rate, particularly in countries with large populations and areas of poverty such as India and Thailand and in many countries of sub-Sahara Africa. It is estimated at the time of this writing that more than 20 million people are known to be infected with HIV worldwide and that by the year 2000, about 40 million people will have become infected. Most of this increase will be in impoverished countries, particularly in those countries with high rates of sexually transmitted diseases (STDs), which are known to be important co-factors in the transmission of HIV. The proportion of new cases involving homo-sexual and bisexual men is dropping, while the proportion of new HIV infections in intravenous drug users, women, and children is rising. The World Health Organization estimates that 1.5 million children are now infected worldwide.

During the first decade of the HIV epidemic it became clear that aggressive educational programs could reduce the transmission of HIV. This mass education had a positive influence on changing high-risk sexual behavior in the United States and other parts of the industrialized world. HIV-infected individuals now live significantly longer, and the quality of their lives has also been improved by the introduction of various antiviral agents and drugs that reduce morbidity and mortality from the myriad opportunistic infections that occur so frequently in the late stages of HIV infection. However, a cure for this deadly disease is nowhere near. But although HIV infection is not yet curable, it is now recognized to be a manageable, albeit chronic and severe, medical condition. Moreover, if HIV infection is detected prior to the development of symptoms, prophylactic administration of the newer anti-HIV agents can have a significant beneficial effect on the overall course of the disease.

Bartlett JG. Update in infectious diseases. *Ann Intern Med.* 1997;127:217–224.

Kessler HA, Bick JA, Pottage JC Jr, et al. AIDS: Part I. *Dis Mon.* 1992;38:633–690.

Virology of HIV

HIV is a retrovirus that is a member of the *Lentivirinae* subfamily. There are currently two lentiviruses known to infect humans:

□ HIV-1, the more prevalent, is seen worldwide

□ HIV-2 is identified primarily in western Africa

HIV-2 virus shares roughly 40% homology in nucleotide sequence with HIV-1 and about 75% homology with simian immunodeficiency virus.

HIV-1 and HIV-2 viruses are each approximately 100 nm in diameter. The virion has a cylindrical nucleocapsid. This capsid contains the single-stranded RNA and viral enzymes, including proteinase, integrase, and reverse transcriptase. Surrounding the capsid is a lipid envelope, which is derived from the infected host cell. This envelope contains virus-encoded glycoproteins. The viral genome contains three structural genes: *gag, pol,* and *env.* HIV-1 and HIV-2 are genetically similar in the *gag* and *pol* regions; the *env* regions, however, are different, resulting in differences in the envelope glycoproteins of these viruses. Such heterogeneity among these viruses leads to specific immune responses and necessitates different HIV-1 and HIV-2 immune assays or Western blot procedures for serologic diagnosis. In addition to the three structural genes, HIV contains six regulatory genes: *tat, rev, nef, vif, vpr,* and *vpu.* Two of these regulatory genes *(tat* and *rev)* are essential for virus replication. HIV isolates show marked heterogeneity in the *env* and the *nef* genes with the following results:

□ Differing tissue and cell tropisms

□ Variations in pathogenesis

□ Disparate responses to therapy

□ Potential challenges in developing a broadly cross-reactive protective vaccine

This viral heterogeneity exists from continent to continent, from one infected individual to another, and even within the same infected host. Spontaneous mutation of the virus, the frequent error rate of the reverse transcriptase enzyme, and/or possibly antiviral therapy may be causes of some of this heterogeneity. See also BCSC Section 2, *Fundamentals and Principles of Ophthalmology,* Part 3, Genetics.

Pathogenesis

Initial events in HIV infection include attachment of the virus to a distinct group of T cells and monocytes/macrophages that display a membrane antigen complex known as CD4. However, other molecules on these cells may also play a role in the attachment of HIV. After attachment the lipid membrane of the virus fuses with the target cell, allowing entry of the viral core into host cell cytoplasm. This viral core is subsequently uncoated and transcribed by reverse transcriptase enzyme, resulting in a complementary strand of DNA. The action of cellular enzymes transforms this DNA into the typical double-stranded form that subsequently enters the cell nucleus.

Once intranuclear, the proviral DNA integrates into the genome of the host cell by means of a viral endonuclease. This host cell can be either latently or actively infected. If latently infected, no viral RNA is produced, and a productive infection may not develop. If actively infected, however, the cell may produce mature virions by transcription of proviral DNA. This transcription also generates messenger RNA (mRNA). In the cytoplasm mRNA is translated into HIV-specific structural proteins that are integrated with the viral core particles.

These assembled virus particles then migrate to the plasma membrane of the infected cell. Final maturation of the virus occurs by a process of reverse endocytosis (budding) at the plasma membrane. Subsequent dissemination of the virus occurs either through free infectious particles that are released by the budding process or, more likely, by cell-to-cell transfer.

The initial target cells of HIV, namely CD4+ helper T cells and macrophages, show different cytopathic effects. The T cells gradually decrease in number as the virus replicates. Helper T cells are known to play a pivotal role in immunologic response, and their decrease in number leads to immune deficiency and subsequent secondary opportunistic infections (see Part 1, Immunology, of this volume). In contrast, the infected macrophages rarely undergo lysis or decrease in number. These circulating infected cells harbor the HIV and may disseminate it throughout the body. HIV alters the immune-related functions of these infected monocytes/macrophages in the following ways:

☐ Decreased migration response to chemoattractants

☐ Defective intracellular killing of various microorganisms such as *Toxoplasma gondii* and *Candida*

☐ Reduced expression of class II MHC molecules, which impairs the processing and presentation of antigen to helper T cells

☐ Excessive production by the macrophages of TNF-α, which leads to dementia, wasting syndrome, and unexplained fever

Weiss RA. How does HIV cause AIDS? *Science.* 1993;260:1273–1279.

Natural History

Although the illness that results from HIV infection differs from one individual to another, various predictable stages ultimately lead to death. In general, infected individuals initially experience an acute primary infection, followed by a relatively asymptomatic infection that can include generalized lymphadenopathy. This progresses to symptomatic disease associated with progressive decline in helper T cells and eventually to advanced HIV disease with the development of opportunistic infections, malignancies, or both. This advanced stage is what was first recognized as AIDS. These AIDS-defining illnesses are summarized in Table XIII-1, which represents the 1993 Centers for Disease Control (CDC) revised classification system for HIV infection and AIDS.

The acute HIV infection usually lasts for about 1–2 weeks and is characterized by symptoms typical of a nonspecific viral illness. Patients then enter an asymptomatic phase of variable duration, from 2 to more than 10 years. During this phase, the CD4 lymphocyte count varies from about 200 to 750 cells/mm^3 (CD4 counts in immunocompetent adults vary from 600 to 1500 cells/mm^3). Advanced HIV disease may last for up to 3 years, and during this stage, the CD4 cells decrease to less than 200 cells/mm^3.

Transmission

Transmission of HIV occurs predominantly by sexual contact, by parenteral (IV drug use) or mucous membrane exposure to contaminated blood or blood products, and perinatally. HIV has been isolated from blood, semen, saliva, cerebrospinal fluid, tears, breast milk, amniotic fluid, vaginal secretions, cervical cells, and bronchoalveolar lavage fluid. A 1997 study broke down the transmission of HIV:

☐ Sexual intercourse accounted for 70% of the cases

☐ Intravenous drug use accounted for 27% of the cases

☐ Blood transfusions accounted for 2%–3% of the cases

☐ Perinatal transmission accounted for about 1% of the cases

TABLE XIII-1

1993 REVISED CLASSIFICATION SYSTEM FOR
HIV INFECTION AND AIDS-DEFINING ILLNESSES

CD4+ T Lymphocyte Categories

Category 1: >500 cells/mm³
Category 2: 200–499 cells/mm³
Category 3: <200 cells/mm³

Clinical Categories of HIV Infection

Category A: One or more of the following conditions, but no conditions in category B or C:
  Asymptomatic HIV infection
  Persistent generalized lymphadenopathy
  Acute (primary) HIV infection

Category B: Symptomatic conditions in an HIV-infected adolescent or adult that are not included in category C (AIDS-defining illnesses) and that meet at least one of the following criteria:
  (1) the conditions are attributed to HIV infection or are indicative of a defect in cell-mediated immunity or
  (2) the conditions are considered by physicians to have a clinical course or to require management that is complicated by HIV infection
  Examples of conditions in category B include, but are not limited to
    Bacillary angiomatosis *(Bartonella henselae, B quintana)*
    Candidiasis, oropharyngeal (thrush)
    Candidiasis, vulvovaginal; persistent, frequent, or poorly responsive to therapy
    Cervical dysplasia (moderate or severe)/cervical carcinoma in situ
    Constitutional symptoms, such as fever (38.5° C) or diarrhea lasting >1 month
    Hairy leukoplakia, oral
    Herpes zoster (shingles), involving at least two distinct episodes or more than one dermatome
    Idiopathic thrombocytopenic purpura
    Listeriosis
    Pelvic inflammatory disease, particularly if complicated by tubo-ovarian abscess
    Peripheral neuropathy

Category C (AIDS): Includes the clinical conditions listed below *(AIDS-defining illnesses):*
  Candidiasis of bronchi, trachea, or lungs
  Candidiasis, esophageal
  Cervical cancer, invasive*
  Coccidioidomycosis, disseminated or extrapulmonary
  Cryptococcosis, extrapulmonary
  Cryptosporidiosis, chronic intestinal (>1 month's duration)
  Cytomegalovirus disease (other than liver, spleen, or nodes)
  Cytomegalovirus retinitis (with loss of vision)
  Encephalopathy, HIV-related
  Herpes simplex: chronic ulcer(s) (>1 month's duration), or bronchitis, pneumonitis, or esophagitis
  Histoplasmosis, disseminated or extrapulmonary
  Isosporiasis, chronic intestinal (>1 month's duration)
  Kaposi sarcoma
  Lymphoma, Burkitt (or equivalent term)
  Lymphoma, immunoblastic (or equivalent term)
  Lymphoma, primary, of brain

Continued

TABLE XIII-1

Category C continued:
  Mycobacterium avium complex or *M kansasii,* disseminated or extrapulmonary
  Mycobacterium tuberculosis, any site (pulmonary* or extrapulmonary)
  Mycobacterium, other species or unidentified species, disseminated or extrapulmonary
  Pneumocystis carinii pneumonia
  Pneumonia, recurrent*
  Progressive multifocal leukoencephalopathy
  Salmonella septicemia, recurrent
  Toxoplasmosis of brain
  Wasting syndrome due to HIV

---

* Added in the 1993 expansion of the AIDS surveillance case definition. In addition, a CD4+ T lymphocyte count of <200/mm³ or a CD4+ T lymphocyte percentage of total lymphocytes <14 is now considered an AIDS-defining condition.

Data from Centers for Disease Control. 1993 revised classification system for HIV infection and expanded surveillance case definition for AIDS among adolescents and adults. *MMWR.* 1992;41:1–19.

Reproduced with permission from Gold JWM. The diagnosis and management of HIV infection. In: *Med Clin North Am.* Philadelphia: Saunders; 1996;80:1286.

There are rare instances in which HIV has been transmitted through transplantation of organs such as the heart, liver, kidney, bone, or pancreas. No cases of HIV transmission have been reported from corneal transplantation.

Diagnosis

Laboratory investigations are essential to establish the diagnosis of HIV infection, which depends on demonstration of virus-specific antibodies by ELISA and Western blot, viral antigen by enzyme immunoassay (EIA), direct isolation of HIV from the blood by culture, or detection of HIV nucleic acid by polymerase chain reaction (PCR). EIA such as ELISA is the most widely used method for screening individuals for antibody to HIV or for direct detection of HIV antigen. The specificity and sensitivity of the commercially available HIV antibody kits (ELISA) are generally in excess of 99%. However, even though the ELISA is a highly sensitive and specific test, false-positive results do occur. Mainly to minimize the reporting of false-positive results, Western blot analysis is carried out to confirm the results of ELISA. The Western blot assay has the advantage of direct visualization of the antibodies directed to specific major proteins of HIV. The additional investigations such as PCR and viral P24 antigen detection are usually employed only when the immunoassays do not provide clearly positive results or in testing seronegative high-risk individuals.

Management of HIV Infection

Systemic Conditions

As the number of HIV-infected individuals increases throughout the world, particularly in impoverished countries, it is important that physicians in these countries become aware of means of managing the viral infection and preventing the complications associated with this deadly disease. The prevention of complications involves not only antiretroviral therapy and prophylactic antimicrobial agents but also immunization (e.g., hepatitis B, influenza, and other vaccines) and early disease detection. Progression of the infection leads to deterioration of the protective immune function, and symptoms such as fatigue, night sweats, malaise, fever, and weight loss will develop. Although thorough clinical examination provides some clues as to the stage of HIV infection, measurement of T lymphocyte subsets, particularly absolute CD4 counts, has become a fundamental aspect of staging HIV infection:

- CD4 counts between 250 and 500 cells/mm^3 are associated with oral candidiasis and disseminated tuberculosis
- Counts between 150 and 200 cells/mm^3 are associated with Kaposi sarcoma, lymphoma, and cryptosporidiosis
- Counts between 75 and 125 cells/mm^3 are associated with *Pneumocystis carinii,* disseminated *Mycobacterium avium* complex, ulcerated herpes simplex, cryptococcosis, toxoplasmosis, and esophageal candidiasis
- Counts lower than 50 cells/mm^3 are associated with CMV retinitis

Medical therapy Anti-HIV agents approved by the Food and Drug Administration (FDA) include *zidovudine (ZDV,* formerly known as *AZT), didanosine (ddI), zalcitabine (ddC), stavudine (d4T),* and *lamivudine (3TC).* All of these are nucleoside analogues that work through inhibition of the reverse transcriptase enzyme. These agents are all associated with toxic side effects, including severe bone marrow suppression, peripheral neuropathy, gastrointestinal irritation, and others. Agents known as nonnucleoside reverse transcriptase inhibitors (NNRTI), such as *nevirapine, delavirdine,* and *DMP-266,* have been found effective in managing HIV-1 infection when used in combination with ddI and ZDV. Nevirapine has been approved by the FDA for use in HIV-1 infection in combination with other agents.

> Havlir DV, Lange JM. New antiretrovirals and new combinations. *AIDS.* 1998;12: S165–S174.

Recently, the FDA approved a new group of antiretroviral agents that inhibit HIV protease. Such inhibition prevents cleavage of a larger precursor viral protein that is required for assembly of infectious viral particles. The approved protease inhibitors include *saquinavir, nelfinavir, indinavir,* and *ritonavir.* These agents are effective in the treatment of advanced HIV infection when used in combination with the reverse transcriptase inhibitors. However, they are also associated with side effects: liver function abnormalities, gastrointestinal irritation, elevated creatinine, nephrolithiasis, and others.

Management of each HIV-infected individual requires an in-depth clinical and laboratory evaluation including

- CD4 T-cell counts
- Determination of plasma HIV RNA level by reverse transcriptase polymerase chain reaction (RT-PCR) or by signal amplification assays like branched DNA (bDNA)
- Detection of AIDS-defining illnesses (see Table XIII-1)

Even though treatment of HIV infection is continually changing as a result of the introduction of new antiretroviral agents and the information gathered from various clinical trials, recent guidelines (1997) have emerged from recommendations by

International AIDS Society–USA. Treatment is indicated for any individual with acute HIV infection or who is within 6 months of seroconversion and in any chronically infected patient when HIV RNA levels are above 10,000 copies/ml or when CD4 count falls below 500 cells/mm^3. The preferred treatment includes a combination of three agents: two reverse transcriptase enzyme inhibitors (e.g., ZVD plus 3TC or ZVD plus ddI, ZVD plus ddC, 3TC plus D4T, and other combinations) and a protease inhibitor (ritonavir, indinavir, nelfinavir).

When the CD4 count falls below 200 cells/mm^3, the patient requires prophylaxis against *Pneumocystis* pneumonia by trimethoprim/sulfamethoxazole (TMP/SMX). It is also important during this stage to rule out tuberculosis, which is a common complication of HIV infection and 500 times more common in HIV-infected individuals than in the general population. HIV patients with positive PPDs require prophylaxis with isoniazid and pyridoxine for at least 12 months. The physician must remember that the PPD is notoriously unreliable in HIV patients because of their altered cellular immune function. Because the skin test reaction is decreased in HIV patients, any skin test that measures greater than 2 mm may be considered a positive result in some patients at high risk for tuberculosis.

HIV patients with low CD4 counts also require prophylaxis against recurrent opportunistic infections such as cerebral toxoplasmosis, cryptococcosis, *Mycobacterium avium–intracellulare* complex (MAI), oroesophageal or vulvovaginal candidiasis, and histoplasmosis. Rifabutin is an agent commonly used for prophylaxis against MAI, and fluconazole is used for the mycotic infections.

Carpenter CC, Fischl MA, Hammer SM, et al. Antiretroviral therapy for HIV infection in 1996: recommendations of an international panel. International AIDS Study–USA. *JAMA.* 1996;276:146–154.

Ophthalmic Complications

Ocular manifestations have been reported in up to 70% of individuals infected with HIV, and it has become apparent that the ocular manifestations almost invariably reflect systemic disease and may be the first sign of disseminated systemic infection. The ophthalmologist thus has the opportunity to make not only a sight-saving, but indeed a life-prolonging, diagnosis in some patients with AIDS. These ocular manifestations include

☐ HIV-related microangiopathy of the retina

☐ Various opportunistic viral, bacterial, and fungal infections

☐ Kaposi sarcoma

☐ Lymphomas involving the retina (primary intraocular lymphoma), adnexal structures, and orbit

☐ Squamous cell carcinoma of conjunctiva

Recent reports suggest that HIV may also cause anterior uveitis, inflammatory reaction in the vitreous, and chronic multifocal retinal infiltrates that are not responsive to corticosteroids and improve with antiretroviral therapy.

HIV retinopathy is the most common ocular finding in patients with AIDS, occurring in about 50%–70% of cases. It is characterized by retinal hemorrhages, microaneurysms, and cotton-wool spots (Fig XIII-1). The cotton-wool spots are usually oriented along vascular arcades and represent focal areas of ischemia in the nerve fiber layer. HIV has been isolated from human retina, and its antigen has been detected in retinal endothelial cells by immunohistochemistry. It is believed that

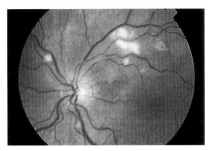

FIG XIII-1—Typical cotton-wool spots in a patient infected with HIV.

such HIV endothelial infection and/or hematologic alterations may play a role in the development of cotton-wool spots and other vascular alterations. The microaneurysms and hemorrhages that characterize HIV retinopathy are also distributed along the nerve fiber layer and in the inner retinal layers. Cotton-wool spots, retinal hemorrhages, and microaneurysms are probably the result of both an underlying microvasculopathy and hematologic abnormalities such as anemia and functional abnormalities of hemostasis.

Other infectious agents that can affect the eye in patients with AIDS include cytomegalovirus (CMV), herpes zoster, *Toxoplasma gondii*, *Mycobacterium tuberculosis*, *M avium–intracellulare*, *Cryptococcus neoformans*, *Pneumocystis carinii*, *Histoplasma capsulatum*, *Candida*, molluscum contagiosum, *Microsporida*, and others. These agents can infect the ocular adnexa, anterior segment, or posterior segment. Visual morbidity, however, occurs primarily with posterior segment involvement, particularly retinitis caused by CMV, herpes zoster, or *T gondii*.

Cytomegalovirus retinitis CMV retinitis is the most commonly seen opportunistic ocular infection in patients with AIDS and can occasionally be the initial manifestation of AIDS. Cytomegalovirus is a double-stranded DNA virus that belongs to the Herpesviridae family, which also includes the herpes simplex, varicella-zoster, and Epstein-Barr viruses. Before the administration of nucleoside analogues in combination with protease inhibitors, generally known as *highly active antiretroviral therapy (HAART)*, came into use against HIV, CMV disease occurring in the retina, colon, lung, and other sites was the most common opportunistic infection in AIDS. Even today CMV disease could be the most common opportunistic infection in AIDS. Among the various affected organs, the retina most commonly presents with clinical manifestations.

Prior to HAART, CMV retinitis was known to occur in 15%–40% of AIDS patients, and the median elapsed time between diagnosis of AIDS and the development of CMV retinitis was about 9 months. However, more recent studies have shown that this infection can occur as long as 3–5 years after the diagnosis of AIDS and usually develops when CD4 cell counts are below 50 cells/mm^3.

The modes of transmission for CMV are not completely understood, although epidemiologic and virologic studies implicate close or intimate contact with infect-

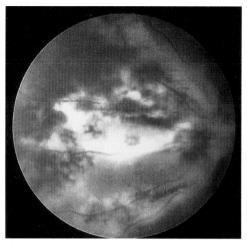

FIG XIII-2—An area of cytomegalovirus retinitis. The infection extends from the disc into the superotemporal quadrant and has the typical hemorrhage.

ed individuals who are shedding virus in their urine, saliva, or other secretions. CMV infection in otherwise healthy adults and children is usually asymptomatic but can occasionally be associated with a mononucleosis-like syndrome. In contrast to the generally benign course of CMV infection in healthy individuals, CMV is a major cause of morbidity and mortality in patients who are immunocompromised. The high incidence of anti-CMV antibodies in the general population is evidence for widespread exposure to this virus. It is possible that CMV retinitis represents a dissemination of systemic infection or a reactivation of CMV that was already present in a latent form.

Well-established CMV retinitis is easily recognized as a full-thickness retinal opacification associated with hard exudates and hemorrhages (Fig XIII-2). The infection typically spreads along one of the major vascular arcades, but it may begin anywhere in the retina, including the far periphery. Because of severe immunosuppression in AIDS patients, the amount of overlying vitreous inflammation is minimal. CMV infection in the peripheral retina shows granular white opacification of the retina with minimal or no retinal hemorrhage. Infections that involve the posterior pole generally demonstrate the more typical picture of full-thickness retinitis with hard exudates and hemorrhages. Occasionally, the CMV retinitis may present with periphlebitis (frosted-branch angiitis) with some retinal necrosis. Very early CMV retinitis lesions may resemble cotton-wool spots.

Diagnosis. The diagnosis of CMV retinitis is based on its characteristic clinical appearance. Serologic investigation and viral culture are of limited value, because a large proportion of individuals show evidence of previous exposure to CMV on serologic testing. In addition, the serologic diagnosis of CMV in patients with AIDS can be equivocal because of the profound immunosuppression of these patients. Although culture-confirmed presence of CMV in the throat, urine, and blood may be more reliable, immunosuppressed patients are often chronic carriers of this virus, so the mere presence of CMV does not necessarily indicate significant infection.

Because of these confounding factors, the ophthalmic examination has taken on great importance, as the diagnosis of CMV infection involving the retina can thus be made easily and reliably. Rarely, molecular techniques such as branch chain DNA and quantitative PCR for CMV DNA are used for diagnosis; however, these investigations are employed primarily for research purposes in predicting which individual may develop CMV retinitis. These techniques are conducted using blood, plasma, or intraocular fluids.

Management. In the United States, four medications are currently approved for treatment of CMV retinitis: ganciclovir, foscarnet, cidofovir, and fomivirsen. Both ganciclovir and foscarnet show an initial response rate of 80%–100%. Moreover, treatment of CMV retinitis may prolong the survival of AIDS patients. Prior to the introduction of HAART, the median survival time following the diagnosis of CMV retinitis was 6 weeks in patients receiving no treatment. Anti-CMV treatment increased the survival time to 10 months in patients who responded completely to ganciclovir treatment and to 3.1 months for those who responded partially. Recent studies show longer survival as a result of improved treatment of HIV infection with antiretroviral agents and management of various opportunistic infections and neoplasms.

Three forms of *ganciclovir* are currently approved for clinical use:

□ Intravenous

□ Oral

□ Intravitreal in the form of an injection or implant

Ganciclovir is usually administered IV. The initial 2-week, high-dose induction therapy (5 mg/kg twice daily for 2 weeks) is aimed at controlling the infection and is followed by long-term maintenance therapy (5 mg/kg once daily 7 days a week, or 6 mg/kg once daily 5 days a week). The primary side effect of ganciclovir is myelosuppression. Concomitant use of granulocyte-macrophage colony-stimulating factor (GM-CSF) can reduce or reverse neutropenia, the most serious component of myelosuppression, and may allow continuation of ganciclovir therapy. Reversal of neutropenia is usually possible but may also necessitate interruption of the drug therapy. Thrombocytopenia has been reported to occur in 5%–10% of patients treated with ganciclovir. At the time of diagnosis of CMV retinitis, patients may already be undergoing treatment with zidovudine. Because ZVD also has toxic effects on the bone marrow, the dosage is usually decreased when used concomitantly with ganciclovir.

Ganciclovir is also available for oral administration, and this route of administration can be used as a maintenance therapy for patients with CMV retinitis who respond well to IV induction therapy with this agent. Drug toxicity is lower in patients maintained on oral administration. However, median time to progression of retinitis on oral ganciclovir (29 days) is less than with IV maintenance therapy (49 days). Moreover, the risk of development of CMV in the fellow eye is greater in patients receiving oral ganciclovir compared to IV maintenance.

Foscarnet is administered IV and, like ganciclovir, it requires an initial 2-week, high-dose induction therapy (60 mg/kg every 8 hours for 2 or 3 weeks) followed by long-term maintenance therapy (90–120 mg/kg daily 5 or 7 days a week). Although foscarnet does not have a toxic effect on the bone marrow and can be used concurrently with full-dose ZVD therapy, it is toxic to the kidneys. Renal dysfunction and metabolic abnormalities of calcium and magnesium have been reported in up to 30% of patients who are receiving foscarnet, and seizures have been reported in approximately 10%.

Although ganciclovir and foscarnet have been approved by the FDA for IV use and ganciclovir for oral administration, patients who cannot tolerate these systemic anti-CMV drugs may receive them through intravitreal injection. Intravitreal ganciclovir or foscarnet can also be considered for patients who have shown progression of retinitis despite high-dose systemic ganciclovir, foscarnet, or combination therapy with both drugs.

Under topical anesthesia, an intravitreal injection of 2000 μg of ganciclovir is given once a week. Foscarnet 1.2 mg in 0.05 ml can be given instead of ganciclovir. Initial success rates are very high, with almost all patients showing early resolution of retinitis. As with IV forms of therapy, relapse occurs in a substantial proportion of patients. The risks associated with repeated intravitreal injections include vitreous hemorrhage, retinal detachment, and bacterial endophthalmitis. Perhaps the most serious drawback of the intravitreal route of administration is that it does not provide the benefits of systemic anti-CMV treatment to the other eye and to extraocular sites of CMV infection.

A second proven method of intravitreal administration of ganciclovir is through an intravitreal device, which is surgically implanted and delivers the drug in effective concentrations over 4–8 months. The intravitreal device would also be a useful alternative for those patients who cannot tolerate IV therapy or do not respond well to it.

Recently, the FDA approved the antiviral *cidofovir* for treatment of CMV disease including retinitis. This agent is administered intravenously with efficacy similar to IV ganciclovir. Cidofovir has a prolonged intracellular half-life and is administered at a dose of 5 mg/kg once a week for 2 weeks for induction, and 5 mg/kg every 2 weeks for maintenance therapy. During the administration of this agent, the patient requires IV hydration and probenecid to avoid severe renal toxicity. Some patients may develop hypotony and/or uveitis while on cidofovir.

Another newly approved agent is an antisense compound *fomivirsen* (Vitravene, ISIS 2922), which is composed of 21 nucleotides. This agent inhibits the virus replication and is administered intravitreally. The agent is recommended at a dosage of 330 μg for the patient whose retinitis has failed to respond to other anti-CMV agents. Fomivirsen has been shown to be effective in controlling early or advanced CMV retinitis for up to 1 year when given as an intravitreal dose of 330 μg. In this study fomivirsen was given weekly for 3 doses, then once every 2 weeks for maintenance therapy. Side effects of fomivirsen include anterior uveitis, vitritis, elevation of IOP, and cataract formation.

When assessing response to treatment, the most important clinical characteristic the physician must evaluate is the size of the lesion. Careful attention to the border of the lesion, not the central area, is essential. The clinical appearance of the lesion can be compared against earlier clinical photographs to detect enlargement or stabilization of its size. The second most important clinical parameter is the degree of activity of the lesion, which is determined by the presence of retinal whitening and hemorrhage at the border of the lesion. Lesions in recurrent disease usually demonstrate fluffy white areas of active retinitis at the border of the original CMV lesion. In some cases of recurrence, lesions may enlarge despite minimal signs of retinal whitening or hemorrhage. As with the primary disease, it is the border of the lesion that reflects disease activity. In chronic stages of the disease, large atrophic holes may develop that can lead to retinal detachment.

Despite the impressive initial response to treatment with the agents described, active retinitis recurs in 18%–50% of patients while on maintenance therapy and in virtually all patients who discontinue anti-CMV therapy. Most investigators believe that, given enough time, all patients will eventually suffer a relapse, although they generally respond to a second course of induction (reinduction) therapy. If a patient has a recurrence while receiving ganciclovir, foscarnet, or cidofovir, consideration must be given to the following choices:

□ Reinduction with the current medication

□ New induction using the second or third medication

□ Concomitant use of two of the medications

Concomitant use is found to be synergistic against CMV in vitro and beneficial in preventing progression of CMV retinitis that fails to respond to either agent administered alone.

Patients on HAART may have an increase in CD4 cell count sufficient to allow a decrease or discontinuation of their anti-CMV therapy. Such patients need to be monitored closely, however, since recurrences of CMV retinitis may occur even with CD4 counts over 100 cells/mm.[3] It appears that such patients may show a *quantitative* increase in CD4 cells, but these cells may be *qualitatively* less immunologically active against opportunistic organisms. Such disrupted immunity against CMV could result from restricted expression of the T-lymphocyte receptor repertoire.

Retinal detachment. An additional complication of CMV retinitis is retinal detachment, which occurs in up to 50% of patients. It may occur either when the retinitis is active or when it is quiescent during successful treatment. In almost all patients with retinal detachment, the CMV lesions extend anteriorly to the pars plana, and the retinitis generally involves more than 50% of the retina. Myopia is an additional risk factor for the development of retinal detachment in patients with CMV retinitis.

Retinal detachments in patients with CMV retinitis are among the most difficult to repair because of extensive retinal necrosis and multiple, often posterior, hole formation. Most investigators agree that these detachments are not amenable to repair by scleral buckling alone; the procedure of choice is pars plana vitrectomy with long-term silicone oil tamponade. Anatomic reattachment can be achieved in 90% of these patients. Functional success, however, depends on the condition of the macula and the extent of affected retina.

Future developments. A current topic of intense research is the possibility of identifying patients at risk for CMV retinitis. Several studies have indicated that, in general, CMV retinitis does not develop unless the CD4 lymphocyte count is lower than 50 cells/mm[3]. Severe immunosuppression may be a prerequisite for CMV retinitis. Disseminated CMV infection and load of CMV in circulation as determined by PCR may play role in the occurrence of the retinal infection.

Progressive outer retinal necrosis (PORN)   A rare infection in AIDS patients, the progressive outer retinal necrosis syndrome may be caused by the herpes zoster virus or other viruses in the herpes family. It may occur in the absence of, at the same time as, or subsequent to a cutaneous zoster infection. It is possible that PORN represents a distinct form of acute retinal necrosis occurring in an immunocompromised host (Fig XIII-3).

In its early stages PORN may be difficult to differentiate from peripheral CMV retinitis. However, its characteristic rapid progression in a circumferential fashion, sparing the retinal vasculature, allows this entity to be distinguished from the acute

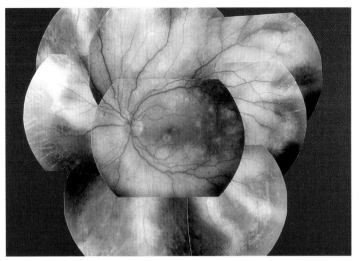

FIG XIII-3—Retinal necrosis with preservation of vessels in a patient with progressive outer retinal necrosis.

retinal necrosis syndrome (ARN) and CMV infection. There is a high incidence of retinal detachment, and bilateral involvement is common. Although no adequate therapy presently exists, ganciclovir or foscarnet in combination with acyclovir may be more effective than acyclovir alone in stabilizing the infection.

Toxoplasma *retinochoroiditis* A number of reports of toxoplasmosis in AIDS patients have revealed important clinical differences from immunocompetent individuals. In general, the size of the retinochoroiditic lesions is larger in patients with AIDS, with up to one third of lesions greater than 5 disc diameters in size. Bilateral disease is seen in 18%–38% of these cases. Solitary, multifocal, and miliary patterns of retinitis have been observed (Fig XIII-4). A vitreous inflammatory reaction usually appears overlying the area of active retinochoroiditis, but the degree of vitreous reaction is less than that observed in immunocompetent patients.

The diagnosis of ocular toxoplasmosis may be more difficult in patients with AIDS. Although this diagnosis in immunocompetent patients is frequently aided by the presence of old retinochoroiditic scars, patients with AIDS rarely demonstrate preexisting scars, which are present in only 4%–6% of AIDS patients with ocular toxoplasmosis. Because the clinical manifestations in this population are so varied and may be more severe than in immunocompetent individuals, ocular toxoplasmosis in AIDS patients may be difficult to distinguish from acute retinal necrosis syndrome and variants of CMV, herpes simplex or herpes zoster virus, and syphilitic retinitis.

The histologic features of ocular specimens from AIDS patients reflect the immunologic abnormalities of the host. In general, the inflammatory reaction in the choroid, retina, and vitreous is less than in patients with an intact immune system. Trophozoites and cysts can be observed in greater numbers within areas of retinitis, and *T gondii* organisms can occasionally be seen invading the choroid, which is not the case in immunocompetent individuals.

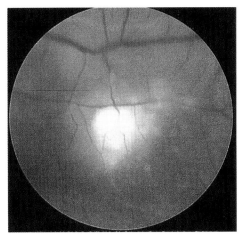

FIG XIII-4—Fundus photograph of a patient with *Toxoplasma* retinochoroiditis.

Ocular toxoplasmosis in immunocompetent individuals is usually the result of reactivation of a congenital infection. In contrast, a high proportion of AIDS patients with ocular toxoplasmosis probably has newly acquired infection or dissemination from a nonocular site of infection. These conclusions are drawn from the observation that preexisting retinochoroiditic scars are rarely present, and *Toxoplasma*-specific IgM titers are found in 6%–12% of patients.

The prompt diagnosis of ocular toxoplasmosis is especially important in patients with immunosuppression because it inevitably progresses if left untreated, in contrast to the self-limited disease of immunocompetent individuals. In addition, ocular toxoplasmosis in immunocompromised patients may be associated with cerebral or disseminated toxoplasmosis, an important cause of morbidity and mortality in AIDS patients.

Antitoxoplasmic therapy with various combinations of pyrimethamine, sulfadiazine, and clindamycin is required. Corticosteroids should not be used because of the risk from further immunosuppression and because the inflammatory reaction is relatively mild in this population. In selecting the therapeutic regimen, the physician should consider the possibility of coexisting cerebral or disseminated toxoplasmosis and the toxic effects of pyrimethamine and sulfadiazine on the bone marrow. Even after the active retinitis has resolved, it is necessary to continue antitoxoplasmic therapy for the life of the patient in order to prevent recurrence.

Syphilitic chorioretinitis The clinical presentations of syphilitic chorioretinitis include uveitis, optic neuritis, and retinitis. Patients may also experience dermatologic and CNS manifestations. AIDS patients with syphilitic chorioretinitis present with vitritis associated with large bilateral pale yellow subretinal lesions that are solitary and placoid. Most of these lesions show evidence of central fading and a pattern of stippled hyperpigmentation of the RPE *(syphilitic posterior placoid chorioretinitis)*. Some HIV-positive patients with syphilis may present with dense vitritis without clinical evidence of chorioretinitis. In these patients vitritis can be the first manifestation of syphilis.

Syphilis may pursue a more aggressive course in patients with AIDS. These patients require treatment with 12–24 million units of intravenous penicillin G administered daily for at least 10 days, followed by 2.4 million units of intramuscular benzathine penicillin G administered weekly for 3 weeks.

Pneumocystis carinii *choroiditis* Patients with AIDS are at much greater risk of developing *Pneumocystis carinii* pneumonia, and this infection can be the initial opportunistic disease to be seen in these patients. Rarely, this infection can disseminate, and patients with such disseminated infection may present with choroidal infiltrates containing the microorganisms responsible.

Fundus changes characteristic of *Pneumocystis carinii* choroiditis consist of slightly elevated, plaquelike, yellow-white lesions located in the choroid with minimal vitritis (Figs XIII-5, XIII-6, XIII-7). On fluorescein angiography these lesions tend to be hypofluorescent in the early phase and hyperfluorescent in the later phases. If disseminated *P carinii* is suspected, an extensive examination is required including

□ Chest radiography

□ Arterial blood gas analysis

□ Liver function testing

□ Abdominal CT

Treatment of *P carinii* choroiditis requires hospitalization for a 3-week regimen of IV trimethoprim (20 mg/kg per day) and sulfamethoxazole (100 mg/kg per day) or

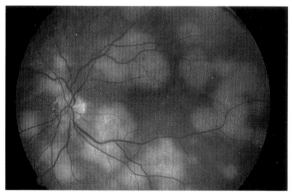

FIG XIII-5—Ophthalmoscopic appearance of disseminated *Pneumocystis carinii* choroiditis.

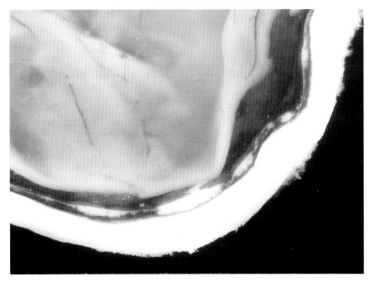

FIG XIII-6—Gross appearance of multifocal infiltrates of *Pneumocystis carinii* in the choroid.

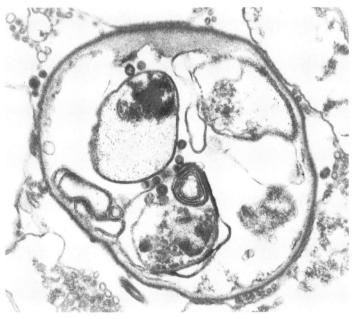

FIG XIII-7—Electron micrograph showing a cyst of *Pneumocystis carinii*.

pentamidine (4 mg/kg per day). Within 3–12 weeks most of the yellow-white lesions disappear, leaving mild overlying pigmentary changes.

Cryptococcus neoformans *choroiditis* The dissemination of *Cryptococcus neoformans* in patients with AIDS may result in a multifocal choroiditis similar to that seen in *P carinii* choroiditis. Some of the patients with *C neoformans* choroiditis show choroidal lesions before they develop clinical evidence of dissemination. Ocular manifestations may presage specific clinical systemic manifestations such as central nervous system disease. The alert clinician may reach an early diagnosis of disseminated cryptococcosis using ophthalmic findings.

Multifocal choroiditis and systemic dissemination Multifocal choroidal lesions from a variety of infectious agents, including those discussed above, are seen in about 5%–10% of AIDS patients. Most of these lesions are caused by *C neoformans, P carinii, M tuberculosis,* or atypical mycobacteria. Although multifocal choroiditis caused by any one of these infectious organisms is seen in many patients with AIDS, occasionally two or more of them in combination can be responsible.

Because it is so often the site of opportunistic disseminated infections, the choroid is a critical structure that needs to be carefully examined in AIDS patients. Although nonspecific, multifocal choroiditis is alarming and should prompt an exhaustive work-up for disseminated infection. Because multifocal choroiditis frequently represents disseminated infection, the ophthalmologist may have a life-prolonging role in the diagnosis and management of these patients.

External Eye Manifestations

Other ophthalmic manifestations of AIDS include Kaposi sarcoma; molluscum contagiosum; herpes zoster ophthalmicus; and keratitis caused by various viruses, protozoa, conjunctival infections, and microvascular abnormalities. All of these conditions affect mainly the anterior segment of the globe and the ocular adnexa. These conditions are also discussed in BCSC Section 8, *External Disease and Cornea.*

Ocular adnexal Kaposi sarcoma Since the initial description of Kaposi sarcoma in 1872, two more-aggressive variants of this tumor have been described. An endemic variety was described in 1959 in Africa; it is especially prevalent in Kenya and Nigeria, where it accounts for nearly 20% of all malignancies. The second variant, *epidemic Kaposi sarcoma,* was first noted in renal transplant patients and currently occurs in 30% of all patients with AIDS. AIDS-associated Kaposi sarcoma is particularly aggressive, disseminating to visceral organs (gastrointestinal tract, lung, and liver) in 20%–50% of patients. Prior to 1981 fewer than 25 patients with ocular adnexal Kaposi sarcoma had been reported, but this condition is now noted to occur in approximately 20% of patients with AIDS-associated systemic Kaposi sarcoma.

Histopathology shows spindle cells mixed with vascular structures (Fig XIII-8). Recent evidence suggests that AIDS-related Kaposi sarcoma may have an infectious origin. Human herpesvirus 8 has been isolated from patients with Kaposi sarcoma. That HIV may play a role in the pathogenesis of Kaposi sarcoma is evident from studies of transgenic mice bearing the HIV-1 transactivator *(tat)* gene under the control of the virus regulatory region (HIV-LTR). The HIV-*tat* protein has been shown to be a potent mitogen for human Kaposi sarcoma–derived cell lines. As in humans, these

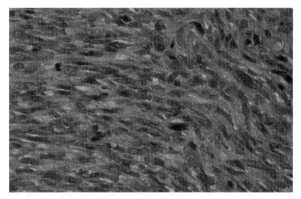

FIG XIII-8—Histopathologically, Kaposi sarcoma is made up of large spindle cells forming slitlike spaces. These spaces contain erythrocytes.

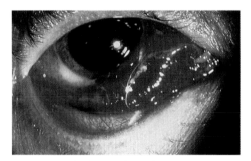

FIG XIII-9—Conjunctival involvement in Kaposi sarcoma; hemorrhagic conjunctival tumor (stage III). (Photograph courtesy of John D. Sheppard Jr., MD.)

lesions in mice occur predominantly in males, which suggests that their development may be hormonally controlled.

Three clinical stages of ocular adnexal Kaposi sarcoma have been described:

□ Stage I and stage II tumors are patchy, flat (less than 3 mm in height), and of less than 4 months' duration

□ Stage III tumors are nodular, elevated (greater than 3 mm in height), and of greater than 4 months' duration (Fig XIII-9)

The treatment of Kaposi sarcoma is based on the clinical stage of the tumor as well as its location and the presence or absence of disseminated lesions. If the lesion is confined to the ocular adnexa, local treatment is appropriate. If the tumor is confined to the bulbar conjunctiva and is stage I or stage II, an excisional biopsy with

1–2 mm tumor-free margins should be considered only if the lesion is symptomatic. Stage III Kaposi sarcoma of the bulbar conjunctiva should be surgically excised, preferably after delineation by fluorescein angiography. Stage I and stage II Kaposi sarcoma involving the eyelid may be treated with cryotherapy. Stage III Kaposi sarcoma of the eyelid may be treated with either radiation or cryotherapy, although radiation is preferred because of a lower recurrence rate. In order to avoid radiation-related complications, however, lesions may be treated with cryotherapy if the patient is aware that recurrence is more likely and may necessitate retreatment.

When evaluating an AIDS patient with ocular adnexal Kaposi sarcoma, the physician should perform a full systemic examination for tumor dissemination. If chemotherapy is administered for systemic Kaposi sarcoma, the ophthalmologist should wait at least 4–6 weeks to observe response to treatment before deciding whether further therapy is warranted.

Molluscum contagiosum Molluscum contagiosum is caused by a DNA virus of the poxvirus family. The characteristic skin lesions show a small elevation with central umbilication. Molluscum lesions in healthy individuals are few in number, unilateral, and involve the eyelids. In AIDS patients, however, these lesions may be numerous and bilateral. If molluscum lesions in AIDS patients are symptomatic or cause conjunctivitis, surgical excision may be necessary. However, in some cases the surgery and cryotherapy may fail to treat these viral lesions.

Herpes zoster Apparently healthy young people who present with herpes zoster lesions of the face or eyelids should be suspected of having AIDS and tested for HIV. Corneal involvement can cause a persistent, chronic epithelial keratitis, and treatment consists of IV and topical acyclovir. See discussion of progressive outer retinal necrosis syndrome earlier in this chapter. Although PORN is rare, these patients should be followed periodically with retinal examination.

Other infections HIV infection does not appear to predispose patients to bacterial keratitis. However, infections that do occur are severe and more likely to cause perforation in AIDS patients than in immunocompetent patients. Bacterial and fungal keratitis can occur in patients with AIDS with no obvious predisposing factors such as trauma or topical steroid use. Although herpes simplex keratitis does not appear to have a higher incidence in patients with AIDS, it may have a prolonged course or multiple recurrences and involve the limbus in these patients (Fig XIII-10). *Microsporida* organisms have been shown to cause a coarse, superficial punctate keratitis with a minimal conjunctival reaction in AIDS patients (Fig XIII-11). Electron microscopy of the epithelial scrapings has revealed the organism, which is an obligate, intracellular, protozoal parasite.

Solitary granulomatous conjunctivitis from cryptococcal infection, tuberculosis, or other mycotic infections can occur in HIV-infected individuals. As with all other infections in AIDS, the possibility of dissemination must be considered and aggressively sought. Orbital lymphomas and intraocular lymphomas have been described in patients with AIDS. These neoplasms are mostly large B-cell lymphomas. Occurrence of conjunctival squamous cell carcinomas have been reported, and in some patients these neoplasms show spindle cells with frequent abnormal mitotic figures.

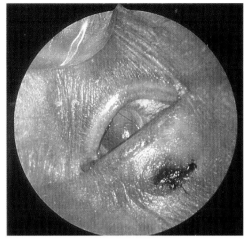

FIG XIII-10—Lesions of the eyelid and cornea in an AIDS patient with disseminated herpes simplex.

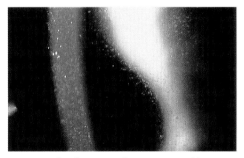

FIG XIII-11—Superficial punctate keratitis caused by *Microsporida*.

The Ophthalmologist's Role

The role of the ophthalmologist in the diagnosis and management of AIDS patients is becoming increasingly important. Not only does the eye reflect systemic disease, but ocular involvement may often precede systemic manifestations. The ophthalmologist treating an AIDS patient truly has an opportunity to make not only a sight-saving, but also a life-sustaining, diagnosis. Therefore, it is the responsibility of the ophthalmologist to provide not only a thorough and accurate ophthalmologic examination but also a careful and pertinent systemic evaluation, timely referrals, and periodic follow-up care.

HIV infection is a major public health problem with almost 100% mortality. It is likely that new drugs to combat HIV infection, and other agents to suppress the opportunistic infections that accompany HIV, will continue to be developed. In the future, an anti-HIV vaccine may be introduced. However, at present, the most productive approach to combating HIV remains prevention of its transmission.

Dugel PU, Gill PS, Frangieh GT, et al. Treatment of ocular adnexal Kaposi's sarcoma in acquired immune deficiency syndrome. *Ophthalmology.* 1992;99:1127–1132.

Holland GN, Sison RF, Jatulis DE, et al. Survival of patients with the acquired immune deficiency syndrome after development of cytomegalovirus retinopathy. UCLA CMV Retinopathy Study Group. *Ophthalmology.* 1990;97:204–211.

Holland GN. Pieces of a puzzle: toward a better understanding of intraocular inflammation associated with human immunodeficiency virus disease. *Am J Ophthalmol.* 1998;125:383–385.

Kuo IC, Kapusta MA, Rao NA. Vitritis as the primary manifestation of ocular syphilis in patients with HIV infection. *Am J Ophthalmol.* 1998;125:306–311.

Lalezari JP, Stagg RJ, Kuppermann BD, et al. Intravenous cidofovir for peripheral cytomegalovirus retinitis in patients with AIDS: a randomized, controlled trial. *Ann Intern Med.* 1997;126:257–263.

Moorthy RS, Weinberg DV, Teich SA, et al. Management of varicella-zoster virus retinitis in AIDS. *Br J Ophthalmol.* 1997;81:189–94.

Nussenblatt RB, Lane HC. Human immunodeficiency virus disease: changing patterns of intraocular inflammation. *Am J Ophthalmol.* 1998;125:374–382.

Rao NA, Zimmerman PL, Boyer D, et al. A clinical, histopathologic, and electron microscopic study of *Pneumocystis carinii* choroiditis. *Am J Ophthalmol.* 1989;107: 218–228.

Reed JB, Schwab IR, Gordon J, et al. Regression of cytomegalovirus retinitis associated with protease-inhibitor treatment in patients with AIDS. *Am J Ophthalmol.* 1997;124: 199–205.

Precautions in the Health Care Setting

Specific precautionary measures against HIV infection have been advocated in the United States by the CDC and other governmental agencies, including the Occupational Safety and Health Administration (OSHA). These agencies insist upon adoption of bloodborne pathogen standards, commonly referred to as *universal precautions.* These precautions should be followed whether or not a patient is known to be HIV positive and include the following:

☐ Taking measures to prevent accidental needle-stick injury

☐ Routine wearing of gloves when collecting and handling specimens

☐ Disposing of contaminated sharp objects in puncture-resistant ("sharps") containers

☐ Proper shielding of eyes and mouth for clinical and laboratory workers

☐ Thorough disinfection of examination equipment that touches mucosal surfaces after each use

☐ Prompt cleaning by a gloved person using 10% chlorine bleach solution of all blood spills in the examining rooms or waiting area

☐ Availability of hepatitis B vaccine to all personnel who come in contact with patient blood

Precautions in Ophthalmic Practice

While it appears that ophthalmology presents a lower level of risk than some other, more hazardous specialties, the American Academy of Ophthalmology has advocated following precautionary measures against HIV infection in ophthalmic practice. These measures are meant to provide protection to patients, ancillary health care personnel, and ophthalmologists.

Even though there are no published reports of HIV transmission in ophthalmic health care settings, hand washing with soap and water and thorough drying with fresh or disposable towels is recommended between various tests on an individual and between patients. If an open wound or weeping lesion is present, disposable gloves should be worn and discarded appropriately.

Tonometers and diagnostic contact lenses should be wiped with an alcohol sponge. Similarly, the Schiøtz tonometer can be disassembled and cleaned with an alcohol sponge. However, the CDC recommends household chlorine bleach (1:10 dilution) to clean such instruments. These items must be carefully rinsed after use of either alcohol or chlorine. BCSC Section 10, *Glaucoma,* gives more specific instructions for infection control in tonometry.

Contact lens trial sets need to be disinfected between patients. For hard contact lenses and rigid gas-permeable contact lenses, hydrogen peroxide disinfection or a chlorhexidine-containing disinfectant system should be employed. For soft contact lenses, hydrogen peroxide or a heat disinfection system should be used.

Barrier precautions, such as disposable gloves, should be used during diagnostic procedures such as injection of dye for fluorescein angiographic studies. During surgical procedures, particularly where contact with blood or blood-contaminated fluids is likely, disposable gloves, masks, and protective eye wear should be worn by all health care personnel in attendance.

Corneal and scleral tissue used for transplantations should be screened for HIV and hepatitis B virus, in accordance with the guidelines provided by the Eye Bank Association of America, which are spelled out in BCSC Section 8, *External Disease and Cornea.*

Updated recommendations for ophthalmic practice in relation to the human immunodeficiency virus and other infectious agents. *Information Statement.* San Francisco: American Academy of Ophthalmology; 1992.

BASIC TEXTS

Intraocular Inflammation and Uveitis

Giles CL. Uveitis in childhood. In: Tasman W, Jaeger EA, eds. *Duane's Clinical Ophthalmology.* Philadelphia: Lippincott; 1991.

Michelson JB. *Color Atlas of Uveitis Diagnosis.* 2nd ed. St Louis: Mosby; 1992.

Nussenblatt RB, Whitcup SM, Palestine AG. *Uveitis: Fundamentals in Clinical Practice.* 2nd ed. St Louis: Mosby; 1996.

Opremcak EM. *Uveitis: A Clinical Manual for Ocular Inflammation.* New York: Springer-Verlag; 1995.

Pepose JS, Holland GN, Wilhelmus KR, eds. *Ocular Infection and Immunity.* St Louis: Mosby; 1996.

Rao NA, Augsburger JJ, Forster DJ. *The Uvea: Uveitis and Intraocular Neoplasms.* New York: Gower; 1992.

Roitt IM. *Essential Immunology.* 3rd ed. Malden, MA: Blackwell Science; 1997.

Smith RE, Nozik RA. *Uveitis: A Clinical Approach to Diagnosis and Management.* 2nd ed. Baltimore: Williams & Wilkins; 1989.

RELATED ACADEMY MATERIALS

Focal Points: Clinical Modules for Ophthalmologists

Dinning WJ. Uveitis and juvenile chronic arthritis (Module 5, 1990).

Dunn JP. Uveitis in children (Module 4, 1995).

Folk JC, Pulido JS, Wolf MD. White dot and chorioretinal inflammatory syndromes (Module 11, 1990).

Holland GN. An update on AIDS-related cytomegalovirus retinitis (Module 5, 1991).

Hooper PL. Pars planitis (Module 11, 1993).

Jaffe GJ. Cystoid macular edema (Module 11, 1994).

Jampol LM. Nonsteroidal anti-inflammatory drugs (Module 6, 1997).

Margo CE. Nonpigmented lesions of the ocular surface (Module 9, 1996).

Mandelbaum S, Forster RK. Infectious endophthalmitis (Module 9, 1983).

Meisler DM. Intraocular inflammation and extracapsular cataract surgery (Module 7, 1990).

Nozik RA. Laboratory testing in uveitis (Module 8, 1983).

Opremcak EM. Topical therapy for iritis (Module 7, 1991).

Palestine AG. Medical therapy of uveitis (Module 8, 1989).

Rosenbaum JT. Practical diagnostic evaluation of uveitis (Module 6, 1993).

Samples JR. Management of glaucoma secondary to uveitis (Module 5, 1995).

Tessler HH. Diagnosis and treatment of ocular toxoplasmosis (Module 2, 1985).

Yannuzzi LA. Cystoid macular edema following cataract surgery (Module 10, 1985).

Publications

Lane SS, Skuta GL, eds. *ProVision: Preferred Responses in Ophthalmology,* Series 3 (Self-Assessment Program, 1999).

Schwab L. *Eye Care in Developing Nations.* 3rd ed. (1999).

Skuta GL, ed. *ProVision: Preferred Responses in Ophthalmology,* Series 2 (Self-Assessment Program, 1996).

Wilson FM II, ed. *Practical Ophthalmology: A Manual for Beginning Residents* (1996).

Slide Script

Tang RA. *Ocular Manifestations of Systemic Disease* (Eye Care Skills for the Primary Care Physician Series, 1996).

Continuing Ophthalmic Video Education

Anand R. *Surgical Technique for Ganciclovir Implant* (1996).

Carlson A. *Evaluation and Management of Postoperative Localized Microbial Endophthalmitis;* and King LP. *Passive Controlled-Needle Evacuation of Subretinal Fluid* (1995).

Kelly MP. *Basic Techniques of Fluorescein Angiography* (1994).

LEO Clinical Topic Updates

Goldstein D, Tessler H, Weinberg R. *Uveitis* (1996).

To order any of these materials, please call the Academy's Customer Service number at (415) 561-8540.

CREDIT REPORTING FORM

BASIC AND CLINICAL SCIENCE COURSE
Section 9

1999–2000

CME Accreditation

The American Academy of Ophthalmology is accredited by the Accreditation Council for Continuing Medical Education to sponsor continuing medical education for physicians.

    The American Academy of Ophthalmology designates this educational activity for a maximum of 30 hours in category 1 credit toward the AMA Physician's Recognition Award. Each physician should claim only those hours of credit that he/she has actually spent in the educational activity.

    If you wish to claim continuing medical education credit for your study of this section, you must complete and return the study question answer sheet on the back of this page, along with the following signed statement, to the Academy office. This form must be received within 3 years of the date of purchase.

> I hereby certify that I have spent _____ (up to 30) hours of study on the curriculum of this section, and that I have completed the study questions. (The Academy, *upon request,* will send you a transcript of the credits listed on this form.)

> ☐ *Please send credit verification now.*

Signature _____
                                                                         Date

Name:_____

Address: _____

City and State:_____ Zip: _____

Telephone: (_____) _____ *Academy Member ID# _____
                area code

*   *Your ID number is located following your name on any Academy mailing label, in your Membership Directory, and on your Monthly Statement of Account.*

Section Evaluation

Please indicate your response to the statements listed below by placing the appropriate number to the left of each statement.

1 = agree strongly
2 = agree
3 = no opinion
4 = disagree
5 = disagree
   strongly

_____ This section covers topics in enough depth and detail.

_____ This section's illustrations are of sufficient number and quality.

_____ The references included in the text provide an appropriate amount of additional reading.

_____ The study questions at the end of the book are useful.

In addition, please attach a separate sheet of paper to this form if you wish to elaborate on any of the statements above or to comment on other aspects of this book.

Please return completed form to: **American Academy of Ophthalmology**
                                             P.O. Box 7424
                                             San Francisco, CA 94120-7424
                                             ATTN: Clinical Education Division

SECTION COMPLETION FORM

BASIC AND CLINICAL SCIENCE COURSE
ANSWER SHEET FOR SECTION 9

Question	Answer	Question	Answer	Question	Answer
1	a b c d e	16	a b c d e	31	a b c d e
2	a b c d e	17	a b c d e	32	a b c d e
3	a b c d e	18	a b c d e	33	a b c d e
4	a b c d e	19	a b c d e	34	a b c d e
5	a b c d e	20	a b c d e	35	a b c d e
6	a b c d e	21	a b c d e	36	a b c d e
7	a b c d e	22	a b c d e	37	a b c d e
8	a b c d e	23	a b c d e	38	a b c d e
9	a b c d e	24	a b c d e	39	a b c d e
10	a b c d e	25	a b c d e	40	a b c d e
11	a b c d e	26	a b c d e	41	a b c d e
12	a b c d e	27	a b c d e	42	a b c d e
13	a b c d e	28	a b c d e	43	a b c d e
14	a b c d e	29	a b c d e	44	a b c d e
15	a b c d e	30	a b c d e		

STUDY QUESTIONS

STUDY QUESTIONS

The following multiple-choice questions are designed to be used after your course of study with this book. Record your responses on the answer sheet (the back side of the Credit Reporting Form) by circling the appropriate letter. For the most effective use of this exercise, *complete the entire test* before consulting the answers.

Although a concerted effort has been made to avoid ambiguity and redundancy in these questions, the authors recognize that differences of opinion may occur regarding the best answer. The discussions are provided to demonstrate the rationale used to derive the answer. They may also be helpful in confirming that your approach to the problem was correct or, if necessary, in fixing the principle in your memory.

1. Which of the following statements about the pathogenesis of ocular inflammation is *incorrect?*

    a. Th1 delayed hypersensitivity to retinal or uveal antigens contributes to the pathogenesis of sympathetic ophthalmia.
    b. Local formation of immune complexes against DNA bound within the vessel wall contributes to the pathogenesis of retinal vasculitis in SLE.
    c. Deposition of circulating immune complexes to bacterial antigens causes HLA-B27 uveitis.
    d. Local immune complexes formed against lens crystallin antigens contribute to the pathogenesis of severe forms of lens-associated uveitis (such as phacoantigenic endophthalmitis).
    e. Innate immunity and scavenging mechanisms contribute to the pathogenesis of mild forms of lens-associated uveitis (such as phacolytic glaucoma).

2. Which of the following statements about immune effector mechanisms is true?

    a. IgE-mediated mast-cell degranulation is important in posterior uveitis.
    b. T cell–mediated delayed hypersensitivity effectors can mediate inflammation in all parts of the eye.
    c. Local synthesis of antibody rarely occurs in ocular tissues.
    d. Deposition of circulating immune complexes mediates many forms of serious uveitis.
    e. Formation of tissue-bound immune complexes fails to induce ocular inflammation.

3. Which of the following statements about the ocular immunologic microenvironment is *incorrect?*

    a. The anterior chamber manifests immune privilege.
    b. The conjunctiva is part of MALT.
    c. The retina has numerous antigen-presenting cells and thus probably has an afferent immune phase.
    d. The absence of lymphatics in the cornea prevents inflammatory effector responses.
    e. Most ocular sites contain plasma-derived immune amplification molecules like complement and kinin precursors.

4. Which statement about the adaptive immune response arc is *incorrect?*

   a. Antigen-presenting cells for CD4 T cells must express class II MHC.
   b. B-cell antigen receptors can recognize intact, unprocessed antigen.
   c. T-cell antigen receptors can recognize antigen only if it is processed and presented by APC.
   d. Immune processing (i.e., initial interaction between antigen, B cells, and T cells; activation of helper T cells; etc) routinely occurs in "peripheral" tissue sites such as the skin or eye.
   e. Immunologic memory is important for both T-cell and B-cell responses.

5. Which statement about the comparison between adaptive and innate immune responses is correct?

   a. Both use the same kinds of triggering stimuli.
   b. Both depend on antigen processing to regulate the response.
   c. Both use nonspecific effector cells (like macrophages) and molecules (like cytokines) to rid the host of the offending stimulus.
   d. Both exhibit memory and specificity.
   e. Innate immunity can rid infections only by causing inflammation, whereas adaptive immunity usually functions subclinically to prevent infection.

6. Characteristics of pars planitis include

   a. Presentation in middle-aged adults
   b. A history of antecedent flulike illness
   c. Heavy choroidal inflammation beneath pars plana snowbanks
   d. Venous sheathing in the posterior pole
   e. Vision loss usually secondary to macular edema

7. Appropriate treatment options for patients with pars planitis include

   a. Observation
   b. Periocular or systemic steroids
   c. Retinal cryopexy
   d. Vitrectomy
   e. All of the above

8. A hospitalized patient on intravenous antibiotics for pneumonia develops floaters and blurred vision in one eye. Funduscopic evaluation reveals multiple yellow-white choroidal lesions with indistinct margins and vitreous fluff balls. Which of the following represents the most appropriate management?

   a. Inquire whether the patient has had recent exposure to cats or uncooked meat.
   b. Culture the patient's blood and catheter tips on multiple media and begin intravenous antifungal medication.
   c. Supplement the intravenous antibiotics with topical and subconjunctival antibiotics to increase ocular penetration.
   d. Prescribe systemic steroids to suppress the vitritis.
   e. Treatment is not necessary. It is reasonable to observe the lesions as long as the optic nerve or macula is not directly threatened.

9. Which of the following statements is true regarding the management of post-operative endophthalmitis?

    a. The absence of pain or hypopyon argues against infection.
    b. An aqueous aspirate will usually provide sufficient material to identify the infecting organism.
    c. All patients with suspected endophthalmitis require immediate vitrectomy.
    d. Negative cultures after 48 hours imply a sterile endophthalmitis that can be managed conservatively.
    e. Intravenous antibiotics are not beneficial in the initial management of postcataract endophthalmitis.

10. Which statement about toxoplasmosis in AIDS is true?

    a. Toxoplasmosis is the most common cause of intraocular infection in AIDS.
    b. Toxoplasmosis produces a characteristic hemorrhagic chorioretinitis that is easy to distinguish from CMV retinitis.
    c. CD4 counts are usually normal.
    d. Antibody titers are helpful in confirming the diagnosis of toxoplasmosis.
    e. All immunocompromised patients with ocular toxoplasmosis should be evaluated for CNS toxoplasmosis.

11. Which of the following is characteristic of Fuchs heterochromic iridocyclitis?

    a. Usually a bilateral condition
    b. Granulomatous keratic precipitates
    c. Frequently associated with glaucoma
    d. Responds well to topical steroids
    e. High incidence of complications with cataract surgery

12. A 64-year-old woman who had undergone cataract surgery 6 months earlier develops an anterior chamber reaction and low-grade anterior vitreous inflammation following Nd:YAG laser capsulotomy of a white plaquelike opacity of the posterior capsule. The uveitis initially responds to topical steroids but recurs as the steroids are withdrawn. The most likely diagnosis is

    a. Phacoantigenic endophthalmitis
    b. Reticulum cell sarcoma
    c. *Propionibacterium acnes* endophthalmitis
    d. Sympathetic ophthalmia
    e. Uveitis-glaucoma-hyphema syndrome

13. Alkylating agents such as cyclophosphamide and chlorambucil

    a. Are contraindicated in the presence of severe inflammatory eye disease.
    b. Should be limited to brief periods of use for up to 1–2 months to minimize adverse side effects.
    c. Exert inhibitory effects on T-cell function while sparing B-cell humoral immunity.
    d. Must be used in conjunction with corticosteroids to achieve maximum anti-inflammatory benefit.
    e. Are first-line drugs in the treatment of Behçet syndrome or polyarteritis nodosa.

14. The most common cause of posterior uveitis in children is

    a. Histoplasmosis
    b. Syphilis
    c. Toxocariasis
    d. Toxoplasmosis
    e. Tuberculosis

15. Which of the following statements is characteristic of ocular histoplasmosis syndrome?

    a. The diagnostic triad consists of peripheral "histo" spots, macular disciform scar, and anterior uveitis.
    b. A histoplasmin skin test is a valuable method to confirm the diagnosis.
    c. It is often associated with active inflammatory cells in the vitreous.
    d. Antifungal agents should be administered if active choroiditis is visible.
    e. Subretinal neovascular membranes between 200 and 2500 µm from the fovea should be treated with focal laser photocoagulation.

16. Which of the following patients would benefit most from steroid therapy?

    a. A 9-year-old girl with JRA, moderate anterior chamber flare, but no cells
    b. A 22-year-old woman with pars planitis, anterior vitreal cells, but no CME
    c. A 44-year-old man with herpes simplex keratouveitis, disciform corneal edema, keratic precipitates, and anterior chamber cells
    d. A 50-year-old woman with Fuchs heterochromic iridocyclitis, fine KP, and anterior chamber cells
    e. All equally likely to benefit from steroid therapy

17. Which of these patients with JRA has the highest risk of developing ocular complications?

    a. A 5-year-old boy with fever, rash, lymphadenopathy, hepatosplenomegaly, and arthritis of one ankle
    b. A 3-year-old girl with arthritis of both hands, wrists, ankle, and knee; a positive ANA result; and negative rheumatoid factor
    c. A 2-year-old girl with mild arthritis of left knee and ankle and a positive ANA result
    d. A 10-year-old boy with arthritis of the hip girdle, negative ANA result, and negative rheumatoid factor
    e. A 5-year-old boy with arthritis involving both knees and both wrists and a rash, negative ANA result, and elevated ACE level

18. Which of the following drugs is *least* likely to cause or aggravate uveitis?

    a. Rifabutin
    b. Cidofovir
    c. Latanoprost (Xalatan)
    d. Metipranolol (OptiPranolol)
    e. Diclofenac

19. A 64-year-old man develops bilateral decreased vision and floaters. Examination reveals clumps of vitreous cells; subretinal infiltrates; and a white, quiet eye. The vitritis is not responsive to steroids. The most likely associated finding would be

    a. Tumor cells in the CSF
    b. Hilar lymphadenopathy on chest x-ray
    c. Positive VDRL serology
    d. Oligoclonal bands in the CSF
    e. *Pneumocystis carinii* in sputum specimens

20. Secondary glaucoma is a common complication of steroid treatment for uveitis. Which therapeutic maneuver would be *least* helpful in managing a patient with uveitis and glaucoma?

    a. Begin timolol
    b. Change prednisolone to rimexalone (Vexol)
    c. Begin pilocarpine
    d. Taper steroid medication to a less frequent dosing regimen
    e. Begin dorzolamide (Trusopt)

21. Complications of systemic steroid therapy include

    a. Muscle weakness
    b. Psychosis
    c. Growth suppression in children
    d. Osteoporosis
    e. All of the above

22. Which of the following is *not* a common HLA association?

    a. HLA-A29—serpiginous chorioretinopathy
    b. HLA-B7—ocular histoplasmosis syndrome and disciform scar
    c. HLA-B27—psoriatic arthritis
    d. HLA-B51—Behçet syndrome
    e. HLA-DR4—VKH syndrome

23. When initiating oral corticosteroid treatment of uveitis, it is usually preferable to

    a. Begin with a low dose of medication and increase gradually in stepwise manner until control of inflammation is achieved
    b. Begin with a high dose of medication and taper back to lowest effective dose
    c. Begin with alternate-day therapy to minimize systemic side effects
    d. Combine with oral nonsteroidal medications to achieve maximum anti-inflammatory effect
    e. Discontinue medication abruptly once inflammation is controlled

24. Which of the following statements is true concerning ocular toxoplasmosis?

    a. Most cases of ocular toxoplasmosis are acquired from recent exposure to cats.
    b. Cysts and tachyzoites of the *Toxoplasma* organism are most frequently found in the choriocapillaris and deeper layers of the retina.
    c. Pregnant woman should routinely be tested for toxoplasmosis.
    d. Siblings of patients with ocular toxoplasmosis usually show similar funduscopic findings.
    e. Treatment should be initiated whenever creamy-colored satellite lesions with active vitreous cells develop next to older atrophic scars.

25. Reasonable treatment protocols for ocular toxoplasmosis include all of the following *except:*

    a. Oral sulfadiazine and pyrimethamine
    b. Oral sulfadiazine and clindamycin
    c. Oral trimethoprim/sulfamethoxazole
    d. Oral tetracycline
    e. Periocular injections of corticosteroids

26. Retinoblastoma and *Toxocara canis* may both cause a leukocoria and intense "endophthalmitis"-like picture with a pseudohypopyon. Findings that favor a diagnosis of retinoblastoma include all of the following *except:*

    a. Family history
    b. Multiple retinal lesions
    c. Presence of calcification on ultrasound or x-ray
    d. Lactate dehydrogenase aqueous–to–serum ratio greater than 1
    e. Eosinophils on cytologic examination of aqueous aspirate

27. Which of the following statements is true regarding toxocariasis?

    a. This disease is caused by an obligate intracellular parasite.
    b. Ocular toxocariasis is frequently associated with visceral larval migrans.
    c. Ova and parasites should be sought in stool samples.
    d. Enzyme-linked immunosorbent assay (ELISA) is the most reliable test for evaluation of antibodies against *Toxocara* organisms.
    e. Ocular toxocariasis requires treatment with thiabendazole or other anti-helminthic agents.

28. Which of the following is true about the HIV virus?

    a. The HIV virus is an encapsulated double-stranded DNA virus with an icosohedral nucleocapsid.
    b. The rate of HIV infection is decreasing on a worldwide basis.
    c. Intravenous drug use is the most common mode of HIV transmission.
    d. HIV has been isolated from the cornea, vitreous, and retina.
    e. The progression from asymptomatic HIV infection to AIDS is marked by gradual reduction in the number of circulating macrophages.

29. Which of the following is true regarding therapy of systemic conditions in patients infected with HIV?

   a. Treatment with antiretroviral agents is not indicated in patients who are asymptomatic.
   b. Opportunistic infections begin to occur once CD4 counts fall below 50 cells/mm^3.
   c. Rifabutin is commonly used as prophylaxis against *Pneumocystis* pneumonia.
   d. Tuberculosis in HIV patients can usually be diagnosed by PPD testing.
   e. Currently available antiviral agents work by inhibiting the HIV reverse transcriptase enzyme or HIV protease enzymes.

30. Peripheral retinal granulomas can be found in all of the following *except:*

   a. Ascariasis
   b. Sarcoidosis
   c. Syphilis
   d. Toxoplasmosis
   e. Tuberculosis

31. Which statement about sympathetic ophthalmia is true?

   a. It only occurs following penetrating injury with uveal prolapse.
   b. It may occur as early as 10 days or as late as 50 years following the suspected triggering incident.
   c. It is characterized by intense lymphocytic infiltration in the choroid and choriocapillaris.
   d. Dalen-Fuchs nodules are pathognomonic findings of sympathetic ophthalmia.
   e. Enucleation does not have any effect on the course of the sympathizing eye once the disease has begun.

32. Complications of uveitis may include

   a. Low intraocular pressure
   b. High intraocular pressure
   c. Cataract
   d. Band keratopathy
   e. All of the above

33. All of the following are associated with uveitis *except:*

   a. Giardiasis
   b. Kawasaki disease
   c. Lawrence-Moon-Biedl syndrome
   d. Tarantula hairs
   e. Whipple disease

34. Which of the following statements concerning Reiter syndrome is true?

   a. It is especially common in the Far East and the Mediterranean basin.
   b. There is often a history of preceding chlamydial infection.
   c. Women typically present with a triad of arthritis, urethritis, and ocular inflammation.
   d. Uveitis is the most common ocular manifestation.
   e. It is often associated with retinal vasculitis.

35. Diagnostic criteria supporting a diagnosis of Behçet syndrome include all of the following *except:*

   a. Arthritis
   b. Erythema nodosum
   c. Genital ulcers
   d. Keratoderma blennorrhagicum
   e. Oral ulcers

36–40. Match the specific therapy with the disease complicated by uveitis for each of the following diseases:

36. Penicillin	a. Tuberculosis
37. Ivermectin	b. Syphilis
38. Isoniazid, rifampin, and pyrazinamide	c. Giardiasis
39. Quinacrine and metronidazole	d. Cryptococcosis
40. Amphotericin B	e. Onchocerciasis

41. All of the following findings are consistent with Vogt-Koyanagi-Harada syndrome *except:*

   a. High-frequency hearing loss
   b. Widespread vitiligo and alopecia
   c. Bilateral exudative retinal detachments
   d. More common in patients of American Indian or Asian ancestry
   e. Systemic anergy

42. All of the following are associated with iris heterochromia *except:*

   a. Fuchs iridocyclitis
   b. Horner syndrome
   c. Iris melanoma
   d. Herpes zoster uveitis
   e. Syphilis

43. The most common noninfectious cause of acute anterior uveitis with hypopyon is

   a. Behçet syndrome
   b. VKH syndrome
   c. HLA-B27–associated iridocyclitis
   d. Sarcoidosis
   e. Toxoplasmosis

44. Findings in ocular sarcoid include all of the following *except:*

    a. Caseating granulomas
    b. Koeppe nodules
    c. "Candle-wax" drippings along retinal venules
    d. Lacrimal gland swelling
    e. Vitreal snowballs

ANSWERS

1. Answer—c. Deposition of preformed circulating immune complexes has been deemphasized as a pathogenic mechanism for tissue-specific diseases in general and probably does not play a major role in anterior uveitis. Rather, T-cell mechanisms are probably more important. The other answers represent current thinking about disease pathogenesis as described in the text.

2. Answer—b. T cell–mediated delayed hypersensitivity is one of the most important effector mechanisms, and examples can be demonstrated in the conjunctiva (i.e., contact hypersensitivity to preservatives in contact lens solutions), cornea (graft rejection, phlyctenules, marginal infiltrates in blepharitis), anterior uvea (acute uveitis), and retina/choroid (sympathetic ophthalmia or VKH). See Table IV-6, p 73. Although mast cells are present in the choroid, IgE-mediated allergy is not believed to mediate posterior uveitis. Local synthesis of antibody by B cells that infiltrate the eye occurs commonly during infections. Local formation of immune complexes in situ, but not deposition of preformed circulating complexes, is thought to be a very important trigger of inflammation in the eye.

3. Answer—d. It is true that the avascular cornea is also devoid of lymphatics and vessels; thus effector cells are not routinely present in normal central stroma, and this absence provides some protection from immune responses. However, clinical experience demonstrates that effector cells can be efficiently recruited into the cornea by the appropriate stimuli in the absence of vascularization, such as innate stimuli (i.e., bacterial keratitis) and adaptive responses (marginal infiltrates caused by DH responses to *Staphylococcus* antigens). The other answers represent current thought about ocular immune microenvironments.

4. Answer—d. Immunologic processing routinely occurs only in lymph nodes, spleen, and specialized MALT compartments such as Peyer's patches, tonsils, and follicles. According to current thinking, it is unlikely that immune processing occurs within the cornea, anterior uvea, or posterior segment. The other answers represent correct statements reflecting current immunologic dogma.

5. Answer—c. Nonspecific effector cells and molecules amplify both innate and adaptive immune responses, which is why it is often difficult to differentiate infection-triggered inflammation (i.e., innate) from immune hypersensitivity inflammation (i.e., adaptive). The other four responses represent false statements. Adaptive responses are triggered by antigen; innate responses by toxins, infection, and cell debris. Only adaptive immunity displays processing, memory, and specificity. Both adaptive and innate immunity usually operate subclinically, but both can also induce inflammation.

6. Answer—e. Pars planitis is primarily a disease of the young, with few cases occurring after age 40. There is a bimodal pattern of incidence, with peaks between ages 5–15 and ages 25–35. Patients appear to have no detectable underlying disease, and a history of antecedent illness is unusual. The disease is distinguished by vitreous condensation and cellular aggregations of macrophages, lymphocytes, and a few plasma cells within the inferior vitreous body. The pars plana snowbanks appear to be primarily a fibrovascular proliferation made up mostly of fibroblasts and vascular endothelial cells. Although some inflammatory cells are present within the exudate, inflammatory activity within the subjacent choroid is minimal. Venous sheathing posterior to the equator is distinctly unusual and suggests an intermediate uveitis associated with an underlying systemic inflammatory disorder such as sarcoidosis or multiple sclerosis. Macular edema is the most common cause of loss of vision in pars planitis.

7. Answer—e. Because of potential side effects associated with currently available forms of therapy, treatment is usually reserved for patients whose vision is reduced to worse than 20/40. Treatment with corticosteroids alone adequately controls inflammation in 70%–80% of patients. These drugs are most effectively delivered through a sub-Tenon's injection, and they may need to be administered several times at intervals of 2–4 weeks before inflammation is controlled. Peripheral retinal cryopexy and photocoagulation have been used to reduce neovascularization within the vitreous base. Vitrectomy can be helpful as both a diagnostic and therapeutic modality in pars planitis. In addition to providing material for cytologic assay, antibody determination, and culture, removal of sequestered cells and mediators may help control inflammation or macular edema unresponsive to steroids or retinal cryopexy.

8. Answer—b. Multifocal chorioretinitis and vitritis in a patient with a history of indwelling catheters, IV drug use, immunosuppression, or antibiotic use should suggest *Candida* endophthalmitis. Blood cultures or cultures from the removed catheters can confirm the diagnosis. Toxoplasmosis may cause a fluffy chorioretinitis and overlying vitritis, but the patients are otherwise healthy and the lesions are typically adjacent to an older, pigmented scar. Intravenous amphotericin B is the treatment of choice (0.5–1.0 mg/kg/day). Other antifungal agents, including fluconazole or miconazole, can be used in certain settings. Severe cases should be treated with vitrectomy and intraocular amphotericin B (5 μg/0.1 ml). Steroids are contraindicated.

9. Answer—e. Early diagnosis and the use of intravitreal antibiotics are the most important aspects of the management of postoperative endophthalmitis. The most common presenting symptom in the Endophthalmitis Vitrectomy Study was blurred vision. It is important to realize that up to 25% of patients had neither pain nor hypopyon. Both aqueous and vitreous specimens should be obtained before antibiotic therapy is initiated because vitreous cultures are often positive even when aqueous cultures are negative. Positive culture rates are similar whether the vitreous sample is obtained by needle aspiration or vitreous biopsy, and there is no advantage to routinely performing immediate

vitrectomy in patients who present with hand motion vision or better. In contrast, patients who present with light perception vision show much greater benefit from early vitrectomy. Systemic antibiotics do not improve the outcome and are not necessary in the initial management of endophthalmitis following cataract surgery.

10. Answer—e. CMV retinitis is by far the most common cause of intraocular infection in AIDS patients, accounting for more than 90% of cases of infectious retinitis. Distinguishing between toxoplasmic retinitis and CMV retinitis can be difficult in immunosuppressed patients. Clinical findings that favor a diagnosis of toxoplasmic retinochoroiditis include dense retinal opacification, smooth-bordered lesions, anterior chamber reaction, vitreous reaction, and absence of retinal hemorrhage. Also, patients with toxoplasmosis tend to have higher CD4 counts than do patients with CMV retinitis. Antibody titers are often not helpful in cases of suspected toxoplasmosis because AIDS patients have often had exposure to toxoplasmosis and may have positive antibody titers despite the absence of active disease. Furthermore, the antibody titer may become negative in the presence of active ocular infection. Any immunocompromised patient diagnosed with ocular toxoplasmosis requires an evaluation for CNS toxoplasmosis, as toxoplasmosis is the most common nonviral intracranial infection in AIDS patients.

11. Answer—c. Fuchs heterochromic iridocyclitis is a chronic anterior uveitis that is usually associated with a low-grade cellular reaction in the anterior chamber, changes in iris color, and mild disturbance of vision. Slit-lamp examination reveals fine stellate keratic precipitates evenly distributed over the corneal endothelium. The inflammation is often recalcitrant to treatment, and it is acceptable to leave a persistent mild cellular reaction untreated. Cataract and glaucoma develop in 50%–100% of patients. The cataracts can generally be successfully managed with standard extraction techniques.

12. Answer—c.

13. Answer—e. Cyclophosphamide and chlorambucil are among the most potent immunosuppressive drugs. They are often the drug of choice for Behçet, polyarteritis nodosa, relapsing polychondritis, and Wegener granulomatosis. Most of these agents have a slow onset of action and are usually used for an extended time. They affect both T cells and B cells. They can be helpful as steroid-sparing agents and may even permit the discontinuation of steroids in many patients. Although the potential for serious side effects necessitates careful and skilled monitoring, these agents can be sight- and life-saving in patients with severe ocular inflammatory disease.

14. Answer—d.

15. Answer—e. Peripheral histo spots, macular disciform scar, and peripapillary pigment changes make up the classic triad of ocular histoplasmosis. The eye is quiet without anterior uveitis or vitritis. The presence of active inflammatory cells in the vitreous should suggest other conditions. A histoplasmin skin test is rarely needed for the diagnosis and not often performed because it may cause the ocular lesions to reactivate. Corticosteroids can be given for acute macular lesions that cause a sudden drop in visual acuity or in preparation for laser therapy. Extrafoveal and juxtafoveal SRNVMs should be treated with focal laser photocoagulation. Antifungal agents have no role in the treatment of ocular histoplasmosis syndrome.

16. Answer—c. JRA is often associated with chronic ocular flare, which represents a breakdown of the blood–eye barrier and, in the absence of cells, is not an indication for treatment. Pars planitis patients who are asymptomatic with old, pigmented cells in the anterior vitreous can be observed and do not require treatment. The inflammation in Fuchs heterochromic dystrophy is often unresponsive to therapy, and a mild persistent cellular reaction may be left untreated. In herpes simplex stromal keratitis, steroids have been shown to reduce the progression of stromal keratitis as well as the time to resolution of uveitis. Concurrent antiviral therapy should be used whenever corticosteroids are used in herpetic keratouveitis.

17. Answer—c. Children with seronegative, ANA positive, pauciarticular (four or fewer joints involved) JRA are at greatest risk for developing chronic uveitis. Eye disease is rare in the acute, toxic form of JRA known as Still disease. Patients with polyarticular arthritis only occasionally develop uveitis. Seventy-five percent of boys with pauciarticular arthritis are HLA-B27 positive, and some go on to develop ankylosing spondylitis later. Childhood sarcoidosis can also cause a large-joint arthralgia, but the uveitis is often granulomatous and frequently involves the retina and choroid as well.

18. Answer—e.

19. Answer—a. Chronic medically unresponsive uveitis, iritis, and subretinal infiltrate in an elderly patient with CNS complaints should suggest non-Hodgkin lymphoma of the central nervous system. MRI and lumbar puncture can confirm CNS involvement. A vitrectomy may help establish the diagnosis. Typical lymphoma cells are large and pleomorphic with scanty cytoplasm and hypersegmented nuclei with prominent nucleoli.

20. Answer—c.

21. Answer—e.

22. Answer—a. Birdshot retinochoroidopathy has a strong association with HLA-A29. HLA-A29 phenotype is present in 80%–96% of patients with this disease. Other entities mentioned also show HLA association; however, the association is relatively less strong.

23. Answer—b. Once the decision is made to commit a patient to oral cortico-steroids, therapy should be started in earnest. The most frequent error is pre-scribing too low an initial dose. It is more efficacious to start out with a high dose, gain rapid control, and begin a judicious taper than to begin "safe" and try to catch up with the inflammation. Alternate-day dosing can be effective for maintenance therapy once control of inflammation is achieved, but many forms of uveitis do not respond well initially to such a dosing schedule.

24. Answer—c. The vast majority of cases of toxoplasmic uveitis in adults and children are thought to be recurrences of a congenital infection. Maternal infection during pregnancy results in a 40% transmission rate to the child. It is believed that if the mother has anti-*Toxoplasma* antibodies before the beginning of pregnancy, then the fetus is protected. Siblings of patients with ocular toxoplasmosis typically do not have eye findings. The organism has a predilection for the superficial layers of the retina, and the contiguous choroid and vitreous are secondarily involved. It is not necessary to treat all cases of active retinal toxoplasmosis; the disease is self-limited in the im-munocompetent person. Small, peripheral lesions with minimal vitritis can be observed. Active lesions that threaten the optic nerve and macula should be treated with antiprotozoal therapy.

25. Answer—e. Immunosuppressive therapy (prednisone) should not be used alone in ocular toxoplasmosis but only under the cover of specific antibiotic therapy. Regional corticosteroids should never be used because of the pro-found local immunosuppression.

26. Answer—e.

27. Answer—d. Toxocariasis is a nematode infection that may cause systemic disease or local ocular disease. The systemic illness, called *visceral larval migrans,* is not usually associated with the ocular disease. *Toxocara canis* can complete its life cycle only in dogs. In humans the life cycle ends in the lar-val stage, so eggs and parasites will not be found in the stool. ELISA is high-ly specific, and the presence of any antibody titer, even in undiluted serum, may be significant. Antihelminthic agents are not helpful in ocular toxocari-asis because the larva incites inflammation and granuloma formation only after its death.

28. Answer—d. HIV is a single-stranded RNA virus with reverse transcriptase (retrovirus). Although the spread of HIV has slowed in the male homosexual community following aggressive education efforts, infection is increasing among women, children, and IV drug users. HIV has a predilection for helper T cells, which decline as the disease progresses. Infected macrophages show impaired function but rarely decrease in number. They harbor the virus and may help disseminate it through the body.

29. Answer—e. The International AIDS Society–USA recommends treatment of any patient who has seroconverted within the last 6 months. CD4 counts below 500 are associated with oral candidiasis and disseminated tuberculosis, while CD4 counts below 200 require prophylaxis against *Pneumocystis* pneumonia by trimethoprim/sulfamethoxazole. The PPD skin test is notoriously inaccurate in patients with AIDS because of altered cellular immunity.

30. Answer—d.

31. Answer—b. Sympathetic ophthalmia is a bilateral, granulomatous panuveitis that occurs after ocular injury. Penetrating trauma, surgical procedures, and nonpenetrating injuries have all been reported to provoke sympathetic ophthalmia. The disease can begin as early as several days after the injury to decades later. Most cases occur within 3 weeks to 3 months after the injury. The choroid shows a prominent epithelioid cell reaction with eosinophils and mild plasma cell infiltration. In general, the choriocapillaris is spared. Dalen-Fuchs nodules are a typical, but by no means a pathognomonic, finding. Dalen-Fuchs nodules can also be found in VKH syndrome and sarcoidosis. Some evidence suggests that once sympathetic ophthalmia has developed, the clinical course can be modified by removing the inciting eye within 2 weeks of disease onset.

32. Answer—e

33. Answer—c.

34. Answer—b. Reiter syndrome is a systemic disorder characterized by arthritis, urethritis, and ocular inflammation. Conjunctivitis is the most common ocular finding. Reiter syndrome may occur after gram-negative dysentery or after nongonococcal urethritis caused by *Chlamydia trachomatis* and *Ureaplasma urealyticum.* White men between the ages of 20 and 40 are diagnosed most frequently with Reiter syndrome. The disease is a difficult one to diagnose in women, who do not typically present with the classic triad.

35. Answer—d. The diagnosis of Behçet syndrome is based on clinical findings. The complete form consists of four main signs: ocular inflammation, oral ulcers, genital ulcers, and skin lesions. The skin lesions usually consist of erythema nodosa or phlebitis. Additional minor criteria such as arthritis, intestinal ulcers, vascular disease, and neuropsychiatric symptoms can assist in the diagnosis. Keratoderma blennorrhagicum is associated with Reiter syndrome.

36. Answer—b.

37. Answer—e.

38. Answer—a.

39. Answer—c.

40. Answer—d.

41. Answer—e.

42. Answer—e.

43. Answer—c.

44. Answer—a. Sarcoid is characterized by noncaseating granulomas.

INDEX

Cotton-wool spots
  in HIV retinopathy, 222, 223*i*
  in systemic lupus erythematosus,
    163, 164*i*
COX. *See* Cyclo-oxygenase
Crohn disease (granulomatous
    ileocolitis), 124
Cryoablation, for pars planitis, 142
Cryptococcus neoformans, choroiditis
    caused by, in HIV infection/AIDS, 232
Crystallins, lens. *See* Lens proteins
CTL. *See* Cytotoxic T lymphocytes
Cutaneous basophil hypersensitivity, 64
Cyclitis, chronic (pars planitis), 141–142.
    See also Intermediate uveitis
Cyclogyl. *See* Cyclopentolate
Cyclo-oxygenase (COX), 76, 77*i*
  in NSAID mechanism of action, 95
Cyclopentolate, for uveitis, 112–113
Cyclophosphamide, for uveitis, 116–117
Cycloplegics
  for uveitis, 112–113, 113*t*, 120, 134
  for Vogt-Koyanagi-Harada syndrome, 195
Cyclosporine, 96
  for uveitis, 117–118
Cysticercosis *(Cysticercus cellulosae),*
    160–161, 162*i*
Cystoid macular edema
  prostaglandins and, 77
  in uveitis, 214
Cytokines, 7. *See also specific type*
  in immune processing, 22*i*, 23
  as inflammatory mediators, 79, 80–81*t*
Cytolysis, immune, 56–57
Cytomegalic inclusion disease, 146
Cytomegaloviruses
  congenital, 146
  retinitis caused by, 145–146, 146*i*
    antiviral immunity in, 68
    in HIV infection/AIDS, 68,
      223–227, 224*i*
Cytotoxic chemotherapy, 95–96
  for uveitis, 116–117
Cytotoxic hypersensitivity (type II)
    reaction, 51*t*, 56–57. *See also*
    Cytotoxic T lymphocytes
Cytotoxic T lymphocytes, 24, 25*i*, 64–69
  mechanisms of, 64–65, 67*i*
  in viral conjunctivitis, 33

d4T. *See* Stavudine
Dalen-Fuchs nodules, in sympathetic
    ophthalmia, 191
Daraprim. *See* Pyrimethamine
DC. *See* Dendritic cells
ddC. *See* Zalcitabine
ddI. *See* Didanosine
Delavirdine, 221
Delayed hypersensitivity (type IV) reaction,
    51*t*, 61–64, 63*i*
  in chronic mast cell degranulation, 71
  response to poison ivy as, 29
  tuberculin form of, 29, 64
Delayed hypersensitivity T cells, 24, 25*i*,
    61–64, 63*i*
Dendritic cells, 14–15
Depo-Medrol. *See* Methylprednisolone
Depot injections, corticosteroid, for
    uveitis, 115
Dexamethasone
  for endophthalmitis, 208*t*
  for uveitis, 114*t*
DH. *See* Delayed hypersensitivity (type IV)
    reaction
Didanosine, 221
Diffuse unilateral subacute neuroretinitis,
    161–162, 162*i*, 163*i*
DMO-226, 221
Domains, immunoglobulin, 53, 53*i*
Donor cornea
  rejection of, 38
  screening of for HIV, 237
Downregulatory T cells, in suppression, 87
Drugs. *See also specific type or agents*
  uveitis caused by, 135
DUSN. *See* Diffuse unilateral subacute
    neuroretinitis

E-selectin, in neutrophil rolling, 45
EBV. *See* Epstein-Barr virus
Effector cells
  immune response using, 10, 24
  lymphocytes as, 24, 25*i*
  macrophages as, 48–50, 49*i*
  neutrophils as, 12, 45–47, 46*i*
Effector phase of immune response arc,
    16, 17*i*, 24, 40–85
  adaptive immunity and, 50–73, 52*t*
  antibody-mediated, 52–61

blockade of, in anterior chamber–
associated immune deviation, 35
cells in. *See* Effector cells
combined antibody and cellular, 69–72
innate immunity and, 40–50, 41*t*
lymphocyte-mediated, 61–69
mediator systems and, 73–85
response to poison ivy and, 28, 29
response to tuberculosis and, 29
Efferent lymphatic channels, definition of, 7
Eicosanoids, as inflammatory mediators,
76–78, 77*i*
Elevated intraocular pressure, in uveitic
glaucoma, 212
Endogenous endophthalmitis, 197, 199*i*,
203–204
Endophthalmitis, 197–210
bacterial toxins affecting severity of, 43
bleb-associated, 197, 198*t*, 203
Candida causing, 153, 201
diagnosis of, 205–207
endogenous, 197, 199*i*, 203–204
exogenous, 197, 198*t*, 199*i*
infectious, 197–204
differential diagnosis of, 205
intraocular specimens for diagnosis of
collection of, 206
cultures and laboratory evaluation
of, 206
Nocardia asteroides causing, 175–176
phacoantigenic, 62, 128, 129*i*
intraocular lens implantation and, 130
postoperative, 197, 198*t*, 199–201, 202*i*
acute-onset, 200, 201*i*
chronic (delayed-onset), 200–201, 202*i*
posttraumatic, 197, 198*t*, 202
prophylaxis of, 205
Propionibacterium acnes causing, 51
signs and symptoms of, 197
in toxocariasis, 159, 160, 161*t*
treatment of, 207–210
medical, 207–209, 208*t*
outcomes of, 210
surgical, 207
Endotoxins, in innate immune response, 41
Enterococcus, bleb-associated
endophthalmitis caused by, 203
Enucleation, for prevention of sympathetic
ophthalmia, 190

Enzyme-linked immunosorbent assay
(ELISA), in HIV infection/AIDS, 220
Eosinophils, 13
Epitheliitis, acute retinal pigment (ARPE),
167*t*, 169, 169*i*
Epithelioid cells, 14, 50
Epitheliopathy, acute posterior multifocal
placoid pigment (APMPPE), 167*t*,
168, 168*i*, 169*i*
Epitopes, 7, 18, 55
Epstein-Barr virus, uveitis caused by,
146–147
Erythema chronicum migrans, in Lyme
disease, 180, 181*i*
Examination, ophthalmologic, HIV
infection precautions and, 237
Exogenous endophthalmitis, 197, 198*t*, 199*i*
Exotoxins, microbial, in innate immune
response, 42, 43
External (outer) eye, HIV infection/AIDS
affecting, 232–234, 235*i*
Extracapsular cataract extraction, in
uveitis, 211–212
Eyedrops, corticosteroid, for uveitis, 114
Eyelids, in uveitis, 101*t*

Fab region (antibody molecule), 53, 53*i*
Fas ligand, 35, 64, 67*i*
FasL. *See* Fas ligand
Fc receptors
definition of, 7
on mast cells, 13
in phagocytosis, 47
Fenton reaction, oxygen radicals produced
by, 83
Fibrin, as inflammatory mediator, 75
Fibrinogen, 75
Filtering bleb
endophthalmitis associated with, 197,
198*t*, 203
for uveitic glaucoma, 213
Floaters, in posterior uveitis, 105
Fluconazole, for endophthalmitis, 208*t*
Fluorescein angiography, in uveitis,
112, 141
Fluorescent treponemal antibody
absorption (FTA-ABS) test, 178–179
Fluorometholone, for uveitis, 114*t*
Fluoroquinolones, for endophthalmitis, 207

FMLP. *See* N-Formylmethionylleucylphenylalanine
Fomivirsen, for cytomegalovirus
retinitis, 226
Foreign bodies, intraocular, retained,
endophthalmitis caused by, 202
N-Formylmethionylleucylphenylalanine
(FMLP), in innate immunity, 43
Foscarnet, for cytomegalovirus retinitis,
225–226
Free radicals (oxygen radicals), as
inflammatory mediators, 82–84, 83*i*
FTA-ABS (fluorescent treponemal antibody
absorption) test, 178–179
Fuchs heterochromic iridocyclitis,
139–140, 139*i*, 140*i*
Fundus
salt-and-pepper
in congenital syphilis, 177–178
in rubella, 147, 148*i*
sunset-glow, 194
Fungi. *See also specific type*
endophthalmitis caused by, 201,
203–204, 204*i*
uveitis caused by, 149–154

Gamma (γ)- interferon, 81*t*
in delayed hypersensitivity, 61–62, 63*i*
Ganciclovir, for cytomegalovirus
retinitis, 225
Gene therapy, retinal, 39
Gentamicin, for endophthalmitis, 208*t*
German measles. *See* Rubella
Giant cells, 14, 50
Glaucoma
in herpetic uveitis, 133
juvenile rheumatoid arthritis–associated
iridocyclitis and, 138
phacolytic, 48, 129–130
uveitis and, 133, 212–214
Glaucomatocyclitic crisis (Posner-
Schlossman syndrome), 127–128
Glucocorticosteroids, 95. *See also*
Corticosteroids
Goldmann-Witmer coefficient, 60
Grafts, rejection of
after penetrating keratoplasty, 38
transplantation antigens and, 91

Granulomas
in sarcoidosis, 187, 187*i*, 188, 188*i*, 189
in toxocariasis, 159, 160*i*, 161*t*
Granulomatous hypersensitivity, 64
Granulomatous uveitis, 103, 107
Growth factors, 79, 81*t*

HAART. *See* Highly active antiretroviral
therapy
Haber-Weiss reaction, oxygen radicals
produced by, 83, 83*i*
Haemophilus influenzae, bleb-associated
endophthalmitis caused by, 203
Hageman factor, in kinin-forming system,
74, 75
Haplotypes, 90
Hapten, 7
poison ivy toxin as, 28
serum sickness caused by, 56
Heavy chains, immunoglobulin, 52–53, 53*i*
Helminths
panuveitis caused by, 186
posterior uveitis caused by, 159–162, 163*i*
Helper T cells. *See also specific type under*
T helper
class II MHC molecules as antigen-
presenting platform for, 18, 19*i*
differentiation of, 20–23
in HIV infection/AIDS, 217–218, 219*t*
in immune processing, 20, 22*i*
Hemorrhages, retinal, in HIV
infection/AIDS, 222–223
Herpes simplex virus
keratitis caused by, in HIV
infection/AIDS, 234, 235*i*
uveitis caused by, 132–134, 144
Herpes zoster
in HIV infection/AIDS, 234
uveitis and, 132–134, 133*i*
Herpes zoster ophthalmicus, vasculitis
and, 134
Herpetic uveitis, 132–134, 133*i*
glaucoma in, 133
Highly active antiretroviral therapy
(HAART), cytomegalovirus retinitis
and, 223, 227
Histamine, as inflammatory mediator, 75
Histiocytic lymphoma (intraocular
lymphoma), 195–196, 196*i*

Histo spots, 149, 149*i*, 151
Histoplasma capsulatum (histoplasmosis),
     149
  ocular, 149–153, 167*t*
     HLA association in, 93*t*
HIV infection/AIDS, 216–237
  adnexal Kaposi sarcoma in,
        232–234, 233*i*
  choroiditis in
     Cryptococcus neoformans, 232
     multifocal, 232
     Pneumocystis carinii, 230–232,
        230*i*, 231*i*
  classification of, 219–220*t*
  cytomegalovirus retinitis in, 68,
        223–227, 224*i*
  diagnosis of, 220
     ophthalmologist's role in, 235–236
  herpes zoster in, 234
  management of, 220–234
     ophthalmologist's role in, 235–236
  molluscum contagiosum in, 234
  natural history of, 218, 219–220*t*
  occupational exposure to, precautions
        in health care setting and, 236–237
  ocular infection/manifestations and,
        216–237
     external eye manifestations,
        232–234, 235*i*
     ophthalmic complications, 222–232
  opportunistic infections in, 222, 234, 235*i*
  pathogenesis of, 217–218
  progressive outer retinal necrosis in,
        227–228, 228*i*
  retinopathy associated with,
        222–223, 223*i*
  syphilitic chorioretinitis in, 229–230
  systemic conditions associated with,
        220–222
  Toxoplasma retinochoroiditis in,
        228–229, 229*i*
  toxoplasmosis in, 155*i*
  transmission of, 218–220
  virology of, 216–217
HLA. *See* Human leukocyte (HLA) antigens
Homing, 26
  MALT and, 32
Horror autotoxicus, 86
Human immunodeficiency virus infection.
     See HIV infection/AIDS

Human leukocyte (HLA) antigens, 18, 19*i*,
     89–94. *See also* Major
     histocompatibility complex
  allelic variations and, 90
  in ankylosing spondylitis, 121
  in anterior uveitis, 93*t*, 94, 121–125
  in Behçet syndrome, 93*t*, 127
  in birdshot chorioretinopathy, 93*t*, 171
  detection and classification of, 90
  disease associations and, 91–94, 93*t*
  in glaucomatocyclitic crisis (Posner-
     Schlossman syndrome), 128
  history of, 92*t*
  in inflammatory bowel disease, 124
  in intermediate uveitis, 93*t*
  in juvenile rheumatoid arthritis, 93*t*, 135
  in multiple sclerosis, 93*t*
  normal function of, 89–90
  in ocular histoplasmosis syndrome, 93*t*
  in Reiter syndrome, 93*t*, 123
  in retinal vasculitis, 93*t*
  in sarcoidosis, 93*t*
  in sympathetic ophthalmia, 93*t*
  transplantation and, 91
  in Vogt-Koyanagi-Harada (VKH)
     syndrome, 93*t*, 195
Humoral immunity. *See* Antibody-
     mediated immune effector responses
Hutchinson's sign, 132
Hybridoma, monoclonal antibody and, 55
Hydrocortisone sodium succinate, for
     uveitis, 114*t*
Hypersensitivity reactions, 50–51, 51*t*
  contact, 64
     response to poison ivy as, 29
  cutaneous basophil, 64
  cytotoxic (type II), 51*t*, 56–57
  delayed (type IV), 51*t*, 61–64, 63*i*
     in chronic mast cell degranulation, 71
     response to poison ivy as, 29
     tuberculin form of, 29
  granulomatous, 64
  immediate (type I/anaphylactic/atopic),
        26, 51*t*, 70, 71*i*
  immune-complex (type III), 51*t*. *See also*
        Immune complexes
  stimulatory (type V), 50, 51*t*, 57–58
Hypervariable region, 53

Hypopyon
   in Behçet syndrome, 126, 126*i*
   in endophthalmitis, 197
   in uveitis, 105, 119, 119*i*
Hypotony, in uveitis, 214

Idiotopes, 55
Idiotypes, 55
Ig. *See under Immunoglobulin*
IL. *See* Interleukins
IL-5. *See* Interleukin-5
Ileocolitis, granulomatous (Crohn
      disease), 124
Immediate hypersensitivity (type I)
      reaction, 26, 70, 71*i*
Immune-complex hypersensitivity (type III)
      reaction, 51*t*. *See also* Immune
      complexes
Immune complexes
   circulating, 55–56, 56*i*
      anterior uveitis caused by, 57
   tissue-bound, 56–60, 58*i*
      Arthus reaction and, 57
Immune cytolysis, 56–57
Immune hypersensitivity reactions. *See*
      Hypersensitivity reactions
Immune privilege
   in anterior uvea, 34
   in cornea, 36
   therapeutic potential of, 36
Immune response (immunity). *See also*
      Immune response arc; Immune
      system; Immunology
   adaptive, 9–10. *See also* Adaptive
      immune response
      effector reactivities of, 50–73, 52*t*
      innate immunity and
         differences from, 11
         similarities to, 10
   immunoregulation of, 86–88
   inflammation differentiated from, 11–12
   innate, 10. *See also* Innate
      immune response
      adaptive immunity and
         differences from, 11
         similarities to, 10
      effector reactivities of, 40–50, 41*t*

ocular, 30–39, 86–96
   of anterior chamber/anterior
      uvea/vitreous, 31*t*, 32–36
   of conjunctiva, 30–32, 31*t*
   of cornea/sclera, 31*t*, 36–37
   of retina/retinal pigment
      epithelium/choroid, 31*t*, 38–39
primary
   immune response arc and, 24–26
   secondary response differentiated
      from, 26
regional, 26–27
secondary
   immune response arc and, 24–26
   primary response differentiated
      from, 26
Immune response arc, 16–29, 25*i*
   clinical examples of, 27–29
   immunologic microenvironments and, 27
   overview of, 16, 17*i*
   phases of, 18–24
      afferent, 16, 17*i*, 18–20
         response to poison ivy and, 28, 29
         response to tuberculosis and, 29
      effector, 16, 17*i*, 24, 40–85. *See also*
         Effector phase of immune
         response arc
         response to poison ivy and, 28, 29
         response to tuberculosis and, 29
      processing, 16, 17*i*, 20–23, 22*i*
         response to poison ivy and, 28, 29
         response to tuberculosis and, 29
      primary or secondary immune responses
         and, 24–26
      regional immunity and, 26–27
Immune system. *See also* Immune
      response
   components of, 12–15
Immunocompromised host. *See also* HIV
      infection/AIDS
   cytomegalovirus retinitis in, 68
   ocular candidiasis in, 153
Immunogen, 18
Immunoglobulin A (IgA)
   structural and functional properties of, 54*t*
   in tear film, 30
   in viral conjunctivitis, 33
Immunoglobulin D (IgD), structural and
      functional properties of, 54*t*

Interleukins, 79, 80t
Intermediate uveitis, 105, 141–142
 causes of, 111t
 classification of, 105
 differential diagnosis of, 108t
 HLA association in, 93t
 in Lyme disease, 181, 182
 signs of, 101t, 103–104
Intraocular culture, in postoperative
  endophthalmitis, 200
Intraocular foreign bodies, retained,
  endophthalmitis caused by, 202
Intraocular lenses
 in Fuchs heterochromic iridocyclitis, 140
 iritis and, 131
 juvenile rheumatoid arthritis–associated
  iridocyclitis and, 138
 phacoantigenic endophthalmitis and, 130
 posterior chamber, in uveitis, 211
 pseudophakia and, 130
 pseudophakic bullous keratopathy and,
  130, 131i
 uveitis-glaucoma-hyphema (UGH)
  syndrome and, 44, 130–131
Intraocular pressure
 elevated, in uveitic glaucoma, 212
 in uveitis, 101t, 103
  corticosteroids affecting, 213
Intraocular specimens, for endophthalmitis
  diagnosis, 206–207
Intraocular surgery, endophthalmitis after,
  197, 198t, 199–201, 202i
 acute-onset, 200, 201i
 chronic (delayed-onset), 200–201, 202i
Intraocular tumors, lymphoma,
  195–196, 196i
Iridocyclitis, 105. *See also* Iritis
 acute, 119–135, 119i, 120i
 in Behçet syndrome, 126
 chronic, 135–140
  in juvenile rheumatoid arthritis,
   135–138, 136i, 137t
  of unknown etiology, 140
  in young girls, 139
 Fuchs heterochromic, 139–140,
   139i, 140i
 in herpetic disease, 132
 HLA associated diseases and, 121–125
 in juvenile rheumatoid arthritis,
   135–138, 136i, 137t
 in Lyme disease, 182

 in sarcoidosis, 188, 188i
 in tuberculosis, 183, 184i
 in varicella, 132
Iridotomy, for iris bombé in uveitis, 213
Iris
 atrophy of, in herpetic inflammation, 134
 immunologic microenvironment
   of, 32–34
 in uveitis, 101t
Iris bombé, in uveitis, 213
Iris nodosa, 178
Iris nodules
 in sarcoidosis, 188, 188i
 in syphilis, 178
 in uveitis, 102i, 103
Iris papulosa, 178
Iritis, 105. *See also* Iridocyclitis
 acute, 119–135, 119i, 120i
 in ankylosing spondylitis, 121–122
 in Behçet syndrome, 126, 126i
 in glaucomatocyclitic crisis (Posner-
   Schlossman syndrome), 127
 in herpetic disease, 132, 134
 HLA associated diseases and, 121–125
 in inflammatory bowel disease, 124
 intraocular lenses and, 131
 in Kawasaki syndrome, 132
 in Lyme disease, 181
 in psoriatic arthritis, 125
 in Reiter syndrome, 124
 in syphilis, 178
 in tuberculosis, 183, 184i
 in varicella, 132
 viral, 134
  treatment of, 134
Isotypes, 7, 52–53, 54t
 in immunologic tolerance, 87
Itraconazole, for endophthalmitis, 208t
Ivermectin, for onchocerciasis, 186
Ixodes ticks, Lyme disease transmitted
   by, 180

JRA. *See* Juvenile rheumatoid arthritis
Juvenile rheumatoid arthritis, 135–138,
   136i, 137t
 HLA association in, 93t, 135
 pars plana lensectomy/vitrectomy for
   uveitis associated with, 138, 211
 pauciarticular, 135, 137t
 polyarticular, 135, 137t
 systemic onset of (Still disease), 135

Kallikrein, 74
Kaposi sarcoma
    epidemic, 232, 233*i*
    ocular adnexal, 232–234, 233*i*
Kawasaki syndrome (mucocutaneous
        lymph node syndrome/infantile
        periarteritis nodosa), 132
Kenalog. *See* Methylprednisolone
Keratic precipitates
    in phacoantigenic endophthalmitis, 128
    in sarcoidosis, 188, 188*i*
    stellate, in herpetic ocular infection,
        132–133
    in uveitis, 102*i*, 103
Keratitis
    in HIV infection/AIDS, 234, 235*i*
    in Lyme disease, 181
    in Reiter syndrome, 123–124
Keratoiritis, in herpetic disease, 132
Keratopathy
    band, in juvenile rheumatoid arthritis,
        136, 136*i*, 138
    pseudophakic bullous, 130, 131*i*
Keratoplasty, penetrating, rejection of
        corneal allograft and, 38
Keratouveitis, 105
    in congenital syphilis, 177–178, 178*i*
Ketoconazole, for endophthalmitis, 208*t*
Killer cells
    in antibody-dependent cellular
        cytotoxicity, 69–70
    lymphokine-activated, 69
    natural, 69
        in viral conjunctivitis, 33
Kininogens, 74
Kinins, 74–75
Koeppe nodules
    in sarcoidosis, 188, 188*i*
    in uveitis, 102*i*, 103
Krill disease (acute retinal pigment
        epitheliitis/ARPE), 167*t*, 169, 169*i*

L-selectin, in neutrophil rolling, 45
LAK cells. *See* Lymphokine-activated
        killer cells
Lamellar bodies, in sarcoidosis, 187
Lamivudine, 221
Langerhans cells, 14–15
Large cell lymphoma (intraocular
        lymphoma), 195–196, 196*i*

Laser therapy (laser surgery)
    for iris bombé in uveitis, 213
    for ocular histoplasmosis, 150–151, 151*i*
Latanaprost, aqueous outflow affected by, 78
LC. *See* Langerhans cells
Lens-associated uveitis, 128–130
    phacoantigenic endophthalmitis as, 62,
        128, 129*i*
    phacolytic glaucoma as, 48, 129–130
    phacotoxic uveitis as, 128
Lens proteins (crystallins)
    in phacoantigenic endophthalmitis, 48,
        128, 129*i*
    in phacolytic glaucoma, 48
    in phacotoxic uveitis, 128
    tolerance to, 88
Lensectomy, pars plana, juvenile
        rheumatoid arthritis–associated
        uveitis and, 138, 211
Leptospirosis, panuveitis in, 182
Leukocoria, in toxocariasis, 159, 160*i*, 161*t*
Leukocytes, 12–15. *See also specific type*
Leukotrienes, 7
    as inflammatory mediators, 78
Light chains, immunoglobulin, 52, 53*i*
Lipids, as inflammatory mediators, 76–79
Lipopolysaccharide, bacterial. *See also*
        Endotoxins
    in innate immune response, 41
    uveitis caused by, 42
Lipoxin, 77*i*, 78
5-Lipoxygenase pathway, eicosanoids
        produced by, 76, 77*i*, 78
Low-zone tolerance, in anterior
        chamber–associated immune
        deviation, 35
LPS. *See* Lipopolysaccharide
Lupus erythematosus, systemic, 59,
        163–165, 164*i*
Lyme disease, 180–182, 181*i*, 182*i*
Lymph nodes, 15
Lymphatics, 7, 18
Lymphocyte-mediated immune effector
        responses, 61–69
    cytotoxic lymphocytes and, 64–69
    delayed hypersensitivity and, 61–64
Lymphocytes, 15. *See also* B cells; T cells
    activation of, 20–23, 22*i*
    effector, 24, 25*i*
Lymphoid tissues, 15

Lymphokine-activated killer cells, 69
Lymphokines, 79
Lymphoma, intraocular, 195–196, 196*i*
Lysis, cell
    complement-mediated, 56–57
    by cytotoxic lymphocytes, 64, 67*i*

M protein, in subacute sclerosing
        panencephalitis, 148
MAC. *See* Membrane attack complex
α_2-Macroglobulin, in innate immune
        response, 44
Macrophage-activating factor, 62
Macrophage chemotactic protein-1, 80*t*
Macrophages, 14
    innate mechanisms for recruitment and
        activation of, 48–50, 49*i*
Macular edema, cystoid
    prostaglandins and, 77
    in uveitis, 214
Macular neuroretinopathy, acute, multiple
        evanescent white dot syndrome
        and, 172
Maculopathy, in ocular histoplasmosis,
        149, 149*i*, 150*i*, 151–152
MAGE. *See* Melanoma antigen genes
Major histocompatibility complex (MHC),
        89–90. *See also* Human leukocyte
        (HLA) antigens
    class I molecules of, 20, 21*i*
    class II molecules of, 18, 19*i*
        primed macrophages as, 49
    history of, 92*t*
    transplantation and, 91
Malignant melanomas. *See* Melanomas
MALT. *See* Mucosa-associated
        lymphoid tissue
Masquerade conditions
    for panuveitis, 195–196
    for posterior uveitis, 175–176
Mast cells, 13
    acute IgE-mediated degranulation of,
        70, 71*i*
    chronic degranulation of plus Th2
        delayed hypersensitivity, 71
Mazzotti reaction, 186
MCP. *See* Multifocal choroiditis and
        panuveitis syndrome
MCP-1. *See* Macrophage chemotactic
        protein-1

MDRTB. *See* Multidrug-resistant
        tuberculosis
Measles (rubeola) virus, 148
Mediators, 7, 73–85, 73*t*. *See also*
        specific type
    cytokines, 79, 80–81*t*
    lipid, 76–79
    neutrophil-derived granule products, 85
    plasma-derived enzyme systems, 73–75
    reactive nitrogen products, 84
    reactive oxygen intermediates, 82–84
    vasoactive amines, 75
Melanoma antigen genes, 70
Melanomas, uveal, immune responses to, 70
Membrane attack complex, 56–57, 73, 74*i*
Memory, immunologic, 11, 24–26
Methotrexate
    for juvenile rheumatoid arthritis, 138
    for uveitis, 116–117
Methylprednisolone, for uveitis, 114*t*
MEWDS. *See* Multiple evanescent white
        dot syndrome
MHA-TP (microhemagglutination assay–
        T pallidum) test, 178–179
MHC. *See* Major histocompatibility
        complex
Microaneurysms, retinal, in HIV
        infection/AIDS, 222–223
Microenvironments, immunologic, 27
    of anterior chamber/anterior uvea/
        vitreous, 31*t*, 32–34
    of conjunctiva, 30, 31*t*
    of cornea/sclera, 31*t*, 36, 37*i*
    of retina/retinal pigment epithelium/
        choroid, 31*t*, 38–39
Microhemagglutination assay–*T pallidum*
        (MHA-TP) test, 178–179
Microsporida keratitis, in HIV
        infection/AIDS, 234, 235*i*
Mimicry, molecular, 89
    autoimmune uveitis and, 89
    HLA disease associations and, 94
Mixed lymphocyte reaction, 91
Molecular mimicry, 89
    autoimmune uveitis and, 89
    HLA disease associations and, 94
Molluscum contagiosum, in HIV
        infection/AIDS, 234
Monoclonal antibodies, 55
Monocytes, 14

Monokines, 79

Moraxella, bleb-associated endophthalmitis caused by, 203

Mucocutaneous lymph node syndrome (Kawasaki syndrome/infantile periarteritis nodosa), 132

Mucosa-associated lymphoid tissue, of conjunctiva, 30–32

Multidrug-resistant tuberculosis, 185

Multifocal choroiditis and panuveitis syndrome (MCP), 167*t*, 175, 175*i*

Multiple evanescent white dot syndrome (MEWDS), 167*t*, 171–172, 171*i*

Multiple sclerosis, HLA association in, 93*t*

Mutton-fat keratic precipitates, 103
  in phacoantigenic endophthalmitis, 128
  in sarcoidosis, 188, 188*i*

Mydriatics, for Vogt-Koyanagi-Harada syndrome, 195

Myeloma, monoclonal antibody and, 55

Nafcillin, for endophthalmitis, 208*t*

Naming-meshing system, for uveitis differential diagnosis, 107, 108–109*t*

Natural (innate) immunity, 10
  adaptive immunity and
    differences from, 11
    similarities to, 10

Natural killer cells, 69
  in viral conjunctivitis, 33

Necrotizing retinitis, atypical, diagnosis of, 61

Nelfinavir, 221

Neoplasms, panuveitis and, 195–196

Neovascular membrane, subretinal, in ocular histoplasmosis, 150, 151*i*

Neural reflex arc, immune response arc compared with, 16, 17*i*

Neuropeptides, as inflammatory mediators, 81*t*

Neuroretinitis
  diffuse unilateral subacute, 161–162, 162*i*, 163*i*
  in syphilis, 178

Neuroretinopathy, acute macular, multiple evanescent white dot syndrome and, 172

Neutralization, antibody, 55, 56*i*

Neutrophil rolling, 45, 46*i*

Neutrophils (polymorphonuclear leukocytes), 12–13
  granule products of, as inflammatory mediators, 85
  innate mechanisms for recruitment of, 45–47, 46*i*

Nevirapine, 221

NHL-CNS. *See* Non-Hodgkin lymphoma of CNS

Nitric oxide, 84

Nitric oxide synthase, 84

NK cells. *See* Natural killer cells

NNRTI. *See* Nonnucleoside reverse transcriptase inhibitors

NO. *See* Nitric oxide

Nocardia asteroides, ocular infection/ inflammation caused by, 175–176

Non-Hodgkin lymphoma of CNS (intraocular lymphoma), 195–196, 196*i*

Nongranulomatous uveitis, 103, 107

Nonnucleoside reverse transcriptase inhibitors, for HIV infection/AIDS, 221

Nonsteroidal anti-inflammatory drugs (NSAIDs), 95
  for uveitis, 116

Non-T, non-B effector lymphocytes (null cells), 24

NOS. *See* Nitric oxide synthase

Nucleoside analogues, for HIV infection/AIDS, 221

Null cells. *See* Non-T, non-B effector lymphocytes

Ocular adnexa, Kaposi sarcoma of, 232–234, 233*i*

Ocular histoplasmosis syndrome, 149–153, 167*t*
  HLA association in, 93*t*

Ocular immunology. *See* Immune response; Immunology

Ocular surgery. *See also specific procedure*
  endophthalmitis after, 197, 198*t*, 199–201, 202*i*
    acute-onset, 200, 201*i*
    chronic (delayed-onset), 200–201, 202*i*
  for uveitis, 118

OHS. *See* Ocular histoplasmosis syndrome

Onchocerciasis, 186

Open-angle glaucoma, uveitis and, 212–213
Ophthalmia, sympathetic, 65–66,
190–193, 190*i*, 191*i*
HLA association in, 93*t*
Opportunistic infections. *See also*
specific type
in HIV infection/AIDS, 222, 234, 235*i*
Opsonization, antibody, 55, 56*i*
Optic nerve (cranial nerve II), in uveitis, 101*t*
Optic neuritis, in Lyme disease, 181
Oral tolerance, 96
Orbit, disorders of, Th1 delayed
hypersensitivity and, 66*t*
Oxygen radicals (free radicals), as
inflammatory mediators, 82–84, 83*i*

P-selectin, in neutrophil rolling, 45
PAF. *See* Platelet-activating factors
Pain
in endophthalmitis, 197, 200
in uveitis, 100
PAN. *See* Polyarteritis nodosa
Panencephalitis, subacute sclerosing,
uveitis caused by, 148
Panophthalmitis, in Lyme disease, 181
Panuveitis, 106, 108–109*t*, 177–196. *See*
also specific cause and Uveitis
in Behçet syndrome, 126–127
causes of, 111*t*
immunologic and granulomatous
diseases, 187–195
infectious diseases, 177–186
classification of, 106
differential diagnosis of, 108*t*
masquerade syndromes and, 195–196
multifocal choroiditis and (MCP), 167*t*,
175, 175*i*
neoplasms and, 195–196
subretinal fibrosis and uveitis syndrome
(SFU), 167*t*, 174, 174*i*
Pars plana
cryoablation of, for pars planitis, 142
in uveitis, 101*t*
Pars plana lensectomy, juvenile
rheumatoid arthritis–associated uveitis
and, 138, 211
Pars plana vitrectomy
for endophthalmitis, 207, 209
for juvenile rheumatoid arthritis–
associated uveitis, 138, 211

for specimen collection, 205
for vitritis, 214
Pars planitis, 141–142. *See also*
Intermediate uveitis
PDGF. *See* Platelet-derived growth factors
Penetrating injuries, endophthalmitis
after, 202
Penetrating keratoplasty, rejection of
corneal allograft and, 38
Penicillin, for syphilis, 179
Pentamidine, for *Pneumocystis carinii*
choroiditis, 232
Perforin, 64, 67*i*
Periarteritis nodosa, infantile (Kawasaki
syndrome/mucocutaneous lymph
node syndrome), 132
Periocular corticosteroids, for uveitis, 115
Peripheral lymphoid structures, 15
PG. *See* Prostaglandin
PG/H synthase (prostaglandin G/H
synthase). *See* Cyclo-oxygenase
Phacoallergic uveitis, 128
Phacoantigenic endophthalmitis, 62,
128, 129*i*
intraocular lens implantation and, 130
Phacoemulsification, in uveitis, 211
Phacolytic glaucoma, 48, 129–130
Phacotoxic uveitis, 128
Phagocytosis, 47
Phospholipase A$_2$, 76, 77*i*, 78
Photocoagulation
for ocular histoplasmosis, 150–151, 151*i*
for pars planitis, 142
Photophobia, in uveitis, 119
PIC. *See* Punctate inner choroiditis
Platelet-activating factors, 77*i*, 78–79
Platelet-derived growth factors, 81*t*
PMN. *See* Polymorphonuclear leukocytes
Pneumocystis carinii infections
choroiditis, 230–232, 230*i*, 231*i*
in HIV infection/AIDS, 222, 230–232,
230*i*, 231*i*
pneumonia, 222
Poison ivy toxin, immune response arc in
response to, 28, 29
Poliosis, in Vogt-Koyanagi-Harada
syndrome, 193, 193*i*
Polyarteritis nodosa, 165, 165*i*
Polyclonal antibodies, 55

Polymorphonuclear leukocytes
(neutrophils), 12–13
granule products of, as inflammatory
mediators, 85
innate mechanisms for recruitment and
activation of, 45–47, 46*i*
PORN. *See* Progressive outer
retinal necrosis
PORT. *See* Punctate outer retinal
toxoplasmosis
Posner-Schlossman syndrome
(glaucomatocyclitic crisis), 127–128
Posterior chamber, in uveitis, 101*t*. *See
also* Posterior uveitis
Posterior chamber intraocular lenses, in
uveitis, 211
Posterior synechiae, in uveitis, 102*i*
Posterior uveitis, 105, 143–176. *See also
specific cause and* Choroiditis;
Retinitis; Uveitis
causes of, 111*t*
classification of, 105
differential diagnosis of, 109*t*
immunologic, 163–175
infectious, 144–162
masquerade conditions and, 175–176
signs of, 101*t*, 104
Postoperative endophthalmitis, 197, 198*t*,
199–201, 202*i*
acute-onset, 200, 201*i*
chronic (delayed-onset), 200–201, 202*i*
Posttraumatic endophthalmitis, 197,
198*t*, 202
PPD test. *See* Purified protein derivative
(PPD) test
Prednisolone
for endophthalmitis, 208*t*
for uveitis, 114*t*
Prednisone
for endophthalmitis, 208*t*
for uveitis, 114*t*
Priming
of effector lymphocytes, 24, 25*i*
of macrophages, 49, 49*i*
Processing phase of immune response arc,
16, 17*i*, 20–23, 22*i*
response to poison ivy and, 28, 29
response to tuberculosis and, 29

Programmed cell death (apoptosis)
by cytotoxic T lymphocytes, 64–65, 67*i*
Fas ligand in, 35, 64, 67*i*
Progressive outer retinal necrosis,
227–228, 228*i*
Propionibacterium acnes
in postoperative endophthalmitis, 51,
199, 201, 202*i*
in pseudophakia, 130
Prostaglandin G/H synthase. *See*
Cyclo-oxygenase
Prostaglandin GD$_2$, mast cells
synthesizing, 13
Prostaglandins
aqueous outflow affected by, 78
as inflammatory mediators, 76–78
NSAID inhibition of, 95
Protease inhibitors, for HIV infection/
AIDS, 221
Proteinase-3, scleritis/retinal vasculitis in
Wegener granulomatosis and, 60
Proteus, in postoperative
endophthalmitis, 200
Protozoa, ocular infection/inflammation
caused by, 154–159
Pseudomonas, in postoperative
endophthalmitis, 200
Pseudophakia, 130–131
Pseudophakic bullous keratopathy,
130, 131*i*
Psoriatic arthritis, 125, 125*i*
Punctate inner choroiditis, 167*t*, 172,
172*i*, 173*i*
Punctate outer retinal toxoplasmosis,
155, 156*i*
Purified protein derivative (PPD) test, 184
in HIV infection/AIDS, 222
immune response arc and, 29
Pyrimethamine, for ocular toxoplasmosis,
157–158

Rapid plasma reagin (RPR) test, 178–179
Reactive nitrogen products, as
inflammatory mediators, 84
Reactive oxygen intermediates, as
inflammatory mediators, 82–84, 83*i*
Receptor activation, in immune
response, 10
adaptive versus innate immunity and, 11

Reflex arc, neural, immune response arc compared with, 16, 17*i*

Regional immunity, 26–27

Reiter syndrome, 123–124, 123*i*, 124*i*
HLA association in, 93*t*, 123

Rejection (graft)
corneal allograft, 38
transplantation antigens and, 91

Remodeling pathway, platelet-activating factors in, 78

Reparative (stimulated) macrophages, 48, 49*i*, 50

Restimulation, of effector lymphocytes, 24

Resting macrophages, 48, 49*i*

Reticulum cell sarcoma (intraocular lymphoma), 195–196, 196*i*

Retina
immune response in, 31*t*, 38–39
necrosis of
acute, 144–145, 145*i*
progressive, 227–228, 228*i*
in systemic lupus erythematosus, 59
transplantation of, 39
in uveitis, 101*t*

Retinal breaks, in acute retinal necrosis, 145

Retinal detachment
in acute retinal necrosis, 145, 145*i*
in cytomegalovirus retinitis, 146, 146*i*, 227
in syphilis, 178, 179*i*
in uveitis, 215

Retinal disease, Th1 delayed hypersensitivity and, 66*t*

Retinal gene therapy, 39

Retinal hemorrhages, in HIV infection/AIDS, 222–223

Retinal pigment epithelium (RPE), immune response in, 31*t*, 38–39

Retinal sheathing, in sarcoidosis, 189, 189*i*

Retinal vasculitis
in Behçet syndrome, 126–127, 126*i*
differential diagnosis of, 109*t*
in herpetic disease, 134
HLA association in, 93*t*
in polyarteritis nodosa, 165, 165*i*
in systemic lupus erythematosus, 59, 163, 164*i*
in Wegener granulomatosis, 60

Retinitis, 105
atypical necrotizing, diagnosis of, 61
Candida, 153–154, 153*i*
cytomegalovirus, 145–146, 146*i*
antiviral immunity in, 68
in HIV infection/AIDS, 68, 223–227, 224*i*
herpetic, 134
measles, 148
rubella, 147, 148*i*
in syphilis, 178, 179, 179*i*, 180*i*
in toxoplasmosis, 155, 156*i*
in Wegener granulomatosis, 165–166, 166*i*

Retinochoroiditis, 105
Toxoplasma causing, in HIV infection/AIDS, 228–229, 229*i*

Retinochoroidopathies, 166–175, 167*t*.
See also specific disorder
birdshot (vitiliginous chorioretinitis), 170–171
HLA association in, 93*t*, 171

Retinopathy
cancer-associated, 59
HIV, 222–223, 223*i*

Reverse transcriptase inhibitors, for HIV infection/AIDS, 221

Rheumatoid arthritis, juvenile. *See* Juvenile rheumatoid arthritis

Rifabutin, uveitis caused by, 135

Rimexalone, for uveitis, 114*t*

Ritonavir, 221

RPE. *See* Retinal pigment epithelium

RPR (rapid plasma reagin) test, 178–179

Rubella
congenital, 147, 148*i*
uveitis in, 147, 148*i*

Rubeola (measles), uveitis in, 148

Sabin-Feldman dye test, for toxoplasmosis, 156

Salt-and-pepper fundus
in congenital syphilis, 177–178
in rubella, 147, 148*i*

Saquinavir, 221

Sarcoidosis, 187–190
HLA association in, 93*t*
panuveitis in, 187–190, 187*i*, 188*i*, 189*i*

Scavenging, 48

Scavenging macrophages, 48, 49*i*

Schaumann's bodies, in sarcoidosis, 187
Sclera
    disorders of, Th1 delayed
        hypersensitivity and, 66*t*
    immune response in, 31*t*
Scleritis, in Wegener granulomatosis, 60
Sclerouveitis, 105
Secondary glaucoma, uveitis and,
    212–214
Selectins, in neutrophil rolling, 45, 46*i*
Self antigens, tolerance to, 86–88
Sensitization, lymphocyte, 20–23, 22*i*
Septra. *See* Trimethoprim/sulfamethoxazole
Seronegative spondyloarthropathies, uveitis
    in, 121–125
Serotonin, as inflammatory mediator, 75
Serpiginous choroidopathy, 167*t*,
    172–174, 173*i*
Serratia marcescens, in postoperative
    endophthalmitis, 200, 201*i*
Serum sickness, 56
SFU. *See* Subretinal fibrosis and uveitis
    syndrome
Sheathing, retinal vascular, in sarcoidosis,
    189, 189*i*
Skin tests. *See specific type*
SLE. *See* Systemic lupus erythematosus
Snowballs
    in intermediate uveitis, 141
    in sarcoidosis, 188
Snowbanking, in intermediate uveitis,
    103, 141
Snowmen, in intermediate uveitis, 141
SO. *See* Sympathetic ophthalmia
Solu-Cortef. *See* Hydrocortisone sodium
    succinate
Specific (adaptive) immunity, 9–10
    innate immunity and
        differences from, 11
        similarities to, 10
Specificity, immunologic, 11
Spleen, 15
Spondylitis, ankylosing, 121–122
Spondyloarthropathies, seronegative,
    uveitis in, 121–125
SSPE. *See* Subacute sclerosing
    panencephalitis
Staphylococcus, in endophthalmitis
    bleb-associated, 203
    postoperative, 199, 200, 201, 201*i*
    posttraumatic, 202

Stavudine, 221
Steroids. *See* Corticosteroids
Still disease, 135
Stimulated macrophages, 48, 49*i*, 50
Stimulatory antibodies, 57–58
Stimulatory hypersensitivity (type V)
    reaction, 50, 51*t*, 57–58
Streptococcus
    in bleb-associated endophthalmitis, 203
    in postoperative endophthalmitis, 200
Sub-Tenon's approach, for periocular
    corticosteroid injection, 115, 115*i*
Subacute sclerosing panencephalitis,
    uveitis caused by, 148
Subretinal fibrosis and uveitis syndrome
    (SFU), 167*t*, 174, 174*i*
Subretinal neovascular membrane, in
    ocular histoplasmosis, 150, 151*i*
Substance P, as inflammatory mediator, 81*t*
Substantia propria, immunologic and
    inflammatory cells in, 30
Suicide induction (cell), by cytotoxic
    T lymphocytes, 64–65, 67*i*
Sulfonamides, for ocular toxoplasmosis,
    157–158
Sunset-glow fundus, 194
Superoxide anion, as inflammatory
    mediator, 82, 83*i*
Superoxide dismutase, as inflammatory
    mediator, 82, 83*i*
Suppression, in immunologic tolerance, 87
Suppressor T cells
    class I MHC molecules as antigen-
        presenting platform for, 20, 21*i*
    role of, 22*i*, 23
Surface markers, lymphocyte, 15
Surgery. *See also specific procedure*
    endophthalmitis after, 197, 198*t*,
        199–201, 202*i*
        acute-onset, 200, 201*i*
        chronic (delayed-onset), 200–201, 202*i*
    for uveitis, 118
Sympathetic ophthalmia, 65–66, 190–193,
    190*i*, 191*i*
    HLA association in, 93*t*
    surgical procedures/injuries leading
        to, 192*t*
Synechiae, in uveitis, 102*i*, 103

Syphilis, 177–180
  chorioretinitis in, 179
    in HIV infection/AIDS, 229–210
  congenital, 177–178, 178*i*
  panuveitis in, 177–180
  secondary, 178, 179*i*
Syphilitic posterior placoid
    chorioretinitis, 230
Systemic drug therapy, corticosteroid, for
    uveitis, 115–116
Systemic lupus erythematosus, 59,
    163–165, 164*i*

T-cell antigen receptors, 86
  HLA disease associations and, 94
T cells (T lymphocytes)
  activation of, 20–23, 22*i*
  class I MHC molecules as antigen-
      presenting platform for, 20, 21*i*
  class II MHC molecules as antigen-
      presenting platform for, 18, 19*i*
  cytotoxic, 24, 25*i*, 64–69
    mechanisms of, 64–65, 67*i*
    in viral conjunctivitis, 33
  delayed hypersensitivity, 24, 25*i*,
      61–64, 63*i*
  downregulatory, in suppression, 87
  effector, 24
  in HIV infection/AIDS, 217–218,
      219*t*, 221
  in immune processing, 20–23, 22*i*
  maturation of, in thymus, 15
  suppressor, role of, 22*i*, 23
T helper 0 cells, 20
T helper 1 cells, 20–23, 22*i*, 61–62, 63*i*
  effector mechanisms mediated by, 66*t*
  in sympathetic ophthalmia, 65–66
T helper 2 cells, 22*i*, 23, 62–64, 63*i*
  in chronic mast cell degranulation, 71
  in *Toxocara* granuloma, 65
Taenia solium, 161
Tapeworm, eye invaded by, 160–161, 162*i*
T$_C$. *See* Cytotoxic T lymphocytes
3TC. *See* Lamivudine
TGF-β. *See* Transforming growth factor–β
Th0 cells. *See* T helper 0 cells
Th1 cells. *See* T helper 1 cells
Th2 cells. *See* T helper 2 cells
Thymus, as lymphoid tissue, 15
Ticks, Lyme disease transmitted by, 180

TNF. *See* Tumor necrosis factor
Tolerance (immunologic), 86–88
  to lens crystallins, 88
  oral, 96
Tonometry, HIV infection precautions
    and, 237
Toxocara (toxocariasis), 159–160
  canis, 65, 159
  granuloma caused by, 65
Toxoplasma dye test, 156
Toxoplasma (toxoplasmosis), 154–159
  gondii, 154, 228
  ocular infection/inflammation caused by,
      154–159
    in HIV infection/AIDS, 228–229, 229*i*
  punctate outer retinal (PORT), 155, 156*i*
  uveitis in, 154–159
Transforming growth factor–β, 81*t*
Transmigration, in neutrophil recruitment
    and activation, 45, 46*i*
Transplantation, retinal, 39
Transplantation antigens, 91
Trauma
  endophthalmitis after, 197, 198*t*, 202
  uveitis caused by, 105
Treponema pallidum, 177. *See also*
    Syphilis
Triamcinolone, for uveitis, 114*t*
Trimethoprim/sulfamethoxazole
  for ocular toxoplasmosis, 158
  for *Pneumocystis carinii* choroiditis,
      230–232
Tubercle, in sarcoidosis, 187, 187*i*
Tuberculin hypersensitivity, 29, 64
Tuberculin skin test, 184
  in HIV infection/AIDS, 222
  immune response arc and, 29
Tuberculosis, 183–185
  in HIV infection/AIDS, 222
  immune response arc in, 29
  multidrug-resistant, 185
  treatment of, 184–185
  uveitis in, 183–185, 184*i*, 185*i*
Tumor necrosis factor
  α, 80*t*
  β, 80*t*
    in delayed hypersensitivity, 62, 63*i*
  in apoptosis, 65
Tumors, panuveitis and, 195–196

ILLUSTRATIONS

The authors submitted the following figures for this revision. (Illustrations that were reproduced from other sources or submitted by contributors not on the committee are credited in the captions.)

David Meisler, MD: Figs VII-1, VII-2, XI-5

E. Mitchel Opremcak, MD: Figs IX-1 through IX-3, IX-6, IX-8 through IX-18, IX-26, IX-29, IX-30, IX-37 through IX-66, X-31, X-32

Narsing A. Rao, MD: Figs XIII-1, XIII-3